BIDAR

ITS HISTORY AND MONUMENTS

BIDAR

ITS HISTORY AND MONUMENTS

G. Yazdani

MOTILAL BANARSIDASS PUBLISHERS
PRIVATE LIMITED • DELHI

First Indian Edition: Delhi, 1995

ISBN: 81-208-1071-6

Also available at:

MOṬILAL BANARSIDASS

41 U.A. Bungalow Road, Jawahar Nagar, Delhi 110 007
120 Royapettah High Road, Mylapore, Madras 600 004
16 St. Mark's Road, Bangalore 560 001
Ashok Rajpath, Patna 800 004
Chowk, Varanasi 221 001

PRINTED IN INDIA

BY JAINENDRA PRAKASH JAIN AT SHRI JAINENDRA PRESS,
A-45 NARAINA, PHASE I, NEW DELHI 110 028
AND PUBLISHED BY NARENDRA PRAKASH JAIN FOR
MOTILAL BANARSIDASS PUBLISHERS PRIVATE LIMITED,
BUNGALOW ROAD, DELHI 110 007

PREFACE

IN 1915 I visited Bidar for the first time. Motor-cars were costly, and further they had not come much into vogue in Hyderabad by that time. The roads were also not so good as they are now. Bidar was a two-days' trek from Hyderabad by the pony tonga. There were no arrangements for relays, and it would have been cruel to use a pair for more than forty miles a day. In such conditions it is apparent that there was little opportunity for the ordinary student or the 'globe-trotter' to visit Bidar. Government also had not taken any action in regard to the repair of 'a mass of ruin', however glorious, which was not easily accessible. The measures recommended by me for the conservation of monuments after my first visit were therefore not very elaborate, and they affected only those remains which were not in an advanced stage of decay. The fort, which is now a great attraction to the tourist, was almost left out, and in the case of the Madrasa only the clearance of its plinth and the setting up of a few props were recommended. But even in my first *note* I had suggested the construction of roads and footpaths as a preliminary measure to facilitate access to these monuments.

The Public Works Department prepared estimates amounting to Rs. 36,000 based on my *note*, and through the active support of the Right Honourable Sir Akbar Hydari, who was then the Secretary to Government in the Archaeological Department, the estimates were readily sanctioned and the work carried out in the years 1917 and 1918. Simultaneously with these measures I read a paper on the beauty and architectural importance of the monuments of Bidar before the Hyderabad Archaeological Society which aroused considerable interest among the general public. This paper was subsequently published in the form of an illustrated booklet, to serve as a guide-book for those who wanted to study the monuments on the spot.[1]

After the carrying out of these measures there followed a cessation for several years in the archaeological activities at Bidar, but luckily it was a time when the Osmania University had been established, and His Exalted Highness's Government, side by side with the development of Higher Education, were pressing forward a vigorous programme of Secondary and Primary Education in the rural areas of the Dominions. Movements were also on foot to open up the country for the economic uplift of the State. These measures were gradually bringing into the minds of people a general reawakening and a sense of national pride. To take advantage of these conditions, in 1927 I submitted to Government a comprehensive programme for the thorough repair and conservation of the monuments at Bidar, and as the estimated expenditure amounted to over two lakhs of rupees, I suggested that the expenditure should be spread over several years, and that a sum of Rs. 25,000 per annum should be ear-marked in the budget for the purpose, this allotment being continued annually until the work was finished. The programme was somewhat ambitious, and I felt considerable doubt as to whether it would be sanctioned, but the Right Honourable Sir Akbar Hydari, who was then at the helm of the finances of the State, fully

[1] This booklet was published under the title *The Antiquities of Bidar* in 1917.

supported the scheme, and through his kind recommendation it was graciously sanctioned by His Exalted Highness.

The carrying out of the scheme has taken nine years, and the work is still in progress. The first measures undertaken were the clearance of jungle and the making of an accurate survey of the sites of the various monuments. For the former we appointed a specially trained staff, so that in cutting down the trees and eradicating the rank vegetation no injury should be done to the masonry of the buildings, which generally were in a precarious condition. The survey work was entrusted to Party No. 6 of the Government of India, who have carried out our instructions with meticulous care. After the accomplishment of this task, we started, on the one hand, the construction of a network of motorable roads to make access to these monuments easy, and, on the other hand, we took up the repair of the remains which had been exposed to view by the clearance of jungle. Simultaneously we started excavations in the fort area at the sites of old palaces, the magnificence of which was extolled in contemporary histories, but the existence of which could be traced only in the shape of huge mounds of debris. These noble edifices were blown to pieces by the royal occupants of the fort themselves at the times of the different sieges, when all hope of relief had been given up, so that their assailants should not live and enjoy themselves in them. As a result of our excavations the famous Ta<u>kh</u>t Maḥall ('throne palace'), the beauties of which had been sung by Ā<u>dh</u>arī in a special poem dedicated to the Baihmanī king Aḥmad <u>Sh</u>āh al-Walī, has now been fully exposed to view, and its pristine grandeur can be admired. In the fort another beautiful palace, called the Rangīn Maḥall ('coloured palace'), has also been cleared from the debris; but the most wonderful portions of the fort now exposed to view are its defences, which were hitherto completely concealed either under a thick growth of rank vegetation or a mass of wrecked masonry. A visitor can now go round the fort, even in a motor-car, and examine the old ramparts, bastions, covered passages, barbicans, and gates, all of which had been most scientifically planned and which had made the fort impregnable against the armament of those days. Parenthetically I must state here that the Honourable Sir Theodore Tasker, Revenue Member, H.E.H. the Nizam's Government, has been most helpful to the Department in the matter of the preservation of the fort; and the 'walk' newly constructed along the glacis is entirely his idea.[1]

The tombs of Bidar, like the sepulchres of Muslim kings in other places, were at one time adorned with lovely gardens, but with the passage of time they fell into ruin, and the lands occupied by the gardens were leased to cultivators by the hereditary custodians of the tombs. The Department experienced no small difficulty in stopping cultivation within the enclosures of the tombs, and in some cases considerable sums have had to be paid as compensation for acquiring possession of lands in the precincts of monuments. The walks of these old gardens have now been restored, and the flower-beds indicated by newly turfed plots.

Almost all the old palaces in the fort were occupied by Government offices, and one was used as the District Jail. The Jail was removed immediately after my first

[1] This walk offers the visitor excellent opportunities of enjoying views of the fort at different points.

report, and several other old buildings have since been vacated. As regards the remaining buildings the Government policy is that they shall be vacated as soon as new offices have been constructed.

In the booklet *The Antiquities of Bidar*, I had expressed the hope of writing a detailed account of the place as soon as the necessary opportunities permitted of this being done. Accordingly, after the sanction of our comprehensive scheme, work was started towards a closer study of the monuments, and architectural drawings and photographs were taken and necessary historical data collected in order to present the subject in correct perspective. The material has been sent from time to time to the University Press, Oxford, which had undertaken to print the volume for the Department. As the volume has been compiled in such hours as could be snatched from official duties the progress of the work has been slow, and I must thank Dr. John Johnson, the Printer of the University Press, for his patience and courtesy in keeping the material standing for such a long time. The text and monochrome plates have both been printed by the University Press, Oxford, while the colour plates have been prepared by Messrs. Henry Stone & Son of London and Banbury.

The expenditure on the production of such a work is necessarily large, and I greatly appreciate the liberality of H.E.H.'s Government in so readily sanctioning the proposal for the publication of the volume, and the kindness of His Exalted Highness who has been graciously pleased to sanction the publication of the book under his special authority.

Lastly I have to thank my esteemed friend, Sir Richard Burn, who has given me most valuable help in the correction of the proofs of the book. I am also grateful to Mr. C. E. A. W. Oldham and Sir John Marshall for most kindly reading the preliminary part of the text and suggesting some useful emendations, and to Dr. J. P. Naish for compiling the index.

G. YAZDANI

ORANGE GROVE, HYDERABAD DN.
June 10, 1944

CONTENTS

PREFACE . . . . v–vii

CHAPTER I

PHYSICAL FEATURES AND TOPOGRAPHY

Situation, climate, geological characteristics of the plateau, soil, agricultural produce, cattle, and monkeys, *pp.* 1–2.

CHAPTER II

HISTORY

Early period, *p.* 3; Muslim conquest, *pp.* 3–4; Ẓafar Khān, founder of the Baihmanī dynasty, made Bidar one of the four provinces of his kingdom, *p.* 4; Bidar a flourishing town during the reigns of the early Baihmanī kings, *p.* 5; transfer of capital from Gulbarga to Bidar by Aḥmad Shāh-al-Walī, *pp.* 5–6; Bidar during Aḥmad Shāh's rule, *pp.* 6–7; 'Alā-ud-Dīn Aḥmad, a cultured monarch, he built a large hospital at Bidar, *p.* 7; reigns of Humāyūn and Niẓām Shāh, *pp.* 7–8; Maḥmūd Gāwān appointed Prime Minister, his services to Niẓām Shāh and Muḥammad Shāh III, *pp.* 8–9; Maḥmūd Gāwān's execution, *p.* 10; reign of Maḥmūd Shāh and the disruption of the Baihmanī kingdom, *p.* 11; Qāsim Barīd, the minister, *de facto* ruler, *p.* 11; the four nominal successors of Maḥmūd Shāh Baihmanī, *pp.* 11–12; Amīr Barīd succeeded his father, Qāsim Barīd, in A.D. 1504, war with Ismā'īl 'Ādil Shāh, *pp.* 12–13; Amīr Barīd died in A.D. 1542 and was succeeded by his son 'Alī Barīd who was the first of the family to adopt the title of Shāh, *p.* 13; 'Alī Barīd joined the confederacy of the Deccan kings in the expedition against Rāma Rāja of Vijayanagar in A.D. 1565, *pp.* 13–14; the rival dynasties of Bijāpur, Golconda, and Ahmadnagar become too powerful for Barīdī kings after the battle of Talīkota, *p.* 14; the kingdom of Bidar reduced to a small principality and ultimately absorbed in the Bijāpur territory, in A.D. 1619, *p.* 14; Aurangzeb conquered Bidar in A.D. 1156 and renamed it Ẓafarābād, *p.* 15; Iftikhār Khān the first Mughal governor of Bidar, A.D. 1656–8, *p.* 15; the successors of Iftikhār Khān until Āṣaf Jāh declared his independence in the Deccan in A.D. 1724, *pp.* 16–17; Bidar fell into further insignificance after the establishment of the Āṣaf Jāhī dynasty, its governors occupying the position of divisional officers, *p.* 17; the *sūbehdārs* of Bidar until A.D. 1846, *pp.* 18–19; with the introduction of the *zil'adārī* system Bidar dwindled to a still lower position, *pp.* 18–19; the signs of revival under the present Nizam, *p.* 20.

CHAPTER III

ARCHITECTURE

Medieval Hindu architecture of the Deccan, *pp.* 21–2; in the fourteenth century A.D. Muḥammad bin Tughluq made strenuous efforts to transfer the whole population of Delhi to Daulatābād which he desired to make the capital of the empire, *p.* 22; as the result of this the earliest Muslim buildings of the Deccan show distinct influence of the contemporary architecture of Delhi, a notable example among them being Fīroz Shāh Baihmanī's tomb at Gulbarga, *p.* 22; Baihmanī kings later employed Persian architects, Rafī' of Qazvīn designed the Great Mosque of the Gulbarga fort in A.D. 1367, *p.* 22; the stilted dome and arch grew rapidly into fashion in the Deccan, and buildings were richly decorated with encaustic tiles, *pp.* 23–4; in the fifteenth century the tradition and craftsmanship of the Tughluq architecture was modified by Persian forms and ideals, as well as by the skill of the local mason who was an adept in the art of carving, *p.* 23; the defences of the Deccan forts entirely rebuilt by Turkish engineers towards the end of the fifteenth century or the beginning of the sixteenth century when gunpowder came into use, *p.* 23; the façade of the Ta<u>kh</u>t Maḥall at Bidar decorated with the device of the tiger and the sun resembling the Persian emblem of the lion and the rising sun, *p.* 24; the walls of the audience hall of the Ta<u>kh</u>t Maḥall embellished with tile-work of Persian design and stone carving of Hindu pattern, *p.* 24; Madrasa of Maḥmūd Gāwān designed in the style of the contemporary schools in Persia and other Islamic countries, *pp.* 23–4; Sir John Marshall's view regarding the lack of contrasted light and shade, or the feeling for plastic form and mass, not justifiable, *pp.* 24–5; during the rule of Barīdī kings the shrinkage of political power affected the vision and taste of the builder, *p.* 25; the Rangīn Maḥall, with all the beauty of its mother-of-pearl work and wood-carving, suffers from the small scale of its dimensions, *p.* 25; the influence of Hindu architecture predominant in the tomb of ʿAlī Barīd, *p.* 26; the employment of Hindu architects for the designing of religious and semi-religious Muslim buildings at the end of the sixteenth century, marks a definite transition in the style of Deccanese architecture, *p.* 26; the sixteenth century was a period of fusion of cultures in the whole of India, *p.* 26; the <u>Ch</u>ār Mīnār at Hyderabad and the Gol Gumbad at Bijāpur, and the palaces at Fatḥpūr Sīkrī show the knowledge and skill of Hindu craftsmen happily blended with Muslim ideals and tradition, *pp.* 26–7; in the seventeenth century the influence of the Hindu mason was predominant in the construction of all kinds of buildings, hence slender minarets, toy-like domes, and profusion of plaster decoration become the salient features of the architecture of the Deccan, *p.* 27; the glory of Bidar architecture waned with the decline of the Baihmanī kingdom and finally disappeared with the extinction of the Barīdī dynasty, *p.* 27.

CHAPTER IV
MONUMENTS

(1) THE FORT ENCLAVE, *pp.* 28-82.

Fortifications built in different periods, *pp.* 28–30; Bidar fort, an irregular rhomboid in shape built on the brink of a plateau, *p.* 30; it has thirty-seven bastions and seven gates, besides the main entrance from the city side, *p.* 31; the <u>Sh</u>arza Darwāza, *pp.* 32–3; the *naqqār-<u>kh</u>āna*, *pp.* 33–4; the Gumbad Darwāza, *pp.* 34–5; the house of the Commandant of the Fort and the watch tower, *p.* 35 f.n. 1; the Large Gun Bastion, *pp.* 35–6; the Māṇḍū Darwāza, *pp.* 36–7; the Kalmaḍgī Darwāza, *p.* 37; the Purāna Qilʿa, *pp.* 37–8; the Fatḥ La<u>sh</u>kar Gun, *pp.* 38–9; the Delhi Darwāza, *p.* 40; the Kalyānī Burj, *pp.* 40–1; the Peṭlā Burj, *pp.* 41–2; the Lāl Burj mounted with a long range gun, *Top-i-Ḥaidarī*, *p.* 42; the Kālā Burj, *p.* 43; the Carnatic Darwāza, *pp.* 43–4; Tasker's Walk, *p.* 44; the Rangīn Maḥall, *pp.* 44–9; the *Shāhī Maṭba<u>kh</u>* or the Royal Kitchen, *pp.* 49–51; the *<u>Sh</u>āhī Ḥammām* or the Royal Bath, *pp.* 51–2; the *Lāʿl Bā<u>gh</u>* or the Ruby Gardens, *pp.* 52–3; the Solah Khamb Mosque, *pp.* 54–6; The Tarka<u>sh</u> Maḥall, *pp.* 57–9; the Gagaṇ Maḥall, *pp.* 60–2; the Hall of Public Audience, *pp.* 62–6; the *Ta<u>kh</u>t Maḥall* or the Throne Palace, *pp.* 66–77; the Octagonal Pavilion, *pp.* 75–6; the underground apartments, *pp.* 76–7; the *Hazār Koṭhṛī* or the Thousand cells, *pp.* 77–8; the old Naubat <u>Kh</u>āna or the Music Gallery, *p.* 78; the Gateway of the Lowlands, *pp.* 79–80; the Long Gun Bastion, *p.* 80; the Vīrasangayya's temple, *pp.* 80–1; the Gunpowder Magazine, *pp.* 81–2.

(2) THE TOWN, *pp.* 82–114.

The defences of the town built in different periods, *pp.* 82–3; the fortifications have a pentagonal plan and comprise thirty-seven bastions and eight batteries, besides the glacis, the moat, and the scarp, *p.* 83; the town entered by five massively built gateways, *p.* 83; the <u>Sh</u>āh Ganj Darwāza, *pp.* 83–4; the *Sarā'i* of Mīr ʿĀlam, *p.* 84, f.n. 1; the Muṇḍā Burj, *pp.* 84–5; the Maḥmūd <u>Sh</u>āhī Gun, *pp.* 85–6; the Fatḥ Darwāza, *pp.* 85–7; Ibrahīm ʿĀdil <u>Sh</u>āh II changed the original name of the gateway and called it the Nauras Darwāza, *p.* 87; the Mangalpeṭ Darwāza, pp. 87–8; the Dulhan Darwāza, pp. 88–9; the Talghāṭ Darwāza, pp. 89–90; the Chaubāra, pp. 90–1; the Madrasa of Maḥmūd Gāwān, pp. 91–100; the Mint (?), p. 100; the Takht-i-Kirmānī, pp. 100–2; the *Manhīyār Ta'līm* or the Bangle-seller's School, pp. 102–3; the Jāmi' Masjid, pp. 103–4; the Ta'līm Pansāl, p. 104; the Khāṣṣ Maḥall, p. 104; the 'Alī Bāgh, p. 104; the Chīta Khāna, pp. 104–5; the Ta'līm of Ṣiddīq Shāh, p. 105; the 'Āshūr Khāna and the Alāvā, pp. 105–6; the monastery of Nūr Samnānī, pp. 106–7; the tomb of Multānī Pādshāh, pp. 107–9; the tomb of Shaikh Ibrāhīm, p. 109; the Khānqāh of Shāh Abū'l-Faiḍ, pp. 109–10; the Ta'līm of Nūr Khān, p. 110; the Khānqāh of Shāh Walī-Ullah, p. 110; the Khānqāh of Shāh 'Alī Ḥusain Quṭb II, pp. 110–11; the Baṛī Khānqāh of Maḥbūb Subḥānī, p. 111; the Chhotī Khānqāh of Maḥbūb Subḥānī, pp. 111–12; the Khānqāh of Makhdūm Qādirī, p. 112; the Khānqāh of Minnat-Ullāh Bī, p. 113; the mosque of Khalīl-Ullah Khān, pp. 113–14.

(3) Baihmanī Tombs, pp. 114–48.

Tomb of Aḥmad Shāh al-Walī, its architecture, pp. 114–17; the paintings of the walls and ceiling, pp. 117–19; the inscriptions, pp. 119–28; the Tomb of Sulṭān Aḥmad Shāh's wife (?), pp. 128–9; the tomb of Aḥmad Shāh's son (?), pp. 129–30; the Tomb of Sulṭān 'Alā-ud-Dīn Shāh II, its tile-work and other decorative features, pp. 130–1; its architecture, pp. 131–2; the Tomb of Sulṭān Humāyūn, its special features, pp. 132–4; the influence of Hindu architecture, pp. 133–4; the Tomb of Sulṭān Niẓām Shāh, p. 134; the Tomb of Sulṭān Muḥammad Shāh III entitled Lashkarī, pp. 134–5; the Tomb of Malika-i-Jahān, pp. 135–6; the Tomb of Maḥmūd Shāh Baihmanī, pp. 136–7; two anonymous Tombs (the Sepulchres of Sulṭān Aḥmad Shāh and Sulṭān 'Alā-ud-Dīn (?), p. 137; the Tomb of Sulṭān Walī-Ullāh, pp. 137–8; the Tomb of Sulṭān Kalīm-Ullāh, p. 138; the Mosque, pp. 138–9; the Tomb of Shāh Rukh Khān (?), pp. 139–40; the Well with the inscription of Mirzā Walī Amīr Barīd, pp. 140–1; The Chaukhaṇḍī of Ḥaḍrat Khalīl-Ullāh, its approach, and special architectural features, pp. 141–2; the tile-decoration, carving, and calligraphic devices, pp. 142–3; other tombs in the court, pp. 143–5; the tombs on a platform under a *nīm* tree, pp. 146–8; and the Tomb of Shāh Rājū, p. 148.

(4) Barīdī Tombs, pp. 148–76.

The Tomb of Qāsim Barīd, pp. 149–50; the Tomb of Amīr Barīd I, its architectural features, pp. 150–1; other tombs in the courtyard, p. 151; the Tomb of 'Alī Barīd, the suitability of the site, pp. 151–2; the southern gateway, pp. 152–4; the architecture of the main building, pp. 154–5; the tile-decoration, pp. 156–8; the inscriptions, pp. 156–8; the Mosque attached to the Tomb, pp. 159–60; the Tomb of Ibrāhīm Barīd, pp. 160–1; *Raṇ Khamb* or Polo Posts, p. 162; the Tomb of Qāsim Barīd II, pp. 162–3; other tombs within the enclosure, pp. 163–5; the 'Idgāh, pp. 165–6; the Barber's Tomb, pp. 166–7; the Tomb of 'Abdullāh Maghribī, p. 167; the Tomb of Khān Jahān Barīd, pp. 167–9; the Tomb of Bībī Bandagī Ḥusainī, pp. 169–70; the Tomb of Ḥaḍrat Shāh Walī-Ullāh, pp. 170–1; the Tomb of the Dog (?), pp. 171–2; the Tomb of Ḥaḍrat Niẓām-ud-Dīn, pp. 172–3; the two anonymous tombs, p. 173; some anonymous Barīdī tombs, pp. 173–4; the Tomb of Ḥaḍrat Shāh Zain-ud-Dīn Kunj Nishīn, pp. 174–5; the two Mosques in the Grove of Ḥaḍrat Shāh Zain-ud-Dīn, pp. 175–6.

(5) Monuments of the Suburbs, pp. 176–213.

Farḥ Bāgh, the Mosque, pp. 176–8; the Mughal garden, pp. 178–80; the Spring and the Temple, pp. 179–80; the shrines of later period in the third stage of the garden, p. 180; the Ḥabshī Koṭ, the popular stories about the hill, pp. 180–1; the Tomb of Ẓafar-ul-Mulk (?), pp. 181–2; other tombs on the plateau, pp. 182–4; the *Dargāh* of Ḥaḍrat Abū'l-Faiḍ, the shrine of the saint, pp. 184–5; the tombs of the descendants of the saint within the enclosure of the *Dargāh*, pp. 185–6; the Tomb of 'Āshūrī Begam, p. 186; the Well attached to the Tomb, pp. 186–7; the Tomb of Ḥaḍrat Shāh 'Alī, pp. 187–8; the Tomb of Shāh Abū'l-Ḥasan, p. 188;

the Tomb of Ḥaḍrat Sayyid Amīr Ḥamza Qādirī, *pp.* 189; Hanūmān's Temple, *pp.* 189–90; the *Dargāh* of Banda 'Alī Shāh Majdhūb, *p.* 190; the *Chaukhaṇḍī* of Mīr Kalān Khān, *p.* 190; the Tomb of Khāṣṣ Maḥall, *pp.* 190–1; the Tomb of Ghālib Khān *alias* Miṭṭhū Khān, *p.* 191; the Tomb of Ḥaḍrat Shāh Nūr Samnānī, *pp.* 191–2; the Tomb of Maḥmūd Gāwān, *p.* 192; the Mosque at Gornallī, *p.* 193; the so-called Kalī Masjid of Aurangzeb's reign, *pp.* 193–5; the Tomb of Ḥaḍrat Muḥammad Ḥusain Imām-ul-Mudarrisīn, *p.* 195; the Kalī Masjid, *pp.* 196–7; the Tomb of Shāh 'Alī, son of Shāh Khalīl-Ullāh, *pp.* 197–8; the Mosque of Barkhẉurdār Beg with the inscription of Aurangzeb's reign, *pp.* 198–9; the Tomb of Shaikh Badr-ud-Dīn, *p.* 199; the Tomb of Fāṭima Bībī (?), *pp.* 199–200; the Tomb of Ḥaḍrat Makhdūm Qādirī, *pp.* 200–1; the Mosque to the north-east of Ḥaḍrat Makhdūm Qādirī's Tomb, *pp.* 201–2; the Tomb of Shāh 'Alī Qādirī, *p.* 202; the Mosque attached to the Tomb with an inscription, dated 1107 H. (A.D. 1695), *pp.* 202–3; the Water Works of Bidar, the Tank at Kamthāna, *pp.* 203–4; the Cistern with masonry margins at the same place, *pp.* 204–5; the Subterranean Canal, *p.* 205; the Subterranean Canals of Naubād and Bidar town, *pp.* 205–6; the Tomb of Qāḍi Shams-ud-Dīn at Naubād, *pp.* 206–7; the Pāpnās Spring, its approach, *p.* 207; the religious sculpture and remains of old structures, *pp.* 207–8; the rock-hewn cells, *p.* 208; the tank, *p.* 208; the Tomb of Ḥaḍrat Sayyid-us-Sādāt, *pp.* 208–9; the Spring with the inscription, dated 910 H. (A.D. 1504), *pp.* 210–11; the Tomb of Fakhr-ul-Mulk at Fatḥpūr, its striking resemblance to the pre-Mughal tombs of Delhi, *p.* 211; the salient architectural features, *pp.* 211–12; the Tomb of Ḥaḍrat Shāh Muḥibb-Ullāh near the village of Malkāpūr, *pp.* 212–13.

Arabic, Persian, and Urdū Index 214

Marāṭhī and Sanskrit Index 218

General Index 218

LIST OF PLATES

I The First Gateway of the Fort.
II The Triple Moat.
III The Sharza Darwāza.
IV The Sharza Darwāza and Parapet: View from the South-west.
V The Ramparts of the Fort facing the South-east.
VI The Guṃbad Darwāza.
VII View of the Interior of the Fort from the Guṃbad Darwāza.
VIII Plan of the Rangīn Maḥall.
IX Tile-Work on the Upper Walls of the Rangīn Maḥall.
X Columns of Wood: Rangīn Maḥall.
XI Designs of Wood Carving: Rangīn Maḥall: (*a*) Muslim Patterns, (*b*) Hindu Devices.
XII Tile-Work on the Doorway of the Royal Pavilion: Rangīn Maḥall.
XIII Mother-of-Pearl work on the Inner Doorway of the Royal Pavilion: Rangīn Maḥall
XIV Tile-Work of the Dado: Rangīn Maḥall.
XV Plan of the Royal Bath.
XVI Plan of the Prayer-Hall of the Solah Khamb Mosque.
XVII The Solah Khamb Mosque: General View. *Before conservation.*
XVIII The Solah Khamb Mosque: Interior.
XIX The Tarkash Maḥall (?): Decorative Features.
XX Plaster-Work of the Tarkash Maḥall (?).
XXI The Tarkash Maḥall (?): Southern Wing.
XXII Plan of the Gagaṇ Maḥall.
XXIII Plan of the Hall of Audience.
XXIV The Hall of Audience: General View.
XXV The Hall of Audience.
XXVI The Minister's Room.
XXVII Designs of the Tile-Work: Audience Hall.
XXVIII Designs of the Tile-Work: Audience Hall.
XXIX Designs of the Tile-Work: Audience Hall.
XXX Pavement of the Royal Chamber: Audience Hall.
XXXI Plan of the Takht Maḥall.
XXXII The Gateway of the Outer Court of the Takht Maḥall.
XXXIII Rooms in the Outer Court of the Takht Maḥall. *Before conservation.*
XXXIV Gateway of the Inner Court of the Takht Maḥall. *Before conservation.*
XXXV The Takht Maḥall: General View during Excavation.
XXXVI Façade of the Royal Chamber: Takht Maḥall.
XXXVII The Tiger and Sun Emblem on the Façade of the Royal Chamber.
XXXVIII Room on the left side of the Royal Chamber after Excavation.
XXXIX Apartments of the Takht Maḥall towards the South-west after Excavation.
XL The Southern Wing of the Takht Maḥall after Excavation.
XLI Pavilion to the South-west of the Takht Maḥall after Excavation.
XLII Gateway to the North of the Takht Maḥall: View from the West.
XLIII Guard-Rooms: View from the East.
XLIV The Kalyānī Burj.
XLV The Double Line of Fortifications.
XLVI The Long Gun.

XLVII The Large Gun.
XLVIII The Monkeys enjoying their Noon Meal.
XLIX The Gun on the Muṇḍā Burj.
L Plan of the Madrasa of Maḥmūd Gāwān.
LI Façade of the Madrasa of Maḥmūd Gāwān.
LII Façade of the Madrasa of Maḥmūd Gāwān: Detail of Tile-work.
LIII Madrasa of Maḥmūd Gāwān: General View. *Before conservation.*
LIV Madrasa of Maḥmūd Gāwān: View from the South-east.
LV Madrasa of Maḥmūd Gāwān: Interior: View from the East.
LVI Madrasa of Maḥmūd Gāwān: Exterior: View from the North-east.
LVII The Fatḥ Darwāza: Bidar Town.
LVIII Plan of the Jāmi' Masjid.
LIX The Jāmi' Masjid: General View.
LX The Jāmi' Masjid: Interior.
LXI The Dulhan Darwāza: View from the East.
LXII The Talghāṭ Darwāza: View from the North.
LXIII The Path leading to the Talghāṭ Darwāza.
LXIV The Chaubāra.
LXV The Takht-i-Kirmānī.
LXVI A Mosque near the Dulhan Darwāza.
LXVII The Baihmanī Tombs: View from the South-east.
LXVIII Plan of the Tomb of Sulṭān Aḥmad Shāh Walī Baihmanī.
LXIX The Tomb of Sulṭan Aḥmad Shāh Walī Baihmanī: View from the North.
LXX Floral and Calligraphic Designs over the Southern Doorway of Aḥmad Shāh Walī's Tomb.
LXXI Geometric and Calligraphic Devices on the Southern Wall of Aḥmad Shāh Walī's Tomb.
LXXII Calligraphic and Floral Patterns on the Eastern Wall of Aḥmad Shāh Walī's Tomb.
LXXIII Floral Designs on the Eastern Arch of Aḥmad Shāh Walī's Tomb.
LXXIV The Ceiling of Aḥmad Shāh Walī Baihmanī's Tomb.
LXXV The *Jangam* with his paraphernalia at the *'Urs* of Aḥmad Shāh Walī Baihmanī.
LXXVI Plan of the Tomb of 'Alā-ud-Dīn Baihmanī.
LXXVII (*a*) The Tomb of 'Alā-ud-Dīn Baihmanī: View from the North.
(*b*) The same: Detail of tile-work: View from the South.
LXXVIII The Tomb of Sulṭān Humāyūn.
LXXIX The Tomb of Maḥmūd Shāh Baihmanī: View from the South.
LXXX The Tomb of Maḥmūd Shāh Baihmanī: View from the North.
LXXXI The Tombs of Walī-Ullāh and Kalīm-Ullāh Baihmanī.
LXXXII Plan and section of Sulṭān Kalīm-Ullāh's Tomb.
LXXXIII Plan of the Chaukhanḍī of Ḥaḍrat Khalīl-Ullāh.
LXXXIV The *Chaukhanḍī* of Ḥaḍrat Khalīl-Ullāh: General View.
LXXXV The *Chaukhanḍī* of Ḥaḍrat Khalīl-Ullāh: Detail of Carving.
LXXXVI A Tomb to the East of Ḥaḍrat Khalīl-Ullāh's *Chaukhanḍī*: View from the South.
LXXXVII A Tomb to the East of Ḥaḍrat Khalīl-Ullāh's *Chaukhanḍī*: Interior: Stucco decoration.
LXXXVIII A Tomb to the South-west of Ḥaḍrat Khalīl-Ullāh's *Chaukhanḍī*: Interior: Stucco decoration.
LXXXIX Plan of the Tomb of Sulṭān 'Alī Barīd.
XC The Southern Gateway of 'Alī Barīd's Tomb.

XCI The Hall on the first floor of the Southern Gateway: Tomb of ʿAlī Barīd.
XCII The Tomb of Sulṭān ʿAlī Barīd: View from the South-east.
XCIII The Tomb of ʿAlī Barīd: View from the West.
XCIV The black-stone Sarcophagus: Tomb of ʿAlī Barīd.
XCV An Inscription on the Western Wall of the Tomb of ʿAlī Barīd.
XCVI The Ceiling of ʿAlī Barīd's Tomb.
XCVII Plan of the Mosque of ʿAlī Barīd's Tomb.
XCVIII The Mosque of ʿAlī Barīd's Tomb: Façade.
XCIX The Mosque of ʿAlī Barīd's Tomb: Interior.
C The Mosque of ʿAlī Barīd's Tomb: View from the North-west.
CI The Tomb of Ibrāhīm Barīd.
CII The Ceiling of Ibrāhīm Barīd's Tomb.
CIII A Carved Pillar: Tomb of Ibrāhīm Barīd.
CIV Plan of the Tomb of Amīr Barīd.
CV (*a*) The Tomb of Amīr Barīd: View from the South-west.
(*b*) The same: View from the South. *Before conservation.*
CVI An Anonymous Tomb: Interior.
CVII The *Raṇ Khamb* or Polo Posts (?).
CVIII The Tomb of Qāsim Barīd II.
CIX An Anonymous Tomb.
CX The Tomb of a Lady (C͟hānd Sulṭāna ?).
CXI The Sarcophagus of a Lady's Tomb.
CXII Plan of the Tomb of K͟hān Jahān Barīd.
CXIII The Tomb of K͟hān Jahān Barīd.
CXIV The Tomb of K͟hān Jahān Barīd: Cut-plaster decoration.
CXV The Barber's Tomb and Mosque. *Before conservation.*
CXVI The Tomb of Ḥaḍrat ʿAbdullāh Magh͟ribī. *Before conservation.*
CXVII (*a*) The Dog's Tomb (?). *Before conservation.*
(*b*) An Anonymous Tomb. *Before conservation.*
CXVIII The Farḥ Bāg͟h.
CXIX The Ḥabs͟hī Koṭ: Principal Tomb.
CXX Plan of the Prayer-Hall of the Kālī Masjid.
CXXI The Kālī Masjid: Façade.
CXXII The Kālī Masjid: View from the South-west.
CXXIII The Tomb of Ḥaḍrat S͟hāh Abū'l-Faiḍ: General View.
CXXIV The Tomb of Ḥaḍrat S͟hāh Abū'l-Faiḍ: Doorway.
CXXV The Tomb of Ḥaḍrat Mak͟hdūm Qādirī: View from the South-east.
CXXVI A Mosque near the Tomb of Ḥaḍrat Mak͟hdūm Qādirī.
CXXVII The *Pāpnās* Spring.
CXXVIII The Tomb of Ḥaḍrat Sayyid-us-Sādāt.
CXXIX Plan of the Tomb at Fatḥpūr.
CXXX The Tomb at Fatḥpūr.

CHAPTER I

PHYSICAL FEATURES AND TOPOGRAPHY

BIDAR town enjoys a picturesque situation, having been built on the brink of a plateau, and thus commanding lovely views of the lowlands (*talghāṭ*) towards the north and the east. Its latitude is 17° 55′ N., its longitude 77° 32′ E., and the height above the sea-level 2,330 feet. The climate is bracing and the temperature in the hottest season does not usually rise above 105°. The distance of the town from Hyderabad is eighty-two miles, but the fringe of the Bidar plateau begins from Kamkol village,[1] and the breast is reached when the visitor has passed a few miles beyond Akelī.[2] The plateau is an irregular oblong, twenty-two miles in length and twelve in extreme breadth, with an area of about one hundred and ninety square miles.

The upper crust of the plateau is of laterite, a soft porous rock with limonitic surface. This crust varies in depth from 100 to 500 feet and rests on a bed of trap, which is of much harder texture and less pervious to water. The volume of water filtered during the monsoons through the laterite stratum is arrested by the trappean bed, and a nursery of springs is formed whose natural level of effluence is the line of contact of the two strata along the base of the cliffs of the plateau. The water in course of time frets out for itself an orifice and macerates and loosens portions of its rocky channel till a rift is produced. The rift gradually dilates into a ravine, and the ravine expands into a vale. These physical phenomena have provided Bidar with some charming sites.[3] The most notable among them are the springs of Pāpnās ('destroyer of sins') and Sayyid-us-Sādāt,[4] and the flowered valley of Farḥ Bāgh ('garden of joy'). The first two have lovely glens, while the last has a shady recess, at the head of which a streamlet gushes out from the cliff after flowing for a considerable distance in the womb of the rock. These sites will be described in greater detail in the sequel.

The surface of the plateau presents wide stretches of red plains, either waved over by light dry grasses alive with coveys of partridges and herds of deer, or mottled by

[1] Kamkol is fifty miles from Hyderabad.

[2] This village is now called Ẓahīrābād; it is sixty-two miles from Hyderabad.

[3] There are seven springs of perennial flow in the vicinity of Bidar. Their names are as follows:

(i) The spring of 'Alīābād, situated some two and a half miles to the north-west of Bidar. It is fed by a *kārez* (کاریز) from Naubād which runs underground through the cliff and can be traced by a series of deep square manholes cut in the hard laterite.

(ii) The spring of Chamkoṛa Maṛī, situated at a distance of a mile and a half from Bidar. Chamkoṛa is a kind of herb which is cultivated there.

(iii) The spring of Sayyid-us-Sādāt. For description, see *infra*, p. 210.

(iv) The spring of Farḥ Bāgh. For description, see *infra*, pp. 176–80.

(v) The spring of Śukla Tīrath, situated at a distance of a mile to the east of Bidar. A pipe-line has been laid from this spring to the village of Agrār.

(vi) The spring of Shaikh Nūr Samnānī, situated at a distance of one mile from the town of Bidar.

(vii) The spring of Pāpnās. For description, see *infra*, pp. 207–8.

[4] The title of a saint whose real name was Sayyid Ḥanīf. For further particulars, see *infra*, p. 208.

every sort of cultivation for which artificial irrigation is not essential. The laterite must everywhere be pierced nearly to the subjacent trap to reach the perennial springs, so that the wells in the vicinity of the edges of the tableland are of extraordinary depth. The stream-fed valleys and the tracts of mixed soil in the lowlands bear prodigally fruits and grains, canes and vines, and every variety of vegetable produce.

Bidar is noted for its cattle and also for the rich quality of the butter made from their milk. To the ordinary visitor, however, the most attractive feature in the fauna of Bidar is the abundance of monkeys which run about freely in large troops amid the shady retreats and ruined abodes of the place. The species has a jet-black face, grey hair all over the body, and a long tail which helps it in swinging and leaping from branch to branch. It is called *langūr* or *hanūmān* (*Semnopithecus*), and is much larger in size than the more common brown monkeys or *bandar* (*Macacus*) of Indian towns. These funny creatures, notwithstanding their predatory raids, enjoy considerable immunity from the people, the reason for this attitude apparently being the religious idea that they are the progeny of the sacred Hanūmān or monkey god who helped Rāma in vanquishing the ten-headed demon Rāvaṇa, and in liberating his beautiful wife, Sītā, from the demon's possession. It was either this reverential regard of the people or the curiosity of the king himself in the antics and frolicsome gestures of these beasts that induced Nawāb Nāṣir-ud-Daula Bahādur (1829–57) to issue a *farmān* sanctioning a handsome grant for the maintenance of the monkeys of Bidar. The grant is still continued, and the monkeys are fed under a large banyan tree near the gateway of the fort every day at noon. It is a pleasing sight to see them approaching the guard who distributes food (Pl. XLVIII).

Bidar is the head-quarters of the district of that name and has a population of over 15,000 persons. It is now accessible from Hyderabad by both rail and road. For the road journey there is an omnibus service running twice daily in each direction.

CHAPTER II

HISTORY

LEGEND has associated Bidar with the ancient kingdom of Vidarbha, to which references are found in early Hindu literature.[1] But the situation of the latter kingdom has been determined by modern research, and it is now considered that Vidarbha occupied the country which is called Berar. The rulers of the kingdom are supposed to have been vassals of the Āndhra rājas,[2] whose dominions covered the plateau of the Deccan and at times extended over a much wider area. Bidar, which is some two hundred miles south-east of Paithan, the capital of the Āndhra kings, must have been included in the territory of the latter, and it has been associated with Vidarbha apparently on account of the similarity in names—Bidar and Vidarbha. The identity of Bidar with Vidarbha was, however, a common belief in Firishta's time, for he, when referring to the romances of the early rulers of Bidar, describes the love-story of Nala and Damayantī;[3] and the latter was undoubtedly the daughter of Rāja Bhīma of Vidarbha.

In the excavations carried out recently by the Archaeological Department, Hyderabad, some sculptures and broken tablets bearing inscriptions have been found in the Bidar fort; but they do not carry back the history of the place earlier than the 10th century A.D., when it was apparently included in the kingdom of the later Chālukyas (A.D. 974–1190), whose capital, Kalyāni, is only thirty-six miles west of Bidar. The power of the Chālukyas, however, rapidly declined during the rule of the last three kings of the dynasty, and a large portion of their territory was occupied by the Yādavas of Deogiri and the Kākatīyas of Warangal, whose kingdoms were at the zenith of their glory in the eleventh and twelfth centuries. Bidar was apparently annexed to the Kākatīya kingdom, for in A.D. 1322, when Prince Ulugh Khān[4] marched upon Warangal, he besieged and conquered the town of Bidar, which was on the frontiers of Telingāna.[5] An inscription of Ghiyāth-ud-Dīn Tughluq, dated A.D. 1323, recently found at Kalyāni, shows that the latter town was also conquered by Ulugh Khān in this expedition, but the absence of Kalyāni's name in this connexion in contemporary history shows that Bidar at that time was a more important town than Kalyāni, the glory of which seems to have faded with the decline of the Chālukyas.[6] In this inscription Kalyāni is mentioned as only a *qaṣba*, or minor town.[7]

The historian Ḍīa-ud-Dīn Barnī, in his account of the conquest of Warangal by Prince Muḥammad (Ulugh Khān), gives further details of the siege of Bidar by

[1] *Mālavikāgnimitra*; *Mahābhārata*; the *Harivaṃśa*, *Bhāgavata*, and a few other Purāṇas.

[2] *Cambridge History of India*, vol. i, p. 600.

[3] Briggs, vol. ii, p. 411.

[4] Afterwards Muḥammad bin Tughluq.

[5] Briggs, vol. i, p. 405.

[6] Firishta writes that Ulugh Khān took the town of Bidar, belonging to the Rāja of Warangal, and some *other places* wherein he left garrisons. Kalyāni, being a minor town at that time, seems to be included in the general term 'other places'. Briggs, vol. i, p. 405.

[7] *Epigraphia Indo-Moslemica*, 1935–6, pp. 1–2.

mentioning the occupation of the outer defences of the fort by the Prince.[1] This fort, dating from Hindu times, was subsequently either demolished by Aḥmad S͟hāh Walī al-Baihmanī, when he built the present fort after making Bidar the capital of his kingdom,[2] or incorporated by him in the new fortifications and lines of defences.[3]

In 1341 Muḥammad bin Tug͟hluq honoured S͟hihāb-ud-Dīn of Multan with the title of Nuṣrat K͟hān and conferred on him the government of Bidar with its dependencies on the condition that he should pay a revenue of one crore of rupees annually into the king's treasury.[4] Nuṣrat K͟hān could not fulfil this condition, and in A.D. 1345 he rebelled. The king ordered Qutlug͟h K͟han, the governor of Daulatābād, to chastize the rebel. Qutlug͟h K͟hān expelled Nuṣrat K͟hān from his government, but at that time, on account of the weakening of the king's authority, general disorder prevailed in the Deccan, and Amīr ʿAlī, one of the new officers who was sent from Daulatābād to collect the revenue of Gulbarga, raised an army and occupied Gulbarga and Bidar on his own account. Muḥammad bin Tug͟hluq again deputed Qutlug͟h K͟hān to subdue the rebellion. When the latter reached the confines of Bidar, Amir ʿAlī gave him battle, but was defeated and obliged to shut himself up in the city. He later capitulated, and Qutlug͟h K͟hān sent him a prisoner to the imperial court. In 1347 Ẓafar K͟hān,[5] a 'centurion' whose real name was Ḥasan, appeared before Bidar with 20,000 horse, but did not attack the place until a large number of troops were sent to his assistance by the Rāja of Warangal.[6] A fierce battle ensued in which the royalists were defeated and ʿImād-ul-Mulk, son-in-law to Muḥammad bin Tug͟hluq, was killed. After this battle Ẓafar K͟hān, at the suggestion of Nāṣir-ud-Dīn Ismāʿīl, was unanimously elected king by the people of the Deccan. The new monarch divided his empire into four provinces, of which Bidar was one, its governor receiving the title of Aʿẓam-i-Humāyūn ('the auspicious chief').

[1] *Tārīk͟h-i-Fīroz S͟hāhī* (*Bibl. Ind.*), p. 449.

[2] Briggs, vol. ii, p. 411.

[3] For a description of the fort, see *infra*, pp. 28–44.

[4] Briggs, vol. i, p. 424.

[5] Ẓafar K͟hān, after his independence, assumed the title of ʿAlā-ud-Dīn Baihman S͟hāh. Recently some inscriptions of Baihmanī kings have been found which record that the Baihmanī kings were descended from the Persian king Baihman, son of Isfandyār. Firis͟hta's remark on this point is interesting. He writes:

> 'It has been asserted that he (ʿAlā-ud-Dīn) was descended from Bahmun, one of the ancient kings of Persia, and I, the author, have even seen a pedigree of him so derived in the royal library of Ahmudnuggur, but it was probably only framed after his accession to the throne, by flatterers and poets, for I believe his origin was too obscure to admit of its being traced. The application of Bahmuny he certainly took out of compliment to his master, Gungoo, the Brahmin, a word often pronounced Bahman. The king himself was by birth an Afghan.' *Firis͟hta* (Persian Text, Bombay lithograph), p. 576.

The title Baihman S͟hāh is mentioned in the Gulbarga mosque inscription, and is also found on the coins of the dynasty. In my opinion it was the most appropriate appellation which the courtiers of ʿAlā-ud-Dīn could suggest for him, taking into consideration the king's sense of gratitude to the Brāhman, Gangū, and the identity of the Persianized form, Baihman, of the caste-name Brāhman, with the name of the great Persian king Baihman, son of Isfandyār. In Gulbarga there is to this day a street called Baihmanīpura, where the majority of the residents are Brāhmans, and some of them describe themselves as the descendants of Gangū.

[6] K͟hafī K͟hān's *Muntak͟hab-ul-Lubāb* (*Bibl. Ind.*), vol. iii, p. 14; Briggs's *Firis͟hta*, vol. ii, p. 289.

Bidar was apparently governed well by A'ẓam-i-Humāyūn during the reign of 'Alā-ud-Dīn, but no reference to it occurs in history until the reign of Muḥammad Shāh, the second Baihmanī king who, during his expedition for the complete conquest of Telingāna, detached A'ẓam-i-Humāyūn with the troops of Bidar for the subjugation of Golconda. As a result of the expedition the hill-fort of Golconda with its dependencies was ceded in perpetuity to the Baihmanī king, who committed it to the charge of A'ẓam-i-Humāyūn. Muḥammad Shāh, on his return from this campaign, disbanded his troops at Bidar and halted there for three months.[1] The salubrity of its climate and the picturesqueness of its environment were apparently the reasons that induced the king to break his journey at the place.

Bidar flourished as a provincial town during the reigns of the early Baihmanī kings, and it is mentioned among the great cities of the Deccan wherein schools for orphans were established by Muḥammad Shāh II (A.D. 1378–97).[2] Later the fortress of Bidar appears in history as the well-protected stronghold wherein the unfortunate Shams-ud-Dīn, the seventh Baihmanī king, was interned to pass the rest of his life in captivity.[3]

The turning-point in the history of Bidar came about the close of the reign of Fīroz Shāh (A.D. 1422), when the two slaves Hoshiyār and Bīdār, who were jealous of the popularity of Prince Aḥmad, led an expedition with the cognizance of the king against the prince. The royalists were defeated in the precincts of Bidar, either at Khanapūr or at Ni'matābād, the former being some ten miles west and the latter only three miles south-west of Bidar.[4] This injudicious action cost Fīroz Shāh his throne, and Prince Aḥmad shortly after his accession made Bidar the capital of his kingdom.

Historians have given various reasons for the transfer of the capital from Gulbarga, among which the old Indian tale of the hunt of a fox by dogs and the extraordinary courage of the latter also occurs.[5] This tale is not worthy of consideration, for it had been told by Indian writers in connexion with the foundation of other ancient towns. The real reasons for the choice of Bidar were its central position in the kingdom, its natural defences, and its invigorating climate. The three principal divisions of the Deccan—Telingāna, the Carnatic, and Mahārāshtra—converge towards Bidar; and the situation of the city on the brink of a plateau about two hundred feet above the adjoining plains would have made it difficult to attack in those days. The perennial springs and the abundance of verdure and fruit trees, which are still the attractive features of Bidar, must have further influenced the king in preferring it to Gulbarga for the seat of his government.[6]

[1] Briggs, vol. ii, pp. 305–6. [2] Ibid., pp. 349–50. [3] Ibid., p. 361.

[4] *Burhān-i-Ma'āthir* (Persian text, Hyderabad edition), pp. 49–50.

[5] *Firishta* (Persian text, Bombay lithograph), vol. i, p. 425.

[6] Firishta and Sayyid 'Alī Ṭabaṭaba, the author of *Burhān-i-Ma'āthir*, both quote the following lines regarding the abundance of springs and the scenic beauty of Bidar:

ز هر سو چشمه چون آب حیوان　　چراغ لاله هر جانب فروزان
بنفشه رسته و سبزه دمیده　　نسیم صبح جیب گل دریده
شقایق بر یکی پا ایستاده　　چو بر شاخ زمرد جام باده

The transfer led to the rebuilding of the old Hindu fortress on an extensive scale and capable of mounting cannon, the use of which had been recently introduced, and against which the previous defences were practically useless. The king built for himself a large palace, regarding the loftiness of which the poet Ādharī composed a poem.[1] Two lines of this were carved on the palace:

حبّذا قصر مشیّد کہ ز فرط عظمت آسمان سدّۂ از پایۂ این درگاہ است

آسمان هم نتوان گفت کہ ترك ادبست قصر سلطان جهان احمد بهمن شاه است

Translation

'How wonderful is this strongly-built palace, compared with the excessive loftiness of which
'The sky is but as a step at its threshold.
' 'Tis an impropriety to compare it with Heaven,
'Verily! It is the palace of the Sulṭān of the world, Aḥmad Baihman Shāh.'[2]

Following the example of the king, the nobles of the court and the important State officials built houses for their residence, and a beautiful city arose, which rapidly acquired fame for the salubrity of its climate, the strength of its defences, and the magnificence of its buildings.

Aḥmad Walī al-Baihmanī had great military and administrative capacity, and during his reign he extended the limits of the Baihmanī kingdom by his campaigns against the King of Mālwa in the north, the Rāi of Warangal in the east, the Rāja of Vijayanagar in the south, and the King of Gujarāt in the north-west. By these campaigns a large portion of the Konkan and a considerable tract of Berar were annexed to the Baihmanī kingdom, and vast sums in cash and large treasures of jewels and valuable commodities realized as tribute or indemnity of war.[3] These riches brought opulence to Bidar, the new capital, and it soon became a centre of culture and progress. Aḥmad Walī's religious propensities attracted to Bidar some divines of repute from Persia, the most important of whom were the son and grandson of Shāh Ni'mat-Ullāh, the famous saint of Kirmān.[4]

During Aḥmad Shāh's reign Bidar was also the scene of great revelry and festivities when Prince 'Alā-ud-Dīn was married to the daughter of Naṣīr Khān Fāruqī of Asīr. The celebrations lasted for two months, and the city was beautifully decorated for the occasion.[5] This alliance strengthened Aḥmad Shāh's government in Rāmgaṛh, Māhūr, and Kallam against the insurrections of the local chiefs and the aggression of the Mālwa king.

[1] The palace was called the Takht Maḥall as it contained a magnificent audience-hall, wherein the famous turquoise throne of the Baihmanī kings was placed. The palace was blown up by gunpowder during a siege of the fort, and huge piles of debris marked its site some twenty-five years ago when the author first visited Bidar. The site has since been excavated by the Archaeological Department and the ground-floor of the palace has been restored to light. For a description of the palace, see *infra*, pp. 66–77.

[2] *Firishta* (Persian text), p. 627; *Burhān-i-Ma'āthir*, pp. 70–1.

[3] *Firishta* (Persian text), pp. 617–35; *Burhān-i-Ma'āthir*, pp. 55–74.

[4] *Firishta* (Persian text), p. 734.

[5] *Burhān-i-Ma'āthir*, p. 56.

Aḥmad Shāh died in A.D. 1436 and was succeeded by his son ʿAlā-ud-Dīn, who built a lofty dome over the grave of his father. The tomb is situated at Āshṭūr, some two miles to the east of Bidar city.[1] The ceiling and walls of this tomb have been decorated with paintings in Muslim style composed of calligraphic devices or floral designs. These paintings are considered to be unique in India for their beauty and elegance.

ʿAlā-ud-Dīn built a large hospital at Bidar and staffed it with expert Muslim and Hindu physicians. A large endowment was made for the cost of medicines and other expenses of the hospital.[2] ʿAlā-ud-Dīn also laid out a delightful garden and built a beautiful palace at Niʿmatābād, a suburb of Bidar.[3] He also built the tomb of Shāh Khalīl-Ullāh and adorned it with carved stone-work and encaustic tiles.[4]

ʿAlā-ud-Dīn was a cultured but pleasure-loving king, and his reign was occupied by intrigues at the court and rebellions in the outlying provinces of the dominions. The most crushing defeat sustained by ʿAlā-ud-Dīn's army was, however, in the Konkan, where a large number of troops under Khalf Ḥasan Baṣarī, the accomplished governor of Daulatābād, were cut to pieces by Sirka, a Konkan chief, and Shankar Rāi the Rāja of Khelna.[5] ʿAlā-ud-Dīn died of a wound in his shin in A.D. 1458 and was succeeded by his son, Humāyūn, who is styled Ẓālim ('the Cruel') in history on account of his atrocious deeds. ʿAlā-ud-Dīn was buried at Āshṭur near the tomb of his father. The magnificent mausoleum which still stands over his grave was apparently built by Humāyūn. The tile-work of this monument has suffered much through climatic conditions, but wherever it is intact the designs and the colour-schemes are most pleasing.[6]

The dark picture of Humāyūn's deeds painted by historians seems to be considerably overdrawn. He was apparently of a peevish nature, perhaps due to indifferent health, for he reigned only a little over three years and died at the early age of twenty-one years. He had rivals for the throne in his own family from the beginning, and when they openly rebelled against him and tried to oust him he showed no mercy to them or to the nobles who had espoused their cause.

Humāyūn appointed his son Niẓām as his successor during his lifetime, and as the boy was only eight years old he ordered that a Council of Regency should transact the affairs of the kingdom. According to Humāyūn's command the Council was to consist of Khwāja Maḥmūd Gāwān, Khwāja Jahān Turk, and the Queen-mother. Khwāja Maḥmūd Gāwān had entered the service of the State during the reign of Humāyūn's father, but distinguished himself by his fidelity to the son.

Humāyūn died in A.D. 1461, and his remains were interred in a tomb built in close vicinity to his father's mausoleum. The dome of Humāyūn's tomb has been destroyed in recent times by lightning, an incident which people of Bidar regard as

[1] For the full description of the tomb, see *infra*, pp. 114–28.

[2] *Burhān-i-Maʾāthir*, p. 87.

[3] Ibid., pp. 76–7; *Firishta* (Persian text), p. 644.

[4] For the description of the building, see *infra*, pp. 141–6.

[5] *Firishta* (Persian text), pp. 644–6.

[6] The building is fully described on pp. 130–2.

divine punishment of Humāyūn's misdeeds. The debris of the dome was lying at the site until A.D. 1917, but it has now been removed by the Archaeological Department of Hyderabad and the damage done to the walls of the building made good by suitable repairs.[1]

The Queen-mother appointed Maḥmūd Gāwān to be Prime Minister and Khwāja Jahān Turk to be Controller of the State (Vakīl-us-Salṭanat), and with their joint advice, which was obtained through a woman called Māh Bāno, began to administer the kingdom on behalf of her young son. Both these ministers were extremely capable and loyal, but in a country where autocratic government was in vogue and the safety of the kingdom depended upon the personal qualities of the ruler, the administration of the Baihmanī kingdom by a Council of Regency gave a welcome opportunity for the neighbouring rulers and chiefs to invade. The first aggressor to march with this object was the Rāi of Orissa, who was joined in his expedition by some refractory chiefs of Telingāna. The Rāi entered the dominions from Rājamundrī and pushed on up to a place some twenty miles from Bidar. There the Baihmanī army met the invaders and attacked them with such valour that the Rāi of Orissa was defeated and had to pay an indemnity of five *lākhs* of silver coins.[2]

After the repulse of the Rāi of Orissa the next aggressor to appear on the scene was Maḥmūd Khaljī, the King of Mālwa, who invaded the kingdom shortly afterwards from the north. Although the young Baihmanī king, accompanied by his ministers and several accomplished generals, marched from Bidar to oppose the invader, their resistance proved unavailing, and Niẓām Shāh had to flee for his life to the capital. Maḥmūd Khaljī marched on triumphantly to Bidar, and ultimately laid siege to the city. Niẓām Shāh, under the advice of the Queen-mother and Maḥmūd Gāwān, committed the charge of the citadel of Bidar to Mallū Khān Deccanī and himself retired to Fīrozābād.[3] The city of Bidar was captured by Maḥmūd Khaljī seventeen days after the departure of Niẓām Shāh, but the fort still held out. In the meantime Maḥmūd Gāwān had written for help to Maḥmūd Shāh of Gujarāt, who readily complied with the request and marched towards the frontier. Later he placed a division of twenty thousand cavalry and several of his trusted officers at the disposal of Maḥmūd Gāwān, who had gone to welcome him on behalf of the Baihmanī king. Sulṭān Maḥmūd Khaljī, who had been unable to capture the citadel, on hearing of the approach of the Gujarāt army raised the siege and retreated precipitately towards Mālwa. Niẓām Shāh dispatched ambassadors with valuable presents to Maḥmūd Shāh of Gujarāt to show his gratitude to the latter for his timely aid. The King of Mālwa again invaded the Deccan in the following year, advancing as far as Daulatābād, but was once more compelled to retreat through the help afforded by Maḥmūd Shāh of Gujarāt.

[1] For a description of the building, see *infra*, pp. 132–4.

[2] *Firishta* (Persian text), p. 665.

[3] A city built by Fīroz Shāh Baihmanī to the south of Gulbarga near the river Bhīma. The ruins of this town still exist, and a description of them is given in the *Annual Report* of the Archaeological Department, Hyderabad, for the year A.D. 1914–15, pp. 44–6.

During the occupation of the city of Bidar by Sulṭān Maḥmūd Khaljī of Mālwa several of its buildings were destroyed. These were, however, built afresh by Niẓām Shāh when he returned to the capital.[1] The young king died suddenly in A.D. 1463, at a time when the Queen-mother had arranged for his wedding, and a nuptial feast with due pomp and magnificence was being prepared. He was buried near the tomb of his father.[2]

The next Baihmanī king after Niẓām Shāh was Muḥammad Shāh III, again a lad nine years old. The Council of Regency appointed during the reign of the last king continued to transact the affairs of government. Khān Jahān Turk, however, acquired unlimited power and influence in every department of the State, and keeping Maḥmūd Gāwān, his colleague, employed in the administration of the frontiers, he became the *de facto* ruler. The Queen-mother, who had a penetrating mind and also possessed considerable political capacity, could not tolerate the aggrandizement of Khan Jahān and arranged to have him put to death.

Muḥammad Shāh III received a good literary education under Ṣadr-i-Jahān Shūstarī, a celebrated scholar of the age, and he is considered by the historians to have been the most learned prince, next to Fīroz Shāh, among the Baihmanī kings. He gave promise of military prowess as well at a fairly early age, and after his emancipation from the tutelage of his mother and the minister, Maḥmūd Gāwān,[3] his first act was to send an expedition for the conquest of the fort of Kherla, which had been a bone of contention between the kings of Mālwa and the Deccan. The fort was captured, but subsequently a treaty was signed, in accordance with which the fort was restored to the King of Mālwa and a mutual understanding was reached between the two monarchs to refrain from molesting each other's dominions.

In A.D. 1469 Maḥmūd Gāwān led an expedition to the Konkan against some refractory chiefs, who were subdued, and finally the port of Goa, which previously belonged to the Rāja of Vijayanagar, was captured. Maḥmūd Gāwān established a strong garrison in the fort of Goa, and when he returned to Bidar after an absence of three years, which the expedition had occupied, the king honoured him by a visit of a whole week and conferred upon him the highest titles with a suit of his own robes.

Other triumphs secured during the reign were the subjugation of Vishagaṛh[4] in the north, of Condapallī[5] and Rājamundrī in the north-east, and of the country as far as Conjeevaram in the south. The success of the reign was, however, marred by a tragedy which was caused by the intrigue of some vicious officials of the court who had become jealous of Maḥmūd Gāwān's popularity and power. These persons forged a letter over the seal of the minister, addressing it to the Rāi of Orissa, who was at that time hostile to the king. The letter was shown to the king at a time when he was intoxicated with liquor, and suspecting treason he forgot all his previous

[1] The coins of Niẓām Shāh's reign bear the title Aḥmad Shāh, a fact which does not find mention in contemporary histories.

[2] For a description of Niẓām Shāh's tomb, see *infra*, p. 134.

[3] Maḥmūd Gāwān succeeded Khān Jahān Turk as Vakil-us-Salṭanat (Administrator of the State on behalf of the King) after the death of the latter. The title of Khān Jahān was also conferred on him.

[4] The fort is mentioned under the name of Vīragaṛh by Firishta, *vide* Persian text, p. 680.

[5] This place is mentioned as Kanchī by Firishta; *vide* Persian text, p. 688.

regard for the minister and gave orders for his immediate execution. The orders were carried out, but the death of the minister caused general alarm and distrust, even among the most devoted officers of the State, who refrained from attending the court when the king invited them. This state of affairs led to the weakening of Muḥammad Shāh's authority and to the gradual disruption of the kingdom.

Maḥmūd Gāwān was perhaps the greatest statesman and general known in the history of the Deccan. The chief reforms introduced during his ministry were: first, the division of the Baihmanī kingdom into eight provinces instead of four as previously established, which had become of unmanageable size owing to the extension of the kingdom; secondly, the assignment of only one fort in each province to the control of the governor, and the retention of other forts of the province, as regards appointment of officers, troops, equipment, munitions, and payment of salaries, in the hands of the king himself; thirdly, the increase in the salaries of army officers, to what were very substantial rates of pay, for Briggs, in a footnote to his translation of *Firishta*, writes that the pay of a body of five hundred cavalry maintained under the Baihmanī kingdom in A.D. 1470 was fifty per cent. more than was necessary to keep an equal number under the British Government in 1828.[1]

Maḥmūd Gāwān was a pious person and was devoted to learning. At Bidar he built a school which stands to this day, and the architecture of which is perhaps unique in India.[2] It was staffed by learned men and divines from various countries of the East, and it contained a large collection of manuscripts for the use of professors and students. Maḥmūd Gāwān was also a poet and a good prose writer, and a collection of his letters called *Riyāḍ-ul-Insha* is still extant in manuscript form. The date of Maḥmūd Gāwān's execution is contained in the chronogram—[3]

قصّۀ قتل بناحق

'*The story of the unjust execution*'

and in another—

بی گنہ محمود گاوان شد شہید

'*The guiltless Maḥmūd Gāwān suffered martyrdom*'

Muḥammad Shāh deeply repented his indiscreet haste in ordering the execution of the minister, and it is mentioned by historians that the sorrow caused by the tragedy undermined his health. He died in A.D. 1482, a year after the minister's death, at the early age of twenty-eight years. His remains were interred in a tomb built near the mausoleum of his brother, Niẓām Shāh, at Āshṭūr.[4]

Muḥammad Shāh III was succeeded by his son, Maḥmūd Shāh, who was only twelve years old when he ascended the throne.[5] The reign of Maḥmūd Shāh, which was a

[1] Briggs, vol. ii, pp. 503–4.

[2] The building is described in detail on pp. 91–100.

[3] Both of these chronograms give the Hijrī year 886 (A.D. 1481) according to the *abjad* system of reckoning.

[4] For the description of Muḥammad Shāh's tomb, see *infra*, pp. 134–5.

[5] Firishta has given a vivid description of the coronation of the king and an extract from it may be of interest to readers, for the coronations of Muslim kings have rarely been described in history:

'The Takht-i-Firoza (Turquoise Throne) was placed in the grand hall of audience, and on each

long one, was a period of troubles and civil wars which ended in the subversion of the Baihmanī dynasty. The king was a mere tool in the hands of his minister, Niẕām-ul-Mulk Baiḥrī, and disturbances broke out frequently in the city of Bidar and other parts of the kingdom. During the king's absence on an expedition to Telingāna, Niẕām-ul-Mulk determined to seize as much of the royal treasure as possible, and then join his son, who was governor of Junīr. The plot was discovered by the governor of Bidar, and Niẕām-ul-Mulk was arrested and executed. In the year A.D. 1490 the Deccanīs and Abyssinians conspired to subvert the influence which the foreigners possessed over the king. Pasand Khān, combining with the Deccanīs, agreed to assassinate Maḥmūd Shāh and place another prince of the royal family on the throne. The king narrowly escaped with his life, and for three days afterwards continuous attacks were made by his troops upon the conspirators and their forces in the city. In order to celebrate his escape from this danger, Maḥmūd Shāh held a magnificent festival lasting forty days, and went in solemn procession through the city, the streets of which were handsomely decorated for the occasion. After this the king neglected the affairs of his government, leaving them entirely to the direction of his favourites. Khafī Khān and Firishta have given vivid accounts of the morals of the court at the time. The latter writes:

'Musicians and dancers flocked to the Court from Lahore, Delhi, Persia and Khorasān, as also story-tellers, reciters of the Shāh Nāmah, and other agents of pleasure. The people, following the example of the Prince, attended to nothing but dissipation: reverend sages pawned their very garments at the wine-cellars, and holy teachers, quitting their colleges, retired to taverns and presided over the wine flask. . . . The consequence of this state of affairs became in a short time apparent, for excepting the province of Telingāna and the districts adjacent to Ahmadābād Bidar, no parts of the kingdom in reality remained in the king's possession.'[1]

Qāsim Barīd, who had succeeded Niẕām-ul-Mulk Baiḥrī as minister, had the king completely in his power, and practically ruled over the kingdom. During this time Malik Aḥmad Baiḥrī Niẕām-ul-Mulk, Fatḥ-Ullāh 'Imād-ul-Mulk, and Yūsuf 'Ādil Khān proclaimed their independence in Ahmadnagar, Berar, and Bijāpur respectively, founding the Niẕām Shāhī, the 'Imād Shāhī, and the 'Adil Shāhī dynasties.[2] A little later Qāsim Barīd also proclaimed his independence in Ausa and Qandhār, but the king made terms with him, and in A.D. 1492 confirmed him as Amīr-i-Jumla, or Prime Minister. Thereafter the Baihmanīs ceased in fact to be a ruling dynasty, though Maḥmūd Shāh had four nominal successors in Bidar, Aḥmad

side of it a chair of silver. Shah Mohib Oolla and Abdul Hanif, the two most celebrated men of the age, having offered prayers for the king's prosperity, placed the crown on his head; then each supporting one arm they assisted him to ascend the throne, which at this time exceeded in splendour and intrinsic value every other in the world. After which the holy men seated themselves on either side on the silver chairs placed for them. Nizam-ool-Moolk Bheiry (minister) and Kasim Bereed then advancing made propitiatory offerings, an example which was followed by all the nobles and officers present. The king then conferred honours and titles on the *oomara* and presented them with *khil'ats* suitable to their respective ranks.' (Briggs, vol. ii, p. 418.)

[1] Ibid., vol. ii, p. 535.

[2] The chiefs continued to send annual presents to Maḥmūd Shāh, and also mentioned his name as the reigning king in inscriptions on buildings and formal documents. See *Epigraphia Indo-Moslemica*, 1925–6, pp. 18–19, and the *Journal of Hyderabad Archaeological Society*, 1918, pp. 89–94.

Shāh II, ʿAlā-ud-Dīn Shāh III, Walī-Ullāh, and last of all Kalīm-Ullāh, who died a fugitive in Ahmadnagar.[1]

Maḥmūd Shāh has left several buildings to his credit at Bidar, the most important of which is the suite of rooms attached to the Gumbad Darwāza, which is referred to as the Shāh Burj ('royal bastion') by Firishta. He writes that the king, after his escape from Pasand Khān's plot, caused a splendid building to be erected on the royal tower which he regarded as auspicious. This building became his favourite abode during the latter part of his life.[2] Maḥmūd Shāh also built the second gateway of the Bidar Fort, which is popularly called the Sharza Darwāza or 'the tiger's gate', on account of the effigies of two tigers carved thereon.[3] The façade of the gateway is decorated with beautiful tile-work and according to an inscription, which can still be read, it was built in A.D. 1503.[4]

Maḥmūd Shāh's mausoleum, built at Āshṭūr, is a monument of considerable dimensions. It was apparently erected by the king himself during his lifetime. The tombs of his successors, who were mere puppets in the hands of their Barīdī ministers, are insignificant structures and possess no architectural interest.[5]

According to Firishta, Qāsim Barīd was of Turkish origin but domiciled in Georgia. He was brought as a young boy to the Deccan by Khwāja Shihāb-ud-Dīn ʿAlī Yazdī and offered for service to Muḥammad Shāh Baihmanī III. Qāsim Barīd was an expert in handwriting and also played well on musical instruments. In the service of Muḥammad Shāh he distinguished himself in subduing the Marāṭhās, and married the daughter of Sābājī to his son Amīr Barīd. Qāsim Barīd obtained the office of Vakīl ('Administrator') during the reign of Maḥmūd Shāh Baihmanī, but he did not behave in a respectful manner towards his royal master. He died in A.D. 1504[6] and was succeeded by Amīr Barīd, who obtained still greater control over the members of the royal family. Amīr Barīd was constantly at war with the newly established Bijāpur kings, and in A.D. 1529 Ismāʿīl ʿĀdil Shāh marched at the head of a large force to Bidar, which he blockaded. Amīr Barīd, entrusting the defence of the citadel to his eldest son, withdrew to the fortress of Udgīr. After the blockade had lasted for some time the besieged made a sortie, and a sharp engagement ensued under the walls of the town. While the siege was still in progress ʿAlā-ud-Dīn ʿImād Shāh came from Berar to intercede with Ismāʿīl ʿĀdil Shāh for Amīr Barīd, but was informed that the injuries which the intriguer had inflicted on Bijāpur could not be pardoned. Shortly afterwards Amīr Barīd was taken prisoner while in a fit of

[1] The exact date of Kalīm-Ullāh's death is not known. Recently some coins bearing his name and the date 952 H. (A.D. 1545) have been found by the Archaeological Department, Hyderabad. They were apparently issued by the Barīd Shāhī king ʿAlī Barīd (A.D. 1542–79)—*Proceedings and Transactions of the VIIth All-India Oriental Conference*, p. 740.

[2] Briggs, vol. ii, p. 535. For a description of the building, see *infra*, pp. 44–5.

[3] The effigies of tigers are frequently found on the Deccan forts, their presence symbolizing the presence of ʿAlī, the son-in-law of the Prophet, whose title on account of his extreme valour was Asad-Ullāh or 'the Lion of God'. The effigies were carved as charms to avert the danger of enemies.

[4] For further information regarding this building, see *infra*, pp. 32–3.

[5] The tombs of Maḥmūd Shāh Baihmanī, Walī-Ullāh, and Kalīm-Ullāh are described on pp. 136–8 *infra*.

[6] His tomb is situated in a pleasant mango grove by the side of the road to Chhidrī.

intoxication, and carried to the Bijāpur king. He begged that his life might be spared and promised to induce his son to give up the fortress of Bidar and the treasures of the Baihmanī family. The son refused to give up the fortress, upon which the Bijāpur king issued orders for Amīr Barīd to be trampled to death by an elephant. However, his life was spared, and after a second parley with his son the garrison evacuated the place and returned to Udgīr, taking a good deal of the Baihmanī jewels with them. Ismā'īl now entered the fort and distributed the treasures amongst his nobles, troops, 'Alā-ud-Dīn 'Imād Shāh, and other neighbouring chiefs, reserving none for himself, to show that he did not make war for the riches of the Baihmanī family.

Amīr Barīd was in attendance on Ismā'īl 'Ādil Shāh at the sieges of Raichur and Mudgal in A.D. 1530, and after the conclusion of the campaign the Bijāpur king restored Bidar to him on condition that he should give up Kalyāni and Qandhār to Bijāpur.[1] Amīr Barīd died at Daulatābād in A.D. 1542,[2] and was succeeded by his son 'Alī Barīd, who was the first of the dynasty to adopt the title of Shāh. He was a cultured prince, specially fond of poetry, calligraphy, and architecture. He built his own tomb at Bidar, which was completed in A.D. 1576, three years before his death. The architecture of this building is very pleasing, being different from the massive and somewhat sombre style of the tombs of the Baihmanī kings.[3] Another delightful building erected by this king is the Rangīn Maḥall ('painted palace'), which has lovely tile and mother-of-pearl decoration. This was apparently built by a Persian architect, for some of the verses inscribed on this palace have a striking resemblance to those painted on contemporary buildings in Persia.[4]

During the reign of 'Alī Barīd Bidar was attacked by Murtaḍa Niẓām Shāh, who wanted to bestow it as *jāgīr* upon his favourite general, Ṣāḥib Khān. Ibrāhīm Quṭb Shāh, being covetous of a portion of the Barīd Shāhī territory, sent troops from Golconda to help Murtaḍa in besieging the city. 'Alī Barīd was for some time in great straits until he applied for help to 'Alī 'Ādil Shāh of Bijāpur. The latter sent a thousand horse at once, and promised to send more on certain conditions. At this time Murtaḍa Niẓām Shāh, hearing of the rebellion of his son in Ahmadnagar, relinquished the siege and hastily returned to his capital.

Another important historical event of 'Alī Barīd's reign was his joining the confederacy of the Deccan kings in the expedition which was led against Rāma Rāja, the ruler of Vijayanagar. 'Alī Barīd took an active part in the campaign, and in the final arrangement of troops for the battle he, with Ibrāhīm Quṭb Shāh, occupied the left wing. The result of the battle, which was fought at Talikota, is well known, but at the same time history is silent as to the territorial gains which 'Alī Barīd

1 The condition was never fulfilled by Amīr Barīd, who was very cunning; hence historians have styled him *Robāh-i-Deccan*, 'the Fox of the Deccan'.

2 The corpse of Amīr Barīd was brought to Bidar by his brother, Khān Jahān Barīd, and interred within the enclosure of his father's, Qāsim Barīd's, tomb. The tomb of Amīr Barīd is described in detail on pp. 150–1 *infra*.

3 For a full description of 'Alī Barīd's tomb, see *infra*, pp. 151–60.

4 See the *Poems of Nizāmī*, by Laurence Binyon, Pl. X. For further particulars regarding this building, see *infra*, pp. 44–8.

secured through this joint triumph of the Deccan kings. ʿAlī Barīd died in A.D. 1580[1] and was succeeded by his son, Ibrāhīm Barīd, who ruled for seven years. His tomb adjoins that of his illustrious father and suffers by comparison with the latter.[2]

In A.D. 1587 Ibrāhīm Barīd was succeeded by Qāsim Barīd II, of whose reign no great event is mentioned in history.[3] After the battle of Talīkota the rival dynasties of Ahmadnagar, Bijāpur, and Golconda became much too powerful for the Bidar kings, who during their later days led a precarious existence, and ultimately their kingdom, which had dwindled to a small principality, was absorbed in the Bijāpur kingdom. In A.D. 1591 Qāsim Barīd II was nominally succeeded by his infant son, but a relative, Amīr Barīd, usurped the throne.[4] Some copper coins of this king bearing the regal title المؤيد بنصر الملك القوى الغنى امير بريد شاه السلطان الغازى have recently been found by the Archaeological Department, Hyderabad.[5]

Amīr Barīd was, however, expelled in A.D. 1601 by Mīrzā ʿAlī Barīd, another member of the family, and compelled to fly to Bhāgnagar (Hyderabad). Firishta, who concluded his account of the Barīd Shāhi kings in 1018 H. (A.D. 1609) writes that Mīrzā ʿAlī Barīd was reigning at Bidar in that year. According to *Basāṯīn* he was succeeded by Amīr Barīd,[6] who was apparently the third sovereign of this name in the dynasty. Fortunately an inscription of this king has recently been found at Bidar which gives both in Persian and Marāṭhī the full name of the king as میرزا ولی امیر برید شاه, and the date 1018 H. (A.D. 1609) in which he evidently ascended the throne. In A.D. 1619 Ibrāhīm ʿĀdil Shāh II marched against Bidar to punish Amīr Barīd, who had maintained the family tradition of hostility to Bijāpur. Bidar fell, and Amīr Barīd and his sons were made captive by Ibrāhīm, who carried them to Bijāpur, where they ended their days under surveillance, Bidar being annexed to the ʿĀdil Shāhī kingdom.

Bidar remained a part of the ʿĀdil Shāhī territory until Aurangzeb began to devise plans for the subjugation of all the kingdoms of the Deccan. Early in A.D. 1656, this prince, then viceroy of the Deccan for his father, the emperor Shāh Jahān, taking with him his son, Muḥammad Muʿaẓẓam, and his generals, Mīr Jumla and Iftikhār Khān, marched from Aurangābād to Bidar. The place was at that time governed by Malik Marjān, an Abyssinian officer, who had been appointed by Ibrāhīm ʿĀdil

[1] The full regal titles of ʿAlī Barīd, as given in the Rangīn Maḥall inscription, were as follows:

المستنصر بنصر الله الملك المالك المجلس المكرم والهمايون الاكرم برید ممالك علي

Of these the last is interesting as meaning 'a messenger to empires'. The historians have described Qāsim Barīd, the first of the line, as a Turk of Georgia, but thrown no light on the significance of the family title 'Barīd', which was retained by all members of the family. Did they hold the position of 'royal courier' before their migration to India?

[2] For a full description of Ibrāhīm Barīd's tomb, see *infra*, pp. 160–1.

[3] The tomb of Qāsim Barīd was situated, originally, in a pleasant garden, by the side of the Udgīr road, to the north of ʿAlī Barīd's tomb. The garden has perished, but the tomb is in a good state of preservation. It is described in detail on pp. 162–4 *infra*.

[4] *Firishta* (Persian text), p. 348.

[5] *Annual Report* for 1930–1, pp. 49–50.

[6] In the *Cambridge History* (iii. 709) the name of the last king is given as ʿAlī Barīd, but *Basāṯīn* (Hyd. lithograph, pp. 272–3) mentions him as Amīr Barīd. As the source of the *Cambridge History* on this point is not known, I have followed *Basāṯīn*.

Shāh II. During the régime of Malik Marjān, which lasted nearly thirty years, the defences of the Bidar fort and the palaces inside it were extensively repaired.[1]

Aurangzeb laid siege to the city, and in a few days succeeded in bringing his artillery to the edge of the ditch, and breached two bastions and a portion of the lower wall. The officers of Aurangzeb's army then scaled the walls and discharged rockets and grenades on Malik Marjān's troops who were defending the breach. One of the rockets accidentally struck a magazine of gunpowder which exploded, severely burning Malik Marjān and his sons. Malik Marjān died of his injuries within two days of the accident, and on the 18th of April, A.D. 1656, after a siege of twenty-seven days, Aurangzeb made a triumphal entry into the fort. Bidar was included in the Mughal Empire, and Aurangzeb by the capture of the place obtained twelve *lākhs* of rupees in cash, ammunition worth eight *lākhs* of rupees, and 230 guns.[2] Aurangzeb, jubilant at his success, proceeded to the great mosque in the fort,[3] and had the *khuṭba* recited in the name of his imperial father, Shāh Jahān. Bidar was renamed Ẓafarābād, and Mughal coins issued under this name from Bidar may still be seen in museums.[4]

Iftikhār Khān, who had taken an active part in the capture of Bidar, was appointed its first governor, and he retained this office for a little over two years until his return to the Faujdārship of Chūragaṛh in Mālwa, which was his permanent post.[5] The next Mughal governor of Bidar was Khān Zamān Mīr Khalīl-Ullāh, who also held this charge for a little over two years, until 1071 H. (A.D. 1660), when he was promoted to the governorship of Mālwa.

Mīr Khalīl-Ullāh was succeeded by Mīr Shams-ud-Dīn Mukhtār Khān, whose name is still kept fresh in the memory of the people of Bidar by the inscriptional tablets which he fixed to the gates of the city and the fort. Mukhtār Khān also built the Farḥ Bāgh Mosque, the inscription on which is a fine specimen of the *nasta'līq* style of writing.[6] He repaired the gates and the defences of Bidar, and Aurangzeb in appreciation of his services promoted him to the governorship of Khandesh in A.D. 1672[7] and appointed Qalandar Khān, who afterwards enjoyed the title of Jān

[1] See *Epigraphia Indo-Moslemica* for 1927–8, p. 26, and *Antiquities of Bidar*, p. 16.

[2] Muḥammad Ṣāliḥ has given a vivid account of the siege, and for detailed information readers are referred to his work, *'Amal-i-Ṣāliḥ* (*Bibl. Ind.*), vol. iii, pp. 249–52.

[3] This mosque has recently been fully repaired, and an inscription discovered which states that the mosque was built by Prince Muḥammad, the son of Aḥmad Shāh Al-Walī Al-Baihmanī in 827 H. (A.D. 1423–4). Previous writers have not been able to determine its exact age, and Muḥammad Ṣālih, also being doubtful, writes in a general way that it was built by Baihmanī kings some two hundred years before the conquest of Bidar by Aurangzeb (*'Amal-i-Ṣāliḥ*, vol. iii, p. 251). For a full description of the building, see *infra*, pp. 54–6.

[4] There is a coin of Shāh Jahān bearing the mint name Ẓafarābād and the year 1067 H. (A.D. 1657) in the cabinet of the Hyderabad Museum. See also Whitehead's *Catalogue of Coins in the Punjab Museum*, p. lxxxviii.

[5] Iftikhār Khān was killed in the battle of Samūgaṛh, which was fought between Jaswant Singh, the governor of Mālwa, and Aurangzeb when the latter was proceeding to Agra to establish himself on the imperial throne. For further particulars regarding Iftikhār Khan, see *Ma'āthir-ul-Umarā* (*Bibl. Ind.*), vol. i, pp. 200–3.

[6] *Epigraphia Indo-Moslemica*, 1927–8, Pl. XVII.

[7] *Ma'āthir-ul-Umarā*, vol. iii, pp. 620–3.

Niṣār Khān, in Mukhtār Khān's place at Bidar.[1] Qalandar Khān's name is preserved in an inscription which records the building by him of a pillared hall in 1088 H. (A.D. 1677).[2] The hall does not exist now, and the inscription which at one time was placed in the Solah Khamb Mosque has been removed for safe custody to the Archaeological Museum in the Bidar fort. Qalandar Khān also built a fine mosque at Gulbarga, which may still be seen.[3]

Qalandar Khān retained the governorship of Bidar until 1092 H. (A.D. 1681), when he was succeeded by Jān Sipār Khān Bahādur Dil, the brother of Mukhtār Khān, the third governor.[4] Jān Sipār Khān's governorship lasted for several years, and according to the *Ma'āthir-ul-Umarā* he was helped in the administration by his son Rustam Dil Khān,[5] who afterwards succeeded him. In Jān Sipār Khān Aurangzeb had great confidence, and in 1098 H. (A.D. 1687), when the emperor, after conquering Golconda, came to Bidar, he deputed Jān Sipār Khān to escort Abū-'l-Ḥasan to Daulatābād, where the unfortunate king afterwards spent the rest of his life in captivity. Jān Sipār Khān was subsequently promoted to the governorship of Hyderabad, and his son Rustam Dil Khān, who was already familiar with the government of Bidar, took up his father's office at the latter place. Rustam Dil Khān was an accomplished administrator and ultimately rose to be governor of Golconda, the Bidar province, after the annexation of Golconda and Bijāpur to the Mughal empire, occupying a minor position in the administration of the Deccan. The local records show that Rustam Dil Khān held the governorship of Bidar for one year and seven months only, until 1099 H. (A.D. 1688), but there is a mosque at Bidar built by Rustam Dil Khān with an inscription of the year 1107 H. (A.D. 1695).[6]

Rustam Dil Khān was succeeded by Aurang Khān, who, owing to his untimely death, held the governorship for a few days only. After Aurang Khān his son Qubād Khān assumed his office, and held it until his demise in 1102 H. (A.D. 1691). Qubād Khān built the Shrine of the Holy Cloak at Bidar. Qubād Khān was followed by Ḥusām-ud-Dīn Khān, who is better known in the history of the Deccan as governor of Udgīr.[7] He was an enterprising officer, possessing both military prowess and administrative ability. He was also fond of music, and was most accomplished in repartee.[8] At Bidar he built a mosque and laid out a garden.[9] He also built a platform near the Talghāṭ Darwāza, whence he enjoyed the view of the lowlands on moonlit nights. The platform was called the Chāndnī Chabūtrā, the 'platform for moon-lit nights'.

1 *Ma'āthir-ul-Umarā*, vol. iii, pp. 863–4. 2 *Epigraphia Indo-Moslemica*, 1927–8, p. 27, Pl. XVI.

3 A description of this mosque and of Qalandar Khān's tomb, which is situated close to the mosque, may be seen in the *Annual Report*, Archaeological Department, Hyderabad, 1925–6, pp. 7–8, Pl. *Xb*.

4 *Ma'āthir-ul-Umarā*, vol. i, pp. 535–7.

5 Ibid., vol. ii, p. 325.

6 The mosque is built in the enclosure of Shāh 'Alī Qādirī. For a description of the mosque, see *infra*, pp. 202–3; also *Epigraphia Indo-Moslemica*, 1927–8, p. 36, Pl. XVIII.

7 *Annual Report*, Archaeological Department, Hyderabad, 1928–9, pp. 27 and 32–4; *Epigraphia Indo-Moslemica*, 1929–30, pp. 23–5.

8 *Ma'āthir-ul-Umarā*, vol. i, pp. 584–7.

9 He laid out a garden at Udgīr also which still exists. *Annual Report*, Archaeological Department, Hyderabad, 1928–9, pp. 27 and 32–4; *Epigraphia Indo-Moslemica*, 1929–30, pp. 23–5.

Ḥusām-ud-Dīn Khān was succeeded by Khāna-zād Khān some time in 1107 H. (A.D. 1695), and he remained in office for nearly a year. Afterwards he proceeded to Delhi, where he was appointed Khān Sāmān, 'Lord Chamberlain', to the Emperor. After Khāna-zād Khān's promotion, Sazāwār Khān received from Aurangzeb the governorship of Bidar.[1] During his régime the famous Madrasa of Maḥmūd Gāwān was struck by lightning. This catastrophe occurred on the 11th of Ramaḍān 1107 H. (4th April, A.D. 1696), destroying one-half of the front of the building and an equal part of the left wing, including the beautiful tower at the south-east corner. The Madrasa was in a ruinous condition until recently, and the fore-court and the interior were filled with debris. It has now been thoroughly repaired and the original plan of the missing portions restored up to the plinth.

Sazāwār Khān was succeeded by Anūp Singh Bundela, who was of a violent temper and murdered one Tondar Mal (Toḍar Mal) Hazārī, who had refused to marry his daughter to the son of Anūp Singh. The followers of Tondar Mal rebelled against Anūp Singh, who shut himself up in the fort of Bidar. Afterwards he secretly escaped from the fort through the help of Rāja Chandra Sen's troops who had come to his rescue. The followers of Tondar Mal represented the matter to the Emperor at Delhi, who appointed Mīr Kalān Khān as governor of Bidar. Mīr Kalān Khān retained the governorship of Bidar for a long time, and when Niẓām-ul-Mulk Āṣaf Jāh, after defeating Mubāriz Khān at Shakar Khelda in October 1724, came to the Deccan and declared his independence, Mīr Kalān Khān offered him a warm welcome. With the establishment of the Āṣaf Jāhī dynasty Bidar fell into further insignificance, its governors gradually occupying the position of district officers.

Mīr Kalān Khān was succeeded in turn by his two slaves, Wāṣil Khān the Senior, and Wāṣil Khān the Junior.[2] Of these, the former was killed by trumpeters at Bhālkī, and the latter was ousted by Khwāja Momīn Khān, who was deputed by Āṣaf Jāh to chastise him in 1153 H. (A.D. 1750). Wāṣil Khān the Junior extended the city of Bidar towards the west by building a large market, which was named Wāṣil Ganj after him. For the protection of this extension he constructed a high wall with three gateways and a moat.[3]

In 1155 H. (A.D. 1752) Nawāb Āṣaf Jāh appointed Muqtada Khān to be governor of Bidar. Later on the latter took advantage of the disturbances which arose during the rule of the sons of Aṣāf Jāh, and levying more than five thousand troops consisting of both cavalry and infantry, began to plunder and lay waste the Telingāna country adjoining the territory of Bidar. Nawāb Ṣalābat Jang besieged Bidar in order to punish Muqtada Khān, but when the latter showed contrition Salābat Jang not only pardoned him but reinstated him in the governorship. Muqtada Khān rebelled again, but on that occasion the siege was resumed by Mīr Niẓām 'Alī Khān,

[1] Sazāwār Khān was the son of Ḥusām-ud-Dīn Khān, whose governorship of Bidar has been noted above. *Ma'āthir-ul-Umarā*, vol. i, p. 586.

[2] Mīr Kalān Khān died at the ripe age of one hundred years, and his remains were interred in the shrine of Multānī Pādshāh at Bidar. He had evinced great solicitude for the upkeep and extension of this shrine during his lifetime.

[3] The market is now called the Shāh Ganj, and the principal gateway the Shāh Ganj Darwāza.

who soon captured Bidar and appointed Siyādat Khān in place of Muqtada Khān as governor.

Subsequently the ill-feeling between the two brothers, Nawāb Ṣalābat Jang and Nawāb Niẓām ʿAlī Khān, became more pronounced, and when Niẓām ʿAlī Khān received a *sanad* from the Emperor of Delhi confirming him in the government of the Deccan, he issued a *farmān* confining Ṣalābat Jang in Bidar. The latter remained in captivity for one year three months and six days until his death on the 20th Rabīʿ I, 1177 H. (28th September, A.D. 1763.)[1]

Siyādat Khān was the governor of Bidar when Ṣalābat Jang was confined there, and as he showed loyalty to the latter, Niẓām ʿAlī Khān removed him from office and appointed ʿAlā-ud-Daula Dilīr Jang in his place. He was a very cruel officer, and it is alleged that he killed Ṣalābat Jang in order to please Nawāb Niẓām ʿAlī Khān. The wicked propensities of Dilīr Jang found vent in other directions also, and ultimately he was deprived of his office by Niẓām ʿAlī Khān, who appointed Mīr Kalān II in his place. Mīr Kalān II remained in office for two years from 1179 to 1180 H. (A.D. 1766–7) and was succeeded by Murtaḍa Khān. In 1187 H. (A.D. 1773) Raghoba marched with a large army upon Hyderabad in order to collect the *chauth*. Niẓām ʿAlī Khān met the Marāṭhā army in the vicinity of Bidar, and ultimately defeated Raghoba in a battle which was fought on the bank of the river Mānjra. The war lasted for twenty days, and during this period Bidar was also the venue of fighting. The garrison of Bidar fort on that occasion used the famous *sāt gazī* gun in order to repel the Marāṭhās.

About the close of the year 1187 H. (A.D. 1773) Murtaḍa Khān was succeeded by Muḥammad Ghauth Saif-ud-Daula,[2] but he died shortly after his appointment, and his brother Saif Jang Najm-ud-Daula Bahādur became governor of Bidar in his place. Saif Jang retained this office for twenty-four years until 1203 H. (A.D. 1789); he did not, however, attend to the duties in person, but appointed deputies to work in his behalf.[3]

The next governor of Bidar was Nawāb Amīn-ul-Mulk Bahādur, popularly called Tārā Mīyān, 'the bright master'. During his administration Bidar suffered from a terrible famine. To relieve the condition of the people Nawāb Niẓām ʿAlī Khān Bahādur came in person from Hyderabad and distributed grain from the stores in the fort. Amīn-ul-Mulk remained in office for three years, but was afterwards dismissed by Nawāb Niẓām ʿAlī Khān, and Nūr Muḥammad Khān was appointed in his place. Nūr Muḥammad Khān stayed in Hyderabad, but sent Dhākir-ud-Dīn Khān as his deputy to manage the affairs of Bidar. About this time a scion of the Āṣaf Jāhī family, named ʿĀlī Jāh Bahādur, rebelled against Nawāb Niẓām ʿAlī Khān; and on the 9th Dhu-'l-Ḥajj 1209 H. (27th June, A.D. 1795) he set out from Hyderabad towards Bidar. Sadāśiva Reddi, a zamīndār, joined ʿĀlī Jāh on the way,

[1] He was buried in the enclosure of Multānī Pādshāh's tomb at Bidar.

[2] According to a *sanad* preserved in the Dīvanī Office another nobleman, Āṣaf-ud-Daula Mīr Aḥmad Khān Bahādur Nuṣrat Jang, held the governorship of Bidar from 1184 to 1187 H. (A.D. 1770–3). Probably he succeeded Murtaḍa Khān.

[3] The names of the deputies were as follows: (1) Ḥusain Khān, (2) Rukn-ud-Dīn Khān, (3) Zain-ul-ʿĀbidīn Khān, (4) Shāh ʿAbd-ur-Razzāq, (5) Rukn-ud-Dīn Khān II, and (6) Ghulām Maḥmūd Khān.

and when the rebels reached Bidar Dhākir-ud-Dīn Khān opened the gates of the fort. Nawāb Niẓām ʿAlī Khān was much upset by the news, and deputed ʿAbdullāh Khān, an Abyssinian officer, with a considerable force to chastise ʿĀlī Jāh and his confederates. ʿAbdullāh Khān, however, was defeated by Sadāśiva Reddi; the former was wounded, and his wife and children were captured by the enemy. Nawāb Niẓām ʿAlī Khān was further annoyed by this defeat, and he then dispatched a larger force under Monsieur Raymond and Sardār-ul-Mulk Ghānsī Mīyān. They ejected the rebels from the fort; ʿĀlī Jāh fled to Aurangābād, while Sadāśiva was captured and imprisoned at Golconda. Nawāb Niẓām ʿAlī Khān, after the quelling of the rebellion, punished Nūr Muḥammad Khān for his disloyalty and appointed Khwāja Munʿim Khān as governor of Bidar in his place. He was exceedingly kind and good to the peasantry, and distributed large sums of money among the people of Bidar to help them to restore their houses which had been destroyed during the late disturbances, but unfortunately he died of paralysis within five months of his appointment. He was succeeded by Khān Jahān Bahādur in the month of Shawwāl 1210 H. (April, A.D. 1796). The latter appointed as his deputy Mīrzā Ḥusain Beg, whom he sent to Bidar to attend to the duties. The Mīrzā was an efficient officer, but Mushir-ul-Mulk, the Prime Minister, did not like Khān Jahān, and when the Prime Minister was released from imprisonment at Poona and returned to Hyderabad he induced the Niẓām to replace Khān Jahān by Yakka Tāz Jang Bahādur, whose real name was Mīr Lillāhī. The latter assumed office in 1214 H. (A.D. 1799). He himself did not go to Bidar, but sent his son Mīr Asad ʿAlī Khān as his deputy. In 1215 H. (A.D. 1800) Yakka Tāz Jang died, and Mīr Asad ʿAlī Khān was confirmed as governor of Bidar in his father's place. He held the appointment for twenty-two years, being succeeded by Sayyid Khalīl-Ullāh Khān Bahādur in 1237 H. (A.D. 1822). After Khalīl-Ullāh Khān eight more governors held charge of Bidar,[1] until 1262 H. (A.D. 1846), when the Niẓām's dominions were divided into districts, and the old system of administration through military officers was abolished. Under the new arrangement Bidar for some time remained the head-quarters of a Ṣadr Taʿalluqdār (Commissioner) and afterwards of a Taʿalluqdār, a position which it still holds. The glory of the town really waned with the decline of the Baihmanī dynasty, although Barīdī kings kept up its beauty during their chequered rule of 122 years. The final signs of decay appeared when it became a provincial town, first under the Mughal kings and afterwards under the Āṣaf Jāhī rulers. The last nail in the coffin was, however, driven when under the *Zilʿa-dārī* system Bidar dwindled to the insignificant position

[1]

Name	*Date of appointment*
(1) Nawāb Naẓar Bahādur Khān	1244 H. (A.D. 1828).
(2) Mīr Ḥasan ʿAlī Khān Bahādur	1254 H. (A.D. 1838).
(3) Kishan Dās Sāhūkār of Gujarāt	1254 H. (A.D. 1838). *Note.* Held charge for two months only.
(4) Nawāb Shams-ud-Dīn Khān *alias* Abban Ṣāḥib	1255 H. (A.D. 1839).
(5) ʿAbdullāh bin ʿAlī	1258 H. (A.D. 1842).
(6) Pindhrī Nāth	20th Rajab 1262 H. (15th July, A.D. 1846).
(7) Nawāb Sulṭān Mīrzā Khān	Ramaḍān 1262 H. (September, A.D. 1846).
(8) Nawāb Shams-ud-Dīn Khān *alias* Abban Ṣāḥib	Dhu-'l-Ḥajj 1262 H. (December, A.D. 1846).

of the head-quarters of a Collector. Having no railway connexion, its industries, among which the Bīdrī-ware was the most notable, fell into decay;[1] its beautiful palaces and public buildings which were once the envy of the great cities of India became a mass of debris; and the people whose piety and learning, military prowess and soldierly bearing were widely renowned,[2] turned into charlatans and professional beggars, or hewers of wood and drawers of water.

Fortunately, under the rule of our benign sovereign, His Exalted Highness Nawāb Sir Mīr Osmān ʿAlī Khān Bahādur, G.C.I.E., G.B.E., a new era of prosperity is dawning in the history of Bidar. It has been linked to Hyderabad by railway; a network of schools has been established to spread literacy among its people; large sums have been advanced for the revival of the Bīdrī-ware industry; and effective steps have been taken for the improvement of the breed of cattle and the uplift of the general life of the peasantry of the district. Further, co-operative societies have been started to ameliorate the condition of the urban population; and for the expansion of the town itself a development scheme has been sanctioned, in which sanitation and aesthetic requirements are the principal features. Lastly, to foster a national pride among the people all the monuments of Bidar have been thoroughly repaired, and roads and paths laid out so that access to them is made easy.

[1] Bīdrī-ware is made of metal composed of zinc 83·5 per cent., copper 12 per cent., lead 3 per cent. These constituents are melted together and then poured into a mould made of baked clay. The article afterwards is turned in a lathe, and artists inlay flowers or other ornaments in silver or gold. They first smear the article over with sulphate of copper and water, which gives the surface a blackish colour and enables the artists more easily to distinguish the pattern which they draw. This they mark with a sharp-pointed instrument of steel, and incise with small chisels of various shapes, and then, with hammer and punch, fill the cavities with small plates of silver, which adhere firmly to the ware. It is then polished preparatory to receiving its finishing coat of black. This is done by subjecting the vessel to a gentle heat and dipping it in a solution of sal-ammoniac, saltpetre, common salt, and blue vitriol. The inlaid silver devices are little altered in colour, but the intervening portions of alloy become permanently jet-black. The work is thus divided into three stages, the mould-making, the smelting, and the inlaying. Bīdrī-ware does not rust, but is brittle and easily broken. The various articles made are vases, washstand basins and ewers, hookahs, spittoons, cups, flagons, dishes, spice and cosmetic boxes, candlesticks, weights, and picture-frames. The industry was originally connected with the silver and gold inlay work on steel of the Arabs and Persians, but the substitution of the alloy for steel was a local development peculiar to India, particularly to the Deccan.

[2] Bidar had four schools for physical training and military instructions in the four quarters of the city. They still exist in name and are called: (1) Nūr Khān kī Taʿlīm, situated in the eastern part of the city; (2) Ṣiddīq Shāh kī Taʿlīm, situated in the western part of the city; (3) Manhīyār ('bangle-seller's') Taʿlīm, situated in the northern part of the city, and (4) ʿAbbās Pansālī ('water-miller's') kī Taʿlīm, situated in the southern part of the city. The schools give instruction in wrestling, club-exercises, and fencing, such as are displayed during the mock-fights of the Muḥarram festival in India.

CHAPTER III

ARCHITECTURE

IN the twelfth and thirteenth centuries A.D. a magnificent style of architecture was in vogue in the Deccan, some specimens of which in the form of religious shrines are still preserved in His Exalted Highness the Nizam's dominions. The salient features of the temples are their star-shaped plans, high plinths, pillared porches and halls, and high spires which generally have receding bands of masonry in horizontal courses. The openings of the halls and corridors are in the post-and-lintel style and the ceilings are generally flat; wherever they are circular they have been built by converting the square spaces into eight-sided, sixteen-sided, or thirty-two sided openings by laying triangular pieces at the angles and ultimately roofing them with circular masonry caps. The principles and methods observed in building a true vault or arch are not followed in these temples, and they were perhaps not known to their builders. For binding the masonry the use of lime or any other kind of mortar is rare, and the pieces of masonry are generally held together by their sheer weight, although in some cases dowels and metal clamps have been used. The majority of these temples have insufficient or no foundations, and the style of building seems to have been evolved from rock or wood architecture which preceded the structural temples in the Deccan.

But notwithstanding these shortcomings these temples show marvellous skill and technical knowledge in the use of large blocks of stone for pavements, pillars, door-frames, lintels, friezes, and ceiling slabs. The walls are also built of huge blocks, and it appears that the architects of these buildings took delight in handling stones of colossal size. In a temple recently excavated by the Archaeological Department, Hyderabad, in the Warangal fort the entire floor of the *maṇḍapa* of the temple consists of a single block of stone, measuring 16 feet each way in length and breadth and 2 feet in thickness. All these pieces, moreover, are so beautifully carved and perfectly finished that sometimes the eye fails to realize their enormous dimensions.

Again, the architects of these temples have shown a highly refined taste in the disposition of the various adjuncts of these buildings. For example, the porticoes and the image-chambers are so arranged in the general plan of the building that their projections break the monotony of the wall surfaces, while the series of vertical carvings divided at suitable intervals by horizontal bands of sculpture produce an effect of light and shade that enhances the beauty of the design. The decorative carving on the exteriors of the temples is quite rich, but it is still richer in the interiors, where the pillars, the architraves, the ceiling stones, the door-frames, and the image-niches are carved and finished with the delicacy and elegance of the goldsmith's work. These lovely carvings coupled with the massive features of the building convey an idea of majestic grandeur which was presumably aimed at by the architects in building abodes for their gods.

The use of bricks was known in the Deccan before the beginning of the Christian era, but the builders of the medieval temples of the Deccan have invariably preferred stone to brick, and have chosen a close-grained variety of hornblende, which is greenish or jet-black according to the geological features of the locality where it has been quarried. This stone takes a beautiful polish and, being hard, has proved an admirable material both for sculpture and building purposes, imparting beauty and strength to the temples.

In the beginning of the fourteenth century A.D. Muḥammad bin Tughluq in his zeal to make Daulatābād, till then known as Deogiri, the capital of the empire made strenuous efforts to transfer the whole population of Delhi to the former place, and although he had to meet serious opposition from the people of Delhi his orders were so imperative that they could not be resisted. As a result of this wholesale migration, the Deccan was flooded by a number of eminent men from Delhi, including apparently architects, engineers, tile-manufacturers, painters, and calligraphists. The architecture of the Deccan must have impressed the new-comers by its magnificence; but as it was something alien in form and spirit to their own works in Delhi, they naturally refrained from copying it in the beginning. Unfortunately we have no building of the Tughluq period in the Deccan,[1] but the tombs of Baihmanī kings, who ruled after the death of Muḥammad bin Tughluq, exist in considerable number in Gulbarga and other places, and they possess the same features as their prototypes in Delhi. They are massive structures with hemispherical domes and battering walls, the latter having been built in this fashion in order to counteract the thrust of the dome. The exteriors are decorated with tiles and in some cases with *jālī* screens, while the interiors have decorative bands of cut plaster along the arch-heads and the base of the dome. The ceilings are adorned with paintings containing calligraphic designs and floral and geometric patterns. The ceiling of the tomb of Fīroz Shāh Baihmanī at Gulbarga has flutings with bands of inscriptions across them, offering a striking resemblance to the flutings of the Quṭb Minār with belts of inscriptions across them.[2]

The most notable building, however, of this period is the Jāmiʿ Masjid of Gulbarga fort, built by a Persian architect named Rafīʿ in A.D. 1367, during the reign of Muḥammad Shāh Baihmanī I. The architecture of this mosque, although plain, possesses considerable fascination because of the sense of proportion and beauty of line displayed in the building. A novel feature of this mosque is that it has no open court in front of the prayer-hall, and the entire area, consisting of the aisles, the central passages, and the prayer-hall, is covered over. Owing to the hot climate of India the plan was not repeated in other places in the Deccan. The architect has in this mosque given a variety of forms to the arches by adopting different spans and using imposts of various heights. For example, the span of the arches of the aisles is extremely wide in comparison with their imposts,[3] thus producing a new form which later became very popular in the buildings of Bijāpur and Bidar. The domes of this

[1] The Deval mosque of Bodhan, containing an inscription of Muḥammad b. Tughluq, is really a temple. The small domes placed artificially on the roof and the pulpit are later additions, and do not form an integral part of the original structure. *Annual Report*, Archaeological Department, Hyderabad, 1914–15, pp. 3–4, Pl. VI*a*.

[2] *Annual Report*, Archaeological Department, Hyderabad, 1925–6, pp. 6–7, Pl. IX *b*.

[3] *Annual Report*, Archaeological Department, Hyderabad, 1915–16, Pl. II *a*; *Cambridge History of India*, vol. iii, Pl. XLVI, Fig. 95.

mosque are a little stilted and not hemispherical like the domes of the earlier Muslim buildings of the Deccan. The stilted dome and arch grew rapidly into fashion in the Deccan, apparently through the influence of Persian architects who were employed by the Baihmanī kings.

Bidar was made the capital of the Baihmanī kingdom in A.D. 1429, when nearly a century and a quarter had passed since the establishment of the dynasty in the Deccan. In this fairly long period the traditions and craftsmanship of the Tughluq architecture had been considerably modified by Persian forms and ideals on the one hand, and by the skill of the local mason, who was an adept in the art of carving, on the other. As a result of these influences the architecture of the Deccan at this period was relieved of the heaviness of the Tughluq style and developed a certain beauty of outline and elegance of detail.

Among the works started by Aḥmad Shāh Walī immediately after the transfer of the capital the building of the fort and his own palace, which also contained an audience hall, deserve special mention. According to Firishta it took nine years to complete the defences of the fort, and public rejoicings were held when the work was finished. But of these defences, except the triple moat, very little remains now, since the fortifications were entirely rebuilt under the superintendence of Turkish engineers towards the end of the fifteenth century or the beginning of the sixteenth century A.D., when gunpowder came into use in the Deccan and the military architecture of the country underwent a complete change.

The triple moat, of which the partitions are hewn out of the solid rock, is a special feature of the Bidar fort.[1] It is apparently the work of Hindu masons whose patience and industry had in previous times produced the famous scarp of the Daulatābād fort and the rock enclosures of the Ellora caves. The fortifications, having been built by Turkish mercenaries, possess a certain resemblance to medieval European forts in the disposition of barbicans, covered passages, and bastions. But there are clear indications of the employment of local talent also, first in the labyrinth-like arrangement of the underground secret passages with safety exits, and secondly in the style of building which gives the bastions, despite their grim appearance, a touch of beauty by the insertion of carved stones and dainty architectural detail at various places.

The major portion of the palace of Aḥmad Shāh Walī had fallen down and the mass of debris completely concealed the plan and architectural features of the building. The excavations carried out recently by the Archaeological Department have, however, exposed to view the remains of this beautiful palace, the praise of which was aptly sung by the poet Ādharī in the highest terms.[2] The palace had two pavilions with lofty arches on each of its wings, while the middle was occupied by a spacious hall with the King's Room behind it, the latter being surmounted by a majestic dome.

The arch of the pavilion on the right wing is still intact, and its stately dimensions and fine proportions can be admired. The façade of the arch was adorned with

[1] Sir John Marshall has kindly sent me the following note for insertion: 'It might be of interest to recall that the city of Syrinx in Hyrcania had three great moats. (Polyb. x. 31. 8 and Tarn, '*The Greeks in Bactria and India*', p. 16).'

[2] See *infra*, pp. 66–75, and Pls. XXXI–XLI.

encaustic tiles, traces of which remain in the spandrels of the arch. Among the designs are the effigies of two tigers with the rising sun (Pl. XXXVII). The royal emblem of Persia is the effigy of a lion with the rising sun; but here the artist has appropriately changed the lion into a tiger, as there are no lions in the Deccan.

The dome of the King's Room rose to a height of nearly 100 feet from the base, and was most massively built, as the portions of the vault, which have recently been removed from the site, attested. The hall had exquisite tile-work on its walls, which were further embellished with designs in pure gold in order to add splendour to the room. The niches, door-frames, and arch-heads of the King's Room and the audience hall are of hornblende, beautifully carved, in both the Muslim and Hindu styles.

The tomb of Aḥmad Shāh Walī, which is intact (Pls. LXVIII–LXXIV), throws further light on the vigour and beauty which was attained by architecture during the reign of this king. The interior of the tomb is decorated with lovely paintings, the designs being floral, geometric, and calligraphic. The colour schemes are extremely rich, the gold patterns appearing on vermilion, turquoise, fawn, and jet-black backgrounds.

The tombs of ʿAlā-ud-Dīn, the son of Aḥmad Shāh, and Ḥaḍrat Khalīl-Ullāh, a contemporary saint, illustrate further the elegance of the Baihmanī architecture. The lovely designs of the tiled panels, the beautiful mouldings and carved bands, the exquisite calligraphic devices and the fine proportion of the arches and other architectural features all bear eloquent testimony to a highly refined taste and sound knowledge of building principles.

The Baihmanī kingdom was established in the Deccan by defying the authority of the Imperial Court at Delhi. The monarchs of the former dynasty therefore drew inspiration in cultural matters from Persian and western Asiatic countries, and their courts were thronged by poets, divines, and artists from those countries. The influence of Persia on the development of the Muslim architecture of the Deccan is thus more prominent than her influence on contemporary architecture in Northern India. A striking example of this influence is the famous Madrasa of Maḥmūd Gāwān at Bidar, which is a unique building of its kind in India, and was apparently copied from some college in Persia. College buildings of this plan are, however, not rare in other Islāmic countries, and the seven great schools of Fez are more or less built in this style, although the wood-carving and cut plaster decoration of these schools are special features of Arab art. The dimensions of the Bidar Madrasa are of course much larger than those of the Madrasas at Fez, the former covering an area of 205 feet by 180 feet.

The Madrasa at Bidar has an open court in the middle, with four sides in which the lecture-rooms, the prayer hall, the library, the professors' rooms, and the students' cubicles are built (Pls. L–LVI). These sides are divided into three stories, and in the middle of each is a lofty arch giving access to lecture-halls on the north, west, and south, and to the gateway on the east. Sir John Marshall has complained of a certain flatness in this building. He writes: 'There is no feeling for plastic form and mass, or for the values of contrasted light and shade. The architect has visualized his subject, as the architects of Eastern Persia habitually did, in two rather than in three dimensions.'[1] These remarks may be true in respect of the building when deprived of two-thirds of its façade, which included another lofty minaret with projecting galleries at intervals and a stately entrance. As the latter is completely missing now it is difficult to say anything about the effect of light and shade in its architectural features; but the balconies of the minarets when complete, as may be visualized from the style of the *denuded* minaret which stands at the north-east angle of the building, would have produced that effect by their horizontal courses of masonry contrasted with the vertical courses of the main tower (Pls. L–LII). The Madrasa was beautifully decorated with encaustic tiles, the arrangement and colour-schemes of which would also have given feelings of depth and light and shade, as the specimens still sticking to the walls sufficiently show.

In completing this brief review of Baihmanī architecture it may be observed that the general character of the buildings remained massive, although the architects used different devices to reduce this effect. Arches of various forms came into fashion and the domes became stilted (turnip-shaped), and where remaining round they were three-fourths of an orb instead of being hemispherical. Love of colour was a conspicuous feature, and increased use was made of tiles and paintings for decorative themes. The work of Hindu masons began to be appreciated in the building of niches, door-frames, corbels, friezes, and pillars, and their skill in carving was utilized for ornamental work. The architecture of this period on the whole exhibits a sound knowledge of building principles and a refined taste in the disposition of the various adjuncts and in the arrangement of the decorative features.

Qāsim Barīd, the founder of the Barīd S͟hāhī dynasty, proclaimed his independence in Ausa and Qandhār during the sovereignty of Maḥmūd S͟hāh Baihmanī (A.D. 1482–1518),[2] but the first ruler of the family to assume regal titles was 'Alī Barīd (A.D. 1542–80), who was fond of architecture and during whose reign a distinct change came over the general character of the buildings of the capital. The two most important buildings of 'Alī Barīd's reign are the Rangīn Maḥall and the tomb which he built during his lifetime and completed in A.D. 1577, three years before his death.[3] The Rangīn Maḥall was so called because it was once decorated with tiles of various colours, traces of which still remain.

The palace has lovely wood-carving and mother-of-pearl work; but it suffers by the narrowness of its dimensions, and incidentally shows how the shrinkage of political power affected the vision and taste of kings in artistic matters. The plan of the palace consists of a hall with four rooms at the sides and four more rooms at the back. The ceiling of the hall is supported on columns of wood which are exquisitely carved. They were apparently made by Hindu craftsmen, whose artistic devices are prominent. The innermost room of this palace, which is called the S͟hāh Nis͟hīn or 'the royal chamber', has a star-shaped plan like that of a medieval Hindu shrine (Pl. VIII). It is therefore not unlikely that the palace was designed by a Hindu architect.

[1] *Cambridge History of India*, vol. iii, p. 636. [2] Briggs, vol. ii, p. 536.
[3] *Supra*, p. 13.

'Alī Barīd's own tomb is not a great architectural creation. Although its proportions have been praised by some writers, yet the building when seen from the front looks top-heavy, its dome being too large for its base. Furthermore, its arches, which are open on all four sides, contravene the rule which ordains that in an Islāmic tomb the opening towards the *qibla* should always be kept closed.[1] In the decorative bands of the tomb, there appear miniature copies of the dome of the building itself, a practice commonly followed by Hindu architects in decorating the exteriors of their temples with miniature towers and shrines.

The tomb is built on a spacious terrace in the midst of a garden, features which have given the building a certain resemblance to contemporary Mughal tombs. Though these innovations impart a sense of charm in contrast with the heavy and sombre features of the Baihmanī tombs, yet the employment of Hindu architects for the designing of religious and semi-religious Muslim buildings marks a definite transition in the style of the architecture of the Deccan, which henceforward became more and more ornate in minor detail, but weak in its constructive elements and somewhat confusing in general expression. These anomalies arose on account of the Hindu masons' different conceptions of beauty in architecture and different ideals of religious expression.

To illustrate the above remarks the architecture of the Kālī Masjid at Bidar, which is also a Barīd Shāhī building, may be taken as an example (Pls. CXX–XXII). The plan of the building consists of a main hall with two minarets, one at each end of the front of the hall. The arches of the façade of the mosque have large spans, and architecturally they required fairly massive towers at each end to counteract their thrusts. But Hindu masons, not being adept in making arches, did not realize the importance of this measure, and they have constructed very slender towers, the workmanship of which, although admirable so far as the carving is concerned, gives an appearance of weakness in the general architectural scheme of the building. These towers are octagonal in shape, with neat bands built in relief round them at various heights. The bases of the towers are further carved in the shape of a casket, and the entire form seems to be more suited for a building of wood or stone in which each part stands independently and is not co-related for durability and strength to other parts. The dome of this mosque is insignificant in size, while the ceiling vaults in the interior are elaborately decorated with plaster-work, and one of them adjoining the *miḥrāb* is divided into a number of squares in imitation of woodwork. These features clearly indicate the preponderance of Hindu workmanship in the building.

It may also be remembered that the sixteenth century A.D. was a period of fusion of cultures in the whole of India. Muslims had been in residence in this country for several centuries, and they had assimilated many Hindu conventions and practices in their social and religious life. The signs of weakness and deterioration at Bidar during this period, however, were due rather to political causes than to modification of building ideals and methods, for almost simultaneously with the Barīd Shāhī buildings some grand buildings like the Chār Minār and the Gol

[1] The direction of Mecca, towards which Muslims face when saying their prayers.

Gumbad[1] were erected at Golconda and Bijāpur respectively, and in Northern India at Agra and Fatḥpur Śikrī the Mughal style was evolved, in which the skill and knowledge of Hindu craftsmen are so happily blended with Muslim ideals and tradition.

The last Barīd Shāhī king, Amīr Barīd II, was taken as a prisoner to Bijāpur in A.D. 1619, and the kingdom of Bidar, which had dwindled to a small principality, was annexed to the ʿĀdil Shāhī territories. Bijāpur at this time was an important centre of architectural activity,[2] but Bidar, being somewhat remote and having become the seat of only a provincial governor, received little stimulus from Bijāpur. There is, however, a small mosque near the Dargāh of Ḥaḍrat Makhdūm Qādirī which was apparently built during the governorship of Malik Marjān.[3] The minarets and the dome of this mosque (Pl. CXXVI) bear a striking resemblance to the minarets and domes of the Bukhārī Masjid and the mosque of Ibrāhīm kā Rauḍa at Bijāpur.[4] In the construction of minor buildings the hand of the Hindu mason was uppermost in almost every place in the Deccan, and the slender minarets, toy-like domes, and profusion of plaster decoration, which are the chief characteristics of the architecture of this period, are the outcome of Hindu methods of building and their ideas of decoration.

In A.D. 1656 Bidar was annexed to the Mughal empire, and thenceforward until A.D. 1724, when Āṣaf Jāh declared his independence, the Governors of Bidar were appointed by the Imperial Court at Delhi. During the Mughal administration some of the gateways of the Bidar fort were extensively repaired, and a few mosques were built; but these buildings have no architectural importance. The glory of Bidar waned with the decline of the Baihmanī dynasty, and the little architectural beauty which shone forth during the Barīdī period finally disappeared with the extinction of that dynasty.

1 The Chār Minār was built in A.D. 1591, and the Gol Gumbad between A.D. 1636 and 1660.

2 See Cousens's *Bījāpūr Architecture*, *A.S.I.*, vol. xxxvii, p. 15.

3 He was governor of Bidar from A.D. 1636 to 1656, *v. supra*, pp. 14–15.

4 Cousens's *Bījāpūr Architecture*, Pls. XLII–III.

CHAPTER IV

MONUMENTS

IN describing the monuments of Bidar the fort is dealt with first, as it contains some buildings which were the earliest to be erected when Aḥmad Shāh Walī Baihmanī transferred the seat of government from Gulbarga to Bidar in A.D. 1429. The next group of monuments comprises the buildings of the town including the fortifications, a large number of which are coeval with the buildings of the fort. The third group embraces the tombs and shrines at Āshṭūr which were erected by the Baihmanī kings from A.D. 1436 to 1535. The Barīdī tombs and the mausolea in their vicinity constitute the fourth group, while the fifth, or last, group includes all monuments of historical, religious, or architectural significance situated within a distance of six miles from Bidar. This order is chronological to a certain extent, but in describing individually the monuments of each group it has been considered expedient to follow the order of their situation along the road or the footpath, so that the visitor may see the monuments continuously without going to and fro, as would have been necessary, if a strictly chronological plan had been followed.

THE FORT ENCLAVE

Fortifications

In the chapter on History it has been shown that there was a fort at Bidar with a double line of defences when Prince Ulugh Khān conquered the place.[1] What the form or the extent of this was, it is difficult to determine exactly now. Tradition, however, says that it occupied the western area of the present fort, from the Kalmaḍgī Gate to the Takht Maḥall site, including the projection on which Vīrasangayya's temple is now built. The large tank would thus have stood at the foot of the old fort, which would have been also defended on three sides by natural precipices. Fragmentary inscriptions, carved blocks of masonry and architectural parts, such as pillars, capitals, and brackets, have been found in abundance in clearing the above area. The tradition is further confirmed by a statement made by Firishta that Aḥmad Shāh Walī built the Government House (Dār-ul-Imāra) at a site where the old fort of Bidar stood in ancient times. Firishta's own words are:

در جای که قدیم الایّام حصار بیدر بود دارالامارة ساختند [2]

The Dār-ul-Imāra is now called the Takht Maḥall or the Throne Palace.

According to Firishta the building of the city and fort of Bidar commenced some time in A.D. 1429, when the king returned from the conquest of Kherla,[3] and the operations lasted for nearly three years, for the same author writes that the fort of Bidar was completed in A.D. 1432, when public rejoicings were held.[4] It was built of stone and mortar, and engineers and architects of various countries were employed

[1] *Supra*, pp. 4 and 6.
[2] *Firishta* (Persian text, Bombay ed.), vol. i, p. 627.
[3] Ibid., p. 626.
[4] Ibid., p. 632.

on its design and construction.[1] As gunpowder had not yet come into use in the Deccan, the form of the fort apparently consisted of long stretches of massive walls defended by a moat which was excavated from the rock on which the fort stood. The moat was apparently the work of Hindu masons, who from very early times were adept in carving scarps out of solid rock, while the massive walls constructed of 'stone and mortar' were designed and built by Persian and Turkish architects who had assembled at the court of Aḥmad S͟hāh Walī. The fortifications of Bidar, as the result of an invasion by Sulṭān Maḥmūd K͟haljī of Mālwa, were destroyed and rebuilt during the reign of Niẓām S͟hāh Baihmanī (A.D. 1461–3), but perhaps no great change was made in their original character until the time of Muḥammad S͟hāh Baihmanī, when gunpowder was used for blowing up walls by laying mines beneath them. Firis͟hta, in describing the siege of Belgām by this king in A.D. 1472, observes that when the garrison thwarted the attempts of the royalists to fill up the moat, they resorted to other devices and began to dig trenches and lay mines which till then had not been used in the Deccan. Firis͟hta has further used the words *bārūt* ('gunpowder') and *top* ('gun') in describing the war material and appliances used in this siege.[2]

Muḥammad S͟hāh's reign was marked by great prosperity, and through the military genius of Maḥmūd Gāwān, his able general and minister, the boundaries of the Baihmanī kingdom were much widened and the construction and equipment of forts were developed along scientific lines. On one occasion when the king ordered Maḥmūd Gāwān to repair an old fort previously built by one of the Delhi kings, he strengthened the defences and equipped it with guns and other war apparatus so thoroughly and with such expedition that the king exclaimed that the Almighty had conferred upon him an incalculable blessing in giving him a servant like Maḥmūd Gāwān.[3]

Although there is no direct reference in contemporary history[4] to the rebuilding of the defences of Bidar fort during the reign of Muḥammad S͟hāh, yet the facts cited above leave no doubt that this king, who was anxious to rebuild even minor forts in his territory, must have planned afresh and remodelled the fortifications of his capital in view of the new material and appliances of war which had come into use during his time.[5] There is both historical and epigraphic evidence to show that

[1] *Firis͟hta* (Bombay lithograph, vol. i, p. 626) writes thus:

مهندسان اقلیدس شعار و طرّاحان مانی آثار بدایع نگار که از اقطار و امصار بپایهٔ سریر ثریّا نظیر جمع آمده بودند بکلک بصارت صورت شهر و عمارت را بر لوح مهارت انگاشتند الخ.

[2] *Firis͟hta* (Bombay lithograph), vol. i, p. 682.

[3] Ibid., p. 687.

[4] Muḥammad S͟hāh changed the name of the city to Muḥammadābād Bidar after his own name; hitherto it had been called Aḥmadābād Bidar after the name of Aḥmad S͟hāh Walī, the founder of the city.

[5] Elliot in his most valuable note on the use of gunpowder in India remarks:

'There is certain testimony to the use of cannon in Gujarat before the arrival of the Portuguese; which is easily accounted for by the constant communication at that time with the Turks of Egypt and Arabia. In A.D. 1482 Mahmud Shah I of Gujarat is mentioned as fitting out a fleet against the pirates of Bulsar, on board of which he embarked gunners and musketeers from Kambay. Two years

some additions to the defences of the fort were made by Maḥmūd S͟hāh Baihmanī,[1] but they were apparently of a minor character, for the reign of this king was disturbed by rebellions at the capital and outside it, and, further, the Barīdī ministers held him completely under their control. Improvements on a large scale, however, may have been made during the reign of ʿAlī Barīd (A.D. 1542–80), who mounted guns, made under his express command, at various vulnerable points of the fort.[2] Later, in A.D. 1618, Malik Marjān, the Bijāpur governor, repaired the walls and bastions of the fort,[3] and afterwards Muk͟htār K͟hān al-Ḥusainī, the Mug͟hal commandant, re-erected and plated and bossed in iron almost all the gates of Bidar, which bear his inscriptions to this day.[4] Muḥammad Ṣāliḥ Kambo, the contemporary historian of S͟hāh Jahān's reign, gives a description of the fort with certain details, which are true even to-day as regards the general disposition of its defences.[5] It is thus clear that since A.D. 1656, when Aurangzeb, as governor of the Deccan, annexed Bidar to the Mug͟hal kingdom, no substantial change has been made in its fortifications, which were rebuilt by Muḥammad S͟hāh Baihmanī under the able superintendence of his general, Maḥmūd Gāwān, after the use of gunpowder was introduced into the Deccan, although they have been repaired and slight additions made during the occupation of the fort by rulers of other dynasties in subsequent years.

Bidar fort is an irregular rhomboid in shape, built on the brink of the plateau with steep sides towards the north and east (Map). On other sides, where the ground-level was not higher than the adjoining lands, a moat has been excavated in the form of a triple channel with partition walls hewn out of the solid rock. These rock-

after, we find him using cannon to breach the walls of Champanir, and even firing shells at the palace of the Raja. It is curious that one of the first applications of gunpowder amongst Muhammadan Indians was in the manufacture of shells. A few years later, Sher Shah met his death by the explosion of one in his own batteries, when besieging Kalinjar. Castanheda, in describing Vasco da Gama's entrance into Calicut in 1498 says, "The procession again set out, preceded by many trumpets and sacbuts sounding all the way, and one of the Nayres carried a *caliver*, which he fired off at intervals." Two years afterwards the Zamorin commanded the Portuguese vessels.' *History of India*, vol. vi, p. 467.

[1] See *Firis͟hta* (Bombay lithograph), vol. i, p. 711, and *Epig. Ind. Mosl.*, 1925–6, pp. 17–18, Pl. VIII.

[2] *Infra*, pp. 35 ff.

[3] *Epig. Ind. Mosl.*, 1927–8, p. 26.

[4] Ibid., p. 24.

[5] Muḥammad Ṣāliḥ may be quoted here:

سدی مرجان قلعه‌دار که از ملازمان قدیم الخدمت ابراهیم عادل خان بود و از مدت سي سال بحراست آن قلعه مي پرداخت و سامان سرانجام و دیگر مواد قلعه‌داري مهيّا داشت و قریب هزار سوار و چار هزار پیاده تفنگچي و باندار همراه داشت باندیشهٔ نگاهداشت قلعه باستحکام برج و باره و سدّ مداخل و مخارج آن پرداخته بکار فرمائيِ ادبار مستعد مواجهه و مقابله گشت ـ شاه آفاق گیر بسبب این حرکت ناهنجار بمجرّد رسیدن از راه همّت بر تادیب او و تسخیر آن حصن حصین که چهار هزار و پانصد ذراع دور و دوازده ذراع ارتفاع و سه خندق عمیق بعرض بیست و پنج گز و ژرفائيِ پانزده گز در سنگ دارد گماشته خود با معظّم خان بگرد قلعه بر آمده اطراف چار دیوار حصاررا بنظر دقت نگر در آوردند — و همه جا ملچارها قرار داده بندهای بادشاهي و ملازمان خود را بمحافظت آن تعیّن نمودند ٭

ʿ*Amal-i-Ṣāliḥ* (*Bibl. Ind.*), vol. iii, pp. 249–50.

partitions are a special feature of the Bidar fort and their long stretches present a grim appearance (Pl. II). The rock is laterite, which by weathering has assumed a dark brown colour. The width of the moat between the glacis and the first partition-wall is 32 feet 6 inches, between the first and second partition-walls 36 feet 4 inches, and between the second partition-wall and the scarp 41 feet 9 inches. The depth of the moat is 30 feet, and the height of the scarp above the rock-base on which it is built varies from 32 feet 8 inches to 43 feet.

The moat and the glacis encircle the fort on all sides, but the rock-partitioned triple channel exists towards the city side only—that is, towards the south-east, the south, and the south-west. The moat was apparently kept dry except between the Kalyānī Burj and the Old Fort bastion, where a sluice has been built to fill it from the tank inside the fort.[1] The external circumference of the defences of the fort is two and a half miles.[2] There are thirty-seven bastions and seven gates, besides the main entrance from the city side. The names of the gates from east to west are as follows:

(1) The Māṇḍū Darwāza,
(2) The Kalmaḍgī Darwāza,
(3–4) Anonymous,
(5) The Delhi Darwāza,
(6) The Kalyānī Darwāza,
and (7) The Carnatic Darwāza.

Some of the bastions are most massively built, and they are generally round or octagonal in shape. A few bastions are, however, square in design. The parapets are honeycombed with machicoulis providing facilities for firing muskets as well as cannon, both at close and long range. The walls near the main entrance appear to have been breached and rebuilt at various periods; the old portions consist of large blocks of stone laid in lime, but the joints are so fine that the lime is not visible. The later portions are built of smaller blocks, but the joints in the masonry are not so fine and the line of mortar is conspicuous between the courses. The stone used is trap, which is not found locally, and must have been brought from quarries in the Gulbarga district. The transport of trap stone sufficient for the construction of the entire fort must have been an undertaking involving both special organization and enormous expense.

In front of the first gate of the main approach there was originally a drawbridge over the moat, but it does not exist now, and the moat at this point has been filled up for the construction of the road. The first gateway is somewhat weak in appearance; if the inscription carved on the door is to be interpreted literally, it was built by Mukhtār Khān al-Ḥusainī, the Mughal governor, in A.D. 1683.[3] The height

[1] This portion of the moat is popularly called the *Paniyā Khandaq*, 'Water-moat'.

[2] The length of the passage along the line of battlements is 2 miles, 1 furlong, and 18 yards. There were 4,176 *kangūras*, of which 644 have fallen down.

[3] The inscription is carved on a metal tablet fixed to the door. The text has been deciphered as follows:

٢٦
روز جمعه ٢٧ شهر رجب المرجب سنه جلوس میمنت مانوس حضرت قدر قدرت جم جاه ملائك سپاه محي الدين محمد

of the gateway up to the top of the parapet is 36 feet, while the entrance arch is 19 feet high and has a span of 12 feet 4 inches. The two small turrets built in front of the parapet over this gateway are incongruous and appear to be later additions. The door of the gateway is fitted with spikes and knobs of iron such as were usually inserted for protection against attack by elephants. The passage through the gateway measures 24 feet 9 inches in length and the roof is vaulted; it is divided into two compartments by an arch which is built in the middle of the passage.

Beyond the first gateway, which faces the north-east, there is a small court and another gateway which faces east-north-east; the first gateway thus serves the purpose of a barbican for the second. The court has rooms for guards on either side; the arches of the rooms on the left side are somewhat squat in proportions, having a span of 14 feet 9 inches with a height of 9 feet 1 inch only. The second gateway is called the Sharza Darwāza on account of the effigies of two tigers carved on its façade. Such effigies are often seen on the Deccan forts, and their presence apparently signifies the Shīʿa belief that the representations of ʿAlī, whose title was Asad-Ullāh al-Ghālib, in this form make the building safe from attack by an enemy.[1]

The Sharza Darwāza is of larger dimensions than the first gateway, its height up to the top of the parapet being 34 feet 3 inches, and the height of the entrance arch 22 feet 7 inches with a span of 17 feet 5 inches.[2] But its façade being covered over with lime plaster and further decorated with tile-work, however lovely in design, lacks vigour and strength, which should be the dominating features of a military building. The top of the gateway was originally decorated with a beautiful parapet of trefoil design, the face of which was adorned with encaustic tiles presenting green and blue patterns tastefully relieved by yellow and white bands. At either end of this parapet stood a slender turret which was emblazoned with tile-work of chevron design. The beauty of this parapet has been marred by another of rough masonry which has been built above it in later times for the purpose of emplacing guns, the heavy arch-shaped blocks of this masonry contrasting woefully with the delicate design of the original parapet. The tile-work of the original parapet has decayed considerably, but wherever it is intact the colours are extremely fresh and charming.

Below this parapet is a long panel of black stone covering the entire forehead of the gateway and containing an inscription which records the building of the gateway

اورنگ زیب بهادر عالم گیر بادشاه غازي خلّد اللّه ملکه و سلطانه موافق . . . . . . هجري نبوي در صوبه داريْ کمترین بندگان مختار
خان الحسیني السبزواري این دروازه صورت اتمام [یافت].

Translation

'On Friday, the 27th of Rajab, the honoured month, in the 26th regnal year from the auspicious accession of His Majesty, (who is) powerful like Fate, glorious like Jamshīd, master of the army of angels, Muḥī-ud-Dīn Muḥammad Aurangzeb Bahādur ʿĀlamgīr, the victorious King (may God perpetuate his kingdom and majesty!), corresponding to 1094 of the era of the Flight of the Prophet, during the governorship of the humblest of servants, Mukhtār Khān al-Ḥusainī as-Sabzwārī, this gate was completed.' *Epig. Ind. Mosl.*, 1927–8, p. 24.

[1] In this connexion the tendency of Hindu masons to decorate buildings with animal figures should not be overlooked.

[2] The passage through this gateway measures 11 feet only in length.

in A.D. 1503, during the reign of Maḥmūd Shāh Baihmanī, by Saif Khān Kotwālbek.[1] The style of writing is *Thulth*, but the letters have been so intertwined that the whole looks like a lace design. There were other inscriptions along this band on the foreheads of the side bastions, but as they were inscribed on tiles they have largely perished. The few pieces which are intact on the left bastion show that the inscriptions were in white on a deep blue background. The following few words may still be read on the left bastion:

Text

مقيم در سلطاني . . . ثاني . . . محكم بنياد او كـ سيف خان ثاني . . . ايوان بارگـ سلطانست

Translation

'Waiting at the royal court . . . the second . . . its solid foundations (were laid) by Saif Khān, the second . . . the portico of the royal court.'

The Sharza Darwāza has a *naqqār khāna* (music gallery) in its upper parts, to which access may be had from the steps built at the back of the guards' rooms near the inner arch of the Darwāza. The entrance room is rectangular in plan, and from it, through a domical chamber, the main apartments of the music gallery are reached. These are three in number; the middle one is crowned by a dome, and the side ones have shallow vaults which are concealed in the thickness of the roof. The dimensions of these apartments are insignificant, their total length being 49 feet 3 inches, but the plaster-work of their vaults is very beautiful, and some of the bands seem to have been copied from woodwork. The side apartments have semi-octagonal projections towards the front, which are pierced by tiny windows fitted with black stone frames and thick iron doors, the latter being decorated with knobs and stars. The windows command views of the lands adjoining the fort from which an enemy could make an attack. Some of the openings of these apartments are

[1] The full text of the inscription is as follows:

اے زمين آستانت آسمان ملك و دين　　آسمانى آسمان گر نقش بندد بر زمين

اشكوب اوّلت سبع سموات طباق　　نقش درگاه تو طبتم فادخلوها خالدين

طاق درگاه تو طغرايست بر منشور ملك　　رسم اركان تو بناديست بر اركان دين

حلقۀ درگاه جاهت گوشوارۀ عز و جاه　　پايۀ صدر رفيعت دستگاه ملك و دين

باني هذا الباب اياز المخاطب بسيفخان كوتوالبك في سنه تسع و تسعماية كتبه محمود شاه بن محمد شاه السلطان البهمني ٭

Translation

'Oh! the earth of thy court is the sky of State and Faith: it can be called a sky if the latter can exist on earth.

'Thy first storey comprises the stages of the seven heavens: the text of the inscription of thy court is: "Ye have been good, wherefore enter ye into *paradise*, to remain therein for ever."

'The arch of thy court is the imperial signature on the mandate of the empire, and the regulations of thy law (*lit.* "principles") are based on the tenets of the (Islāmic) Faith.

'The ring of the threshold of thy glory is the ear-ring of greatness and dignity, the plinth of thy exalted court is the support of the State and Faith.

'The builder of this gate (is) Ayāz, entitled Saif Khān, Kotwālbek: in the year 909 H. (A.D. 1503). Written by Maḥmūd Shāh son of Muḥammad Shāh as-Sulṭān al-Baihmanī.' *Epig. Ind. Mosl.*, 1925–6, p. 18.

filled up with trellis-work of elegant designs. To keep up the old military traditions of the fort, music is still played from this gallery four times a day at the beginning of each watch.[1]

From the entrance of the music gallery a good view of the fortifications is obtained. On the left stretches the line of ramparts, interspersed with bastions and having a passage along the battlements for the use of the garrison firing at, and hurling missiles on, the enemy at the time of a siege (Pls. IV and V). To the north-west stands the Guṃbad Darwāza, which is a most massive structure, the grim appearance of which presents a striking contrast to the somewhat weak and decorative features of the first two gateways of the fort (Pl. VI). The distance between the Sharza Darwāza and the Guṃbad Darwāza is considerable, but they are connected by a broad passage which is defended on both sides by low curtains of massive construction. Two to three thousand soldiers could easily be posted between these two gateways for purposes of defence in time of danger.

The architecture of the Guṃbad Darwāza forms an important landmark in the history of the monuments of the Deccan. Its battering walls, its low arch-shaped parapet, its fluted corner turrets (*guldastas*), and its hemispherical dome are all reminiscent of the contemporary (14th–15th centuries) architecture of Delhi, but the shape of its outer arch with its significant stilt and the proportions of its span and its altitude disclose that Persian influence which gradually became more and more prominent in the buildings of the Deccan. The span of this arch is 29 feet and the height up to the apex 39 feet 8 inches, but the springing points being low, the general appearance of the arch is somewhat squat (Pl. VI).

With a view to greater security the entrance of the Guṃbad Darwāza is through a recessed arch of much smaller dimensions than the outer one, and it is fitted with doors plated and bossed with iron.[2] The thickness of the walls, combining the depths of both arches, is 22 feet 3 inches, and they rise to a height of 45 feet, above which the dome is built. The internal diameter of the dome is 38 feet, the external 48 feet, thus showing a thickness of 10 feet in the masonry of the dome. The thickness of the domes of the Deccan gradually decreases in their upper parts, as has been revealed by examination of the masonry of those specimens which have partly fallen down, when their thickness can be measured at different heights. The interior of the gateway has platforms on either side of the passage for the accommodation of guards.

From its style of architecture the gateway seems to be of the earliest period, and it is not unlikely that it was built by Aḥmad Shāh Walī when he laid the foundations of the fort in A.D. 1429.[3] The bastions adjoining the front of this gateway seem to be

[1] Bidar fort still has a *corps de garde* which is called the *aḥshām*.

[2] The span of the recessed arch is 12 feet 4 inches, and the height 19 feet 9 inches.

[3] From the roof of the gateway an excellent view of the southern ramparts of the fort may be had. As they have been built in front of the triple rock-hewn moat they are apparently of a later date, after artillery had come into use. The triple moat has been filled up with earth and there are traces of a garden, which seems to have been laid out after the ramparts were built. The garden had fountains and paved walks, the outlines of which can still be seen. The total length of the garden is 193 yards and the breadth 25 yards. The ramparts have an arcade, built in two stages, at their back. The arcade may have been used for the accommodation of the guards of the fort. The back wall of the arcade has loop-

later additions, built at different periods according to the exigencies of the times. Architecturally they are not welded into the main body of the building, as they cover portions of the original wall and appear as if superimposed (Pl. VI). The bastion on the right is barrel-shaped, while that on the left is circular; the latter is more massive and perhaps of later date. For the defence of the right side another bastion, octagonal in shape, has been built in front of the cylindrical one. From the entrance of the Guṃbad Darwāza the first object to attract attention in the interior of the fort is a banyan tree of colossal size and great antiquity (Pl. VII). In spring, when the berries ripen, the herds of monkeys and the flocks of birds that visit it add to the picturesqueness of this tree.

To continue the description of the fortifications it will be best to take the road which goes in a north-easterly direction on entering the fort from the Guṃbad Darwāza.[1] Proceeding some 250 yards along this road, first a bastion is noticed in two stages, each equipped with machicoulis. Farther on there is a tower, perhaps utilized as the 'keep', for it commands a complete view of the city walls up to the Ḥabshī Koṭ and of the lowlands in the south-east as well as of the fort ramparts towards the south-west. The interior of the tower is beautifully finished with plaster-work. The plan of the building is square at the base, measuring 11 feet 6 inches each way. The ceiling is domical, with ribs in imitation of a wooden structure. On either side of the tower, towards the south-west and north-east, there are remains of halls. At a lower level, from this tower towards the north-west there are some rooms, the walls of which are extremely thick, with arches heavy in proportion but stilted at the top. The rooms are at present in possession of the descendants of the old guards of the fort who apparently have been living there for several generations.

The road leads farther on to the Large Gun Bastion which stands by the side of the Māṇḍū Gate. This bastion is most massively built, and in its construction large blocks of masonry have been used. It has two stages; the lower is loopholed for the use of minor fire-arms including cannon of small size, while the upper is mounted with a magnificent specimen of ordnance, bearing the name of 'Alī Barīd, during whose time (A.D. 1542–80) the bastion was apparently built and the gun made. M. Thevenot saw the gun in A.D. 1667 and roughly calculated its mouth to be 3 feet wide. Its actual dimensions are:

Length	14 ft. 9 in.
Bore	1 ft. 7 in.
Diameter near the muzzle	3 ft. 6 in.
Circumference near the butt	11 ft. 9 in.

holes for muskets as well as for cannon. In the middle of the arcade is a massive arch, the proportions of which are almost the same as those of the outer arch of the Guṃbad Darwāza.

[1] Adjoining the Guṃbad Darwāza towards the north there is a vast enclosure with two gates opening upon the road. One of these gates is close to the Guṃbad Darwāza and the other in the middle of the enclosure wall towards the west. There are traces of several rooms within the enclosure and also remains of a rectangular cistern with jets. The remains of a room adjoining the ramparts show tile-work in which blue pieces are still intact. The main part of the building seems to have been on a platform, below which there was a court, 144 feet from north to south and 174 feet 5 inches from east to west. As this building is of large dimensions and is attached to the Guṃbad Darwāza, the main entrance to the fort, it was apparently meant for the residence of the Commandant of the Fort.

Six inscribed panels with ornamental lettering adorn the body of the gun.[1] The inscriptions, besides the name of the king, mention the date 977 H. (A.D. 1572) and the weight of the shot and powder with which the gun was to be charged. The text in regard to the latter has been deciphered as follows:

غلولہ دوازده من و نیم | بارود دو من و نیم

Translation

'Shots twelve and a half maunds, powder two and a half maunds.'

The maund here is apparently the *kachcha man* of the Deccan weighing twelve seers or twenty-four English pounds avoirdupois. The gun has a highly polished surface, and is built of bars of laminated metal, bound with hoops which have been welded together beautifully. The size and the finish of this gun show that in the latter half of the sixteenth century very high scientific knowledge and technical skill in the manufacture of guns had been acquired in the Deccan (Pl. XLVII). The bastion commands an extensive view of the lowlands toward the east, and this large gun was apparently used for long-range firing.

Adjoining the bastion towards the north-west are the barbicans of the Māṇḍū Gate which opens on the moat and faces the north. The barbicans are in two stages, the upper one is a little lower than the ramparts of the fort, and is equipped with machicoulis for the use of both large and small fire-arms. The curtains of the upper barbican have been built in haste, for carved slabs originally belonging to other buildings seem to have been indiscriminately used in the construction of the curtains. A notable example of this is a pair of tablets bearing the *Āyat-al-Kursī* ('throne verse') built in near the entrance of the barbican. But, notwithstanding this haphazard selection of stones, the curtains are most massively built and are circular in plan so that the garrison might be able to shoot from all angles. Steps from the upper barbican lead down to the lower one, which has almost the same arrangement, except for the existence of a narrow arcade along the line of battlements. As the level of the barbican at this stage is almost the same as that of the glacis, a roofed protection was necessary for the garrison when defending the

[1] The full text of the inscriptions has been deciphered as follows:

وضعہ اللّٰہ اطیب عیش ❖ توپ الٰهي یکی از غرایب علامات وضع کارخانۂ خاصہ شاهي همایون اکرم حضرت علي برید شاهي تمّت في تاریخ سنہ ۹۷۷ الهجریة النبویہ ❖

غلولہ دوازده من و نیم دارو دو من و نیم اگر خواهد کہ ازین زیاده صافي کند از ده سیر زیاده نہ اندازد ❖

Translation

'May God make his (the king's) life the sweetest! The Top-i-Ilāhī ("divine gun") is one of the most wonderful specimens manufactured by the royal factory of His August and Benevolent Majesty, 'Alī Barīd Shāh. Finished in the Hijra year of our Prophet, 977 H. (A.D. 1572).'

'Shot twelve and a half maunds and powder two and a half maunds. If [the gunner] desires to increase the charge he should not increase it by more than ten seers.'

The texts of both these inscriptions are repeated in other panels; and in one of them the date, instead of being given in figures, is given in words:

في تاریخ سنہ سبع وسبعین و تسعمایة الهجرة النبویہ

fort from the lower stage. For further protection the passage which leads to the entrance has been built in a zigzag manner so that it could be choked with live coal or other materials at any point.

In the Deccan the term *parkoṭa* is applied to such barbicans as are built below a bastion (*koṭ*) guarding a passage as an additional measure of defence.

From the Large Gun Bastion the road proceeds in a north-westerly direction, and at a distance of a furlong and a quarter excellent views of the ruins of the fort may be had from the ramparts. After going some two furlongs the Kalmaḍgī Gate is reached. In the construction of this, special precautionary measures have been observed as the descent to the adjoining ground is not very steep at that point. The passage to the gateway is through a tunnel cut in the rock, but before entering it the visitor should not miss seeing the beautifully carved pillars of Hindu design which support the roof of a room built above the tunnel.

The passage through the rock is 12 feet wide and 126 feet long, and at its end it has a rectangular opening which was once fitted with a door, as the sockets above the opening indicate. The opening leads into an S-shaped court which is 233 feet in length and varies in width from 23 to 44 feet at different points. The court is defended by lofty and massive bastions, which present a grim appearance owing to their dark trap masonry. At the northern end is an arcade fitted with machicoulis both at the top and the bottom so that the garrison could discharge fire-arms from two levels. At both its eastern and western ends the court has steps which lead to another line of fortifications (*parkoṭa*) at a lower level. The passage between this line of fortification and the line behind is narrow, being only 10 feet wide. At the southern end the passage has steps which lead down to a gate facing the east and having a barbican built in front of it for protection; at its western end it abuts on a small court which has a gate at the north-west corner. The gate opens upon the moat. The various lines of fortifications in defence of the two openings of the gate referred to above are so arranged that the progress of an enemy could be checked at various points, while he would always be exposed to the fire of the garrison in his attempt to enter the fort.

Proceeding three-quarters of a furlong farther westward along the road, the enclosure of the Purāna Qilʿa is entered. The defences inside the Qilʿa are all of the Muslim period, but as the site may originally have been occupied by the old Hindu fort, the name Purāna Qilʿa has survived. The enclosure wall has two entrances, one leading to a Darwāza, the name of which is not known with certainty now, and the other to the interior of the Purāna Qilʿa. The archway giving access to the anonymous Darwāza has been blocked up; that leading to the interior of the Purāna Qilʿa is open, but it is of small dimensions, although on the inner side it is defended by a massive bastion.

The outer arch of the entrance to the anonymous Darwāza from the interior of the fort is most massively built, although it is rather narrow at the top. The span is 12 feet 8 inches, and the height up to the apex 18 feet. The passage beyond this entrance is hewn through the rock, and has been given a slope in order to reach ultimately the level of the moat to which it leads. After a distance of 36 yards it passes under three massive arches, the spans of which are 16 feet 6 inches and which have no imposts, the arch-heads springing from the rock on either side. These three arches were once connected by a common roof, which has fallen down. Beyond this point the passage continues, with abrupt turns, for a distance of 110 yards, when a second gateway is reached. Both the outer and inner arches of this gateway show a fine sense of proportion, and the inner arch which is open now has a span of 12 feet 9 inches and a height up to the apex of 22 feet 9 inches. Above this arch there was originally a frieze on which *Qur'ānic* texts were carved in an artistic manner. Some of the slabs of the frieze are still intact, and these have been conserved by the Department. The left side of the arch had fallen down, and has been rebuilt. Between the two arches of this gateway there were rooms at either side of the passage, for the accommodation of the guards.

Passing through this gateway the passage leads to a court, almost circular in plan,[1] which is defended on the moat side by a double arcade, arranged in two storeys. The arcade has ample accommodation for guards, while at its back it is provided with loopholes in both the upper and lower stages, which show that it could be used for attacking the enemy in time of siege. At the south-east end of the court there is an arched gateway which opens on the moat.

In the interior of the Purāna Qilʿa there are no traces of quarters for guards, but the disposition of the fortifications is of interest to students of the military architecture of that period. The passage along the battlements is wider so that troops could go up there in larger numbers for the purpose of defence. In the northern part of the Qilʿa, behind the ramparts, another line (traverse) has been built up, apparently to enfilade attacking columns. From the bastion at the extreme north point of the Qilʿa to the Kalyānī Burj in the west the line of ramparts has been doubled, the reason being that the lowlands towards the north and north-west of the fort have no steep descent, and there is also a small hillock to the north of the Purāna Qilʿa which, if occupied by the enemy, would enable him to bombard the fort. The bastion at the northern point has been most massively built, and in its lower stage it has a *parkoṭa* from which fire could be opened on an enemy making an attack from the lowlands.[2] On the bastion is mounted a fine piece of ordnance, bearing the name Fatḥ La<u>sh</u>kar ('triumph of the army') and the date 988 H. (A.D. 1580). It is smaller in size than the Large Gun[3] and the weight of the charge inscribed on it is—

[1] The width of the court (east to west) is 86 feet, and the length (north to south) 90 feet 6 inches.

[2] To the west of the bastion there are steps which lead through an arched doorway to a *parkoṭa* which in its upper stage extends 45 yards only. The second stage, which is approached by steps from both the eastern and western ends of the upper stage, is, however, much larger, extending to a length of 180 yards and being defended by bastions at various points. Ultimately, steps from the western limit of the second stage lead to a third one, where there are three bastions and an archway. The latter faces west and leads to the moat. The third stage of the *parkoṭa* measures 21 yards from north to south and 46 yards from east to west.

[3] The exact dimensions of this gun are as follows:

Length	11 ft. 4 in.
Bore	1 ft. 2½ in.
Diameter near the muzzle	2 ft. 6½ in.
Circumference near the butt	8 ft. 4 in.

'shot five maunds and half a seer (121 lb. avoirdupois) and powder one maund and ten seers (44 lb. avoirdupois)'.[1] The date falls within the reign of Ibrāhīm Barīd, who ruled from A.D. 1580 to 1587, and it appears that the bastion and the ramparts at this point were either built or strengthened under his orders.

In going round the 'traverse' the road makes a loop and descends to a lower level, where the remains of two gun-foundries and an old well may be seen. The well is very deep, its bottom being on a level with the bed of the tank which is situated below the precipice towards the south. A pipe-line had been laid from the well, traces of which may still be seen along the edge of the plateau.

[1] The full text of the inscription has been deciphered as follows:

Text

Panel I

Bismi'llah

Panel II

غلوله پنج من و نیم سیر بارود یك من و ده سیر و اگر خواهد که ازین زیاده صافي کند دیگر ده سیر زیاده باندازد ◆

Panel III

Qur'ān, ch. xlviii, verses 1–3

Panel IV

فتح لشکر که ز سهمش دل اعداست حزین   راست چون برق فرود آمده بر روی زمین

چون پشنك در دهن اژدر پیٔ خیل بود   اژدهای که سر خصم فرو برده بکین

Panel V

تیار شد توپ ظفر پیکر مسمی بفتح لشکر در زمان دولت اعلیٰحضرت عالیجاه امیرزا شاهي محمود المخاطب بهمایون اکرم برید
شاه خلد الله ملکه و سلطانه في تاریخ سنه ۹۸۸ هـ ◆

Panel VI

Abbreviations at the commencement of certain chapters of the *Qur'ān*. Written by Yada'llāh.

Panel VII

Qur'ān, ch. lxi, verse 13

Panel VIII

Nādi 'Alī

Translation

Panel II

'Shot five maunds and half a seer (121 lb. avoirdupois) and powder one maund and ten seers (44 lb. avoirdupois). If the gunner desires to increase the charge he may increase it by ten seers (20 lb.).

Panel IV

Verse

'The Triumph of the Army, by the awe of which the heart of the enemy is filled with grief,
It has come down to earth like a bolt from the blue.
It is like the dragon which held Pashang in its mouth, and in pursuing the enemy
It is a serpent which in fury swallows the head of the enemy.'

Panel V

'The gun bearing the emblem of victory, called Fatḥ Lashkar ("triumph of the army"), was made during the reign of His Majesty, the exalted Amīrzā, the praised sovereign, entitled Humāyūn-i-Akram (the auspicious and the most benevolent) Barīd Shāh—may God perpetuate his kingdom and authority! In the year 988 H. (A.D. 1580).'

To complete the circuit of the fort, the visitor should leave the road and descend from the Purāna Qilʿa by the flight of steps which are cut in the rock to the side of the path which goes along the margin of the tank. The roof of this rock-hewn staircase has been lined with masonry in the form of an arch. After descending from the steps, which are fifty in number, the visitor should proceed in a north-westerly direction until he climbs to the higher ground running parallel to the counterscarp. At the south-western end of this is a slope which leads to the inner entrance of the Delhi Darwāza (Map). This is of small dimensions,[1] but is fitted with a massive door, which was locked until recently.[2] To the left of the entrance is the mouth of a big drain, called the Jumna Morī, through which the rain-water flowed from the lowlands of the fort to the nullahs outside it.[3]

Beyond this entrance is a court defended by walls, and another gate which faces the north-east. The court and the line of fortifications round it serve the purpose of a barbican for the inner entrance of the Delhi Darwāza. In the walls of the court some carved stones from old buildings have been used. They bear floral designs, figures of deities, acrobatic performances, and hunting scenes.[4] The entrance of the Delhi Darwāza has an Γ-shaped plan, the passage first going straight and then turning to the right. The arches of this entrance are of small dimensions, but they show a fine sense of proportion, and the masonry used in the building is neatly dressed.[5]

From the court of the Delhi Darwāza a good view of the Kalyānī Burj may be had (Pl. XLIV). It stands to the west of the Darwāza and rises to a height of about 100 feet from the level of the court. It is constructed in three stages which are defended by curtains and have ample space for the accommodation of troops. A flight of steps from the court leads to the apartments built below the bastion in the first stage. The arches of these apartments show a fine sense of proportion, and from their style seem to be contemporary with some of the arches of the Ta<u>kh</u>t Maḥall. The apartments may have been used for the accommodation of the guard posted at the Delhi Darwāza, or they may have been utilized for storing arms.[6] The masonry of the Kalyānī Burj shows that it has been built from the material of old buildings, for the stones are of different varieties and some of them are sculptured. The style of architecture is, however, massive, and the use of carved stones does not detract from the strength of the building. The top of the bastion commands a good

[1] The dimensions of the entrance arch are: span, 11 feet; height up to the apex, 16 feet 9 inches. The door of this entrance is heavily plated and bossed in iron.

[2] The lock is of a primitive type weighing 30 lb. It is exhibited in the fort with other antiquities discovered there.

[3] The mouth of the drain is rectangular, measuring 7 feet 7 inches by 4 feet 7 inches. It is fitted with an iron grating.

[4] These subjects are beautifully carved and originally belonged to a Hindu edifice. In one panel a warrior is shown holding two wild elephants by their hind legs. The animals are vainly struggling to free themselves from his giant grip.

[5] The dimensions of these arches are as follows:

Inner arch—span, 11 feet 3 inches; height up to the apex, 16 feet 3 inches.

Outer arch—span, 8 feet 8 inches; height up to the apex, 12 feet 8 inches.

[6] There is an arcade for the accommodation of the guards in the second stage of the bastion as well.

view of the country towards the north and the table-land towards the west, the latter being almost on a level with the plateau on which the fort has been built. The bastion also offers an excellent view of the double line of the fortifications from the Delhi Darwāza to the Purāna Qil'a (Pl. XLV). As during the monsoon the water of the fort area is drained towards the north, the land on that side is utilized for cultivation, and the green patches of vegetation present a delightful contrast to the otherwise red soil of Bidar.

This bastion must originally have been mounted with a long-range gun, but this is now missing, and an insignificant piece, bearing the maker's name, Muḥammad Qāsim, is lying in its place. Guns by this maker are found in great abundance in the Deccan forts, but they are always of inferior class both in size and workmanship. From the dates given on Muḥammad Qāsim's guns it appears that he flourished during the reign of Nawāb Niẕām 'Alī Khān Bahādur, the second Niẕām of Hyderabad, who ruled from A.D. 1763 to 1803. Nawāb Niẕām 'Alī Khān, however, appointed Monsieur Raymond as Comptroller of Ordnance in A.D. 1796, but earlier than that the post may have been occupied by Muḥammad Qāsim, for Raymond's name appears on guns which are of a later date than those of Muḥammad Qāsim.

About 250 yards farther south is situated the Peṭlā Burj ('the Fat-belly Bastion'), so called on account of its curtains and base protruding prominently from the main line of fortifications. It rises some 83 feet higher than the Kalyānī Burj, the reason for this precaution being that the table-land beyond the moat opposite this bastion is higher than that opposite the Kalyānī Burj. The bastion has a *parkoṭa* which defends the passage leading to the Kalyānī Darwāza. The entrance to the passage from the interior of the fort is through a window built at the base of ramparts to the north of the bastion. The passage beyond this window is very narrow, being 8 feet 4 inches only in width, but it is strongly defended by a line of battlements. After a distance of some 30 yards the passage has steps which lead to another window facing the south.[1] Beyond the latter window is some open space, and farther on a T-shaped gateway with arches at the entrance points. The gateway is strongly built, and the arches, though small, are well proportioned. The first two have a span of 7 feet 6 inches and a height up to the apex of 9 feet 8 inches. The other two, one at each end of the top of the T, are still smaller, being 7 feet in span and 7 feet 6 inches in height. The northern of the last two arches was originally fitted with a door which opened on another court with a line of battlements. This formed the second stage of the *parkoṭa*. Beyond this stage there are steps and a gate leading to the moat. The gate faces the north, and has an arched opening, measuring 11 feet in height and 7 feet 9 inches in width. This gate was called the Kalyānī Darwāza on account of its facing that town. It is likely that in early times the road to Kalyānī also started from that point.

The Peṭlā Burj is mounted now with a gun by Muḥammad Qāsim, bearing the date 1193 H. (A.D. 1779); but originally it must have had a long-range gun which was subsequently removed either to the Red Bastion or the Black Bastion, both

[1] The dimensions of the window are: height, 5 feet 6 inches; width, 4 feet 10 inches.

of which were built at a later date and are mounted with long-range guns of earlier make. The Peṭlā Burj faces west, and as the plateau extends a long way in that direction it is pleasant to watch the sunset from the bastion—the last rays of the sun imparting a lovely radiance to the domes of the Barīdī tombs which are seen in the distance and form a delightful outline on the horizon.

The Lāl Burj or the 'Red Bastion' is so called on account of the red masonry (laterite) of which it is built. The bastion stands some 25 yards behind the main line of fortifications (Map), and was apparently built as an additional measure of defence for the Takht Maḥall, which could be bombarded if earthworks and batteries were raised on the plateau outside the Kalyānī Darwāza to the north-west of the bastion. The construction of the Lāl Burj is not very solid; it seems to have been built in haste, but it is mounted with a long-range gun of an elegant design. The name, Top-i-Ḥaidarī,[1] and the date, Ramaḍān, 996 Shahūr San (February, A.D. 1596), are carved on the gun. It also bears the name of the king, Qāsim Barīd II, and the statement that it was *begun* during his reign, which extended from A.D. 1587 to 1591. The date, February, A.D. 1596, is apparently that of the completion of the gun, when Qāsim Barīd II had died and a usurper, styled Amīr Barīd, was on the throne.[2] The exact dimensions of the gun are as follows:

Length	12 ft. 2 in.
Bore	1 ft. 2½ in.
Circumference near the muzzle	8 ft. 1 in.
Circumference near the butt	11 ft.

[1] Ḥaidar was the title of 'Alī, the son-in-law of the Prophet Muḥammad. The gun was named after him on account of his proverbial valour in the battle-field.

[2] The full text of the inscription carved on the gun has been deciphered as follows:

Text

Top Panel

چون توپ حیدري بسعادت نظام یافت   قاسم برید شاه ممالك بكام یافت

Middle Panel

بطالع دولت ابد پیوند حضرت عالي جاه عالم پناه ابتدا كرده شده این توپ حیدري مشتري در ایّام اعلیٰحضرت خداوند سلیماني جمشید مكاني قاسم برید شاه ثاني خلّد اللّه تعالیٰ ملكه و سلطانه

Bottom Panel

و اعلیٰ امره و شانه في شهور سنه ست و تسعین و تسعمایة ◆ شهر رمضان

Translation

Top Panel

'As the Ḥaidarī Gun was made (or manufactured) at a felicitous time
The King, Qāsim Barīd, found the dominions submissive.'

Middle Panel

'Through the ever-increasing good fortune of His Exalted Highness, the refuge of the world, the (making of the) Ḥaidarī Mushtarī Gun was commenced during the time of His Majesty, possessing Solomon's authority and Jamshīd's dignity, Qāsim Barīd Shāh II; may God Almighty perpetuate his kingdom and sovereignty!'

Bottom Panel

'May God elevate his authority and rank!
In Ramaḍān, *Shahūr San* 996 (February, A.D. 1596).'

About three-fourths of a furlong farther south from the Lāl Burj is another bastion, styled the Kālā Burj, on account of the dark trap masonry of which it has been built. The Kālā Burj also is constructed behind the main line of fortifications (Map) and its object, like that of the Lāl Burj, was to strengthen the defence line at this point for the protection of the Takht Maḥall against a cannonade from the plateau outside the fort. The Kālā Burj is most massively built, and it has a battery on its top mounted with a long-range gun, which bears the name of King ʿAlī Barīd and the date 977 H. (A.D. 1569). The gun has a highly polished surface and is adorned with ornamental panels containing inscriptions in the *Ṭughrā* style of writing. The inscriptions are identical with those carved on the Large Gun,[1] although in size the Kālā Burj gun differs from the latter. The dimensions of the Kālā Burj gun are also not inconsiderable, the length being 18 feet 5 inches, bore 1 foot 7 inches, circumference near the muzzle 9 feet, and circumference near the butt nearly 12 feet. The charge marked on the gun:

Shot 12½ maunds (300 lb. avoirdupois)
Powder 2½ maunds (60 lb. avoirdupois)

gives an idea of the havoc which this large engine of destruction would have caused when fired.

At a short distance to the south-east of the Kāla Burj the line of fortifications has been doubled, apparently to guard a passage which leads from the fort to the Carnatic Darwāza (Map). The entrance to the passage was through a massive arch built under the ramparts, but this had been blocked with masonry at a later date.[2] The Archaeological Department, Hyderabad, has recently opened this arch and repaired and cleared the passage leading to the Darwāza. On entering through the arch there are steps which descend to another arch, which is of smaller dimensions[3] and was originally fitted with a door. Passing beyond the latter arch there is a court divided into two parts by a rock-wall in which an aperture has been made to give access from one part of the court to the other. The court has an arcade, which has been increased in depth in places where the posting of troops in larger numbers was necessary for purposes of defence.[4] The arcade has a line of battlements at the top, and it is provided with loopholes for both small and large fire-arms. Fire thus could be opened on the enemy from both the roof and the interior of the arcade. The court in front of the arcade is defended by several massive bastions.

In the southern part of the arcade is a gateway which has arched openings at each end[5] and rooms for the guards along the passage through it. The outer opening of the gateway was originally fitted with a door, as is proved by the presence of sockets. The roof of the gateway is vaulted.

Beyond the gateway there is another court with rooms for guards along its sides.

[1] *Supra*, p. 36.

[2] The dimensions of this arch are: span, 8 feet 4 inches; height up to the apex, 12 feet 6 inches.

[3] The span of this arch is 5 feet 3 inches, and the height up to the apex, 9 feet 6 inches.

[4] The total length of the arcade is 200 feet.

[5] The dimensions ot these arches are as follows:

Inner arch—span, 8 feet 9 inches; height, 11 feet 8 inches.
Outer arch—span, 8 feet 6 inches; height 10 feet 9 inches.

At the end of the court there is another gateway which faces north and opens upon the moat.[1] This is the third gateway, counting from the archway built under the ramparts, providing an exit from the interior of the fort. The elaborate arrangements of the defences of this Darwāza show that a regular system for the lay-out of the fortifications in the Deccan was developed subsequent to the introduction of fire-arms.

Close to the arch leading to the passage of the Carnatic Darwāza is the northern entrance to the Ta<u>kh</u>t Maḥall enclosure, but instead of entering it, it will be best to proceed to Tasker's Walk opposite the outer gateway of the Carnatic Darwāza, and follow it along the glacis until the main gateway of the fort from the city side is reached and the circuit of the ramparts is completed. The walk affords excellent views of the triple moat and the fortifications at various points, particularly at the place where the city walls touch the fosse. For the convenience of sightseers following the walk a bridge has been built by the Archaeological Department over the city moat. Proceeding eastward a glimpse of the balconies and windows of the royal palaces may be had, their dainty outlines in the midst of long sweeps of grim walls and formidable bastions looking somewhat romantic.[2]

In giving an account of the palaces and the other royal buildings in the fort a start may be made from the Rangīn Maḥall which adjoins the Guṃbad Darwāza towards the south-west (Map).

Rangīn Maḥall

Rangīn Maḥall literally means the 'Coloured Palace', and this name was apparently given to it on account of its walls being originally decorated with tiles of different hues, traces of which still exist on the façade of the eastern halls (Pl. IX). Near the Guṃbad Darwāza a royal tower has existed perhaps since the time when Aḥmad <u>Sh</u>āh Walī built the fort (A.D. 1429–32). From this tower, which is mentioned as the <u>Sh</u>āh Burj in contemporary history, the Baihmanī kings often reviewed their troops, which assembled outside the gate of the fort. In 892 H. (A.D. 1487) when a party of Abyssinians and Deccanīs revolted against Maḥmūd <u>Sh</u>āh Baihmanī and tried to murder him, he took refuge in the <u>Sh</u>āh Burj. The rebels were subsequently punished, but as the king had despaired of his life he considered the shelter afforded by the <u>Sh</u>āh Burj as auspicious, and he had a lofty palace built in its close vicinity.[3] The southern apartments of this palace were rebuilt by ʿAlī Barīd (A.D. 1542–80), who adorned them with wood-carving and mother-of-pearl work.[4] In modern times the palace has been used as the court of the First Taʿalluqdār of Bidar,[5] and a veranda and several partition walls have been built, which not only

[1] The dimensions of the inner and outer arches of this gateway are as follows:
Inner arch—span, 10 feet 2 inches; height, 13 feet 2 inches.
Outer arch—span, 8 feet 4 inches; height, 10 feet 9 inches.

[2] The outlines of these windows have recently been altered, and corrugated iron sheds have been inserted over them to protect the interiors of the rooms against sun and rain. These eyesores will be removed as soon as the Rangīn Maḥall and the adjoining palaces shall be made over by the Revenue authorities to the custody of the Archaeological Department.

[3] *Firi<u>sh</u>ta* (Persian text), Part I, pp. 709–11.

[4] See inscription of ʿAlī Barīd, *infra*, p. 47.

[5] The office of First Taʿalluqdār under the Nizam's Government is analogous to the office of Collector in British India.

mar the general appearance of the building, but make it difficult to trace its original plan.

Access to the building is now obtained by two flights of steps which lead to a landing[1] from which, by passing through some rooms, the interior of the palace is reached (Pl. VIII). One of these rooms opens on a veranda which is modern (Pl. IX), but there are two halls at its back towards the east, which from the style of their architecture appear to be of the Baihmanī period (Pl. VIII). The hall at the north-east end is square in plan, but has a high-vaulted roof which is supported by squinches in corners. The hall measures 25 feet 4 inches each way at the base, and the domical ceiling is 23 feet 9 inches above the centre of the floor. The hall has a rectangular projection towards the east, and a window at the extreme end which opens in the south-eastern wall of the fort and commands views of the ramparts and the part of the city that is situated on that side. The walls of the hall are extremely thick, and the general style of the building gives an effect of heaviness.

To the south of this hall there is another which was originally connected with it by an opening in the wall on that side. The latter hall also is square in plan, but is smaller than the former. It measures 18 feet each way, and has a pentagonal projection towards the east with a window at the end which opens upon the ramparts. This hall is entered from the veranda by an arch, the proportions of which are rather squat, the span being 11 feet 5 inches and the height up to the apex 13 feet 5 inches. This hall also seems to be of the Baihmanī period, and may have been added by Maḥmūd Shāh Baihmanī after the revolt of 892 H. (A.D. 1487). It has a rectangular extension towards the south, which has also an arched opening to the veranda (Pl. VIII). This narrow room was utilized either as a toilet chamber or as a wardrobe. From the plan (Pl. VIII) it will be noticed that there are three small rooms at the southern end of the veranda and two at the northern end. To the west of the latter there is a double room which opens on the court and has also a door towards the steps. All of these six rooms are of small dimensions, and their architecture is such that they may belong to any period, Baihmanī, Barīdī, or even later.

From the court a view of the upper walls of the palace may be had. These were once richly adorned with tile-work arranged in arch-shaped and rectangular panels. The colour scheme now visible consists of white patterns on a dark blue background. There may have been other colours also, but as the tiles have been exposed to the inclemencies of the weather for several centuries, they have completely faded. The designs consist of floral and calligraphic devices exhibiting a highly developed technique and refined taste. Among the religious texts inscribed on the walls an invocation (*du'ā*) may still be read:

واتّخذه بحرمت نبينا محمد مقاما مخلّدا محمودا مرضيا

Translation

'And provide him [the King] through the grace of our Prophet, Muḥammad, with an abode which may be everlasting, exalted, and delightful.'

[1] The landing has recently been roofed over, and round masonry pillars have been built to support the roof towards the east.

The court had a water-channel with fountains and a cistern in the middle.[1] These were filled up with rubbish in the course of time, but the Archaeological Department has recently cleared them.

At the southern end of the court is the hall and pavilion built by ʿAlī Barīd, who was the first of the Barīdī dynasty to assume the regal title after his two predecessors had carved out a territory for themselves from the Baihmanī kingdom. The plan of the hall has been disturbed by the insertion of some modern walls and doors, but originally it had two apartments, each containing five bays (Pl. VIII). The total length of the hall is 52 feet and the width 20 feet. The divisions are arranged by means of columns, which are of wood and most beautifully carved (Pl. X). The designs are both Muslim and Hindu (Pl. XI). An interesting feature is presented by the ornamental scalloped arches arranged by means of struts, which appear to be the forerunners of the cusped arches of the Mughals in later times (Pl. X). The walls of the hall were originally decorated with tile-work which unfortunately has been destroyed in the course of repairs made in comparatively recent times, but specimens of it may be seen in the spandrels of the doorway which leads to the royal pavilion. This doorway is built at the back of the hall and consists of two arches, one at the outside and the other inside, with a passage between them. The outer arch is a little larger in size, its span being 6 feet and its height up to the apex 8 feet 3 inches. This arch has a black stone moulding above the imposts, while below are tiny shafts most elegantly carved. The moulding is of the rope pattern type. In the spandrels are lovely floral designs worked out on tiles, and above the doorway is a Persian verse inscribed on the same. The verse because of its appropriateness is worthy of being quoted here:

شاه نشین چشم من تکیه گاه خیال تو   جای دعاست شاه من بی تو مباد جای تو

Translation

'Since in my eye (lit. "the royal chamber of my eye") always rests thy image,
It is my prayer (Oh King!), that my sight may remain only as long as that vision.'

It will be interesting to cite here a parallel verse inscribed in tile-work on a royal pavilion reproduced in Plate X of the *Khamsa of Nizāmī*, edited by Laurence Binyon:

رواق منظر چشم من آستانهٔ تست   کرم نما و فرود آ که خانه خانهٔ تست

Translation

'The balcony of my eye is thy abode,
Gracefully alight therein, for this house is thy own.'

Besides the similarity in these two verses, the style of architecture and the tile decoration represented in Plate X, as also in several other plates of the *Khamsa*, have a striking resemblance to the tile-work and architecture of the Shāh Nishīn of Bidar, and it is not unlikely that the latter was designed by a Persian architect.[2]

[1] The dimensions of the cistern are: length, 9 feet 6 inches; breadth, 6 feet 10 inches; depth, 2 feet 6 inches.

[2] The date of the *Khamsa* illustrated MS., described by L. Binyon, is A.D. 1539–43, which is almost the same as that of the building of the Rangīn Maḥall (A.D. 1542–80).

The inner arch of the doorway is decorated with mother-of-pearl work, which, being inlaid in jet-black stone, appears all the more brilliant.[1] Beyond this arch is a square room, 12 feet 4 inches each way, which served as an antechamber between the royal pavilion and the hall. This room was also once richly decorated with tiles, which are to be seen now only on the dadoes. The designs are floral, and the colours—pink, green, blue, and yellow—are all arranged and contrasted most tastefully. The room, besides leading to the royal pavilion, has two more rooms attached to it, one towards the east and the other towards the west (Pl. VIII). The latter rooms are almost square in plan, each measuring 12 feet by 10 feet 3 inches. The room towards the east has a window opening in the fort wall.

The arch between the middle room (antechamber) and the royal pavilion has been filled up now, and a wooden door has been fitted. It is an eyesore and will be removed as soon as the Rangīn Maḥall has been vacated by the Taʿalluqdār's court, which the Revenue Department has kindly promised to arrange at an early date. The royal pavilion also is of small dimensions, the main room, square in plan, measuring 12 feet 6 inches each way. It has, however, deeply recessed windows towards the east and west and a pentagonal projection with three windows towards the south. There are also projections at the corners of the room which have given it a star-shaped plan similar to that of a medieval Deccan temple. The beauty of the room, however, lies in its rich decorations, which consist of mother-of-pearl work and tile-mosaics. The former is fairly intact on the entrance arch (Pl. XIII), which is built of basalt of a very dark variety. The floral patterns and calligraphic texts have been depicted by inlaying mother-of-pearl of the finest quality. The effect is lovely and further enhanced by the architect's romantic choice of the verses which he has inserted in the decorative scheme. These verses may be quoted here:

هر درّ ثمین کہ در صدف دارد عشق   از بهر نثار درگهت آرد عشق

عاشق شود آنکس کہ در آید ز درت   گویا ز در و بام تو مي بارد عشق[2]

Translation

'Every precious pearl which cherishes love in its shell
Cherishes the desire to be given in alms at thy court.
Any one who enters thy door is inspired with thy love
As if love pours down from thy portico and balcony.'

ای منظر دیده از جمالت روشن   وی کرده چو درّ در صدف سینہ وطن

بخرام بشہ نشین خلوتگہ دل   کہ از بهر تو آراستہ شد این گلشن

[1] The dimensions of the inner arch are—span, 3 feet 10 inches; height up to the apex, 6 feet 4 inches.

[2] Below these verses is inscribed a line in prose which gives the name of the king. It has been read as follows:

المستنصر بنصر اللّه الملك المالك المجلس المكرّم و الهماين الاكرم بريد ممالك علي

Translation

'Invoker of divine help, the supreme King, Majlis-i-Mukarram, Humāyūn-i-Akram, Barīd-i-Mamālik, 'Alī.' *Epig. Ind. Mosl.*, 1927–8, p. 25.

Translation

'O Thou! who hast brightened the sight of mine eye,
Who hast taken thy abode in my breast (lit. "taken thy abode in the bosom like the pearl in the shell"),
Gracefully enter the chamber of my heart,
For that pleasance has been adorned for thee.'

The pavilion originally had a fountain in the middle, the basin of which is now lying in the outer court of the palace between the two flights of steps referred to above. It is made of dark hornblende, and has an octagonal shape with cusps at the margin. The basin measures 2 feet 6 inches across. The love of Mughal kings for fountains and water-channels has become proverbial, but the Baihmanī and Barīdī kings were equally fond of them, and it will be noticed later from this book that in all their palaces the lay-out of the waterworks was an important feature of their architectural and decorative schemes.

The Rangīn Maḥall, however beautiful its wood-carving and however fascinating its tile-mosaics and mother-of-pearl work, suffers by the smallness of its dimensions and betrays a feebleness of spirit and lack of vision on the part of the builders. But the plan of the palace and its structural parts have been altered so extensively at various periods that it is difficult to visualize it in its original form or to appraise correctly its beauty and its defects.

Adjoining the western wall of the court, steps descend to another part of the palace which is now occupied by the Local Fund Office. The building here consists of a hall with a lofty façade decorated with stucco work. The arches of the northern openings of the hall rise to a considerable height, and their dimensions show a fine sense of proportion. The hall itself measures 29 feet 6 inches by 14 feet 10 inches, and has a recess 9 feet 9 inches deep towards the south which is fitted with windows opening on the ramparts of the fort. The hall was once decorated with encaustic tiles, traces of which may still be seen in the upper parts of the walls. The roof of the hall, which is vaulted, has been divided into three compartments by arches which have been built across the width of the hall. The elegant form of these arches combined with their large dimensions[1] gives an air of dignity to the hall. The vault of the middle compartment has a small cupola in the form of a lantern above it. Although there is no inscription in this part of the palace, the style of architecture shows that the hall was built during the Baihmanī period.

To the east of the hall steps rise to the roof, where another hall and two rooms are built above the Shāh Nishīn of ʿAlī Barīd. But before describing them, mention should be made of the vault above the steps, which has a lantern-like shape. The hall on the roof measures 29 feet 2 inches by 11 feet 6 inches, and is flanked by two rooms, one on each side towards the east and west. The latter rooms are almost square in plan, each measuring 12 feet 8 inches by 10 feet 6 inches. As the hall and the rooms are being used as a part of the office of the First Taʿalluqdār of Bidar they have been fitted with modern doors, and the annual whitewashing by the Department of Public Works has concealed all features of their previous beauty and

[1] Span, 13 feet 10 inches; height up to the apex, 25 feet 3 inches.

elegance. The ceiling of the hall and rooms consists of shallow vaults which are concealed in the thickness of the roof. From the top a good view of the interior of the fort and Bidar city is obtained, and the ladies of the harem at times must have enjoyed fresh air and moonlit nights there.

In the basement of the Rangīn Maḥall there is a series of rooms, which were apparently occupied by the guards and the menial servants of the palace. The ceilings of these rooms are vaulted, being most massively built with a view to supporting the weight of the royal apartments above. The arched openings of these rooms, nine of which may be seen from the road, are somewhat squat in form, having a width of 11 feet 2 inches with a height of 11 feet 9 inches only.

The Shāhī Maṭbakh, or the Royal Kitchen

This adjoins the Rangīn Maḥall towards the west and is situated to the left of the road, a few steps from the venerable banyan tree. The building at one time may have been used for the royal kitchen, but it is too large to have been originally built for that purpose, and from its plan it would appear to have been the residence of a prince or of some court dignitary. After the annexation of Bidar to the Bijāpur kingdom in A.D. 1619,[1] Malik Marjān, an Abyssinian general in the service of the latter kingdom, was appointed governor of Bidar, and he resided in the fort, apparently in this palace, for there is an inscription on the inner entrance which mentions Malik Marjān's name.[2] When I first visited the fort in A.D. 1916, the building was used as the District Jail, but immediately after the submission of my

[1] *Supra*, p. 14.

[2] The text of the inscription has been deciphered as follows:

بتوفیق اللّٰه قادر و سبحان   عمارات شاهان دیرینه دوران

ز مسجد و کوت محلها و ایوان   مجدّد نموده ملك شان امرجان

سنه ۱۰۲۷

Translation

'By the grace of the Holy and Almighty God,
The buildings of bygone kings:
Comprising mosques, forts, palaces, and halls,
Were repaired by the sovereign-like (governor),
Malik Amarjān.' 1027 H. (A.D. 1619).

There is another inscription in a room adjoining the inner entrance, which records the conquest of the Deccan by the Bijāpur king, Ibrāhīm 'Ādil Shāh II in A.D. 1619. By the conquest of the Deccan apparently the annexation of Bidar is meant. The inscription has been read as follows:

شه زمانه چو بد براهیم   نبود جز او کریم کامل

دکن سریرش چو شد مسخّر   بود مورّخ معزّ فاضل

سنه ۱۰۲۸

Translation

'When Ibrāhīm was the king of the age,
None was so perfect in bounty as he.
When the capital of the Deccan was conquered by him
The "*honoured scholar*" was the recorder of events.'

The words '*Mu'izz-i-Fāḍil*' give the date 1028 H. according to the *abjad* system. *Epig. Ind. Mosl.*, 1927–8, p. 26, Pl. X *a–b*.

note the Government were pleased to order the removal of the jail and the making over of the building to the Archaeological Department.

The building is entered from the roadside by an arched gateway which leads to an open court measuring 70 feet 6 inches by 81 feet 8 inches. Along the eastern, western, and northern sides of this court runs a modern colonnade with masonry piers and semicircular arches. The south wing of the court is, however, old and comprises an inner gateway and seven rooms with double apartments. The arches of these rooms are extremely squat in their proportions, each having a span of 11 feet 2 inches with a height of 11 feet 7 inches only. The arch of the inner gateway, however, shows a better sense of proportion, its span being 8 feet and its height up to the apex 14 feet 2 inches. The passage of this gateway is 11 feet wide and 32 feet 9 inches long, and on either side of it are rooms for guards. The ceiling of the gateway consists of a single vault. The arches of the guards' rooms are again very squat in their proportions, the span being 18 feet 2 inches, the height from the floor up to the apex 14 feet 9 inches, and the height of the columns up to the springing-points 5 feet 8 inches. The rooms themselves measure 22 feet 3 inches by 14 feet 10 inches, and they have vaulted ceilings which are almost flat.

On passing through the inner gateway a court is reached which measures 180 feet 5 inches from east to west, and 67 feet 5 inches from north to south. At the southern end of the court is a spacious platform, five steps higher than the court level, measuring 51 feet 7 inches in width and 162 feet 2 inches in length. There is a small cistern in the middle of the platform, and it appears that originally there were fountains and water-channels in this palace as well. The main building of the palace faced north, and comprised a series of rooms and chambers with two domical halls, one at the eastern and one at the western end. The two domical halls are still standing, but the rooms and chambers in between have been replaced by some modern halls which were erected when the building was used as the District Jail.[1] The new halls are not in alignment with the old rooms, and the plan of the building has thus been considerably disturbed.

The domical halls are very massively built. The interiors are star-shaped in plan, comprising a square space in the middle with projections on all four sides. The middle space measures 21 feet 2 inches each way. There are spacious arches on all four sides from which the projections start, the span of the arches being 20 feet 10 inches and the height up to the apex 17 feet 6 inches. There are squinches at the corners which make the plan of the hall octagonal above the arches, and higher up there are niches, three in each corner, which make it twenty-four sided, thus passing easily into the circular base of the dome above. The shape of the latter gives an impression of heaviness. It is probable that this palace was originally built by the Baihmanī kings.

At the northern end of the courtyard is a modern veranda with a tiled roof, and on the western side is the office of the Excise Department; these modern accretions have spoiled the effect which the decayed remains of the palace, by their grey

[1] The back part of the middle room is still intact. This room had an elegant plan, with an alcove at the southern end. The ceiling is barrel-vaulted.

masonry and soft outline, would otherwise have produced. Marks of beauty may, however, still be traced here and there; for example, the proportions of the arches outlined on the western and eastern walls are extremely fine, and there is some delightful stucco work in a room in the upper storey behind the dome at the north-western corner.

There are traces of several other rooms and of a cistern in the upper storey, and it appears that there were rooms on the southern side as well, as the vaults which served as their base are still to be seen. There is a series of these vaults with low squat arches which continue up to the ramparts. The vaults were evidently utilized for the accommodation of palace guards and for storing provisions and royal paraphernalia.

Behind the western enclosure wall of the palace is a large well, which is approached by a ramp on the left side of the road. The masonry work of the well has been raised to a great height, so that the water when drawn to that level might flow into the cistern and fountains in the upper storey of the palace.

Shāhī Ḥammām, or the Royal Bath

The road near the north-eastern corner of the Shāhī Maṭbakh enters through an arch in the enclosure of the Royal Seraglio, locally called the Zanāna Maḥallāt, and passes by the steps of the Shāhī Ḥammām, which is situated within the enclosure. The building was, some time ago, used as the Civil Court and afterwards as the office of the Inspector of Schools, but on the representation of the Archaeological Department it has recently been made over by the Government to the latter department for preservation as an ancient monument. During the occupation of the building by the Civil Court and the office of the Inspector of Schools the platform in front of the building was extended towards the east and west, and a veranda with round columns was also constructed in front of the middle part of the building. In the plan reproduced in Plate XV these modern additions have been omitted. The platform rises to a height of 4 feet from the road, and has a length of 67 feet from east to west and a width of 61 feet from north to south. In front of the middle part of the building there is a pavement a little higher than the platform, measuring 29 feet by 23 feet. Behind the pavement was a double hall with five bays in each half, the four corner bays being larger than the middle ones. The divisions are arranged by means of arches which have wide spans and low imposts, a common feature of the architecture of Bidar. The total length of the hall is 63 feet and the depth 27 feet. The ceiling is divided into vaults. The hall extends towards the south in the form of two wings, each consisting of a double apartment with vaulted ceiling (Pl. XV).

The middle part of the building was apparently used as the waiting-hall, from which those who wanted to take the bath proceeded to the intermediate stage, which consists of three apartments, as shown in the plan, adjoining the hall towards the east. The original roof of the southern two apartments of this stage fell down some time ago, and the present roof is modern. These three apartments were used for dressing. Beyond this stage was another towards the east, consisting of a single domed chamber. Here, the temperature being warmer, the bathers waited for a few minutes to prepare themselves for the still warmer atmosphere of the interior. Those who came out of the bath here laid aside their wet clothes and were provided with towels. The dadoes of this chamber were once adorned with encaustic tiles, but they have disappeared, and now only the black stone margins, indicating the outlines of the tile panels, are to be seen.

The plan of the innermost hall consists of a middle apartment, measuring 8 feet 9 inches each way, with a narrow corridor 3 feet 8 inches wide all round. Towards the east, at the ends of the corridor, there was a more spacious apartment, measuring 5 feet 6 inches in width and 22 feet 2 inches in length. This apartment was purposely made broader for the accommodation of the bath attendants, who had to resort to it freely for drawing water from the hot and cold tanks which adjoined it on the east (Pl. XV). The rectangular tank apparently contained the hot water, and the square one the cold. The doors in the back and side walls of these reservoirs have been opened recently with the object of utilizing the building for modern purposes. The passage from the hot and cold water cisterns to the middle apartment, where the bath was taken, is also wide, measuring 8 feet 9 inches.

The ceiling of this hall is vaulted, being divided into compartments and having a variety of forms, hemispherical, barrel-type, and dish-shaped. The arches are also of two types, wide and squat, and narrow and slim. The contrasts and variety in forms have added to the picturesqueness of the architecture of the hall.

Corresponding to the eastern apartments of the building there are rooms on the western side, but their plan is different, and they were apparently used as retiring-rooms or for other social purposes. They consist of two halls, each divided into three apartments. The total length of each hall is 22 feet 6 inches, and the breadth 12 feet. The ceiling is vaulted, being divided into compartments with hemispherical and casket-like forms.

The exterior of the building is somewhat inconspicuous, perhaps owing to the alterations which have been made in recent times for utilitarian purposes. On the roof of the building there was originally a parapet of pleasing design representing overlapping arches. As this design is generally found in the later Baihmanī and Barīdī buildings it appears that the Ḥammām was built either by the later Baihmanī kings or by the rulers of the Barīdī dynasty. Portions of this parapet still exist above the western and northern walls.

Lā'l Bāgh, or the Ruby Gardens

On the other side of the road facing the Shāhī Ḥammām was the Lā'l Bāgh, so styled either on account of its beautiful lay-out or the abundance of red flowers once blooming therein. The garden has completely perished, and to add insult to its past glory some mud huts and tiled structures had sprung up in the middle, which were occupied by sweepers and other menials. Some five years ago these unsightly dwellings were pulled down by the Archaeological Department, and the site has been thoroughly cleaned and enclosed by a wall. It is now planned to relay the garden on a modest scale, for water is scarce inside the fort, and an electric pump will have to be installed in one of the three old wells in the immediate vicinity of the garden, which originally supplied it with water.

The total length of the garden is 136 yards and the breadth 70 yards. Originally it had a pavilion in the middle, through which a delightful water-channel passed. Traces of the water-channel still exist in the courts of the gardens. After entering the garden from the road-side there is first seen a cistern of elegant design. It is built

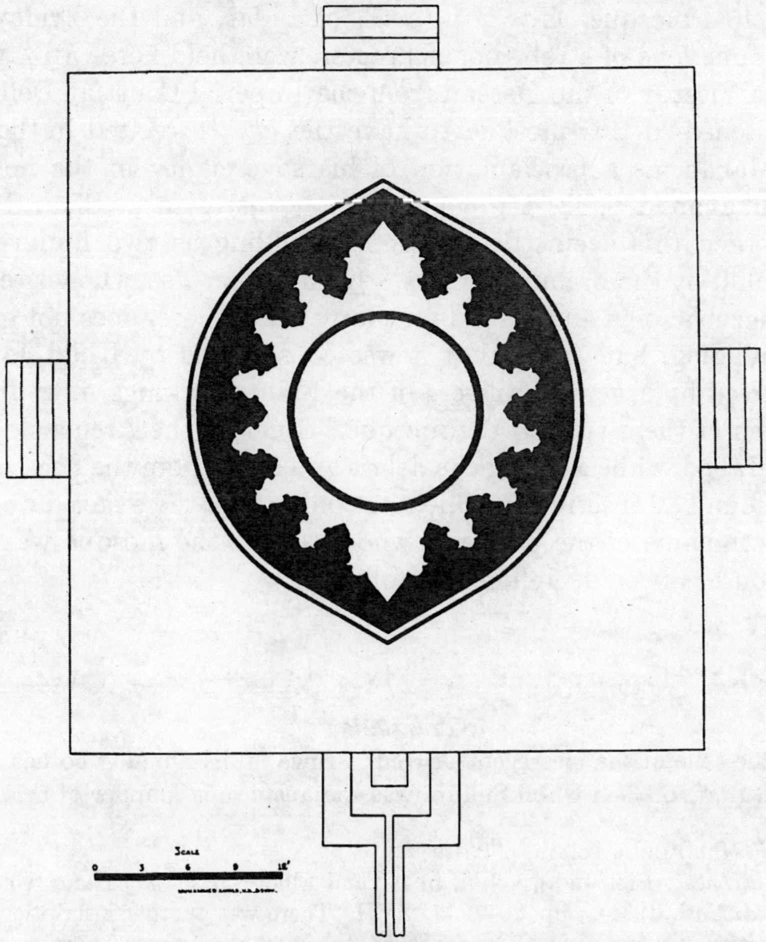

Plan of the cistern in the Lā'l Bāgh.

in the middle of a platform 4 feet high and 41 feet square. The cistern is 3 feet 4 inches deep, and has a beautiful black stone margin which is arranged in ornamental cusps giving the cistern a fourteen-sided oval form.

Proceeding towards the south the remains of a channel, 2 feet 10 inches wide, are seen, and farther on a narrow cistern with five jets. The length of this cistern is 60 feet, and the breadth, including the margins, 8 feet 8 inches. A carved slab built in a slanting position on the northern side of the cistern shows that a small cascade had been arranged there. Traces of another cascade of this design are to be seen in the wall of the palace at the southern extremity of the garden. The water feeding the latter came from a reservoir built in the higher apartments of the palace, which in turn received their supply from a well situated close to the southern wall.

The Zanānī Masjid or the Solah Khamb Mosque

Both these names have been given in comparatively recent times; the first on account of the building being situated in the Zanāna enclosure, adjoining the Lāʿl Bāgh towards the west, and the second on account of the presence of sixteen columns (*solah khamb*) in the middle part of the prayer-hall, which was screened off from the rest of the building after the latter had fallen into ruin. Originally it was the principal mosque, *Masjid-i-Jāmiʿ*, of Bidar, and the Friday prayers, as well as State functions of a religious character, were held here. In A.D. 1656 when Aurangzeb, as Viceroy of the Deccan from the Imperial Court at Delhi, conquered Bidar, he hastened to this mosque to have the *khuṭba* recited in the name of his father Shāh Jahān, as a proclamation of his sovereignty in the newly acquired territory. Muḥammad Ṣāliḥ, the contemporary historian of Shāh Jahān's reign, who has recorded this event, describes the building as two hundred years old, having been built by the Baihmanī kings.[1] Khāfī Khān also, who visited the Deccan during Aurangzeb's reign and stayed for many years there, does not give the exact date of the building, but writes that it was constructed by Khān Jahān. As this title was enjoyed by several ministers of the Baihmanī kings, it is difficult to say precisely which of them erected the mosque.[2] Luckily the Archaeological Department of Hyderabad, while clearing the debris and earth from the decayed part of the mosque, has found an inscription which not only gives the exact date of the building but also the name of the prince in whose régime the mosque was constructed. The inscription has been deciphered as follows:

اندر زمن خليفۂ يزداني   سلطان محمد کے ندارد ثاني
در هشصد و بيست و هفت اين مسجدرا   شد باني‌ء خير قبلي‌ء سلطاني

Translation

'During the time of the viceregent of God; Prince Muḥammad, who has no equal;
'In 827 H. (A.D. 1423–4) Qublī Sulṭānī was the auspicious founder of this mosque.'[3]

[1] *ʿAmal-i-Ṣāliḥ* (Bibl. Ind.), vol. iii, p. 251.

[2] *Muntakhab-ul-Lubāb* (Bibl. Ind.), vol. ii, p. 452 and Elliot's *History of India*, vol. vii, p. 125.

[3] See *Epig. Ind. Mosl.*, 1931–2, pp. 26–7, Pl. XVII. There was another inscription in this mosque recording the erection of a portico by Qalandar Khān, the Mughal governor (*supra*, p. 16), in A.D. 1677. As this inscription had no connexion with the mosque, it has been removed to the Archaeological Museum in the Bidar fort. The text of the latter inscription also has been deciphered and it is as follows:

بدور شاه عالم‌گير غازي   که از عدلش شده گيتي منوّر
قلندر خان بهار باغ دولت   که از بويش جهان گشته معطّر
به پيش آفتاب دست جودش   بود دريا و کان از ذرّه کمتر
رواقی ساخت بهر يادگاری   که باشد زير اين فيروزه منظر
پیء تاريخ او از طارم چرخ   ندا آمد که خال روی بيدر

۱۰۸۸ هـ

Translation

In the reign of Shāh ʿĀlamgīr, the victorious,
By whose justice the world has been illumined,—
Qalandar Khān, the bloom of the garden of the State, (*concluded*, p. 55.)

Prince Muḥammad was the son of Aḥmad Shāh Walī al-Baihmanī, and he held the viceroyalty of the province of Bidar before the transfer of the seat of government from Gulbarga to Bidar city. The mosque is therefore the earliest Muslim building in the city of Bidar, and its style of architecture and vast dimensions deserve careful study.

The building has a long front, nearly 310 feet from the north to the south, but as its height is only 28 feet 6 inches, and all the arched openings of the façade are of a uniform size, there is considerable monotony, besides an effect of flatness in the general appearance of the building (Pl. XVII). The architect, however, had planned to remove this effect by building a parapet of pleasing design above the row of front arches and also by giving a high clerestory with windows of beautiful *jālī*-work round the dome, whilst the dome by itself takes away the impression of flatness when the building is seen from a distance. But these features are completely lost when the building is seen from near, and the long stretch of nineteen uniform arches wearies the eye.

The form of the arches taken separately shows a fine sense of proportion, their span being 11 feet 4 inches, and their height up to the apex 20 feet. The columns are, however, too massive, and although in the front, where they are square in design, they do not appear obtrusive, yet in the interior where they are round in form they do offend the eye (Pl. XVIII). The square columns measure 4 feet 2 inches on each side and the round ones have a girth of 13 feet 9 inches at the base, but they decrease in bulk slightly as they rise.

The prayer-hall measures 294 feet 9 inches from the north to the south and 80 feet from the east to the west. The rows of columns divide the prayer-hall into five apartments lengthwise and nineteen breadthwise (Pl. XVI), thus making ninety-five bays, but the space of the nine middle bays near the western end is occupied by a hall which is crowned by a majestic dome. This hall is square in plan at the base, measuring 38 feet 4 inches each way, but higher up it has been made octagonal by the insertion of squinches at the corners. The squinches are rather massive in proportions and they are supported by struts of the elephant-trunk shape. The squinches and the struts counteract the outward thrust of the dome and also form a pleasing feature of the interior of the building by breaking the monotony of the otherwise plain surfaces of the walls.

Above the squinches the plan of the building becomes sixteen-sided by the arrangement of a series of arched windows which are filled with tracery of exquisite design, the patterns being geometrical. The tracery work, like the painted glass

Whose sweet odour has perfumed the country.
Before the sun of whose generous hand
The treasures of the ocean and the mine dwindle to a particle—
Built a balcony as a memorial,
To last long under the azure window of Heaven.
For the date of its erection from the balcony of the sky
These words were heard—'The beauty spot' (lit. mole) on the face
of Bidar. 1088 H. (A.D. 1677).

Epig. Ind. Mosl., 1927–8, pp. 26–7, Pl. XVI.

panes of the Gothic cathedrals of Europe, adds to the beauty of the interior of the prayer-hall, and further admits fresh air and light to the building. The series of windows form a sort of clerestory on which the dome rests, the latter rising some 70 feet above the floor of the prayer-hall.[1] The side walls of the hall are extremely massive, being 8 feet 6 inches in thickness; the idea of the architect was apparently to make them strong enough to support the weight of the superstructure of the clerestory and the dome. The western wall has a pentagonal niche, entered by an arch of fine proportions. The niche points out the direction of the Kaʿba which the congregation faces when saying its prayers. The niche, technically called the *miḥrāb*, also marks the place of the Imām who conducts the prayers.

The roof of the remaining part of the prayer-hall, which is divided into square bays, comprises a series of small domes which are visible at the top, but concealed from view by the parapet when seen from the ground level. The interior of the mosque has become very dark on account of the royal palaces which were built at a subsequent date and which have covered the south-eastern part of the façade of the building. To admit light into the southern part of the hall five domes have openings at their apexes, and one of them has a lantern-shaped projection like the domes of the Zachcha Bachcha at Delhi.[2]

There is a well beyond the southern wall of the mosque from which water was obtained for the ablutions of the congregation. Traces of a water channel may still be seen along the top of the western wall of the mosque. There is also a water reservoir on the roof of the mosque, from which water was distributed to the cisterns in the ground-floor of the mosque.

The building, through the neglect of centuries, had fallen into a sad state of disrepair; several of the domes of the room had fallen down, many others had developed cracks, the floor of the building was practically destroyed, and the walls were in a parlous condition. In recent times an enclosure wall had also been built almost in the middle of the court of the mosque, and it not only obstructed the view of the building but by its clumsy masonry and indifferent style of architecture was a real eyesore. The mosque has now been thoroughly repaired by the Department, the floor restored, the drainage improved, and the enclosure wall pulled down and another built, which is at a considerable distance and does not mar the view of the building.

The mosque, although one of the largest in India, suffers by comparison with its contemporary at Māṇḍū or its predecessor at Gulbarga.[3] It has neither the grandeur nor the elegance of the former, nor does it possess the classical chastity and beauty of the latter; on the contrary, there is considerable monotony and heaviness in the general style of the building, and the only pleasing feature is the middle hall crowned by the large dome.

[1] Outwardly the clerestory rises 25 feet higher than the roof level and the dome rises 27 feet still higher above the top of the clerestory. At the apex of the dome there is a gilded copper finial, measuring 9 feet 6 inches in height. The total height of the dome up to the top of the finial is 84 feet from the ground level.

[2] These domes are situated along the Quṭb Road in the vicinity of the Ḥauḍ Khāṣṣ.

[3] The Māṇḍū mosque was built in A.D. 1454 and the Gulbarga in A.D. 1367.

Tarkash Mahall

It was perhaps so styled on account of its having been built for a Turkish wife of the king, but about this time it appears that a certain conventionality was also observed in giving names to the royal buildings, for Tarkash Maḥalls, Gagaṇ Maḥalls, and Nagīna Maḥalls are mentioned in contemporary records as the names of palaces at Bijāpur, Golconda, and Bidar. The rulers of the contemporary dynasties at these places evidently vied with one another in the glory of their architectural works and chose the same names for their palaces as were adopted by their rivals in the other kingdoms.[1] The Tarkash Maḥall at Bidar may have originally been begun by the Baihmanī kings, but the upper parts of the building are decidedly of the Barīdī period,[2] and the palace has undergone so many alterations through the caprice of various rulers at subsequent periods that it is impossible now to determine its original plan.

The uppermost apartments of the building are approached at the present time from the steps which are built at the western end of the building and lead also to the roof of the Solah Khamb mosque. The roof of these apartments has fallen down, but the walls are more or less intact and they give an idea of the design of the building. In the middle there was a hall measuring 28 feet 6 inches in length and 14 feet 6 inches in width. It had arched openings[3] and was beautifully decorated with tiles and stucco work. There are also a great number of small arched niches in the walls of this hall, such as we find in the buildings of Jahāngīr and Shāh Jahān in North India. They may have been used for holding china and sundry articles of toilet, but apart from this utilitarian purpose their presence detracts from the solidarity of the building because of their tiny dimensions. The roof of the hall has fallen and originally there was another apartment above it, the remains of which in the shape of two arches may still be seen. These arches rise highest among the present buildings of the fort and are seen from a long distance, representing a distinguishing feature in the panorama of old dark-grey piles of ramparts and towers. They are also richly decorated with stucco work, and although their spans are a little too wide in relation to their height,[4] yet their general appearance is very pleasing. There are smaller rooms on either side of the middle hall, those on the eastern side disfigured by later additions, but those on the western side more or less intact, and they comprise a square room with two narrow rooms in the form of corridors in front and behind respectively. The square room measures 11 feet 10 inches each way, and it was at one time beautifully adorned with encaustic tiles, traces of which may be seen on the dadoes of the room. The upper parts of the walls and the ceiling are decorated with cut-plaster work.

The corridor in front of the square room measures 14 feet 3 inches in length and

[1] There was a Gagaṇ Maḥall at Mudgal as well, built by the Bijāpur king, Muḥammad 'Ādil Shāh, in A.D. 1643. See *Epig. Ind. Mosl.*, 1935–6, pp. 18–19, Pl. XI *b*.

[2] The decorative emblem, chain and pendant, which is a special feature of the Barīd Shāhī ornamentation, appearing even on the tombstones of the kings of this dynasty, is to be seen prominently in the upper apartments of the Tarkash Maḥall.

[3] The width of these arched openings is 6 feet 9 inches and height up to the apex 8 feet 6 inches.

[4] The span of these arches is 10 feet 4 inches and height up to the apex 10 feet.

6 feet 1 inch in width. The ceiling of the corridor is flat and was originally decorated with stucco work, the designs being floral. The back corridor is still narrower, its width being 4 feet 6 inches and length 11 feet 9 inches. The ceiling of this corridor also is flat. From it a covered passage along the back of the building leads to the steps.

In front of these apartments there is a terrace 137 feet 6 inches long and 22 feet 8 inches wide, with a projection 29 feet long and 13 feet 8 inches deep in the middle. The terrace has a beautiful fountain to which water was apparently supplied from the well near the northern end of the building, for the level of the terrace is higher than the reservoirs built on the roof of the Solah Khamb mosque and near the north-west angle of the Shāhī Maṭbakh. The basin of the fountain is hexagonal in form, measuring 4 feet 6 inches across. It has a masonry margin with a cusped design.[1]

The storey below these apartments is now occupied by the Taʿalluqdār's Court as Records Office. The principal apartment consists of a hall divided into eight bays by the insertion of arches which are very massive in construction. The span of these arches is 11 feet 5 inches, their height up to the apex 10 feet 7 inches, and the thickness of the masonry 4 feet 10 inches. The total length of the hall is 110 feet, and its width is 17 feet 6 inches. The roof is vaulted, each bay having a separate vault. The style of architecture shows a solidarity combined with picturesqueness of detail; but the modern repairs accompanied by alterations and additions have robbed the hall of much of its original charm. New walls have been built across the hall and the old stucco ornament filled up and concealed by successive layers of whitewash.

At the back of this hall towards the north there were two more halls of the same length but a little narrower. The span of the arches which support the roof of the latter halls is 9 feet 6 inches, and their height up to the apex is 10 feet 3 inches. Beyond these two halls is an open space, and traces of an old parapet prove that the uppermost apartments of the Tarkash Maḥall were built at a later date.

Below this storey on the ground floor is a series of rooms which were utilized for storing sundry articles of domestic and state use, even ammunition, for in recent times rockets have been found in great numbers in these rooms. They are built in four rows one behind the other, and have vaulted roofs.

To the east of the hall, now occupied by the Records Office, there is a double hall, measuring 35 feet 6 inches in length and 23 feet 6 inches in depth. The floor of the hall seems to have been raised in later times and consequently the arches which support the ceiling now look somewhat squat. Their span is, however, the same as that of the arches of the Records Office, that is, 9 feet 6 inches. In front of the double hall towards the north there is another hall, in the southern wall of which a pipe-line is plainly visible. The line is connected with the well to the west of the building. The floor of the latter hall is much lower than that of the former.

There are some more rooms with vaulted ceilings, adjacent to the last two halls, and it appears that originally they formed the eastern wing of the building. They

[1] There are traces of several other rooms, but their roofs have collapsed.

are now occupied by Arab guards who have built mud walls for the purpose of partitioning and have thus disfigured the beauty of the old arches and elegant plaster-work.

At present the structure called the Tarkas͟h Maḥall forms the western side of another palace, styled the Gagaṇ Maḥall, which is described below.[1] But another building situated to the east of the latter is also called the Tarkas͟h Maḥall. It is in an extremely ruined condition now, but the plan of the building as far as this can be made out from its present remains shows that it had two storeys and that the rooms in the upper storey were probably occupied by the royal ladies, whilst those on the ground floor were either occupied by guards or used as storerooms. The plaster decorative work of the western wall comprises designs and patterns which are frequently found in the ornamentation of Barīdī architecture, and it is not unlikely that the palace (Tarkas͟h Maḥall) was built, or extended, by the kings of the Barīdī dynasty, who according to contemporary history kept large *harems*, comprising ladies of different nationalities, such as Persian, Georgian, Circassian, and Turkish. The western wall has also a large number of arched niches, the heads of some of which are of the trefoil pattern.

In the northern side of the building rooms with vaulted ceilings are preserved on the ground floor, but the apartments in the upper storey have almost perished, and only their western wall and the pedestals of some pillars and a cistern now exist. The plinth of the western wall was originally decorated with encaustic tiles of hexagonal pattern and the arch-heads with plaster-work of floral design (Pl. XX). The vaulted rooms of the ground floor are arranged in four rows, one behind the other in the depth of the building.

The southern wing of the palace has also fallen into considerable decay, and some later additions have further disfigured the appearance of the building (Pl. XXI). The rooms on the ground floor had arched openings towards the court, their shape resembling the four-centred arch of Tudor design. The façade of the building was decorated with plaster-work, which has peeled away, and only traces of it can be noticed here and there.

The apartments of the upper storey have also suffered a great deal; their remains comprise a screen of arches facing the court and a hall with five arched openings in the western side of the terrace. There was an octagonal room in the front, a portion of which in the form of a balcony projects over the court. The balcony, although much dilapidated, can still be clearly made out (Pl. XXI). The lower part of the balcony is decorated with a knob at the end and several circular bands of carved masonry above it. The design of the carving resembles that of the finials of the medieval temples of the Deccan. Finials of this type are also noticed on the early tombs of the Muslim kings of Northern India. The court of this palace measures 99 feet from east to west and 95 feet 9 inches from north to south.

At one time the vaulted rooms of the northern wing of the palace were used for the Tahsil Office of Bidar, but the latter has been removed since the establishment of the Archaeological Department in Hyderabad.

[1] *Infra*, pp. 60–2.

The Gagaṇ Maḥall

Gagaṇ is a Sanskrit word (गगण) meaning heaven.[1] The Gagaṇ Maḥall, therefore, means the Heavenly Palace. It was originally built by Baihmanī kings, but later the Barīdī rulers made certain alterations and additions in the plan of the building, notably in the northern wing of the palace and the apartments on the roof of the southern block. The rooms belonging to the ground floor of the latter block are, however, of the Baihmanī period, and they show a style of architecture in which strength is combined with beauty.

The palace has two courts, the outer apparently used by the male staff and the guards of the palace. The entrance to the outer court is at the back of the Solah Khamb mosque. It comprises a four-centred arch of Tudor type, the span of the arch being 12 feet, its height up to the springing points being 13 feet 5 inches, and up to the apex 16 feet 10 inches. On the southern side of the court is a series of rooms and halls built in rows one behind the other. They have eight arched openings towards the court, but their inner arrangement can best be studied from the plan given in Plate XXII. Their length from the east to the west is 125 feet, and the depth of the first four rows of halls is 52 feet 6 inches. There are masonry piers to support the arches which divide the ceiling of these halls into a number of vaults, decorated with plaster-work of elegant designs. There is a hall with a small court near the inner entrance of the palace.[2] The hall measures 47 feet 3 inches in length and 17 feet in depth and has four arched openings towards the court.

The entrance to the inner court comprises a covered passage, 41 feet in length, with three arches, one at each end, towards the east and the west, and one in the middle. These arches are lofty in proportions, rising to a height of 18 feet 6 inches from the ground level and having a span of 11 feet 4 inches. There are rooms on either side of the covered passage for the accommodation of the guards.[3]

The inner court of the palace measures 137 feet north to south and 96 feet 3 inches east to west. There were arcades on three sides of the court, the remains of which may be seen towards the east and the west, but the arcade towards the north has been incorporated in the basement rooms of the Tarkash Maḥall,[4] which was built at a later date than the Gagaṇ Maḥall. The eastern and western arcades have each ten openings towards the court, their form indicating a fine sense of proportion. The main building of the palace is towards the south and has rooms both on the

[1] It is interesting to note that the Muslim kings from the beginning introduced into their vocabulary Sanskrit words which were used in the various dialects spoken by their subjects. This tendency subsequently gave rise to a new language, called Urdū, or the common tongue of the army which embraced units of various nationalities. During the rule of the Quṭb Shāhī kings this language was further developed to such an extent that Muḥammad Qulī Quṭb Shāh and Muḥammad Quṭb Shāh, the fifth and sixth rulers of the dynasty, have left a large number of poems composed by them in this language. These poems are preserved in the Hyderabad State Library and several other libraries in India and abroad.

[2] The small court measures 47 feet 9 inches by 33 feet.

[3] From a room on the northern side of the passage a flight of steps leads to the roof of the Solah Khamb mosque and also to the upper storey of the Tarkash Maḥall.

[4] *Supra*, pp. 57–9.

ground floor and on the roof. The arrangement of the rooms on the ground floor is indicated in the plan shown in Plate XXII. In the middle there is first an open space in the form of a pavement. It measures 48 feet 8 inches by 32 feet 5 inches. The main doorway of the rooms is in the middle of the southern side of the pavement. It has a pointed arch with low imposts at its outer side.[1] The arch is adorned with a stone margin which is beautifully carved, the design being a trefoil creeper. Passing through the doorway a double hall may be seen, which is divided into six bays by massive arches. Each of these bays measures 18 feet 3 inches square and has a shallow vault for its ceiling. Vaults of this type are frequently found in Baihmanī buildings, and as they are generally supported by low piers and wide-spanned arches the general effect of the architecture is somewhat heavy.

At the back of this double hall is a narrow corridor, 3 feet 7 inches wide, with deeply recessed windows opening on the moat. From these the ladies of the *harem* enjoyed the animal fights which were held in the moat below, and sometimes the unlucky victims of the king's displeasure may also have been thrown down from these windows to be devoured by wild beasts, a large number of which were kept in the moat and let loose at the time of a siege, or on an occasion when a person guilty of treason or some other grave offence was to be disposed of silently.

The arches on the right side of the double hall are blocked, hence it is difficult to determine whether there was any passage connecting the latter with the halls in the southern wing of the outer court (Pl. XXII). The rooms on the left side of the double hall are, however, open, and may be entered from the door in the left side of the pavement. The first room is rectangular in plan, 30 feet in length and 18 feet 8 inches in width. It has a vaulted ceiling, the section of the vault being in the form of a pointed arch. The room has arched openings both towards the north and towards the south. The opening towards the south gives access to a pair of rooms which are connected together by a massive arch. The total length of these rooms is 27 feet 6 inches and width 13 feet. They have vaulted ceilings, the vaults being of a shallow type, but neatly decorated with stucco work done in relief. At the northern end of the eastern room of these two there is another pair built along the eastern wall of the palace. The latter two rooms also have vaulted ceilings and they are joined together by a well-proportioned arch, the dimensions of the latter being: span, 12 feet 6 inches, height up to the apex, 15 feet 6 inches. These rooms at the floor level are square in plan and measure 15 feet each way.

The inner aisle of the main hall of the palace is connected towards the east with two more rooms which are joined by an arch. These two rooms together measure 30 feet in length, and have a uniform width of 10 feet 2 inches. The northern of these rooms has a vaulted projection towards the east, whilst the southern is connected with two more rooms, now occupied by the Arab guards of the Bidar District Treasury, which is housed in the entire southern wing of the palace.

From the south-west corner of the pavement a staircase leads to the apartments on the first floor of the building. From the first landing a series of rooms are approached which are divided into three aisles. These rooms are also accessible

[1] The span of the arch is 9 feet 6 inches and the height up to the apex 10 feet 5 inches.

from the steps built in the western side of the outer court of the palace (Pl. XXII). A door in the front aisle of the rooms gives access to a hall which must have been magnificent at one time, but as its roof has fallen much of its splendour is lost. It is divided into two apartments by lofty arches, their height from the floor being 23 feet 3 inches and span 18 feet 6 inches. The walls of the hall are richly decorated with small niches and carving in which the pendant and chain devices are prominent. The dimensions of the hall are: length, 48 feet 6 inches and width, 22 feet 11 inches. The hall was apparently meant for the use of the king, and that is perhaps also the reason why it can be approached both from the outer and from the inner courts, independently. There are two series of vaulted chambers to the north and east of the great hall, which during the residence of the king were probably occupied by the ladies of the *harem*.

In the front aisle of the rooms on the west of the hall, steps may be noticed at its northern end which lead to the uppermost storey of the palace. There in the middle of an extensive terrace two halls were built, one behind the other. The outer hall is the more spacious of the two, measuring 35 feet by 21 feet 6 inches. The inner is narrower, its depth being only 12 feet. The walls of the outer hall are profusely adorned with stucco work.

Towards the east of these halls, at a lower level, is another suite of rooms, the arches of which have very graceful proportions. In the northern wall there are outlines of three arches, the middle one being wider in span than the two side ones. Their exact dimensions are:

Middle arch. Span 10 feet; height up to the apex 19 feet.
Side arches. Span 5 feet 10 inches; height up to the apex 19 feet.

The arrangement of these arches with differing spans is very pleasing to the eye. The terrace commands a good view of the various buildings of the fort and of the country around, which together offer a picturesque pancrama.

The Dīwān-i-ʿĀm, or The Hall of Public Audience (?)

This building was called the *Jālī Maḥall,* on account of some screens of trellis-work which were visible at the top of the huge pile of debris lying on the site until some twelve years ago. Since then excavations have been conducted on an extensive scale by the Archaeological Department of Hyderabad, and they have disclosed not only the plan of the building but also such remains as reveal, in their architectural and decorative features, the original grandeur of the whole.

The building is situated to the west of the Zanāna enclosure, and it is approached by a road which proceeds straight from the latter enclosure. The outer wall of the Dīwān-i-ʿĀm is preserved up to a considerable height on the southern side (Pl. XXIV), but on the remaining three sides it rises only a few feet above the plinth and has been exposed to view by recent excavations. The building has two entrances, one through the eastern wall and the other through the western, but they do not face each other. The excavations have exposed to view the original pavement of the eastern entrance, but the masonry of its outer and inner gateways, which must have comprised large blocks of carved stone, has all disappeared, perhaps carted away for use in modern buildings. The entrance on the outer side measures 9 feet in width, but on the inner side it has become wider, apparently owing to the decay of the side walls at this end.

Passing through the entrance, we approach the court of the building, which measures 166 feet from east to west and 133 feet from north to south. In the latter direction it is, however, divided into two parts. The southern part is paved and has a width of 96 feet 3 inches. The northern part is some 16 inches lower than the former and has a width of 36 feet 9 inches only.

The principal hall of the building, which was probably used for public audiences, is on the southern side and approached by five steps from the pavement. The steps extend along the entire length of the hall and are built of a black stone of close texture (hornblende ?) which has kept its beautiful polish to this day.[1] The steps are, however, not comfortable to climb, being high and also narrow.[2] But this defect is found in all Indian buildings, whether Buddhist, Brahmanical, or Muslim, down even to the eighteenth century A.D.

The hall is divided into three apartments by rows of pillars, six of them being arranged in each row (Pl. XXIII). These pillars also divide the hall breadthwise into seven avenues, the interspacing between the pillars in all the avenues being uniform (13 feet), except in the middle avenue, the fourth from each side, where it measures 15 feet 9 inches. The total length of the hall is 109 feet and depth 52 feet 6 inches. The pillars of the hall were probably of wood, and they have all perished. The stone pedestals on which the wooden shafts rested are, however, intact, and their carving shows beautiful workmanship. The pedestals are square in plan, being wider at the base than at the top, where they measure 1 foot 11 inches each way.[3] The shafts also, as indicated by the rough surface of the top, were square in plan, measuring 1 foot 9 inches on each side approximately. The walls of the hall were originally decorated with panels of tile-work, some of which have survived the havoc caused by human vandalism and nature's unpropitious hand since the hall was built, and they are reproduced in Plates XXVII–XXIX. The colours of a majority of the panels are not so fresh as shown in the plates, for the tiles have remained buried under debris and earth for a long time, and the salts generating through various causes reached the surface of the tiles together with the monsoon water, percolating through the overlying mass of rubbish, and destroyed the glaze, also affecting the colours. By the kind advice of Dr. Plenderleith, of the Chemical Laboratory of the British Museum, the surface of the tiles has been treated scientifically, and they are now preserved against further damage from the pernicious effect of salts. The colours on such pieces as were not affected by salts have retained their freshness and resemble those shown in the plates. The predominant colour is blue, of which several shades may be seen, while green, yellow, and buff have been

[1] The stone is found in trap-dikes and has been used extensively for pillars, lintels, friezes, and images of Brahmanical temples.

[2] The height of each step is nearly a foot.

[3] Two of these pedestals seem to have been removed from the site after the ruin of the building, but they are now discovered in a mosque called *Qaṣṣābon-kī-Masjid* (Butchers' Mosque), built along the principal street of Bidar town.

used for purposes of contrast. In the middle of some rosettes spots of red may also be noticed, but this colour has been used very sparsely. The designs are floral, geometrical, and calligraphic, combined in a pleasing manner and resembling in some aspects those seen on Persian book covers and carpets. The panel (*b*) reproduced in Plate XXVII, has a calligraphic device arranged in the form of a *svastika*. It contains the name of ʿAlī, the son-in-law of the Prophet Muḥammad, repeated four times in the *Kufic* script. The subject (*a*) in Plate XXIX represents leaves of a vine-creeper, showing considerable affinity to the style in which they are carved to-day on wood in Kashmir. In this panel, above a representation of leaves in white, there are some green leaves also, the lower ends of which have been given fancy shapes, the design resembling both Chinese and Persian patterns. The tiles were probably made by Persian craftsmen, for artists and technicians of the latter country were much patronized by the Baihmanī kings.

The ceiling of the hall, like the pillars, may have been of wood painted and gilded over in the style of the so-called Āt͟hār Maḥall of Bijāpur.[1] The latter building was of course constructed over a hundred years after the audience hall of Bidar was erected, but the shape and style of its pillars and ceiling convey an idea of what the pillars and ceiling of the former may have been like. In the hall was placed the *Tak͟ht-i-Fīroza*, Turquoise Throne, which according to Firis͟hta, 'exceeded in splendour and intrinsic value every other in the world'.[2] In this hall were celebrated the accessions of Baihmanī kings, with a magnificent display of their opulence and power; and in this hall foreign embassies bringing rare and costly presents from their respective countries waited on the sovereigns of this dynasty.

At the back of the hall the remains of three rooms may be noticed (Pl. XXIII); the middle one was probably the king's chamber where he sat before appearing in the audience hall. This room has a square plan at the base, measuring 18 feet 6 inches each way. The floor has a mosaic design comprising geometric patterns, such as hexagons and stars (Pl. XXX). The walls, like those of the main hall, were richly decorated with tiles, and the arch-heads above the doorways had elegantly carved black stone margins. Several slabs of the margin have been found in the excavations, a few of which may be seen in the room itself, while the rest are exhibited in the museum now established in the Royal Bath. On either side of the king's chamber were rectangular rooms, the floors and the lower ends of the walls of which have now been exposed to view. They are connected by doorways with the main hall towards the north. These two rooms have uniform dimensions, being 25 feet 10 inches long and 16 feet 10 inches wide. Beyond the latter rooms, both towards the east and west, there are two more rooms, one on each side, measuring 25 feet 10 inches by 16 feet 10 inches. The latter, however, are separated from the former rooms by narrow corridors, measuring 19 feet in length and 4 feet 7 inches in width. The corridor on the western side has a small door in its northern projection.

The last-mentioned two rooms have openings towards the north, which connect them with the halls built on the eastern and western side of the great hall. They

[1] Cousens, H., 'Bījāpūr Architecture', *A.S.I.*, vol. xxxvii, Imperial Series, pp. 91–2.

[2] Briggs (English tr.), vol. ii, p. 520.

were probably ministers' halls, being spacious and adorned with tile-work in the style of the former hall (Pl. XXVI). Their exact dimensions are: length, 45 feet 6 inches, width 21 feet 6 inches. At the northern end of the ministers' rooms are steps which lead to balcony-like apartments, opening on the court, whence the ministers or other responsible officers of the court apparently received petitions.

At the back of the ministers' rooms, towards both the east and the west, there is another room, a little narrower in width but of the same length as the former (Pl. XXIII).[1] These two rooms are connected at their northern ends with the colonnades built along the eastern and western sides of the court, and at their southern ends with two square rooms built at the extreme ends of the back apartments of the building described above. The square rooms measure 16 feet 3 inches each way. Their walls in their present condition do not bear any traces of ornamentation, but the arches built along their sides have very pleasing proportions, exhibiting a fine style of architecture. These arches are of considerable dimensions, the span being 12 feet 10 inches and the height up to the apex 17 feet.

The remains of walls preserved in the south-eastern and south-western parts of the building show that there was an upper storey which had an arched screen built along its sides (Pls. XXIV–XXV). Some arches of the screen still exist, and they contain terra-cotta *jālīs* of geometrical designs.

The court had colonnades on either side of it, and remains of them have been found during the excavation. In the midst of the colonnade towards the west the traces of an entrance have also been found. As it faces the royal palace (Ta<u>kh</u>t Maḥall) it is not unlikely that it was a sort of special entrance, meant only for the use of the king and the high officials of the State. The passage of the entrance is narrower than that of the other entrance in the eastern side.

The two colonnades, excepting the gaps caused by the entrances, connected the southern wing of the building with that towards the north. The latter wing has suffered much more than the former, and but for the basement, the remains of an octagonal cistern, two small fountains, and an ornamental cascade, arranged along the northern wall, nothing has survived. The presence of decorative niches in the walls, however, suggests that there was a series of rooms in this wing also which corresponded in arrangement to some extent to those in the southern wing. For example, at the north-east and south-west corners of this wing the foundations of two rooms have been discovered, which show that the rooms were square in plan, measuring 16 feet 3 inches each way. These dimensions correspond with those of the square rooms in the back apartments of the southern wing at the corners. The plinth of the northern wing rises 4 feet 6 inches above the floor of the court on that side.

The remains of the cistern alluded to above have been found near the southern end of the pavement of this wing. The cistern is octagonal in plan, each side of the octagon being 5 feet 1 inch in length. The marginal slabs of the cistern were of polished blackstone, but after the ruin of the building they were removed to Bidar town and used in some modern structure where they were conspicuous by their

[1] The dimensions of the back rooms are: length 45 feet 6 inches, width 16 feet 3 inches.

incongruity with the other material employed in it. A clever Taʿalluqdār had them pulled out of that structure and made of better use by inserting them along the margin of the platform in the District Club bungalow. Subsequently, when the excavations conducted by the Archaeological Department exposed the cistern to view, it looked bare notwithstanding its attractive design. The Department therefore was on the look-out for slabs of polished black stone among the debris in order to restore the margins of the cistern. In the meantime the Darogha of the Department reported that the black marginal slabs of the Club bungalow were of identical dimensions and perhaps originally belonged to the cistern. This suggestion was followed up, and when it was found to be correct the Department requested the Revenue Department kindly to arrange for the return of the slabs. Sir Theodore Tasker, then Revenue Member of His Exalted Highness' Government, readily agreed to the proposal of the Department, and through his good offices the old black stone marginal slabs have now been restored to their original position.

Ta<u>kh</u>t Maḥall or The Throne Palace

The name Ta<u>kh</u>t Maḥall is modern, for it is not mentioned in contemporary history, although the magnificence of the royal palace built by Aḥmad <u>Sh</u>āh al-Walī at Bidar is extolled by Sayyid ʿAlī Ṭabaṭaba in his work entitled, *Burhān-i-Maʾā<u>th</u>ir*. This author mentions a palace and a forecourt—قصر و پیشگاهی, but does not give any name of the palace.[1] The name was apparently given by the literati of Bidar,

[1] It may be interesting to quote here the Persian text of Sayyid ʿAlī Ṭabaṭaba's description which, in spite of its poetic exaggeration, gives certain features of the building, such as its high basement, its lofty arches and towers, and its blue tiles, which still distinguish the palace from other buildings of its kind in India. Further, Ṭabaṭaba cites the two verses of the poet Ā<u>dh</u>arī which he composed in praise of the palace, and which were subsequently written in the form of an inscription by the calligraphist <u>Sh</u>arf-ud-Dīn Māzandrānī and set up on the gateway of the palace. The poet Ā<u>dh</u>arī at that time was on a visit to the court of Aḥmad <u>Sh</u>āh al-Walī, and he received a gift of a lākh and a quarter silver coins of the Deccan for composing the two verses. ʿAlī Ṭabaṭaba's words are as follows:

درین سال سلطان فریدون خصال در درون قلعهٔ محمدآباد بیدر بمعماریء دولت روز افزون و باهتمام همّت همایون قصر و پیشگاهی بنیاد نهاد که مهندس روزگار با آنکه معمار عالم‌کون و فساد است مثل آن عمارتی در معمورهٔ ربع مسکون و در زیر سقف این سپهر بوقلمون نساخته و نه پرداخته بود — ارتفاعش بدرجهٔ که بپایمردیء مدارج وهم و اندیشه عروج بر معارجش از قبیل ممتنعات نمود — و شیاطین‌را از بیم ناوك پاسبانش بقدم استراق پیرامون آسمان گشتن از جملهٔ محالات بود — از لطافت و صفای آن قصر فردوس آسا حوران بهشت‌را هوس دنیا در سر و مانند جنت الماویٰ محنت و عنا از آنجا بر در — و چون فردوس در و دیوارش منوّر و معطّر از اشعهٔ شمسه‌اش خورشید ضیا گستر و غرفات شرفاتش مطالع شمس و قمر —

اساس قصر ازین خوبتر توان افگند که دست همّت آن شاه کامران افگند
علو کنگرهٔ او بغایتی برسید که آسمان‌را از چشم اختران افگند
شب سیاه فروغ بیاض دیوارش مؤذّنان‌را از صبح در گمان افگند
چو خشت عرصهٔ او داشت رنگ فیروزه فلك بمغلطه خود را در آن میان افگند
بخود فرو شده صد بار وهم دور اندیش که تا کمند نظر چون بر آن توان افگند
ستارهای فلك جملە آفتاب شدند چو شمسهاش اشعه بر آسمان افگند
نخست بارگهٔ اقبال باز کرد درش سعادت آمد و خود را بر آستان افگند

(*cont. on p. 67.*)

who had read glowing accounts of the splendour of the royal throne, as given by Firishta and Sayyid ʿAlī Ṭabaṭaba, and who did not find a more appropriate edifice among the ruins of Baihmanī buildings which according to their conception of things could be associated with the throne. The audience hall, where the throne was really placed, was a mass of debris, as stated above, and nothing could be made out of its plan or of the rich decorations of its walls and pillars. The plan of the so-called Takht Maḥall (Pl. XXXI), however, agrees in its general outline and decorative features with that of the 'palace and fore-court' built by Aḥmad Shāh al-Walī for his residence, and it should not be confused with the audience hall where the royal throne was kept and the remains of which have been discovered in the course of excavations conducted by the Archaeological Department within the fort area in recent years and described above.

The palace adjoins the audience hall towards the north, and has an imposing entrance facing the east. The façade is much damaged, but such arches as are intact show strength combined with beauty in the style of their architecture (Pl. XXXII). They differ in span and also in shape, indicating the architect's love of variety. The stilt of the apex shows Persian influence, which is also apparent in the decorative schemes of the building which will be discussed later in this account. The outer arch has a span of 8 feet 2 inches, whilst its height from the floor to the apex is 17 feet 4 inches. Behind it is another arch which is four-pointed in design and resembles a Tudor arch. The span of the latter is 9 feet 7 inches and its height up to the apex 16 feet. Between the outer and inner openings of the entrance there is a covered passage, measuring 70 feet in length and 15 feet 6 inches in width. The ceiling was supported by massive arches, three of which stood across the width of the passage between the inner and outer openings of the entrance. On either side of the passage towards the north and the south are halls for the accommodation of the guards, these being 62 feet in length and 18 feet 4 inches in depth. The roofs of the covered passage and of the two side-halls have fallen down. The massive proportions of the arches supporting the ceiling of the passage may be judged from

بالجمله چون بیمن اهتمام خسرو کیوان غلام عمارتی بآن لطافت و هوا و خرّمي و صفا اتمام یافت شیخ آذري که از کمال شهرت به توصیف و تعریف محتاج نیست در آن حین بشرف زمین بوس پادشاه روی زمین استعداد یافته این دو بیت دو وصف قصر سلطنت انشا نموده بعرض رسانید —

حبّذا قصر مشیّد که ز فرط عظمت　　آسمان پایهٔ از سدّهٔ آن درگاهست
آسمان هم نتوان گفت که ترك ادبست　　قصر سلطان جهان احمد بهمن شاهست

سلطان فریدون خصال دست دریا نوال از پی جایزهٔ دو بیت آن طوطيء شکر مقال سحاب مثال کشوده مبلغ صد هزار تنکهٔ دکن که تخمینا یك هزار تمن بوده باشد بآن شاعر شیرین سخن عطا فرمود — شیخ آذري گفت لا تحمل عطایاکم الّا مطایاکم — سلطان خندان شده بیست و پنج هزار تنکهٔ دیگر بجهت خرج راه و کرایهٔ حمل آن بر انعام سابق افزود — شیخ مذکور بوفور نعم و احسان سلطان مسرور گشته بشکر ایاديء انعام و اکرام خسرو عالي مقام رطب اللسان و عذب البیان و دستکام و مقضی المرام بوطن مألوف معاودت نمود — درین سخاوت و احسان که از سلطان فلك احتشام صدور یافت نام پادشاهان جهان‌را از جریدهٔ کرام منسوخ ساخته رایت نیکنامي و کرم تا انقراض عالم درمیان اولاد آدم بر افراخت — مولانا بشرف الدین ماژندراني که یکی از مریدان شاه نعمت اللّه بود این دو بیت شیخ آذري‌را بخط خوب بر دروازهٔ قصر ثبت نمود و صاحب قرآن جهان باو نیز دوازده هزار تنکه عطا فرمود ❖

Burhān-i-Maʾāthir, pp. 70–1 (Persian MSS. Society ed.).

the arch behind the inner opening of the entrance (Pl. XXXII). The dimensions of the latter arch are: span, 15 feet 6 inches, height up to the apex, 22 feet 4 inches.[1]

On passing through the entrance the forecourt (*peshgāh*) of the palace is reached, which measures 320 feet 6 inches from east to west and 239 feet from north to south. The excavations conducted by the Archaeological Department in recent years have disclosed the foundations, and remains of the walls and piers, of a series of chambers and halls which were originally built on all the four sides of the court. Of these the apartments adjoining the northern wall of the entrance, and a hall projecting from the northern wall of the court near its eastern end, are prominent (Pl. XXXI). The latter hall originally had nine domes in its ceiling, five of which are intact whilst four have fallen down (Pl. XXXIII). The domes are rather flattish in shape, resembling their prototypes in Northern India, built by the early Sulṭāns of Delhi during the fourteenth and fifteenth centuries A.D. The arches of the hall, but for the stilt at their apex, would have looked rather squat on account of their dimensions, which are: span, 9 feet 2 inches, and height 10 feet. The hall itself measures 35 feet 6 inches in length and 29 feet 7 inches in depth. The excavations have revealed the traces of a small court also in front of the hall.

In selecting the site for the palace and its forecourt the architect has observed extreme care regarding the safety of the inmates against an attack by disloyal members of the garrison of the fort, or by the enemy from outside. The site abuts upon lowlands towards the north and west and is defended by a massive wall, varying from 50 to 120 feet in height, and further strengthened by bastions at the corners. A good view of the wall and bastions is obtained from the gateway leading to the lowlands of the fort, built towards the north-west of the palace. The epithet مشیّد (strongly defended) given by Ādharī to the palace seems appropriate when one contemplates the height and the solid construction of its enclosure wall.[2]

The inner entrance of the palace is at the north-west corner of the forecourt. Its side walls are solidly built, but to relieve them of the monotony of a uniform surface, arches of elegant proportions have been designed on the exterior (Pl. XXXIV). The masonry of the walls was originally plastered over and traces of tile-decoration have also been found in the spandrels and side-walls of the arches. The span of the arches designed on the façade of the southern walls of the inner entrance is 12 feet 9 inches and their height up to the apex 24 feet. Access is arranged through an arch of slimmer proportions, the span of which is 7 feet 4 inches and its height up to the apex 19 feet. On entering through the latter arch a small court is reached which is open, but flanked with halls for the accommodation of guards towards the north and the west. The dimensions of the court are: length 63 feet, width 27 feet. The hall on the western side has three arched openings towards the court and measures 40 feet 6 inches lengthwise and has a depth of 19 feet. The arches of the openings have a distinct stilt at the apex, although their

[1] The masonry of the inner and outer openings of the entrance has been recently repaired by the Archaeological Department, and the building does not look so dilapidated as it appears in the photograph (Pl. XXXII).

[2] *Khizāna 'Āmira*, by Ghulām 'Alī Āzād, pp. 20–1 (Hyderabad lithograph).

proportions are pleasing to the eye, the span being 9 feet 4 inches and the height up to the apex 16 feet 6 inches. The hall on the northern side of the court has only two arched openings, and its inner measurements are: length 27 feet 6 inches, depth 15 feet 10 inches. From the small court the passage turns towards the left (west), and the visitor before entering the inner court of the palace has to pass through two more arches. The passage between these two arches is roofed and the ceiling is in the form of a cone with eight facets. The dimensions of the latter two arches are not uniform, the span of the outer arch being 7 feet 6 inches and its height 16 feet, while the span of the inner arch is considerably wider, that is, 10 feet 3 inches, and its height up to the apex 15 feet 6 inches. The position of these two arches in the plan of the inner entrance of the palace provides privacy in the interior, and also that stricter control over the egress and ingress which a turn in a passage generally offers to the watchmen.

The interior of the palace, until a few years back, was a huge mound of fragments of stone and wreckage of building material, all made into a compact mass by the passage of time and overgrown with cactus. Only the room at the northern end of the west wing of the palace was visible, which, on account of its lofty plinth, its stately arches, and the pleasing design of the tile-decoration, was considered by the local people to be the Throne Room of the Baihmanī kings, and hence the name Ta<u>kh</u>t Maḥall given to it. The excavations have, however, exposed to view the entire plan of the building, and in the few blanks which remained (Pl. XXXI), foundations of halls and rooms have been traced and identified by the recent operations there as well.

In describing the various apartments of the palace, it would be convenient to begin with the court. It measures 206 feet north to south and 145 feet east to west. Excavations carried out in 1940 showed that the southern part of it, immediately in front of the main apartments of the building, is paved. It measures 85 feet 6 inches by 145 feet. The dividing line between the paved and unpaved parts is not shown in the plan reproduced in Plate XXXI, since it was printed before the recent excavations. The unpaved part of the court was flanked with halls and rooms on three sides, towards the east, the west, and the north. The hall towards the east was found in the better state of preservation. It is divided into two apartments by arches built in the middle of its width. The length of the hall is 74 feet 3 inches and its depth 33 feet 10 inches. It has two square rooms, 10 feet 4 inches each way, at its northern end. Their floor is lower than that of the hall, and they are further separated from the latter by walls. The hall has five arched openings towards the court, the dimensions of the arches being insignificant, span 8 feet and height up to the apex 9 feet 11 inches. The hall is also divided into square apartments by arches built in its length. The span of the latter is much wider than that of the front arches, 12 feet 5 inches as opposed to 8 feet. They, however, look squat because of their height, which is 9 feet 6 inches only.

On the northern side of the court the excavations have revealed the foundations of two rectangular halls with a square room between them. The hall nearest the entrance was 95 feet long and 12 feet 9 inches deep, and it had five openings towards the court. The middle room, as indicated by its remains, measured 12 feet 9 inches each way, and had only one opening towards the court. The other hall, on the west side of the square room, would have measured 61 feet 9 inches by 12 feet 9 inches, and had three openings towards the court. Whether the two long halls were dormitories for servants or kitchens it is difficult to determine from the remains which have been discovered.

There were halls and rooms on the western side of the court as well, and their arrangement and arched openings probably corresponded to those of the apartments on the eastern side. Their total length was 91 feet 7 inches and their depth 34 feet, but at the north-western corner of the court there were some more apartments, the plan of which cannot be determined now owing to the scanty and irregular character of the foundations.

The apartments on the southern, eastern, and western sides of the paved court were occupied by the king and his family, and their arrangement may be of interest to those students who desire to know how kings lived in those days. As the room at the northern end of the western wing has been found in a comparatively good state of preservation, and it could be visited even before the excavations, it will be convenient to start the description of the royal apartments from that room. It has a magnificent façade decorated with arches and encaustic tiles of elegant pattern and great beauty (Pls. XXXV–XXXVII). The approach to the room comprises a flight of seven steps arranged in a circular design which is unusual among the Muslim buildings of India. The steps lead to a narrow rectangular porch, above which, however, a lofty arch rises (Pl. XXXVI). The span of the arch is 19 feet and the height of its apex from the floor 34 feet 7 inches. It has a margin of polished black stone and the spandrels are filled with tiles of geometric pattern among which the effigies of tigers with the rising sun are prominent (Pl. XXXVII). The royal emblem of Persia comprises the effigy of a lion with the rising sun, and it appears that the craftsmen who were employed by Aḥmad S͟hāh al-Walī for the decoration of the palace with tiles were probably imported from Kās͟hān, or some other centre of tile industry in Persia, in the fifteenth century A.D.; and they, being familiar with the royal emblem of their mother country, inserted the same design in the decoration of the Baihmanī palace, with the slight alteration of converting the Persian lion into a tiger, a beast which they would often have seen in the suburbs of Bidar during their stay.[1]

The door which gave access to the room was deliberately designed of a small size with a view to safeguarding the lives of the inmates on the one hand and for the purpose of privacy on the other. It is built in the trabeate style, the width of the opening being 3 feet 5 inches only. For the purpose of ventilation and light, however, pairs of arched windows are arranged in all the four walls of the room (Pls. XXXV–XXXVI). The plan of the interior of the room is octagonal with projections on each side, this arrangement giving a pleasing form to the design (Pl. XXXI).

[1] Before the cleaning of the monuments in Bidar fort it had become a favourite haunt of panthers, and the writer saw a large-sized beast in the lower fortifications of the fort while surveying the monuments in the Purāna Qil'a area in 1930.

Each side of the octagon measures 9 feet 3 inches, and the width of the room across is 27 feet 9 inches. The floor and the dadoes were adorned with tiles, the lime beds of which are plainly visible. The walls of the room rise to a height of 46 feet 6 inches from the floor, and above them was a dome which has perished, but its base can still be seen on the roof. Sayyid ʿAlī Ṯabaṯaba mentions خشت کبود, blue tiles, in the decoration of the palace. They may have been predominant in the scheme, but tiles of all colours except red are found in the remains of the palace, and some beautiful specimens of a green shade may be noticed in the arch-head above the door of the room facing the north. Red is not altogether absent from the decorative scheme of the palace, for pieces of hand-painted tiles with designs in red and gold have been discovered in the debris cleared from the principal hall of the building.

The western projection of the room ends in an opening which offers lovely vistas of the lowlands, stretching to a considerable distance from the foot of the plateau on which the palace is built. From this point of vantage the king and the other inmates would have enjoyed the view of the country and the gardens which were probably laid out in the lowlands of the fort adjoining the large tank.

A door in the southern side of the octagonal room opens on another of a rectangular plan. Its dimensions are: length 43 feet, width 26 feet 8 inches. The room has three arched niches in the depth of its western wall which faces the Kaʿba. The presence of the niches suggests that the room was perhaps used as a mosque by the inmates of the palace. This surmise may be supported by the existence of two small cisterns, the remains of which have been found near the steps in front of the room (Pl. XXXI). The jambs of all the three niches are of black stone, carved in Indo-Muslim style, the patterns representing the leaf and the vase, which are peculiar to Hindu sculpture, and arabesque and geometric designs, a speciality of Muslim workmanship. The room has three openings towards the east, which originally had arches with stone margins. The arches have perished completely, but the remains of masonry columns which supported the arch-heads have been found during the excavations, and may be seen on Plate XXXVIII. According to the position of these columns the span of the arches was 4 feet 9 inches approximately.

A door from the latter room leads to another built on its southern side.[1] This room, although square in plan, measuring 25 feet 3 inches each way, by the addition of projections has assumed the form of a star-shaped octagon. This room has also a stately arch in each of its four principal sides; the arches bear traces of encaustic tiles which once adorned them. In a corner of this room a black stone fountain has been found which does not appear to be in its original place, because it is not connected with any water-channel. The fountain is square in plan along its margins, but in the middle it has a cavity and a hole.[2] It has also four props carved in the style of the legs of a throne.

[1] The carving of the jambs of this door is worthy of notice, notably the mixed geometric and ornamental pattern worked out in relief in square compartments.

[2] The dimensions of the fountain along the margins is 4 feet on each side, while the cavity is 1 foot 7 inches deep.

Beyond the square room, farther towards the south, is a rectangular hall with two vestibules or antechambers, one on each of its northern and southern ends. The rectangular hall was probably the bedroom of the king and the two vestibules were meant for the guards, or were used as dressing-rooms, for the vestibule at the southern end is connected by a passage with a small room which appears to be a privy. The hall measures 36 feet in length and 17 feet 9 inches in width. The dimensions of the two vestibules are uniform, their length being 17 feet and depth 11 feet. In the thickness of the northern wall of the hall are two round funnels, for the passage of air or smoke (?), which go up to the roof-level of the room. The roof, however, has perished completely, and consequently the exact purpose for which the funnels were constructed cannot now be determined. In the north-western corner of this hall the remains of a lead pipe were discovered during the excavation; this was probably used for the supply of water to the hall.

The hall has three openings in its eastern side which lead to a paved court, 51 feet by 48 feet, with a swimming-bath in its middle and alcoves in its northern and southern sides. The bath is almost square externally, measuring 33 feet 3 inches by 29 feet 2 inches; in the middle it has a pleasing design faced with polished black stone.[1] The alcoves had originally encaustic tiles in their floors and walls, fragments of which may still be seen. The king and the ladies of the *harem* watched the bathers from the alcoves, and these were also used for changing clothes. In the south wall of the court are steps which led to the upper storey of the palace. The latter does not exist now, for it has perished completely.

A door from the eastern side of the court leads to the Royal Hall, which was crowned with a large dome. It was probably the highest dome in the fort and rose over 100 feet from the floor, which itself is nearly 15 feet higher than the ground on its southern and eastern sides. The hall is square in plan, measuring 51 feet each way, but the architect has given it an ornamental form by the insertion of arches and niches at appropriate places (Pl. XXXI). The niches in the side walls have, however, a Hindu appearance, resembling their prototypes in the interior of a medieval temple for the accommodation of statues of gods and goddesses. The reason for this is obvious, since in the construction of the palace a large number of Hindu masons and sculptors must have been employed, whose fancy irresistibly found an expression in spite of the close supervision of the Persian architects and engineers over the building and decorative schemes of the palace. The general style of the hall is Muslim, as shown by its lofty and massive arches, and also by the magnificent tile-work and luxuriant hand-paintings in gold and vermilion. A fragment of one of the arch-heads of the hall was found in clearing the heap of debris which once lay at the back of the building, and it has since been preserved at that place in order to enable the visitor to judge the strength and the colossal size of the arches which were built in the sides of the hall and supported its dome.

The floor of the hall had black stone margins which are intact and may still be seen. Black stone was also used for arch-heads, lintels, and jambs, all of them being beautifully carved. Some specimens, which have been found during the excavations,

[1] The design resembles that of the cistern in the Lā'l Bāgh (*supra*, p. 53).

may be seen at the Archaeological Museum in the Royal Bath. They exhibit the love of the sculptor for intricate arabesque patterns, with which are also combined geometric and calligraphic devices. The last mentioned are generally in relief, the script being *Thulth* of a very attractive style. Among the carving are also represented Hindu designs, such as chain patterns, leaf and floral devices, and pot motifs of various shapes. Tiles of various hues and designs have also been found in the debris, and their technique represents three different categories. The majority of them have a smooth glazed surface, the coloured clays being inlaid before the tiles were placed in the fire for the finishing operation. A few show mosaic-like work, the pieces representing different colours being fired separately and then joined together to form the design. Such tiles also have a smooth surface. The third class represents flowers, leaves, tendrils, and Arabic and Persian texts in relief, the patterns being represented in different colours. These tiles were evidently pressed in special moulds before being placed in the fire for completion and glazing.

The colours represented in these tiles are: blue comprising several shades; green of two classes, light and deep; yellow; grey; black and white. Red is also noticed, but rarely; on the other hand it is prominent among the colours laid on plaster in which gold is lavishly used. A large collection of these tiles is exhibited in the Archaeological Museum, and students who are interested in Islāmic ceramics will find their visit to the Museum of value because they will be able to examine the technique as practised in India, although, as mentioned above, Persian craftsmen and artisans were probably imported to do the work. Along with specimens of tiles students will notice in the Museum an extensive display of fragments of old china, embracing various classes of celadon and Persian blue ware. These are pieces of bowls, dishes, water-flagons, and jars, which were originally kept in the niches of the palace for both decoration and use.[1] Chinaware was much valued by the Baihmanī kings, and it was brought to the Deccan by Persian merchants, and also imported direct by the sea route. Among the choice presents offered by Maḥmūd Gāwān to the Baihmanī king, Muḥammad Shāh III, there were 'one hundred dishes of superb china porcelain, to be seen no where excepting in the palaces of a few great princes'.[2]

In this hall the Baihmanī kings may have given audience to the high dignitaries of the court, thus using it in the same way as the Dīwān-i-Khāṣṣ was employed in the Mughal forts of Delhi, Agra, and Lahore. An opening in the eastern side of the hall leads to another which measures 50 feet from north to south and 40 feet from east to west. The remains of a cistern have been found in the middle of the latter room, but the cistern is of a much smaller size than the one in the open court on the western side of the royal domed hall. The presence of cisterns and fountains

[1] In the Museum a large collection of steel and iron weapons and implements is also exhibited. The specimens have been found in the course of excavation at various places in the fort. They represent swords, arrow- and spear-heads, breast-plates, helmets, coats of armour, and fragments of horses' armour and trappings. Some of the mouth-bits are of colossal size and must have been used for large-size sturdy horses. Among specimens of fire-arms there are rockets of various types and also star-shaped thorns (گوکھرو) which were poisoned and loaded in shells. There are also locks of huge size, one of them being 2 feet 10 inches in length and weighing nearly 30 lb.

[2] *Firishta*, English tr. by Briggs, vol. ii, p. 490.

in the various apartments of the palace, however, indicates the love of Baihmanī kings for the display of fresh running water in various forms. Adjoining the latter room towards the east was another, which probably had windows opening on the outer court (*peshgāh*). In the plan reproduced in Plate XXXI both the latter rooms are shown as one, because the foundations of the partition wall between them have been discovered only recently.

On returning to the royal domed hall and passing through an opening in the middle of its northern wall, one reaches another spacious hall which faces the main court of the palace. It is rectangular in plan, measuring 72 feet by 36 feet. The hall is divided into two apartments by pillars, the pedestals of which are intact, but the wooden shafts perished in the fire caused by an explosion of fire-arms, remnants of which were found during excavation. The explosion also damaged the floor and the steps near the north-eastern corner of the hall.[1]

The position of the stone pedestals shows that the central aisle of the hall was wider than the two side ones, the former measuring 26 feet 10 inches in breadth, as opposed to the 16 feet 6 inches of the latter. The wooden shafts were probably of the same dimensions as those of the audience hall (*Dīwān-i-ʿĀm*), and were gilded and decorated with paintings. The dadoes of the hall were adorned with tiles, which were also used in the adornment of the plinth of the flight of steps, starting from the paved court and making an impressive approach to the hall. The steps extend to a length of 72 feet; but their height and depth, one foot each way, do not show good proportions. The steps are made of large slabs of black stone, the polish of which may still be admired.

On either side of the rectangular hall is a room 31 feet 3 inches square (Pl. XXXI). The room on the eastern side has two bathrooms attached to it, which are also connected with the room on the eastern side of the royal domed hall.

In the eastern wing of the palace there was probably a hall corresponding to the one in the western wing, which has been identified as a mosque. But this part of the palace was completely destroyed, and even the enclosure wall, which is shown in the plan (Pl. XXXI), has been restored recently. Beyond this empty space towards the north the ruins of an octagonal room have been found which corresponds in plan to the royal octagonal room with the tiger's effigies in the western wing. The remains of walls indicate that this room was larger in dimensions than the latter, and as its windows opened on the forecourt (*peshgāh*), the king and the ladies may have watched from it the parade of the royal guards, or the retinues of the nobles and the dignitaries who were privileged to enter the enclosure of the royal palace and wait on the king at his residence.

Adjoining the southern wall of the palace, almost at the back of the swimming-

[1] It is difficult to determine exactly when the explosion took place, for Bidar fort was besieged several times, first by Sulṭān Maḥmūd Khaljī of Mālwa (A.D. 1461–3), when several of its buildings were destroyed, and later by Murtaḍa Niẓām Shāh (A.D. 1572–6), Ibrāhīm ʿĀdil Shāh II (A.D. 1619), and Aurangzeb's troops (April, A.D. 1656). Aurangzeb's army discharged grenades and rockets and one of them struck a magazine which exploded, severely burning Malik Marjān and his sons. It is also possible that the royal apartments may have been blown up by the inmates of the palace themselves as an act of despair during one of these sieges.

bath, there are the remains of a hot bath. It has a massive arch in front, the dimensions of which are worthy of notice, the span being 22 feet and the height up to the apex 27 feet 6 inches. The opening of the arch was apparently filled with a glazed screen, such as were used in hot baths to stop air on the one hand and to admit light on the other. The bath has two floors, the upper comprising a square hall in the middle and two rectangular rooms, one on each side of the former, on its eastern and western sides. The square hall measures 22 feet on each side, whilst the rectangular rooms are each 22 feet by 7 feet 9 inches. The roof of the middle hall is vaulted, the ceiling being adorned by stucco work. The ceilings of the side rooms are divided into three compartments, each having a conical vault of a pleasing design. Behind the rectangular room towards the west there is a small chamber, measuring 7 feet 3 inches by 5 feet 9 inches, which was apparently used as a privy. A narrow staircase leads to the lower floor of the bath, which has octagonal cisterns of artistic cusped design.

There were arcades in the eastern and southern sides of the court of the hot bath, the remains of which still exist. The arcade on the eastern side has a frontage of 52 feet. There was also a cistern in the open court which has been excavated recently and is shown by dotted lines in the plan (Pl. XXXI). It was probably used as an open-air bath in summer.

In the close vicinity of the palace, towards the south-west, the remains of a royal pavilion were found during recent excavation (Pl. XLI). The pavilion is built on the brink of the plateau and commands a good view of the lowlands. The plan of the building comprises a hall in front with an octagonal room at its back and some more rooms on its northern side. The hall measures 46 feet 8 inches in length and 30 feet in width. It is divided into two aisles by pillars, the pedestals

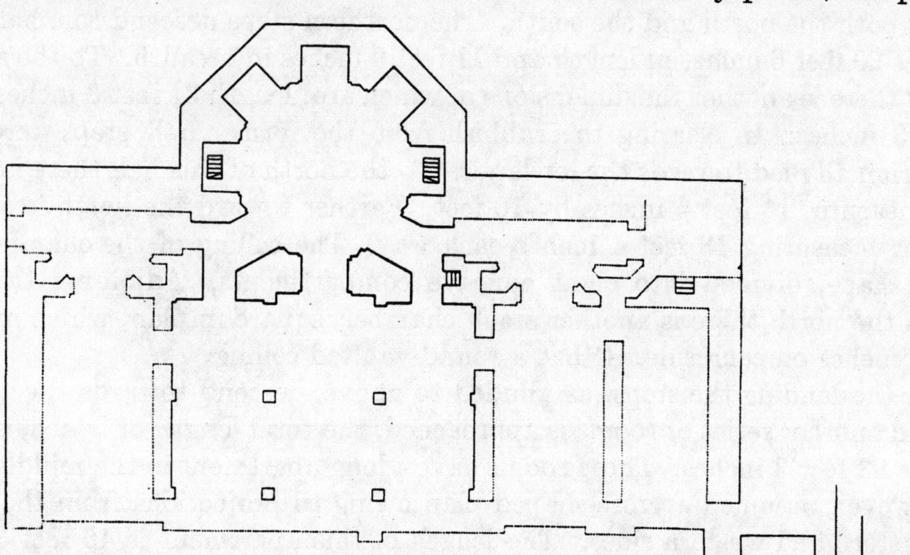

Plan of the Royal Pavilion
Scale: 30 feet to an inch

of which are intact, though the wooden shafts have perished. The pedestals are of black stone, beautifully carved and polished like the pedestals of pillars in the audience hall and the royal palace. The dadoes of the walls of this hall were decorated with mosaic-tiles, fragments of which may still be seen. Among the colours, yellow, green, and blue are prominent. The designs worked out on the tiles are chiefly floral.

The octagonal room at the back of the hall was crowned by a lofty dome, for the walls rise to a considerable height. Each side of the octagon measures 11 feet 3 inches internally and 16 feet 9 inches externally, the thickness of the wall being 5 feet 5 inches for the support of the dome. There are projections on each side of the room, those towards the north and the west have openings at their backs to admit light and air, and also to afford a view of the country below. Towards the interior of the room the projections have arches, in building which the architect has shown a fine sense of proportion. Their span is 7 feet 2 inches and their height up to the apex 17 feet 6 inches.

The rooms adjoining the northern and southern sides of the hall are much ruined, and it is difficult to judge of their architectural or decorative schemes in their present condition, but their plans can be grasped from the sketch given above. The octagonal pavilion and the hall and the rooms adjoining it formed a sort of annexe to the royal palace, which was occupied by one of the consorts of the king, or by some royal prince and princess.

A staircase from the base of the rooms on the north side of the pavilion leads down to some underground halls and chambers, which were used either for residence in summer or for storage of arms and other royal paraphernalia. By a descent of seven steps a landing is reached near the western end of which steps again start towards both the north and the south. The northern steps descend to a hall which measures 30 feet 6 inches in length and 11 feet 3 inches in breadth. To the south of this hall there is another the dimensions of which are: length 31 feet 3 inches, width 11 feet 3 inches. In clearing the rubbish from the former hall, steps were found which originally led towards the lowlands. To the north of this hall there is a room which measures 14 feet 6 inches by 10 feet. Farther toward the north is a square chamber, measuring 13 feet 4 inches each way. The ceiling of the chamber has a conical shape, divided into eight concave compartments. Adjoining this room towards the north there is another small chamber, square in plan, which measures 6 feet 6 inches on each side. It has a round vaulted ceiling.

From the landing the steps, as alluded to above, descend towards the south as well, and another series of rooms is approached, the total length of which, north to south, is 83 feet 3 inches. These rooms have a long apartment in the middle, which has, however, assumed a cross-shaped plan owing to projections from the middle of its eastern and western sides. The length of this apartment is 46 feet 3 inches and its breadth, excluding the projections, 15 feet 8 inches. The ceiling is vaulted in the form of a barrel. Beyond the western projection of this apartment is an entrance room or porch, because steps descend to its floor from three sides, the north, the south, and the west.

The middle apartment has double rooms towards both the north and the south, which are of uniform plan and dimensions. These double rooms have a rectangular apartment at the back and a square one in front, the two being joined together by an arch. The dimensions of each of the rectangular apartments in the back are: length, 27 feet 3 inches, breadth 13 feet 10 inches, while each of the square apartments in front measures 14 feet approximately each way.

Outside the walls of the palace, towards the south, is a well, near the head of which a high reservoir is built. The reservoir was filled with water drawn from the well by large leather buckets to which ropes were attached. Pairs of oxen were yoked to pull the ropes on account of the colossal size of the buckets and the great depth of the well. Baked clay pipe-lines as well as narrow channels, built in brick and lime, carried the water to the various apartments of the palace; traces of both the pipe-lines and the brick and lime channels still exist.

The Thousand Cells (Hazār Koṭhṛī) and the Subterranean Passage

About half a furlong to the south of the royal palace is another group of underground rooms, which are styled the *Hazār Koṭhṛī*. The rooms do not number one thousand, but the designation is based on a tradition that this part of the fort was at one time honeycombed with underground vaults and secret passages. These vaults are approached by steps from three directions—north, east, and west. On

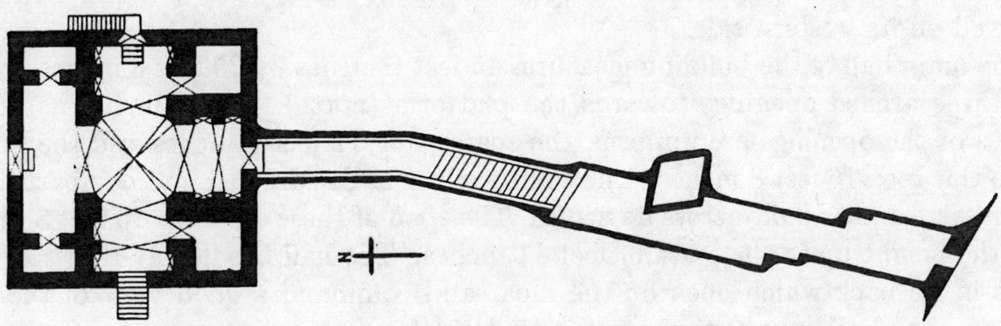

Plan of the underground rooms and the subterranean passage
Scale: 40 feet to an inch

entering by the northern steps a large rectangular room is reached which measures 31 feet lengthwise and 12 feet breadthwise. It is flanked by two small chambers, one each towards the east and the west. Both the chambers are of uniform dimensions, each measuring 12 feet by 5 feet. Adjoining the large rectangular room is another towards the south, which is more spacious than the former and measures 48 feet 3 inches in length and 14 feet 1 inch in width. The ceiling of this hall is vaulted, being divided into compartments by arches which spring from masonry piers, and overlap one another in the middle of the ceiling.

This hall has three apartments adjoining its southern side; the middle one is of larger dimensions than those on each side of it, and it measures 14 feet 8 inches by 14 feet 1 inch. The dimensions of the two side rooms are uniform, viz. length 10 feet 6 inches, width 9 feet 11 inches. From the southern side of the middle apartment a subterranean passage begins which has a vaulted masonry ceiling up to a distance of 70 feet. The width of the passage for these 70 feet is 6 feet 8 inches. Farther on there is a flight of steps which bring down the passage 13 feet lower than its previous level, and henceforward it is cut in the laterite rock and has no masonry covering its walls or ceiling. From the steps the passage extends to a distance of 89 feet in the solid rock until it opens on the moat. At a distance of 19 feet from the steps there is a well, the walls of which are 9 feet 6 inches wide on all four sides, but as they have not been built at right angles to one another, they present the form of a trapezoid. The well has an opening at the top for light and air.

The arrangement of the rooms and the passage shows that they were constructed as a safety exit for use if ever the surrender of the fort might seem imminent.

The Old Naubat Khāna

The building from its position and style of architecture appears to be the abode of one of the commandants of the fort, rather than a Naubat Khāna, 'Music Hall', because below this building the city wall joins the ramparts of the fort and at that point a close watch would have been necessary for the purpose of defence. The name Naubat Khāna, like several other names associated with the old buildings of the fort, may have been given in modern times. The plan of the building includes a spacious hall with a side room towards the west and a platform in front. At the northern end of the platform is a large reservoir to which water was supplied from the well on its western side.

The main hall of the building measures 45 feet 6 inches by 25 feet 3 inches, and it has three arched openings towards the platform (north). The dimensions of the arches of the openings are uniform, the span being 12 feet 6 inches and the height up to the apex 16 feet 8 inches. The ceiling of the hall is divided into compartments by massive arches built across its width. The span of these arches is 15 feet 8 inches and the height up to the apex 17 feet 11 inches. The hall has deeply recessed windows in its back which open on the moat and command a good view of the city wall and the buildings of the town on that side.

The side room, on the west side of the hall, measures 25 feet 3 inches in length and 18 feet 10 inches in width. It has a vaulted ceiling, which is shaped like a casket, the flat part of the vault being divided into small squares by plaster-work with a view to decoration. This room also has a recessed window in its back and a projection towards the west; the latter was probably used as a privy. There is also a large arched opening towards the platform to match with the openings of the main hall in that direction.

The platform in front of the building is quite extensive, and it would have been pleasant, particularly in summer, to sit there and to enjoy the view of the splashing waters of the reservoir at its foot. The latter is square in plan, 81 feet each way and 6 feet deep. But there is a landing, running on all four sides, in the middle of the depth of the reservoir, which shows that it was also used for swimming, the water being kept at different levels according to the practice and the age of the swimmers.

The Gateway of the Lowlands

This is a massive structure, built of black trap masonry finely chiselled and laid in lime. The surface of the walls at one time must have been coated with lime-plaster which has now completely disappeared, and the building looks rather bare. The arches show a large variety, both in the size of the spans and in the form of their heads (Pls. XLII–XLIII). Some of them have a marked stilt near the apex, while the shoulders of a few, like those of an ogee arch, have an inward bend which is not pleasing to the eye. The gateway is defended by bastions which are round in shape, but increase in girth from top to base, apparently with a view to maintaining their architectural strength (Pls. XLII–XLIII). The outer arch of the gateway is of considerable dimensions, its span being 17 feet 10 inches and its height up to the apex 29 feet 6 inches. The arch of the entrance itself, which is built behind two ogee arches outlined on the wall, is, however, smaller in dimensions than the outer arch, and has a span of 10 feet 3 inches, and its height up to the apex is 17 feet 6 inches. From this arch a covered passage, 14 feet 4 inches wide and 40 feet 4 inches long, extends to the outer opening of the gateway which faces the lowlands. The roof of the covered passage has fallen down, but the arches which supported it are intact, and their dimensions and shape are identical with those of the arch of the entrance. On either side of the covered passage are halls for the accommodation of guards, but the openings of the hall on the left (south) are blocked with masonry, and hence its exact inner dimensions cannot be determined with certainty. The openings of the hall on the right (north) are, however, not blocked, and its inner plan comprises a single apartment, 37 feet 2 inches by 9 feet 3 inches, with deeply recessed niches in its back. The roof of this hall has fallen down.

Close to the gateway, towards the north, are the remains of some rooms and a house, the roofs of all of which have collapsed. The walls of these structures are, however, intact, and those forming their façades have arches with pleasing proportions. The house has a high plinth and its front contains five arches, the middle one of which has a wide span, being 15 feet 3 inches at the base. The architect, however, in order to improve upon the form of the arch-head, has given several offsets near the springing points and reduced the span to 12 feet 3 inches, as opposed to 15 feet 3 inches at the base. The house has several apartments in its interior, their total dimensions being: length 60 feet 8 inches, depth 19 feet 6 inches. This house was probably occupied by a responsible officer of the garrison, who controlled the egress and ingress of traffic at this point. The rooms built adjoining it towards the south were apparently occupied by the guards (Pl. XLIII).

The average level of the lowlands, immediately below the edge of the plateau on which the royal palace was built, is nearly 200 feet lower than that of the plateau, and to facilitate the ascent sixty stages are built which make a not uncomfortable approach to the gateway. The stages are lined with masonry, and on one side, towards the east, defended by a massive wall from the top of which missiles could be thrown on to the enemy and his advance adequately checked. The lands are now cultivated for food grains, but originally fruit and flower gardens were laid out there, which presented a beautiful show of colours when looked at from the terrace or the windows of the palace. On the lowlands remains of some old houses and of a gateway may be seen. The arch of the latter is in a comparatively fair state of preservation, and its proportions show a refined taste. The span of the arch is 9 feet and its height up to the apex 14 feet. In the midst of the rock wall the opening of a tunnel may also be seen from which during the monsoons the rain-water of the town and the plateau of the fort flows down to the lowlands and ultimately fills up the tank which is at the back of the north-western wall of the fort. The surplus water of the tank was drained off through a sluice to the Paniyā Khandaq, between the Kalyānī Burj and the Purāna Qilʿa (Pl. XLV). The sluice and the remains of an embankment may still be seen in the western and northern sides respectively of the tank. The tank also replenished through a channel the well built in the Purāna Qilʿa, from which water was distributed by pipe-lines to the various buildings in that area of the fort.[1]

The Long Gun Bastion and Vīrasangayya's Temple

A spur of the plateau of the fort runs in a north-westerly direction almost along the middle of the lowlands (Map). At the tip of the spur a bastion has been built on which is mounted a gun of extraordinary length. It measures 29 feet from the butt to the muzzle, and has a circumference of 6 feet near the former. The bore of the gun is 6 inches, but the diameter across its mouth, including the thickness of the metal, is 1 foot 9 inches. The gun is beautifully carved, the patterns representing the chain, the bead (*rudraksha*),[2] leaves with stalks, and birds (Pl. XLVI). The workmanship is in a Hindu style and the gun was probably made by mechanics professing that faith.

On the eastern side of the bastion is a temple, the *sikhara* (spire) of which has a modern appearance. As the buildings of religious shrines are frequently restored and renovated through the zeal of votaries, it is not unlikely that the temple, in spite of its modern features, may have a long history, and it may have existed in some other form even before the coming of Muslims into the Deccan.

At present its plan comprises a court, with arcades on its southern and western sides, a hall, and two chambers. The court measures 52 feet 6 inches from east to west and 25 feet 3 inches from north to south. The arcades are rather narrow, having a depth of 6 feet only. They have six openings towards the court on the eastern side and two on the western. The hall and the two chambers are built along the northern side of the court, and their joint base measures 46 feet 9 inches externally. The hall, like the arcades, is narrow in plan, having a length of 25 feet in contrast to a breadth of 7 feet. The two chambers, which are built one at each end of the hall, on the east and the west, are uniform in dimensions and measure 9 feet 8 inches by 8 feet 10 inches each. The western chamber contains the *samādhī* of a local hero, known as Vīrasangayya, who is said to have been a *Lingayat*. A *yonī-linga*, the Śaivite emblem of worship, is also to be seen in this chamber, but

[1] *Supra*, p. 39.

[2] The word means Rudra's (Śiva's) eye. Śaivite devotees generally wear rosaries of such beads.

it is explained that the latter was installed there at a later date. The eastern chamber contains no icon but it has a cell below its floor, which is approached by steps built in the base of the building towards the west, entrance being from outside the chamber. The cell may have been used for meditation.

The Gunpowder Magazine

There were a large number of magazines in the fort for storing arms and explosive materials, the remains of which may still be noticed behind the ramparts near all the important bastions (Map). The principal magazine, however, is situated on the left side of the road which goes from the Gumbad Darwāza to the Māṇḍū Gate. In its present condition the magazine comprises two blocks, with a terrace between, which has vaults below it. The terrace measures 45 feet 6 inches by 26 feet 6 inches and has two circular apertures to give air and light to the chambers below. The latter are two in number and measure 35 feet 6 inches by 19 feet 3 inches jointly. The walls of these chambers are more than 3 feet in thickness, and as they are built below the ground level, it appears that the vaults were meant for storing gunpowder. The space between the western and eastern blocks of the magazine is 100 feet approximately. The former block is ¬ shaped, having two wings, the northern being smaller than the western.

The western wing comprises seven vaults towards the south and five double rooms towards the north. Three of the latter have arches opening on to the court. These arches show a good sense of proportion in their dimensions, the span of each being 12 feet 6 inches and its height up to the apex 17 feet 3 inches. The depth of the double rooms measuring from the western end of the court is 35 feet. Of the seven vaults, the five adjoining the double rooms have bastion-like constructions towards the court. Their inner plan is also circular, and each vault on the floor level measures 29 feet 6 inches across. The bastion-like shape was apparently adopted to make the building adequately strong for the storage of high explosives. The remaining two vaults of this wing, which are built at its southern end, have a masonry wall towards the court, but their inner plan and dimensions are the same as those of the five vaults mentioned above. In the western wing there are also two staircases leading to the roof, which has fallen down. One staircase is between vaults 1 and 2, starting from the north, and the other between vaults 3 and 4, following the same order. Until quite recently remnants of old matchlocks, muskets, small cannon, and bullets could be seen in these vaults, but they are now stored in other parts of the fort.

The northern wing of this block has a plan uniform with that of the double rooms at the northern end of the western wing, and it appears that both of them were built at the same time, while the five bastion-shaped vaults were added afterwards. The external dimensions of the northern wing are: length 94 feet 3 inches, width 42 feet. This wing has five arched openings towards the court and also a staircase leading to the terrace. The staircase is built between the second and the third arches, starting from the east.

Close to the northern wing, in the open court, there are steps leading to some underground chambers which have not been cleared so far, and hence their plan cannot be described. The eastern block of the magazine has a rectangular plan externally and measures 170 feet from north to south, and 40 feet from east to west. The interior of the building is divided into five apartments, which have a square plan at the floor level,[1] but are crowned by circular vaults, the transition from the square plan being arranged by squinches and overlapping arches built at corners. The plinth of this block is high, and access to the apartments is through doors of rather small size, each being 6 feet 3 inches high and 4 feet wide. There are two staircases leading to the roof in this block also. As the architecture of the block is massive and the doors are small and built at a considerable height from the ground level, it appears that the building was designed for storing such articles as rockets, shells, and other explosives of similar character, specimens of which can still be seen in the fort.

For the purpose of defence the magazine had an enclosure wall and a ditch all round, the remains of which may be noticed at the back of the eastern block. The entrance was through an arched doorway, still visible when one approaches the magazine from the road towards the east.

THE TOWN

Fortifications

It has already been stated in the chapter on history that Bidar was a town of considerable strategic importance long before the transfer to it of the seat of government by Aḥmad S͟hāh al-Walī from Gulbarga in A.D. 1429;[2] and as such it must have been defended by a wall of the Hindu style of architecture, similar to those to be noticed round pre-Islāmic forts of the Deccan.[3] But as the requirements of the capital would have called for a larger area within the defensive system, the old enclosure wall of the Hindu period may have been demolished and new fortifications built around the expanded town. The present ramparts and bastions of the town are, however, of the later Baihmanī period, the last quarter of the fifteenth century A.D., when cannons as war weapons came into vogue in the Deccan. A gun placed on the Muṇḍa Burj, which will be described in its proper place in this account, bears an inscription mentioning the name of the gun as *Top-i-Maḥmūd S͟hāhī*, Maḥmūd S͟hāh's Gun, and thus confirming this view. There is also a strong tradition that the parapets and batteries of Bidar town were built by Barīdī kings,[4] which does not seem unlikely, for Bidar was not only under a continuous menace from the rival kingdoms of Ahmadnagar, Bijāpur, and Golconda, but it was actually besieged by Ismā'īl 'Ādil S͟hāh in A.D. 1529, by Murtaḍa Niẓām S͟hāh in A.D. 1579, and by Ibrāhīm 'Ādil S͟hāh II in A.D. 1619. The last-mentioned ruler annexed it

[1] These apartments are uniform in dimensions, measuring 25 feet each way.

[2] Briggs' *Firis͟hta*, vol. i, p. 405.

[3] The forts at Warangal, Bhongīr, and Golconda, which were originally built by Hindu kings, have enclosure walls of cyclopean type, built of huge blocks of masonry, the courses of which are irregular, but the joints perfectly fitting.

[4] Muḥammad Sulṭān, the author of *Ā'īna-i-Bīdar*, writes that the enclosure wall of Bidar town was built by 'Alī Barīd during 962–5 H. (A.D. 1555–8). *Ā'īna-i-Bīdar* (Gulbarga lith.), pp. 17–18.

to his kingdom and appointed governors to administer the territory attached to the conquered town. The Bijāpur governor, Sīdī Marjān, is also reported to have repaired and extended the defences of the town,[1] and inscribed tablets fixed to several gates show that Mughal governors also, after the capture of the town by Aurangzeb in A.D. 1656, added to the fortifications of the place.[2] The strengthening of the defences of the town appears to have been maintained during the régime of early Āṣaf Jāhī rulers, for a record carved on the Mangalpeṭ Darwāza states that during the reign of Nawāb Nāṣir-ud-Daula Bahādur, Āṣaf Jāh IV (A.D. 1829–57), a gateway was built facing the Maḥmūd Ganj.[3]

At present the fortifications of the town have a pentagonal plan; the two sides facing the west and the south-west run almost straight, but those towards the south-east and north-east are crooked, and the defences bend and project in an irregular manner at short distances according to the shape of the edge of the plateau (Map). The northern side of the town touches the fosse of the fort and extends from a point opposite the Naubat Khāna to the first gate of the fort (Map). The town fortifications terminate at both ends of its northern side, for at those points they join the works of the fort.

The defences comprise a glacis, a moat, which is 33 feet 6 inches deep and 51 feet wide, and a scarp. The last is built of black trap masonry laid in lime and crowned by arch-shaped battlements. The total height of the scarp including the battlements is 42 feet from the bottom of the moat. The battlements are loopholed for the use of both muskets and small-sized guns, which can be fired at various angles according to the approach of the enemy. Behind the battlements is a passage, running almost the entire length of the ramparts, but varying in width from 55 feet to 17 feet according to the vulnerability of the line of fortifications to the attack of the foe. For further defence there are bastions, very massively built and arranged at appropriate distances from one another. Originally they were all surmounted by heavy long-range guns, but now these are to be seen on only a few bastions. The total number of bastions is thirty-seven, and in addition there are eight batteries on which are placed smaller pieces of artillery.

The town is entered by five gateways, the names of which are as follows:

(1) The Shāh Ganj Darwāza
(2) The Fatḥ Darwāza
(3) The Mangalpeṭ Darwāza
(4) The Dulhan Darwāza
(5) The Talghāṭ Darwāza.

The circuit of the ramparts is nearly three miles, and the area of the town less than a square mile, although at some points it stretches east to west and north to south quite a mile. Starting from the north-west side of the town the ramparts extend almost straight to the Shāh Ganj Darwāza, a distance of some 500 yards in which they are defended by two bastions only. The passage behind the parapets in this portion of the fortifications is only 17 feet wide, thus indicating that owing

[1] *Epig. Ind. Mosl.*, 1927–8, p. 26. [2] Ibid., pp. 36–8. [3] Idem, p. 38.

to the close vicinity of the fort-walls, which were surmounted by heavy artillery, military strategy did not require the building of a wider passage in which to post troops in large numbers for defence.

The Shāh Ganj Darwāza is a comparatively modern name given to the Makkī Darwāza (Mecca Gate) as it faces Mecca. During the régime of Nawāb Nāṣir-ud-Daula Bahādur a grain market, called the Shāh Ganj, was constructed outside the town near this gate; hence the change in the name from the Makkī Darwāza to the Shāh Ganj Darwāza.[1] The gateway comprises two arches, one of which is fitted with a pair of massive wooden doors studded with iron knobs and bands. The dimensions of the inner and outer arches are uniform, the span being 12 feet 7 inches and the height up to the apex 17 feet. The total height of the front wall of the gateway including the parapet is 34 feet 6 inches.[2]

Near the inner arch of the gateway, towards the south, are steps leading to the passage built on the ramparts behind the battlements. This is 51 feet wide; and this width continues up to the Muṇḍā Burj, where the western side of the pentagon ends and the fortifications turn towards the south-east. The distance between the Shāh Ganj Darwāza and the Muṇḍā Burj is only 360 yards, but for the purpose of

[1] The Shāh Ganj locality is now densely populated, for a mushroom growth of houses has sprung up among which the Sarā'i of Mīr 'Ālam is comparatively old. Mīr 'Ālam served as Vazīr to Nawāb Nāṣir-ud-Daula Bahādur and the Sarā'i was apparently built at the same time as the grain market. It has a large enclosure inside which there is an arcade towards the west and small rooms for the accommodation of travellers in the three other directions. The arcade has in its middle a mosque with three arched openings towards the east. The court in the middle of the four wings of the building is fairly extensive, and may have been used for the parking of carts and the penning of animals bringing grain and other commodities to the market.

[2] A metal tablet bearing an inscription is fixed to the wooden door of this gateway. The inscription records the building of the gateway by Mukhtār Khān al-Ḥusainī in 1082 H. (A.D. 1671), during the 14th regnal year of Aurangzeb. As the bastions and the enclosure wall of Bidar were destroyed in several places during the siege of the town by Aurangzeb in A.D. 1656, it is very probable that the defences of Bidar, wherever they were breached, were repaired or rebuilt under the orders of the king by his governors. Mukhtār Khān al-Ḥusainī was the third Mughal governor at Bidar, and he had charge of this office from A.D. 1660 to 1672, until his promotion to the governorship of Mālwā (*supra*, p. 15). The inscription consists of four lines of Persian prose written in *Nasta'līq* characters of a pleasing form. The text has been deciphered as follows:

Text

(۱) روز چهار شنبه پانزدهم شهر شوال سنه ۱٤ جلوس میمنت مانوس حضرت

(۲) قدر قدرت جم جاه ملایك سپاه محي الدین محمد اورنگ زیب بهادر عالم گیر بادشاه

(۳) غازي خلد الله ملكه و سلطانه موافق سنه ۱۰۸۲ هجري نبوي در صوبه داريء كمترين

(٤) بندگان مختار خان الحسیني السبزواري دروازه صورت اتمام پذیرفت.

Translation

'On Wednesday, the 15th of Shawwāl, in the 14th year of the auspicious reign of His Majesty, powerful like Fate, glorious like Jamshīd, the lord of the army of angels, Muḥī-ud-Dīn Muḥammad Aurangzeb Bahādur 'Ālamgīr, the victorious King (may God perpetuate his kingdom and majesty), corresponding to the year 1082 of the Flight of the Prophet, during the governorship of the humblest servant (of the Court) Mukhtār Khān al-Ḥusainī as-Sabzwārī, this gate was completed (A.D. 1671).'

Vide *Epig. Ind. Mosl.*, 1927–8, p. 37.

defence, besides the broad passage alluded to above, there are two bastions which originally must have had heavy guns on them. The ground beyond the fortifications of the town on this side is flat, which explains the presence of this precaution in order to strengthen the defences against an attack.

The Muṇḍā Burj is the most massive of all the bastions of the town. It is built in two stages which are approached by steps built along the back wall of the bastion itself. The second stage commands a good view of the country to the west and south-east of the town, and it is surmounted by a large gun which has an inscription in six ornamental panels on its body (Pl. XLIX).[1] The third and fourth panels of the inscription contain the name of the gun as *Top-i-Maḥmūd Shāhī*, and also the date of its completion in Muḥarram 1000 H. (October, A.D. 1591), during Qāsim Barīd Shāh's reign. It is not unlikely that the gun was originally manufactured following a plain design during Maḥmūd Shāh Baihmanī II's reign (A.D. 1482–1518), but was improved in calibre and embellished with calligraphic panels at the instance of Qāsim Barīd II in 1000 H.[2] The gun industry received a distinct impetus during the rule of the Barīd Shāhī kings, for the magnificent specimens mounted on the Māṇḍū Gate bastion, the Purāna Qil'a bastion, and the Lāl Burj bear the names of the kings of this dynasty.[3]

From the Muṇḍā Burj to the Fatḥ Darwāza the distance is approximately 5 furlongs, and as the fortifications of the town are exposed to attack from the table-land on the south, the width of the passage on this side has been increased from 51 to 56 feet at certain places, and seven bastions have been constructed at vulnerable points. The Fatḥ Darwāza, being the principal entrance to the town, was designed with considerable care. It has two solidly built towers in front of the bridge over the moat (Pl. LVII), beyond which is a tortuous passage planned between the walls of the gateway, the entire arrangement presenting the form of a barbican. The gateway itself comprises two lofty arches with a passage, 17 feet in length and 12 feet 6 inches in width, between them. The gateway has a vaulted roof, and at one end it is fitted with a wooden door, the iron spikes and bands of which are of

[*For footnotes, see over.*]

[1] The full text of the inscription has been deciphered as follows:

Text

(۱) حبّذا توپی پر آشوبی که از رعد بلند — کر کند گوش فلك را بر کند کوه از وطن

(۲) از پیء خصمان شاهنشه دهن بکشوده است — تا کند یکبارگي خصمان شه اندر دهن

(۳) شاه معدلت گسترے قاسم برید شاه آنکه او — صاحب هند و سند است و مالك ملك دكن

اختتام توپ در شهر محرم بوده است — توپ محمود شاهي شد نامش سپاه صف شکن

(٤) افضلي میجست تاریخش سروش غیب گفت — توپ بی‌مثلی بود تاریخ او اندر وزن

۱۰۰۰ هـ

(٥) یا حافظ این توپ‌را در امان خویش نگاه داراد بمحمد و آله الامجاد بالصاد و النون

(٦) نصر من الله و فتح قریب وبشر المؤمنین فاللّه خیر حافظا وهو ارحم الراحمین

Translation

Panel 1 How awful is the terror-striking gun whose thunder
Deafens the ears of the sky and dislodges the mountain.

Panel 2 It has opened its mouth wide against the enemies of the emperor
In order to swallow them in one gulp.

Panel 3 The just king, Qāsim Barīd Shāh, who is
The master of Sind and India, and the lord of the kingdom of the Deccan.
The gun was completed in the month of Muḥarram,
The *Top-i-Maḥmūd Shāhī* (the Gun of Maḥmūd Shāh), entitled the Destroyer of the Flank of the Army.

Panel 4 (As) Afḍalī searched for the chronogram, the inspirer of the unknown said,
The chronogram is in the phrase *Top-i-be mithli* (the Matchless Gun) which completes the metre of the verse.

Panel 5 O Protector! May He guard this Gun under His care. Through the benediction of Muḥammad and his distinguished progeny, (and) the grace of the chapters of the *Qur'ān* beginning with *Ṣād* and *Nūn* (xxxviii and lxviii).

Panel 6 '*Help from God and a speedy victory. And do thou bear good tidings to the true believers.*' (*Qur'ān*, lxi. 13.) '*But God is the best guardian; and He is the most merciful of those who show mercy.*' (*Qur'ān*, xii. 64.)

[2] Briggs in his translation (vol. iii, p. 499) has given 1000 H. as the date of Qāsim Barīd's demise, but in the original Persian text (vol. ii, p. 348, Bombay ed.) only the durations of the reigns of Qāsim Barīd II and his father Ibrāhīm Barīd are given. Haig (*Camb. Hist.*, vol. iii, p. 709), apparently on the basis of the latter, has fixed the chronology of these two kings as follows:

Ibrāhīm Barīd Shāh, 987–94 H. (A.D. 1579–86).
Qāsim Barīd Shāh II, 994–9 H. (A.D. 1586–9).

But as the chronogram, *Top-i-be mithli*, contained in the present inscription gives the date 1000 H. and the name of the king, Qāsim Barīd Shāh, is also clearly mentioned, there remains no doubt that he was alive in that year. In the light of the above facts the chronology of the two Barīdī kings mentioned above might be revised as follows:

Ibrāhīm Barīd Shāh, 987–95 H. (A.D. 1580–7).
Qāsim Barīd Shāh II, 995–1000 H. (A.D. 1587–91).

Further, as Firishta gives only the year (987 H.) of 'Alī Barīd's demise, and the inscriptions carved on his tomb also mention simply the year and do not state the month in which he died, I would suggest that the A.D. year corresponding to 987 H. should be taken as 1580 and not 1579, because Firishta's statement that Ibrāhīm Barīd ruled for seven years fits in with 1580 better than with 1579. According to Swāmīkannu Pillai's *Ephemeris* (vol. v, pp. 360–2) the Hijrī year 987 began on the 28th of February 1579 and ended on the 16th of February 1580.

[3] *Supra*, pp. 35–6 and 39–40.

the same style as those of the Shāh Ganj Darwāza.[1] The side-walls of the inner façade of the gateway show a batter which has added further to the solidity of the building.

The name Fatḥ Darwāza was given to this gateway by Aurangzeb when his forces marched through it triumphantly in A.D. 1656.[2] The gateway was previously called the Nauras Darwāza, but this also cannot be its original name, for the title *nauras* was coined by Ibrāhīm ʿĀdil Shāh II of Bijāpur, who probably renamed the gateway as Nauras Darwāza after his conquest of Bidar in A.D. 1619.[3]

From the Fatḥ Darwāza to the Mangalpeṭ Darwāza, which is built at a distance of a little over three and a half furlongs from the former, the fortifications have a zigzag plan owing to the abrupt curves of the edge of the plateau on which they are built. As the level of the ground adjoining the glacis on this side is considerably lower than that of the lands of the town, this natural advantage was duly taken

[1] The Fatḥ Darwāza also has an inscriptional tablet fixed to its door, the text of which shows that this gateway, like the Shāh Ganj Darwāza, was rebuilt by Mukhtār Khān under the orders of Aurangzeb in A.D. 1671. The inscription consists of three lines which have been deciphered as follows:

Text

(۱) روز جمعه ۱۵ شهر ربیع الثاني سنه ۱٤ جلوس میمنت مانوس حضرت قدر قدرت جم جاه ملایك سپاه ابو الظفر

(۲) محي الدین محمد اورنگ‌زیب بهادر عالم گیر پادشاه غازي خلد اللّٰه ملکه و سلطانه موافق سنه ۱۰۸۲

(۳) هجري نبوي در صوبه‌داري٭ کمترین بندگان مختار خان الحسیني السبزواري این دروازه صورت اتمام پذیرفت.

Translation

'On Friday, the 15th of the month of Rabīʿ II, in the 14th year of the auspicious reign of His Majesty, powerful like Fate, possessing Jamshīd's glory and having angels in his train, the victorious king, Muḥī-ud-Dīn Muḥammad Aurangzeb Bahādur ʿĀlamgīr, the conqueror (may God perpetuate his kingdom and majesty!), corresponding to the year 1082 of the Flight of the Prophet, during the administration of the humblest servant (of the Court), Mukhtār Khān al-Ḥusainī as-Sabzwārī, this gate was completed.' Vide *Epig. Ind. Mosl.*, 1927–8, p. 37.

[2] Aurangzeb gave the same name to the eastern gate of the Golconda fort whereby his army entered in October 1687.

[3] Mirzā Ibrāhīm Zubairī has given an interesting history of the origin of the term *nauras* in his book, styled *Basātīn-us-Salāṭīn*, from which the following extract may interest the reader:

طبع رنگین بادشاه (ابراهیم عادل شاه ثاني) که نورس چمن مکنت و سلطنت و نوباوهٔ گلشن جهانداري و خلافت بوده لفظ نورس‌را چنان خوش کرده بود که در هر جا و بهر چیز استعمال آن لفظ بکار برد — سکهٔ نورس نام مهر خاص که بر عقیق یمني بجای نام مبارکش این لفظ رقم یافته امروز برکت خاص بادشاهي دیده مي شود — و علم نورس و نشان نورس که هر یك زرد نشان عادل شاهیان است — و محل خاص که از سائر محلها بزیادتي منظوري و مقبولي اختصاص یافته هم بنورس موسوم گردیده — و کتابی که بزبان دهریت در فنّ موسیقي تالیف یافته و آن‌را به بادشاه مخصوص میکنند هم بنورس مشهور است — و فلوس که از آن عهد تا زمان حال مشهور و مروّج است هم بفلس نورس معروف است — ***** و عید نورس که چون ماه نهم روز جمعه واقع گردد — و نورس که طوایف قوّالان و سازندگان و نوازندگان نادرهٔ حق اند — تا آنکه سبب مقبول و مطبوع آمدن این لفظ بر خاطر نازك پسند بادشاه نازك پسندان عصر نیز بموجب الناس علی دین ملوکهم این لفظ پسند کرده به استعمال خودها آورده اند — چنانچه ظهوري نام دیباچه که در مدح آن ممدوح زمان گفته دیباچهٔ نورس نام گذاشت — و محمد قاسم فرشته کتاب مؤلّف خود که در فن تاریخ پرداخته نورسنامهٔ فرشته موسوم گردانیده — عبد القادر نورسي که شاعر فصیح‌گو بود تخلّص خویش نورسي قرار داده ٭

Vide Hyderabad lithograph, pp. 249–50.

into consideration by the builders of the fortifications. Accordingly the width of the passage behind the parapet has been reduced from 51 feet to 22 feet only, but at each curve of the line of ramparts a bastion has been constructed to maintain the strength of the fortifications. There are altogether five bastions and one battery between the Fatḥ and Mangalpeṭ gateways.

Mangalpeṭ Darwāza is perhaps the old name of the gateway, given to it on account of its vicinity to the suburb wherein a market was held every Tuesday—*peṭ* being an abbreviated form of the Sanskrit word *Penṭh*, meaning a market, and *Mangal* corresponding to Tuesday. A new market styled the Maḥmūd Ganj was established at the site some time later, for an inscription of Nawāb Nāṣir-ud-Daula Bahādur, which is carved on the Darwāza, mentions the name Maḥmūd Ganj.[1] The latter name seems to have been used only for a short time because the old name Mangalpeṭ still survives, while Maḥmūd Ganj is entirely forgotten.

The Mangalpeṭ Darwāza, as it stands at present, was rebuilt by Shams-ud-Dīn Khān *alias* Abban Ṣāḥib, the Taʿalluqdār of Bidar, in A.D. 1850. The general style of the building is the same as those of the other gateways, namely, the entrance comprising two arches with a space of 9 feet between them, and two bastions which with the enclosure wall form a sort of barbican in front of the gateway. The dimensions of the two arches are uniform, viz. span 12 feet 8 inches and height up to the apex 18 feet 1 inch. The door is strengthened by iron bars and studded with iron spikes to repel an attack by elephants.

The distance between the Mangalpeṭ Darwāza and the next gateway towards the north, styled the Dulhan Darwāza,[2] is three and a half furlongs approximately. The ramparts are built on laterite rock and have some sharp turns near the latter gateway (Map). In view of the existence of a hillock, called the Ḥabshī Koṭ, which is situated in the vicinity of the town and from which the latter could easily be bombarded, the defences have been strengthened by the construction of seven

[1] The inscription is carved on a metal tablet fixed to the door, and consists of three lines of Persian prose. The text has been deciphered as follows:

Text

(۱) حسب الفرمان جليل الشان اعليحضرت قدر قدرت حضور پر نور نواب ناصر الدوله بهادر آصف جاه خلد الله ملکه و سلطانه

(۲) بروز یکشنبه یازدهم شهر ربيع الثاني مطابق سنه ۲۲ جلوس همايون در تعلقداري و ز حسن ارادت بندهٔ جانفشان شمس الدين خان

(۳) عرف ابن صاحب تیاري دروازهٔ حصار قلعه روبروی محمود گنج فی سنه ۱۲۶۶ هجري النبوي زيب اتمام پذيرفت لله الحمد و المنت.

Translation

'By the high command of His Exalted Highness, powerful like Fate, of luminous presence, Nawāb Nāṣir-ud-Daula Bahādur, Āṣaf Jāh (may God perpetuate his kingdom and majesty!) the gate of the walls of the Fort facing Maḥmūd Ganj, was completed on the 11th of Rabīʿ II, 22nd year of the reign (of Nawāb Nāṣir-ud-Daula), corresponding to the year 1266 of the Flight of the Prophet (A.D. 1850), through the sincere devotion of the loyal servant Shams-ud-Dīn Khān *alias* Abban Ṣāḥib, during his term of office as Taʿalluqdār, and to God be the praise and the glory.'

[2] *Dulhan* literally means a bride; Dulhan Darwāza therefore signifies either the Bride of the Gateways, or the gateway associated with some bride whose history is not known.

bastions and as many batteries. The bastions must have originally been furnished with heavy guns, while the batteries were apparently meant for lighter pieces of short range. The width of the passage behind the parapet has, however, been reduced,[1] which suggests that for the defence of the town in this part the presence of troops generally armed with muskets was considered not so essential, because their firing could hardly cause any damage to an enemy in occupation of the Ḥabs͟hī Koṭ.

The Dulhan Darwāza appears to have been rebuilt in comparatively recent times, but its wooden door is still missing, and there are, besides, no battlements on the roof of the gateway. The span of the arches of the entrance is 12 feet 8 inches, and their height up to the apex 21 feet 2 inches. The passage from the entrance has an abrupt curve towards the outside (east) and is further defended by two massive towers, one on each side of the approach (Pl. LXI). As the lands to the east of the Darwāza lie 100 to 150 feet lower than the verge of the town-plateau, the likelihood of an attack from this direction was considered to be small.

As the edge of the plateau to the north-west of the Dulhan Darwāza is more abrupt than it is towards the south-east, the fortifications have been built with sharp turns between this gateway and the Talghāṭ Darwāza, which is situated at a distance of three and a half furlongs from it. The line of fortifications is, however, defended by a bastion at each turn, and there are altogether six bastions between these two gateways. The width of the passage behind the battlements in this part has been slightly increased, being 20 feet, in contrast to 18 feet between the Mangalpeṭ and Dulhan Darwāzas.

The Talghāṭ Darwāza is the most picturesque of all the gateways of the town, both as regards the style of its architecture and the motley character of the traffic which daily passes through it to the lowlands of the Marāṭhā country and vice versa (Pls. LXII–LXIII). As the decline from the table-land of the town is considerable at this point, the path has been divided by terraced levels and paved with stones. The traffic is chiefly pedestrian, but carts laden with grain or other produce of the country are frequently seen going up and down, rattling and jolting, the effort of hauling them putting no small strain on the bullocks by which they are drawn.

This gateway, like the others previously described, has two lofty arches, one on each side of its inner and outer faces. The space between these two arches, which measures 16 feet 5 inches, has been roofed over.[2] The span of the arches is approxi-

[1] The passage on the ramparts between the Mangalpeṭ Darwāza and the Dulhan Darwāza measures 18 feet only in width.

[2] This gateway was also repaired by the order of Aurangzeb, and an inscription mentioning this fact is carved on a metal tablet which is fixed to the door of the gateway. The record is in Persian, comprising three lines which have been read as follows:

Text

(۱) روز دو شنبه شهر ذي قعده سنه ١٥ از جلوس ميمنت مانوس حضرت قدر قدرت جم جاه ملايك سپاه

(۲) ابو الظفر محي الدين محمد اورنگ زيب بهادر عالم گير بادشاه غازي خلد اللّٰه ملكه و سلطانه موافق سنه ١٠٨٢

(۳) هجري نبوي در صوبه داريء كمترين بندگان مختار خان الحسيني السبزواري اين دروازه صورت اتمام يافت.

Translation

'On Monday, the 20th of Dhū-Qa'da in the 15th year of the auspicious reign of His Majesty, powerful

mately 10 feet and their height up to the apexes 17 feet 2 inches. The total height of the building including the parapet is 28 feet 10 inches. At the head of the path are two bastions which form the principal defence of the gateway, although the latter itself is most massively built and furnished with machicolations (Pl. LII). These two bastions are octagonal in plan, but there are two others which are round in shape and built midway for the defence of the path, one being on each side of it (Pl. LXIII).

The town enclosure beyond the Talghāṭ Darwāza up to the point where it joins the ramparts of the fort consists of a parapet only, this being considered a sufficient defence because the fall from the plateau of the town to the lowlands below is almost perpendicular, and ascent would be extremely difficult. This parapet is, however, provided with loopholes which open both vertically and horizontally so as to enable the garrison to fire at assailants from different positions according to the approach of the latter.

The Chaubāra

This is a cylindrical tower built in the middle of the town where the two principal thoroughfares of Bidar cross each other; the tower thus constitutes the hub of the town (Pl. LXIV). One of the two thoroughfares extends from the fort to the Fatḥ Darwāza, its alinement being north to south, and the other connects the Mangalpeṭ and the Shāh Ganj Darwāzas, the direction of the latter being east to west, excepting the little diversion near the Shāh Ganj Darwāza (Map). The plan of the town is more or less on the gridiron principle, there being parallel streets, linked together by roads which run crosswise.

The tower is reported to have been built in the pre-Islāmic period, but its style of architecture is Islāmic, and it was probably constructed as an observation post simultaneously with the other fortifications of the town by Aḥmad Shāh al-Walī, or his immediate successors. It rises 71 feet above the ground level, and from the top commands a view of the entire plateau and also of the lowlands stretching beyond it in every direction. The prefix *Chau* in Hindī as well as in Persian signifies the four directions, while *bāra* in Persian means a fortified place, and in Hindī (*bāṛa*) a house. The word therefore in both these languages means a central building facing in four directions. The entire structure is most massively built and its shape resembles that of the towers of some of the early mosques of Western Asiatic countries, notably that of the Great Mosque at Samarra.[1]

The tower has a circular base, 180 feet in circumference and 16 feet 9 inches in height, with arched niches built along its lower parts (Pl. LXIV). These may have been occupied by the guards who kept watch here, or resorted to by pedestrians

like Fate, glorious like Jamshīd, the lord of the army of angels, the victorious (king) Muḥī-ud-Dīn Muḥammad Aurangzeb Bahādur 'Ālamgīr the conqueror (may God perpetuate his kingdom and sovereignty!), corresponding to the year 1082 of the Flight of the Prophet, during the governorship of the humblest servant (of the Court) Mukhtār Khān al-Ḥusainī as-Sabzwārī, this gate was completed.'

Vide *Epig. Ind. Mosl.*, 1927–8, p. 38.

[1] The steps leading to the top of the Samarra tower are built along the outer surface of that structure, but its counterpart at Bidar has the steps built in its interior.

when taking short rests during their journeys. The front of the base in recent times was disfigured by a police station built facing the north, but thanks to the help and cultured tastes of Sir Theodore Tasker, the ex-Revenue Member, and his able and energetic successor, Mr. W. V. Grigson, this police station has been pulled down and the façade of the Chaubāra fully exposed.[1]

The steps which lead to the terrace of the basement start from a door which faces the east.[2] The girth of the tower at the terrace level is 114 feet, and a space of 8 feet 5 inches has been left all round it in order to enable visitors to walk round at the foot. In the northern side of the building on this level is a door from which a winding staircase comprising eighty steps leads to the top of the tower. The summit is 53 feet above the basement, and the parapet round it rises 3 feet 6 inches still higher. The circumference of the tower along the base of the upper parapet is 85 feet 7 inches. The entire tower is built of black trap masonry laid in lime and strengthened by circular bands at two places in its height. The dimensions of the tower are no doubt colossal, but pillars of this shape are frequently to be noticed in the Islāmic buildings of the fourteenth and fifteenth centuries in India, and the corner columns of the prayer-halls of the Fīroz Shāh Koṭla mosque at Delhi, Mubārak Khaljī's mosque at Daulatābād, and the Baihmanī 'Īdgāh at Bidar itself are notable examples of such masonry. The staircase of the tower has an arch-shaped vaulted ceiling which is not to be found in pre-Islāmic buildings. The tower has four rectangular openings pierced in its walls to let in light and air.

The Madrasa of Maḥmūd Gāwān

Proceeding about 350 yards from the Chaubāra towards the fort the visitor will notice on the left side of the road a time-worn but magnificent structure styled the Madrasa of Maḥmūd Gāwān. It is not only the most imposing building of the Baihmanī period, but in its plan and in the general style of its architecture it is a unique monument of its kind in India. In the descriptions of the Takht Maḥall and the Rangīn Maḥall it has been already shown that the Persian architects employed by the Baihmanī kings often copied in their Indian work buildings with which they had been associated in their motherland,[3] and the Madrasa is a notable example of that tendency. Maḥmūd Gāwān, the founder of the Madrasa, had himself come from Gīlān, and as even during his stay in the Deccan he was continually in correspondence with eminent personages in Persia, it is not unlikely that he brought engineers and craftsmen from that country to design this building. The plan, however, for such institutions in Islāmic countries had become stereotyped in the beginning of the fourteenth century A.D., if not earlier; for the Madrasas at Marrakesh, Fez, Rabat, and other places in north-west Africa, have almost the same plan, although they do not possess either the stately round minarets which existed here, or such grand entrances as that which once adorned the eastern façade

[1] Simultaneously with the building of the police station, a large clock was installed on the top of the tower, which, although adding to the amenities of the life of the town, looked somewhat incongruous. This has also been removed at the request of the Department.

[2] These steps are 20 in number.

[3] *Supra*, pp. 46 and 70.

of the Madrasa of Bidar. The latter features evidently came into the Deccan from Persia, and a striking resemblance may be noticed between the plan, the architectural style, and the decorative detail of this building and those of the Madrasa of Khargird near Meshhed.[1] The latter was built in A.D. 1444 by order of Abū'l-Muẓaffar Khān son of Shāhrukh Mirzā, and the mosaic workers were two artisans from Shiraz. The Madrasa of Maḥmūd Gāwān was built in A.D. 1472,[2] that is, twenty-eight years after the Madrasa at Khargird, which, according to the authorities who have visited the school, in its palmy days was the finest building of its kind in Khurasan.[3] Another school which enjoyed a high reputation both for the beauty of its architecture and for the high standard of its learning, particularly mathematical studies, was Ulugh Beg's Madrasa at Samarqand built in 828 H. (A.D. 1425). According to Firishta, Maḥmūd Gāwān was a great scholar and 'in Mathematics he had few equals'.[4] That he was familiar with the college of Ulugh Beg at Samarqand is thus extremely likely, and this surmise is strengthened when we learn further that Maḥmūd Gāwān 'remitted annually valuable presents to several learned men in Khorassan',[4] some of whom apparently were on the staff of Ulugh Beg's College. Maḥmūd Gāwān, under the aegis of the Baihmanī kings, who were enthusiastic patrons of learning and architecture, was thus able to found a college at Bidar on the same magnificent lines as its prototypes in Khurasan and other Islāmic countries, and he not only staffed it with eminent divines, philosophers, and scientists, but also equipped it with a library of 3,000 valuable manuscripts.[5]

In 1107 H. (A.D. 1696) the building suffered great damage from lightning which deprived it of half of its front and half of its southern wing,[6] and it deteriorated

[1] Ernst Diez's *Churasanische Baudenkmäler*, Band I, pp. 72–6 and Plate XXXI.

[2] The chronogram which gives the date of the building is as follows:

Text

این مدرسهٔ رفیع و محمود بنا   تعمیر شده است قبلهٔ اهل صفا

آثار قبول بین کہ تاریخش   از آیت <u>ربّنا تقبّل مِنّا</u>

Translation

'This exalted school with a high (lit. praiseworthy) basement,
Has been built as the place of adoration (*qibla*) for the pure-minded.
Look at the signs of its Divine acceptance that its chronogram
(Is contained) in the *Qur'ānic* verse, "Our Lord, accept it from us".'

The numerical value of the verse according to the *Abjad* system gives the date 877 H. corresponding to A.D. 1472.

[3] P. M. Sykes, 'A Fifth Journey', *G.J.L.* xxviii, 1906, p. 581, and Yate's *Khurasan and Sistan*, p. 129.

[4] Briggs, vol. ii, p. 510.

[5] Idem, p. 514.

[6] The words خراب شد according to the *Abjad* system give the year of the incident, but Briggs in a footnote of his English translation of Firishta (vol. ii, p. 510) gives a different version of the havoc caused to the building. He writes:

'After the capture of Bidar by Aurangzeb, in the latter end of the 17th century, this splendid range of buildings was appropriated to the double purpose of a powder magazine and barracks for a body of cavalry, when by accident the powder exploding, destroyed the greater part of the edifice, causing dreadful havoc around.'

further subsequently through neglect and climatic conditions, so that in 1914 when the Archaeological Department took it in charge the building presented a miserable spectacle of decay and vandalism. The inner court was blocked with heaps of debris, the walls were overgrown with rank vegetation, the upper band of the surviving portion of the façade had developed a large crack and threatened to fall any moment, all the roofs leaked, and the land in front of and surrounding the building was littered with piles of filth, since the Madrasa in its ruinous condition had been found by the people of the locality to be a convenient place for dumping all kinds of rubbish.

The building has now been thoroughly cleaned, and an enclosure wall built with a view to stopping the encroachments of undesirable visitors. The roofs have been made water-tight, the gaping cleft in the façade repaired in such a way as to show no signs of patching, the decayed trellis-work of the arches has been appropriately restored, the interiors of the halls and the inner court have been cleared of debris and silt, and the plinth of the building has been fully exposed. Further, a lightning conductor has been fixed to the top of the surviving minaret with a view to protecting it against another stroke of lightning. As the left half of the entrance arch of the southern hall had perished, either in a thunderstorm or in the gunpowder explosion, alluded to above, the masonry of the right half of the arch has been propped up by a massive pier, but as this looks incongruous it has been proposed to the Government that the arch and some of the rooms adjoining it on the left should be restored.

Notwithstanding the extensive decay and destruction of the building it still retains enough of the original architectural features and decorative work to afford some notion of its pristine splendour and beauty. The building has a high basement, but to make the approach convenient two terraces have been built in front of it, each about 4 feet high, the total height of both being 8 feet. The main entrance has vanished, but its floor has been exposed by excavations carried out in recent times and the plan shows that the whole comprised an outer arch 21 feet in span and an inner arch 10 feet 5 inches in span, with a recess 5 feet deep between the two arches which corresponded to the thickness of the walls flanking the entrance on either side. The height up to the apex of the outer arch must have been more or less the same as the average height of the three main arches in the interior of the building, that is some 45 feet from the floor level. Beyond the entrance there was a portico, square in plan at the base, measuring 15 feet 4 inches each way. But as the corners of the square are cut by masonry projections, the plan at the floor level looks almost octagonal (Pl. L). The portico above its roof probably had a dome similar to those above the roofs of the semi-decagonal projections in the northern, western, and southern wings of the building (Pls. LV and LVI). These latter rise to a height of 90 feet approximately from the floor level. From the portico two passages, each 8 feet 8 inches wide, lead to the interior of the building. The roofs of the passages have perished, but the pavements and the remains of walls still exist.

The minaret at the northern end of the façade and the wall adjoining it towards the south are comparatively the best preserved portions of the Madrasa, although their tile-decoration and trellis-work have survived only in fragments. The minaret has an octagonal base, 67 feet 4 inches in girth at the ground level, but as it has a round shape at the point whence it springs, five bands of carved masonry have been built above the octagonal base, these gradually decreasing in dimensions in order to fit in with the circumference of the tower, which is 45 feet immediately above the uppermost band of the basement (Pl. LII). The tower has three storeys, the first and second having balconies which project from the main body of the tower in a curvilinear form but have no brackets to support them such as are generally noticed below the balconies of Indian minarets. The absence of brackets again shows that the architect was a Persian, for the balconies of towers in Persia have a curvilinear form without any struts. The lower part of the Madrasa tower was originally decorated with encaustic tiles arranged in a chevron pattern, the colours being yellow, light green, and white. Owing to rain-water which percolated through fissures in the lime beds into which the tiles were fixed many of them have fallen down, but a considerable number of them are still intact, and these convey a clear idea of the decorative scheme of the tower. For the purpose of variety in each storey at the neck point there was a band of calligraphic devices containing religious texts. These were reproduced in mosaic tiles, the letters being white fixed to a deep blue background, on which some floral designs in green and yellow were also worked out. Above this band immediately below the balcony are horizontal courses of light green tiles, apparently to give the eye some relief after looking at the intricate pattern of the calligraphic motifs. The balconies in their present condition are denuded of any kind of decoration, nor have they any trace of the parapets which originally must have been an attractive feature of the ornamentation of the tower. The height of the tower up to the balcony of the first storey is 78 feet 8 inches.

The tile-work of the second storey of the tower has almost completely perished, and it is difficult to determine the designs of the lower two bands (Pl. LI). The third band probably, like the neck band of the first stage, contained religious texts reproduced in an ornamental style of writing, while the portion immediately below the balcony of this stage would have contained horizontal courses of tiles of a single colour only (green ?). The height of the second balcony from the first is 29 feet, and from the ground level 107 feet 8 inches. The tower has a tapering form, gradually decreasing in girth as it rises.

The third storey of the tower looks still more naked, for its tile-decoration has completely disappeared. The height of the tower from the second balcony to the base of the dome is 12 feet; the latter rises some 8 feet higher still and is crowned with a pinnacle 3 feet high. The total height of the tower is thus 131 feet from the ground level. As regards architectural effect, the top of the tower looks somewhat dumpy, possessing neither the grace of the slender apexes of Turkish minarets nor the picturesqueness of the pillared kiosks of the Mughal *mīnārs* of India.

The wall adjoining the tower towards the south forms the façade of a mosque built in the north-eastern part of the building. This wall extends at present to a length of 59 feet 2 inches from the tower, and has an elevation of 65 feet approximately from the floor of the upper terrace. The architect in order to produce an effect of light and shade in the building has divided the façade into several compartments, two of which have deeply recessed arches with screens of trellis-work at their backs, and the lowest compartment has a series of double windows, the upper row being arch-shaped and the lower rectangular (Pl. LII). The windows of this compartment are also adorned with trellis-work, and when the sunlight is blazing on the exterior of the building the trellis screens fixed in the deep recesses of the arches have a shimmering effect. Sir John Marshall, and following him Mr. Percy Brown, have complained that 'the building does not rely on its composition of lines and forms, or on the variety and distribution of its solids and voids, or play of light and shade, but depends entirely on its surface treatment for the effect for which its walls are specially prepared'.[1] How far this criticism is justified may be judged from the architect's design of the front of the building; by his placing two stately minarets one at each end, the massive bases of which project 22 feet 2 inches from the main line of the façade; by his building a lofty entrance in the middle, the outer arch of which has a deep recess and at the top is crowned with a dome, the outline of the latter in combination with the tapering minarets at the corners presenting an architectural silhouette of no small charm to the eye. Further, the division of the wall into a number of panels with windows of various forms and dimensions, the majority of which are deeply set in the building, offers a play of light and shade. All these features indicate clearly the architect's anxiety to impress the connoisseur by the beauty of architectural form in the component parts of the building, and in no way show that he has tried to attract the attention of the latter simply by decorative work.

Details of the façade include a band of tile-work containing a parapet design showing *kangūras* of a cusped pattern, frequently to be seen on the Muslim buildings of the Deccan.[2] The design is worked out in white, yellow, and blue tiles arranged in an artistic manner. Below this band comes another broader one containing an extract from the *Qur'ān* (ch. xxxix, verses 73–4),[3] written in the *Thulth* style by

[1] *Cambridge History of India*, vol. iii, p. 636, and Percy Brown's *Indian Architecture*, vol. ii, p. 71.

[2] For the various patterns of such *kangūras* see Cousens's *Bījāpūr Architecture*, Plate LX.

[3] The full text of the inscription is as follows:

قال اللّه تعالیٰ. وسیق الذین اتّقوا ربّهم الی الجنّة زمرًا حتی اذا جآؤها و فتحت ابوابها وقال لهم خزنتها سلام علیكم طبتم فادخلوها خالدین. وقالوا الحمد للّه الذی صدقنا وعده و اورثنا الارض نتبوّأ من الجنة حیث نشآء فنعم اجر العاملین. صدق اللّه. كتبه العبد علي الصوفي.

Translation

Thus saith God Most High: 'But those who shall have feared their Lord, shall be conducted by troops towards paradise, until they shall arrive at the same: and the gates thereof shall be ready set open; and the guards thereof shall say unto them, "Peace be on you! ye have been good: wherefore enter ye into paradise, to remain therein for ever." And they shall answer, "Praise be unto God, who hath performed his promise unto us, and hath made us to inherit the earth, that we may dwell in paradise wherever we please!" How excellent is the reward of those who work righteousness!' God's word is true. Written by the servant 'Alī aṣ-Ṣūfī.'

a calligraphist, 'Alī aṣ-Ṣūfī, whose name occurs at the end of the inscription. The writing exhibits art of a high order, and as in tile-decoration the painter and the calligraphist worked out jointly the designs for the craftsman, the services of 'Alī aṣ-Ṣūfī seem to have been specially requisitioned to prepare the decorative schemes of the Madrasa in collaboration with other artists and artisans.

Below the calligraphic band, which is of a rather intricate pattern, there is another comprising little squares arranged in the form of stars. The design is very simple, but at the same time most effective, and shows the ingenuity of the artist in placing it near an elaborate pattern for the purpose of contrast. The tiny squares are shown in white, yellow, light green, light blue, and deep blue, thus producing a kaleidoscopic effect.

Below the three bands of tile-work there is a broad compartment, containing five arches, the spandrels and side-walls of which are again decorated with encaustic tiles, the designs being floral in this place. The decoration has suffered a great deal from moisture and neglect, but the keen eye of the artist can easily follow the patterns on the wall surface. The arches for the sake of variety have been made with different spans, the middle one being the widest, having a span of 9 feet 5 inches with a height of 9 feet 9 inches up to the apex. The span of the next two arches, one on either side of the middle arch, is 7 feet 9 inches and the height up to the apex the same as that of the middle arch. The two rectangular panels, one at each end of this compartment, contain in their upper parts arch-shaped windows of small size. These are filled with trellis-work of elegant design. The masonry immediately below these windows being new it is difficult to determine whether originally there were rectangular windows below the former, such as are to be seen in the corresponding panels of the second compartment (Pl. LII). Behind the arches lies a passage 3 feet deep, the back wall of which has tiny windows filled with lattice-work, affording air and light to the mosque in the interior of the building. The artistic effect of these windows, in both the exterior and the interior of the structure, is unquestionable.[1]

The second or the middle compartment also contains arches, the side-walls and spandrels of which, like those of the top compartment, were adorned with encaustic tiles. The middle arch of this compartment is of the same dimensions as those of the first, but the height of the two side arches, towards the right and left of it, is a little smaller. Further, in the panels near the northern and southern ends of the compartment there are pairs of tiny windows, the top ones being rectangular and the lower arch-shaped. The third compartment, which adjoins the plinth of the building, comprises five rectangular panels which are rather slim in their proportions. The middle one has a small doorway in its lower part and an arch-shaped window above it. The window has a *jālī* screen. The next two panels, one on each side of the middle one, have pairs of windows, the top window being arch-shaped and the lower one rectangular. These windows also are adorned with *jālīs* of delicate patterns. The two extreme panels, one near each end of the compartment, have no opening, and originally they were decorated with encaustic tiles, the traces of which may still be observed on the wall.

[1] Cf. pp. 55–6.

The adornment of the entire façade of the building with tiles, in the arrangement of which the decorators have exhibited a refined taste in the choice of colour and pattern, would indeed have made a grand display, but in the apparent charm of this adornment the art-critic cannot overlook the beauty of line and form, depth and volume, shown in the architectural features of the building.

The interior of the mosque has the plain but lofty style of architecture appropriate to a place of worship. The building comprises a single hall, 49 feet 9 inches in length and 24 feet 10 inches in width. The prayer-niche (*miḥrāb*) is built in the thickness of the western wall in the form of a semi-decagon, while towards the north there is another projection of rectangular design, measuring 19 feet 2 inches by 11 feet 10 inches. This latter projection is separated from the main hall by a massive arch. The ceiling of the mosque is vaulted, divided into three compartments by two stately arches which rise to a height of 33 feet 8 inches from the floor level. The walls and arches of the mosque are very strongly built, having a thickness varying from 4 to 5 feet. The *jālī* screens built at different heights from the floor in the northern and eastern walls of the mosque, admit subdued light to the interior, which adds to the mystic effect proper to a house of God.

Corresponding to the mosque, and adjoining the minaret at the south-eastern angle of the Madrasa, was the library, which has completely perished (Pl. L). But as architects in the East generally design the wings of a building of a uniform plan, it is not unlikely that the plan of the library was a replica of that of the mosque.

By entering the building through the opening where the main gateway once stood, and following either of the two passages to the right and left of the porch, the inner court is reached, which measures 103 feet 2 inches square and has a dodecagonal cistern in the middle. Each side of the latter measures 7 feet in length, the total circumference of the cistern thus being 84 feet. The marginal slabs of this cistern are missing, and its present depth is only 3 feet 1 inch.[1]

As the northern and western wings of the building are in a better state of preservation than those on the corresponding sides, it would be best to begin the description of the different apartments of the Madrasa from its northern wing. At the extreme eastern end of this wing, adjoining the mosque described above, is a square hall with a dome-shaped ceiling which is on a level with the ceilings of the cubicles in the uppermost storey of the building. The hall measures 27 feet 2 inches on each side at the base, but its corners are slightly cut, and further there are projections in the middle of each side, which have given a pleasing design to the floor.[2] The walls are plain, but the series of receding arches built as squinches at the corners of the hall, and the band of niches below the drum of the vault, combined with tracery of an elegant design in the northern projection of the hall, take away any impression of monotony from the building. An opening in the eastern projection originally gave access to the mosque, but it is now blocked. The hall was apparently meant for

1 The water for the cistern was apparently supplied by a subterranean channel from the well in the forecourt of the building.

2 The projections are rectangular in plan, and each of them measures 9 feet 11 inches by 6 feet 3 inches approximately.

the residence of the principal teacher of the Madrasa who would have acted also as *Imām*. At the north-eastern and north-western corners of the hall are doorways leading to small chambers which may have served as storerooms for the occupant of the hall.

Corresponding to this hall there was another in the southern wing of the building which has completely disappeared, but its plan has been determined by the excavations carried out by the Department in recent years (Pl. L). Beyond the latter two halls the plan of the northern and the southern wings of the Madrasa is uniform, comprising a large hall in the middle with pairs of students' rooms built on either side of it (Pls. L and LIV). These rooms rise to three storeys, and the plan of all the rooms is the same, each being divided into three apartments. In the front they have a small veranda with an arched opening towards the court. The dimensions of the arch are considerable, the height up to the apex being 14 feet 2 inches and the span 11 feet 6 inches; but the depth of the veranda is insignificant, being 6 feet 1 inch only. Behind the veranda is a room, measuring 10 feet 8 inches by 7 feet 9 inches. At the back of the latter there is another room, almost square at its base, the dimensions being 10 feet 8 inches by 10 feet 4 inches. The two rooms perhaps provided sleeping accommodation for three students. The back rooms of these apartments have also projections fitted with windows opening on the grounds surrounding the building. These projections are rectangular in plan, their dimensions being 9 feet 7 inches by 5 feet 4 inches. The windows of the projections were originally filled with *jālīs* of elegant design which have recently been restored. The arrangement of the apartments shows that the architect in designing them had taken into consideration the comfort of students in all the seasons of India. The veranda was meant for occupation in the morning and the afternoon, the projection at the back with the *jālī* screen for use at noon, when the glare of the sun becomes intolerable, and the two middle rooms for sleeping in at night. There are thirty-six suites of these rooms in all the three storeys of the building, and according to the estimate made above, if we consider each suite to be intended to provide accommodation for three students, the Madrasa was capable of accommodating 108 students.

Each of the middle halls has a lofty arch opening on the court, the dimensions of which in the northern and southern wings are uniform, and the height up to the apex is 40 feet and the span 26 feet 8 inches (Pls. L and LII–LV). The arch of the western hall is still loftier, measuring 46 feet 3 inches from the floor level. The plan of the middle halls on all three sides is uniform, having a rectangular apartment in the front with a semi-decagonal projection at the back. Each of the front apartments towards the north and south measures 34 feet 3 inches by 26 feet 8 inches, and their semi-decagonal projections have a uniform depth of 16 feet.[1] The ceilings of the front apartments are vaulted, in the form of a barrel, but instead of being round at the top they have the shape of an arch. Originally the ceilings were lavishly decorated with encaustic tiles representing floral designs and Arabic texts, but these have almost completely perished except a few pieces left here and there.

[1] The depth of the projection of the western hall is slightly larger, being 18 feet 7 inches in contrast to the 16 feet of the projection of the northern and southern halls.

The specimens of *Kūfic* writing preserved in these pieces show calligraphic art of a high order.

The semi-decagonal projections are divided from the front apartments by means of arches which have very pleasing proportions, although they are a little smaller in height than the arches in the front, the height of the former being 34 feet in contrast to 40 feet which is the height of the front arches of the hall in the northern and southern wings. The projections had *jālī* screens of elegant patterns in their backs. These had decayed badly owing to climatic conditions and to vandalism, but have been fully restored according to their original design by the Archaeological Department. The halls were apparently used as lectures-rooms like their prototypes in the Madrasas of North African countries.

At the north-west and south-west corners of the building the architect has planned rooms for professors, which are not only comfortable for living in but have pleasing designs. These rooms are built on the ground floor (Pl. L) as well as in the upper storey. The rooms on the ground floor are approached from the court by doors of modest dimensions, opening into a porch which gives access to the central apartment and also contains a staircase leading to the rooms in the upper floor of the building. The plan of the central apartment is almost square at the base, measuring 17 feet 5 inches each way, but the four projections on each of its four sides, and four more at each of its four corners, have given it an octagonal form. The walls of these projections at their tops have formed a ring for the support of the circular ceiling of the central apartment (Pl. L). The ceiling has the shape of a shallow vault. The four projections at the corners are square in plan, measuring 9 to 10 feet on each side, while for light and air they have screens of trellis-work and also traces of shelves for books. The latter were made of wood and have completely perished, their planks having been either destroyed by white ants or pulled out deliberately from the wall by vandals. The projections on the four sides of the central apartment are also square in plan, although a little smaller in dimensions than the corner ones. The rooms remain cool in summer and warm in winter, and each suite would have offered accommodation to a professor with one or two of his junior colleagues, or some of the advanced students. The six suites of these corner rooms would have accommodated twelve, if not more, members of the teaching staff.

The semi-decagonal projections of the middle halls of the Madrasa have vaulted ceilings; but the vaults, although visible above the roof, have more imposing domes built over them. The latter rise from octagonal bases and their height on an average is 36 feet 6 inches from the level of the roof and 86 feet from the floor of the Madrasa. The domes make a pleasing feature in the contour of the building, for the long stretches of walls though crowned with parapets and pierced by *jālī* screens, would have looked monotonous without them (Pl. LVI). The base of the dome above the northern projection has a girth of 80 feet at the roof level, and a height of 20 feet 6 inches up to the springing-point of the dome. The latter itself at this point has a circumference of 72 feet, thus a masonry band of 4 feet is left all round to take the thrust. The base of the dome for further security is embedded some 6 feet in the thickness of the roof.

The architect has built a platform all round to make the structure still more secure, and in consideration of the height of the walls, which rise 56 feet approximately up to the parapet, has given a batter to them which is quite apparent in the northern and southern walls (Pl. LVI). Further, he has strengthened the corners of the building by short but massive buttresses which do not offend the eye. The minarets in the front and the semi-decagonal projections crowned with domes, in the middle of the walls, also serve the same purpose, but at the same time, as we stated above, they add to the stately appearance of the building. The exterior of the Madrasa has a sombre look towards the north, south, and west, on account of its weather-stained walls, but as they were originally ornamented with bands of mosaic tiles and panels of delicate tracery, the artistic effect would have been quite different at that time.

The walls of the Madrasa measure externally 242 feet from east to west and 220 feet from north to south. They are built of rough-tooled trap masonry, which has been covered with plaster and emblazoned with tiles.

Mint (?)

To the south of the Madrasa is a small dome called the Mint (*Taksāl*). The dimensions of the structure are insignificant, measuring 13 feet on each side at the base internally. The walls of the building rise 12 feet from the ground level and are crowned by an elliptical dome. It has a circumference of 45 feet and a height of 7 feet above the walls. This small building may have been used for stamping coins which would have been minted in a larger structure situated adjacent to it. But no trace of a large building which can be identified as having been a mint is to be found in the vicinity.

Takht-i-Kirmānī

At a short distance from the Madrasa, proceeding towards the fort, is a gateway built along the northern side of the main road (Pl. LXV). At present it has a hall at its back, but originally it may have been connected with other apartments occupied by Ḥaḍrat Khalīl-Ullāh and his descendants, who migrated to Bidar from Kirmān at the invitation of Aḥmad Shāh al-Walī in 834 H. (A.D. 1431).[1] The building is now called the Takht-i-Kirmānī (Throne of Kirmān) on account of its containing a couch associated with the saint Khalīl-Ullāh.

The gateway possesses certain features of the Baihmanī architecture, although its plaster decoration may strike one at first sight as being comparatively modern. The medallions and other motifs represented in the latter, however, on close study prove the building to be of the Baihmanī period. The gateway has a large arch in the middle, rising 22 feet 6 inches from the threshold and having a span of 14 feet 9 inches. The facets of the columns supporting the arch-head have given them a cluster-like effect, the device being apparently copied from the carving of the stone columns of the medieval Hindu temples of the Deccan. The string of *rudraksha* beads carved on the border of the arch-head is another Hindu decorative motif, but

[1] Briggs, vol. ii, pp. 419–20.

such devices are frequently to be observed on the early Muslim buildings of the Deccan, for the masons employed were generally Hindu, and although Muslim architects designed the main features of the building, the detail was often filled in by the Hindu craftsmen. The spandrels of the arch are, however, adorned with medallions and floral patterns of Muslim design. The medallions represent religious texts arranged in the *Ṭughra* style.

The main arch has four smaller arches, built in its sides, the latter being arranged in two rows, one above the other. The recessed façades of these arches have a pleasing effect. At the back of the smaller arches are niches, of which those in the lower row may have been occupied by the guards of the house or by occasional wayfarers. The niches in the upper row are ornamental, for they are not accessible from any apartment of the building. They may, however, have been used for flower vases and other similar articles on festive occasions.

Above the arches the gateway has two bands of ornamental plaster-work and on the top a parapet of trefoil design (Pl. LXV). At each end of the parapet is a miniature column lavishly adorned with niches on all four sides and crowned with an orb which springs from lotus leaves. The diminutive columns in this style and the parapet of trefoil pattern both came into fashion during the Baihmanī period, and some fine specimens of them may be noticed on the tombs of this dynasty at Āshṭūr.[1]

The threshold of the building comprises a sort of landing in the middle of the steps which lead from the road to the hall.[2] This landing is arranged in the recess of the main arch, the back wall of which is decorated with niches and the effigies of two tigers.[3] The door of the hall is in the pillar-and-lintel style, and is fitted with wooden shutters of a plain design which may not be very old.

The hall measures 30 feet 7 inches by 35 feet 7 inches, and is divided into three apartments by arches which are built across both its length and its breadth. The span of the arches built in the length of the hall is 10 feet, in contrast to the 8 feet 5 inches of the arches built across its width. The height of both is uniform, that is 11 feet 10 inches from the floor to the apex. The arches rise from low masonry columns and support a flat ceiling.

In the middle of the hall is a platform of wood on which a couch is placed. The platform is 6 feet 9 inches wide, 8 feet 9 inches long, and 1 foot 5 inches high, being supported by round feet. The couch has a wooden frame, and the seat is to-day

[1] *Vide* Plates LXIX, LXXVII, and LXXXVI. The parapet of the trefoil pattern still remained in vogue during the rule of Barīdī kings and it is frequently to be seen on their tombs. See Plates XC, XCII, CI, CVIII, CX, and CXIII.

[2] The threshold is approached by three steps from the road; and four more steps from the former lead to the interior of the building.

[3] The effigies of tigers are a common feature of the gateways of forts in the Deccan. They are emblematic of power and majesty and also have some connexion with the lion-headed representation of Vishnu, styled Narasiṁha. In Persian heraldry a lion is the representation of 'Alī, the son-in-law of the Prophet Muḥammad, who gained the title of Asadullāh, 'the lion of God', on account of his extraordinary valour. The fondness of the sculptors and the masons of the Deccan for this device is apparently due to these various traditions.

made of woven cotton tape. The dimensions of the couch are: length 6 feet, width 4 feet, and height 1 foot 10 inches; but the back of the couch rises 2 feet 9 inches above the seat level, and it has a length of 4 feet 8 inches. The woodwork of the couch is elegantly carved and gilded in Persian style. The couch has also a canopy of cloth above it which is supported by poles fixed into the platform. This relic, on account of its association with the saint Khalīl-Ullāh, is held in great reverence by the people of Bidar, who assemble to see it in large numbers during the month of Muḥarram.[1]

Manhīyār Ta'līm or the Bangle-seller's School

The four schools for physical training in the four principal divisions of the town have already been mentioned in Chapter II (*supra*, p. 20, n. 2), and here a description of the building in which the Bangle-seller's school is located will be given. The gateway and the enclosure wall of the school have suffered considerably, partly owing to the change in the policy of Government regarding the maintenance of these institutions, but mainly on account of lack of interest of the people of the town in learning old military exercises, such as fencing, cudgelling (*paṭa*), and wrestling.

The only architectural feature of the gateway to attract the attention of the visitor is the incongruity of its pillars, which do not seem to be in their original place and may have been brought from some other building after the decay of the latter. On entering through the gateway the principal building within the enclosure is an 'Āshūr Khāna,[2] which comprises a single hall with three arched openings in the front and a small room for storing relics at the back. The hall measures 19 feet 3 inches by 10 feet 6 inches. The pillars of the hall also seem to have been brought from some other old building.

[1] Between the Madrasa and the Takht-i-Kirmānī there are remains of two old buildings, the first being an arch which, although at present not connected with any building, bears an inscription of the Mughal period showing that the house to which the arch was originally attached belonged to Sayyid Murtaḍa, a descendant of the famous Muslim saint, Makhdūm-i-Jahānīyān Jahān-Gasht. The text of the inscription has been deciphered as follows:

Text

(۱) باني• اين عتبۂ عالي مكان   سيد مرتضی ابن سيد ميران

(۲) بحضرت مخدوم جهانيان نسلش   چون خطابست جهان گشت زمان

في سنہ ۱۱۱۸ هجري نبوي صورت اتمام يافت.

Translation

Verse

(1) The builder of this lofty gate is Sayyid Murtaḍā, the son of Sayyid Mīrān.

(2) His genealogy is connected with Makhdūm-i-Jahānīyān whose title is Jahān-Gasht.

Prose

In the year 1118 H. from the 'flight' of the Prophet (A.D. 1706) it was completed.

The other building is now the official residence of the Ta'alluqdār of Bidar, and as such has entirely changed its old features. In this building Nawāb Nāṣir-ud-Daula Bahādur, the fourth Niẓām (A.D. 1829–57), was born, and his father Nawāb Sikandar Jāh lived in it for three years.

[2] 'Āshūr Khāna, a building wherein religious ceremonies of the Shī'ite faith are performed during the month of Muḥarram. In the 'Āshūr Khāna religious flags ('*alams*) and other relics are also housed and displayed.

In the court of the 'Āshūr Khāna there is another hall which has no roof, being quite modern. According to local tradition the four schools (Ta'līm Khānas) were also called Tahdīd Khānas (Punishment Houses), since culprits, by the orders of the king, or the governor, received punishment under the surveillance of the staff of these institutions.

The Jāmi' Masjid

Retracing our footsteps to the Chaubāra and proceeding towards the Fatḥ Darwāza, the Jāmi' Masjid, or the Assembly Mosque of the town, is approached. It is situated on the west side of the road, being enclosed by a modern wall with a gate in the front. The visitor has to ascend four steps in order to reach the inner court, a plan of which is given in Plate LVIII.

The courtyard has a path in the middle with a pair of flower-beds on either side of it and another pair near the water cistern, which is close to the northern end of the court.[1] The dimensions of the entire court are 144 feet 4 inches from north to south and 141 feet 8 inches from east to west. At the head of the court is a pavement two steps higher than the court itself and having a depth of 41 feet 3 inches. Votaries can approach the cistern for ablutions from the pavement as well as from the court side. The cistern has a masonry margin 3 feet 4 inches wide all round, and in the middle, the area which is filled with water measures 30 feet 8 inches by 28 feet.

The prayer-hall has an imposing façade towards the court, being divided into seven arches, the middle one of which is slightly larger in dimensions than those on each side (Pl. LIX). The span of the middle arch is 17 feet in contrast to the 16 feet 2 inches of the others, and its height up to the apex is 18 feet 9 inches as opposed to the 18 feet 2 inches of the latter. The arch-heads rest on low but massive columns and support the ceiling, which is divided into twenty-one vaults. The prayer-hall contains several rows of arches across both its length and its breadth, and comprises three apartments from east to west and seven from north to south. The architectural effect of the interior of the building on account of the rows of arches and the squinches, which support the vaults of the ceilings, is extremely pleasing to the eye (Pl. LX). The hall has no decorative features, but the arrangement of the arches and their fine proportions have given the building a certain elegance in spite of its plain style. The hall has a length of 144 feet with a depth of 65 feet.

The *miḥrāb* as usual projects from the hall and has a pentagonal plan at the base. The apartment of the prayer-hall, adjoining the *miḥrāb*, whence the Imām conducts the service and recites the holy texts, has a domed ceiling of considerable height, in the style of the lantern-shaped vaults of the *Jāmi' al-Zaitūna* at Tunis and of several other early mosques in North Africa. But the dome-shaped ceiling at Bidar has another dome over it, which springs from an octagonal base built on the roof of the building. Each side of the base measures 12 feet in length; thus the total girth of the base is 84 feet, and its walls rise to a height of 10 feet 6 inches above the roof. The dome itself has a circumference of 76 feet at its springing-point on the top of the base, and rises 19 feet above that. The height of the dome including its finial

[1] The flower-beds are in a ruinous condition, and they can now be traced only by the marginal stones which still remain in a few places.

is 32 feet 9 inches from the level of the roof and 66 feet from the floor of the prayer-hall.[1] The object of building a high-vaulted ceiling for the apartment adjoining the *miḥrāb* was to produce an impressive resounding effect for the chantings of the *Qur'ān* by the Imām, perhaps the same aim as that kept in view in building the high-vaulted roofs of cathedrals in Europe so as to fill the hall with the echoes of organ music and the recital of sacred hymns.

The front wall of the prayer-hall has a parapet of trefoil pattern at its top which is interspersed with tiny minarets (Pl. LX). The shape of the latter has been considerably changed during modern repairs. The chain and pendant device which is a prominent decorative design of Barīdī architecture may also be noticed in the spandrels of the arches of the front wall. This device may have been added in the repair or restoration of the building carried out during the rule of the Barīdī kings, but from the shape of its main dome and the style of its arches it can probably be assigned to the Baihmanī period. Its general appearance, however, shows it to be of a much later date than the Baihmanī mosque in the fort (Pl. XVII).

Ta'līm Pansāl

Proceeding towards the Fatḥ Darwāza by the main road, the premises of another old school for physical training may be visited. It is called the Pansāl Ta'līm or Water-miller's school.[2] The various apartments and buildings connected with this institution possess no architectural importance. They, however, comprise an 'Āshūr Khāna, a mosque, and a tomb. The 'Āshūr Khāna consists of a single hall with a screen of wooden arches in its front. The mosque also is a small structure, comprising a prayer-hall and a court in front of it. The prayer-hall has three arches opening on the court. A veranda has recently been built in front of the hall to protect votaries from the heat and glare of the sun.

The tomb consists of a single chamber with an arched opening towards the east. The proportions of the latter are somewhat squat and clumsy. The chamber contains the grave of Ustād Yār Muḥammad, who was at one time in charge of the school. On the façade of the building an inscription has been set up recently.

Khāṣṣ Maḥall, 'Alī Bāgh and Chīta Khāna

These buildings are situated on the road which starts from the Chaubāra and runs almost parallel to the main thoroughfare of Bidar towards the Shāh Ganj Darwāza. Of the Khāṣṣ Maḥall now only an enclosure wall and some chambers with arched openings are left. The latter were utilized, until quite recently, as the quarters and stables of the police *sawārs*,[3] but now they are being used as the hostel of the Art and Crafts School, Bidar. The arches of this building have a very wide span in relation to the height, and thus do not show a happy sense of proportion.

The site of the 'Alī Bāgh is now occupied by the High School, the rooms of which have recently been built round the old reservoir of the garden, which at present measures 82 feet 10 inches square and has a depth of 5 feet 4 inches.

Beyond the 'Alī Bāgh towards the north is the Chīta Khāna or the Leopard's

[1] The finial is 3 feet 3 inches high. [2] *Supra*, p. 20, f.n. 2. [3] Mounted police-guards.

House. Judging from the style of the building this cannot be its original name, and may have been given to it at a time when under the orders of some whimsical king or governor of Bidar the building may have been utilized for housing the leopards tamed by him for hunting deer.[1]

The building has a high plinth, being constructed on a platform 5 feet 11 inches in height. The black stone pillars fixed at the south-east and south-west corners of the plinth of the platform are carved in the style of the stone margins of the arches of 'Alā-ud-Dīn Baihmanī's tomb at Āsh̲ṭūr (*infra*, p. 130). The platform has a flight of steps which are built along its western side. The upper dimensions of the platform are: length, east to west, 62 feet 11 inches, and width, north to south, 43 feet. It has a cistern in the middle which is square in plan, measuring 27 feet 9 inches on each side. The present depth of the cistern is 4 feet 7 inches, and the water was apparently supplied to it from the well situated towards the west.

At the northern end of the platform was a colonnade which has completely disappeared now, except for the traces of some arch-heads the stone margins of which are carved in the Baihmanī style. Adjoining the colonnade towards the north were some apartments, which are more or less intact, although on account of the housing of the Art and Crafts School therein, some modern features, such as doors and partition walls, now spoil their original appearance. The present plan of these apartments comprises a hall in the middle with two rooms, one on each side of the latter towards the east and west. The middle hall measures 32 feet 9 inches in length and 13 feet 3 inches in width, and has a vaulted ceiling which is divided into three compartments by the arches built across the width of the hall. The two side-rooms are of uniform dimensions, being square in plan and measuring 13 feet 11 inches on each side.

Below the platform there are cells which may have been utilized for the accommodation of servants or for storing goods. These cells, however, indicate no plan which would support the view that they were designed for housing leopards originally.

Ta'līm Ṣiddīq Sh̲āh

Close to the Kh̲āṣṣ Maḥall are the Physical School and the Tomb of Ṣiddīq Sh̲āh, neither of which has any pretension to architectural merit. On the contrary the latter has quite a modern appearance, comprising a pavilion with an arcade on all four sides. The middle arches of the pavilion are cusped, a feature which is noticeable in the buildings of Bidar after its occupation by the Mug̲h̲als in A.D. 1656.[2] The apartment containing the grave of Ṣiddīq Sh̲āh has four turrets of fancy design on its roof. The tomb is built of laterite masonry.

To the north-east of the tomb is an 'Āsh̲ūr Kh̲āna and in front of it an *alāvā*. The *alāvā* is built almost in the middle of the road. It consists of a pit where fire and incense are kept burning during the first ten days of the month of Muḥarram. As far as their origin is concerned such pits may remind one of the fire-temples of Iran, but in India they are associated with 'Āsh̲ūr Kh̲ānas, where, as explained above,[3]

[1] Leopards are still trained and kept for hunting purposes by some of the Indian chiefs.

[2] *Supra*, p. 15.

[3] *Supra*, p. 102, n. 2.

the religious banners and other relics sacred to the S͟hīʿas are exhibited. As regards the derivation of the word *alāvā* (الاوا) it may be connected with the Hindī word *alāo*, meaning a fire heap.

Close by is the Taʿlīm of Ṣiddīq S͟hāh which has almost the same plan as the other physical training schools, i.e. it comprises an open court and an ʿĀs͟hūr K͟hāna. The latter is built along the northern wall of the school and consists of a hall with a room at its back. The front of the hall has three arched openings.

K͟hānqāh of Ḥaḍrat Nūr Samnānī

He was one of those holy men whom the religious inclinations of the Baihmanī kings attracted to Bidar where they settled down and ultimately passed away; but their memory is still sacred to the inhabitants of the place.[1] The K͟hānqāh has within its enclosure a hall for the accommodation of the disciples who assembled to learn the teachings of the S͟haik͟h or his *sajjādās* (successors), and a mosque wherein they prayed. The latter comprises a room, measuring 22 feet 3 inches from north to south and 19 feet from east to west. The room has three arches in its eastern side, the middle one of which is much larger in dimensions than those on each side, which look very small in comparison with it. The dimensions of the middle arch are: span 10 feet 8 inches and height up to the apex 10 feet 2 inches.[2]

The hall of the K͟hānqāh has a cell at its back, perhaps for the meditation of the S͟haik͟h. The hall itself measures 33 feet 6 inches by 15 feet 3 inches, and has three arched openings towards the east. The ceiling is divided into three compartments

[1] The tomb of S͟haik͟h Nūr Samnānī is described in the sequel (*v. infra*, pp. 191–2).

[2] The mosque has the following inscriptions:

I

Text

باني• اين مسجد ردون وقار　　　خاص خدا است ميان يادگار

از پے• تاريخ بنايش نوشت　　　مسجد عاوي بناه نامدار

۱۰۷۲ هـ

Translation

(1) The builder of this heavenly mosque is the chosen one of God, Miyān Yādgàr.

(2) For the date of the building (the poet) composed this chronogram: 'The ʿAlavī mosque is a well-known building.' 1072 H. (A.D. 1662).

The hemistich, however, gives the date 572, and there remains a deficiency of 500 years which it is not clear how the poet has made up.

II

Text

شکر حق تا مسجدی شد جانفزای دل پسند　　　ذبح نفس خویش کرده دل بحق باید دهند

سجده کاصلش ریختن (با ؟) بار سر گردد یقین　　　در عبادت با اطاعت ترك خود باید کنند

Translation

(1) Thanks to God, that a soul expanding and heart cherishing mosque has been built: the votaries should sacrifice their (lower) self and offer their heart to God.

(2) Real 'prostration' means throwing down the burden of conceit: in prayer based on (genuine) devotion they should forsake self.

each having a vault. The spandrels of the arches on the external side are adorned with plaster-work. The plinth of the hall is 3 feet 2 inches above the small court in front of it.

The Tomb of Ḥaḍrat Multānī Pād<u>sh</u>āh

The tomb is situated in the north-west corner of the town and may be approached either by the road which turns towards the north at a short distance from the <u>Kh</u>āṣṣ Maḥall group of monuments, or by the road which starts from the Club Bungalow and runs parallel to the southern glacis of the fort. The full name of Ḥaḍrat Multānī Pād<u>sh</u>āh is Abu'l-Fatḥ <u>Sh</u>ams-ud-Dīn Muḥammad al-Qādirī, and he was born in 862 H. (A.D. 1458), and died on the 1st of <u>Sh</u>awwāl, 935 H. (8th June, A.D. 1529). He is one of the most popular saints of Bidar, and his tomb is still visited by a large number of votaries daily. The title al-Qādirī is attached to his name because he belonged to the order of saints established by <u>Sh</u>ai<u>kh</u> ʿAbdu'l-Qādir Gīlānī.[1] The name Multānī he evidently got from his father, Ḥaḍrat <u>Sh</u>ai<u>kh</u> Ibrāhīm, who was a native of Multan and migrated to Bidar some time during the reign of ʿAlā-ud-Dīn Aḥmad Baihmanī (A.D. 1436–58), if not earlier. The son Muḥammad was probably born at Bidar.

The tomb has a large enclosure, and is approached from the main street by a lofty arch whence a branch road leads to the gateway of the tomb.[2] The gateway has an arch at each end towards the north and south and also a pair of rooms, built on either side of the passage. The latter are occupied by watchmen and drummers in the service of the shrine and also by dervishes visiting the tomb. Beyond the gateway a paved walk first passes through a large cemetery containing the graves of the followers of the saint. Several of these graves bear inscriptions, which may interest those who are fond of studying chronograms.[3]

[1] For ʿAbdu'l-Qādir Gīlānī see *Encyclopaedia of Islam*, vol. i, pp. 41–2.

[2] There is a cistern in front of the gateway of the shrine. To the left of the gateway there is also a mosque which has only one arched opening towards the east. It is, however, wide enough (12 feet 3 inches) considering the modest dimensions of the prayer-room which measures only 17 feet 3 inches by 13 feet. The arch springs from low masonry pillars, the height of which is not as much as 3 feet. On the right of the prayer-room is a chamber, intended either for storing the carpets and religious books of the mosque or for the dwelling of the *Imām*.

[3] One of these inscriptions is carved on a tomb built to the right of the passage, almost midway between the main entrance and the sepulchral chamber of the shrine. The inscription consists of two lines of Persian verse and reads thus:

Text

رخت بربست زین جهان دني   آن ولي زمانه آل نبي

سال تاريخش از خرد جستم   گفت اندر بهشت سيد ولي

١٠٨٢

Translation

'From this low world packed up his chattel,
The saint of the world, an offspring of the Prophet.
I inquired of Wisdom the chronogram of his demise,
It communicated, "*Sayyid Walī is in Heaven*".'

(*continued on p. 108*)

The tomb of the saint is built on a platform which has a plinth, 3 feet 2 inches high. The tomb has been repaired on an extensive scale several times, as the result of which much of its original character has been lost. The latest repairs were carried out in 1343 H. (A.D. 1923), and the visitor will notice tile and marble decorations in the front of the building which have marred the simple dignity of the original tomb. The sepulchral chamber measures 18 feet square inside and 25 feet 4 inches externally. There is a corridor 6 feet 6 inches deep all round the sepulchral chamber. In the plinth of the platform towards the west an incribed tablet is fixed which contains the chronogram of S͟hāh Isḥāq's death. S͟hāh Isḥāq was one of the five sons

(*continued from p. 107*)

The phrase اندر بهشت سيد ولي gives the date 1082 H. (A.D. 1671) which falls in Aurangzeb's reign (A.D. 1659–1707). The style of writing is *Nastaʿlīq* of the Mug͟hal period.

Almost opposite Sayyid Walī's tomb, on the other side of the passage (towards the west), is the tomb of Mukkā Bī, which has an inscription recording an endowment for the maintenance of the tomb. The style of writing as well as the language of the inscription is crude, and as it is dated 1258 H., it shows that public taste in literary matters at that time was at a very low level.

Text

. . . . . . مصطفیٰ . . . . . . محمد . . . . . . صلی

محي الدين جيلاني قادري ۱۲۵۸ . . . . . مكّا بي	لا الٰه الّا اللّه محمّد رسول اللّه مكّا بي زاهد كنيزك قطب محمد ملتاني قادري	دو حسين ۸۱۲

و يك چاه عالمگيري و ده چاه شيخ باوي خريدي خود بہ نان و حلواوات و قرآن خوان و روغن درگاه با ديها و زمين و انبہ وغيره زير مقبره مكّا بي وقف نمودم آنكہ طمع نمايد فردا از ديدار خدا و شفاعت رسول محروم . . . . .

پياسيكو تو پاني كيا لي بهوكيا ونت روٹي

بسم اللّہ الرحمٰن الرحيم

چوري گر كردي مكّا بي ناك كٹي يا چوٹي

Translation

. . . . . . the Chosen, Muḥammad . . . . bless . . . . .

There is no god but God and Muḥammad is the Prophet of God.

Mukkā Bī, the pious slave of Quṭb Muḥammad Multānī Qādirī.

Enclosed (right). Muḥī'u-'d-Dīn Jīlanī Qādirī. 1258 H. Mukkā Bī.

Enclosed (left). Ḥusain. 812.

'And one well built by ʿĀlamgīr (or during ʿĀlamgīr's reign) and ten wells of S͟haik͟h Bāwī, purchased by me (are an endowment for the distribution of) bread and sweets, for the fees of the *Qur'ān* reciters, and for the expenses of oil (for the lamps of the *dargāh*). I also dedicate the villages, lands, mango-trees, etc., attached to the tomb of Mukkā Bī. Whoever shows avarice in respect of this endowment may he be deprived to-morrow (the Day of Judgment) of the Divine vision and the intercession of the Prophet!

In the name of God the most Merciful and Compassionate.

Verse

'The thirsty may drink the water and the hungry enjoy the bread, but if thou committest a theft it is tantamount to thy cutting the nose or the tresses of Mukkā Bī.'

Vide *Epig. Ind. Mosl.*, 1927–8, p. 23, Pl. XXI.

of Ḥaḍrat Multānī Pād<u>sh</u>āh, and according to the chronogram he died in 887 H. (A.D. 1482). The letters of the inscription are much worn, but the few words which can be made out are as follows:

Text

گفتم یا حسین تاریخ . . . . . خان گو

گفت تاریخ . . . اسحاق . . . علم از هند رفت

۸۸۷ هـ

Translation

I asked Ḥusain to compose the chronogram of . . . .
He said, 'The chronogram of Isḥāq's death may be found in *Knowledge departed from India.*'
887 H. (A.D. 1482).[1]

There is also a mosque close by to the north of the shrine which comprises a double hall, measuring 26 feet 10 inches by 26 feet 2 inches over both parts. The arches of the hall show a marked stilt at their apex.[2] An enclosure attached to the mosque towards the south contains the tomb of Ḥaḍrat Ibrāhīm Multānī, the father of the saint.

<u>Kh</u>ānqāh of Ḥaḍrat <u>Sh</u>āh Abū'l-Faiḍ

Bidar has several monasteries wherein the descendants of the saints who exercised considerable influence on the kings of Bidar still reside, and are supposed to impart religious teaching according to the doctrine of the special order of dervishes to which they belong. Among these the monastery of Ḥaḍrat Abū'l-Faiḍ is the most important. It is situated on the right side of the road when proceeding from the <u>Ch</u>aubāra to the Mangalpeṭ Darwāza.

The saint, who was born in 811 H. (A.D. 1408) and passed away in 879 H. (A.D. 1474), was a contemporary of Aḥmad <u>Sh</u>āh al-Walī, 'Alā-ud-Dīn Aḥmad, Humāyūn, and Niẓām <u>Sh</u>āh Baihmanī. These kings had great respect for the saint, and there are *sanads* in the possession of the present *sajjāda* which show that he was addressed by them in terms of the highest reverence.[3]

The monastery has a large enclosure, the eastern, western, and southern walls of which are old. The approach is through an arched gateway. The posts and the arch-head of the gateway are of polished black stone and carved in the Baihmanī style. The main building within the enclosure comprises a hall with some rooms attached to it. The style of the hall and the rooms has been altered considerably during the repairs carried out from time to time at the instance of the *sajjādas* according to their tastes and requirements. In the monastery are some *sanads* and also a few relics, the most important among the latter being the tunic of Ḥaḍrat

[1] *Epig. Ind. Mosl.*, 1927–8, p. 22, Pl. IX *b*.

[2] Close to the shrine of Multānī Pād<u>sh</u>āh are the Ṣūfīya School, Ṣūfīya Mosque, and Ṣūfīya Arch; although none of them possesses any special architectural beauty, yet these buildings are reminiscent of the time when Bidar was a great centre of religious learning.

[3] In a *sanad* he is addressed as follows:

سیادت و نقابت دستگاه هدایت و نجابت انتباه مرتضی ممالك اسلام مقتدی طوایف انام افتخار آل طٰه و یٰسین قدوة اولاد سید المرسلین شمس فلك سیادت و هدایت اشرف العباد . . . . . .

Farīd-ud-Dīn Shakar Ganj and the cap of Ḥaḍrat Banda Nawāz Gesū-darāz which the *sajjāda* puts on when he is installed on the carpet of his predecessor.[1]

The Ta'līm of Nūr Khān or the Physical Training School of Nūr Khān

It is situated close to the Mangalpeṭ Darwāza and has more or less the same plan as the other three schools,[2] that is, it comprises an open court with an 'Āshūr Khāna and a mosque built therein. Both the buildings are small, the mosque being made up of a prayer-hall with a court in front of it.[3] The 'Āshūr Khāna consists of two apartments which measure jointly 26 feet 5 inches in length and 22 feet in width. There are three arched openings in each apartment, the openings being of small dimensions.

The Khānqāh of Shāh Walī-Ullāh al-Ḥusainī

From the Chaubāra-Mangalpeṭ road a street branches towards the north, almost opposite the Khānqāh of Shāh Abū'l-Faiḍ, and after proceeding a few steps in that street the Khānqāh of Shāh Walī-Ullāh is reached.[4] The main building in the monastery comprises a spacious hall which is divided into two aisles in its depth. The hall has three arched openings towards the court. The arches of the openings are rather wide in relation to their height; the span of the arches is 10 feet 11 inches and their height up to the apex 12 feet 6 inches. The arch-heads are supported by masonry pillars, which although quite massive, rise only 4 feet 6 inches above the floor. The architectural effect of the building is therefore somewhat heavy.

The main hall has rooms built in its sides towards the east and west, and also a small room in its back which is technically styled the *Shāh-nishīn*, or the room for the retirement of the saint. At present heirlooms of the family are kept therein, which comprise some beads reported to have belonged originally to Ḥaḍrat 'Alī, the son-in-law of the Prophet Muḥammad, a manuscript of the *Qur'ān* in *Kufic* characters, and some old apparel of the saints of the family.

Towards the east of this Khānqāh is a small dome which is now enclosed in the *zenana* part of the residence of the *sajjāda*. The dome has also an independent approach through an arch of massive proportions.

The Monastery of Shāh 'Alī Ḥusain Quṭb II

The building is in a decayed condition, but may be visited from the Khānqāh of Shāh Walī-Ullāh Ḥusainī, since it is situated close to the latter. It has an enclosure built of trap masonry with an arched gateway towards the street. The roof and the walls of the main hall of the monastery have fallen down, but a colonnade along its western wall is still intact.

The gateway has a parapet of the trefoil design of the later Baihmanī or Barīdī

[1] The tomb of Ḥaḍrat Shāh Abū'l-Faiḍ is situated outside the Mangalpeṭ Darwāza, half a mile to the south of the latter. It is described in the sequel (pp. 184–7).

[2] *Supra*, p. 104.

[3] The prayer-hall is 21 feet 10 inches in length and 13 feet 6 inches in breadth.

[4] The tomb of Walī-Ullāh al-Ḥusainī is situated to the west of the Mausoleum of Khān Jahān Barīd and described elsewhere in this book (*infra*, p. 170). He was a descendant of Shāh Abū'l-Faiḍ and the son-in-law of the Bijāpur governor, Sīdī Marjān.

style, and its façade is further decorated with plaster-work which may also be assigned to the same period (sixteenth century A.D.).

The Great Monastery of Maḥbūb Subḥānī

Maḥbūb Subḥānī, meaning the chosen one of the Holy God, is the epithet applied to Ḥaḍrat Shaikh ʻAbdu'l-Qādir Gīlānī by the devotees of his order. Bidar, it appears, was at one time a great centre for the teaching of the Qādirīya school of Islāmic doctrine, since there are several monasteries of the votaries of this order in the town. The Great Monastery or the Baṛī Khānqāh, as it is called, may be approached either from the road which branches from the Madrasa–Fort main road towards the east,[1] or from the lane close to the monasteries of Shāh ʻAlī Ḥusain and Shāh Walī-Ullāh.

The monastery has several buildings inside its enclosure, among which a mosque is interesting because its parapet consists of overlapping arches, a pleasing feature of the Baihmanī style. The turrets are slender and crowned with orbs, but they seem to have been built at a later period, perhaps during some repair of the mosque. The prayer-hall has three arched openings towards the east which are of uniform dimensions, the span of their arches being 7 feet 4 inches and the height up to the apex 10 feet 7 inches. The prayer-hall measures 28 feet 11 inches in length and 18 feet 9 inches in depth, and has a vaulted ceiling divided into three compartments.

The Small Monastery of Maḥbūb Subḥānī

This monastery, styled the Chhoṭī Khānqāh, is situated in the same locality in which the Baṛī Khānqāh is found, the distance between the two being some 100 yards. The Chhoṭī Khānqāh has an inscription on its gate which mentions the name of its builder as Fīroz Khān.[2] There is another inscription on the mosque within the

[1] The distance from the Madrasa is about 200 yards.

[2] The inscribed tablet is fixed over the doorway of the *Khānqāh* and measures 2 feet 8 inches by 2 feet. The inscription consists of two Persian couplets and the chronogram, which is also in verse. The couplets are written in *Naskh* characters while the chronogram is in *Nastaʻlīq*.

Text

قال غوث الاعظم

با ما دو سه دل مباش دل يكدله كن   وز هر چه كه غير باشد آنرا يله كن

يك صبح باخلاص بيا بر در من   گر كار تو بر نيايد آنگه گله كن

چو تاريخ دهليز قدسي مكان   بخواهي بنا دان بفيروز خان

Translation

The great saint (lit. the great refuge) has said,

Couplets

(1) 'In our company thou shouldst not be double or triple-minded but be single-minded, and free thy heart from that which is not-God;

(2) Come one morning in a sincere mood to my door, and if thy craving be not fulfilled, then thou shouldst complain.'

Chronogram

If thou wantst the date of this sacred threshold, (know it from the phrase) '*Built by Fīroz Khān*'. The numerical value of this phrase according to the *Abjad* system gives the date 1054 H. (A.D. 1644–5).

monastery enclosure which contains the date 1069 H. (A.D. 1659) and the name Aḥmad Khān Kheshgī.[1] Bidar was annexed to the Mughal empire in A.D. 1656, and as the Kheshgī Afghans played an important role in the army of the kings of this dynasty, it appears that Aḥmad Khān Kheshgī was one of the officers who were left by Aurangzeb at Bidar after his conquest of the town.

The plan of the monastery comprises a gateway, a mosque, and an assembly hall with a court in front of it. The gateway has a covered passage in the middle and a vaulted room on either side towards the east and west. These rooms are of uniform dimensions, measuring 26 feet 3 inches in length and 14 feet in width. The court has a cistern of neat design with margins of polished black stone. The assembly hall measures 48 feet 8 inches in length externally, which measurement covers also the width of the rooms built on either side of the hall towards the east and west. There is also a chamber, built at the back of the hall, to house the relics of the monastery.[2]

The Khānqāh of Makhdūm Qādirī

This monastery is situated towards the east at a short distance from the *Chhoṭī Khānqāh* of Maḥbūb Subḥānī, but it may also be approached from the Madrasa–Dulhan Darwāza road. The monastery has several buildings within its enclosure, among which the main block comprises a double hall with five arched openings towards the court. The hall has also a small room at its back for keeping the relics. The turrets on the roof of the hall have a fanciful appearance, but they are modern. Ḥaḍrat Makhdūm Qādirī, with whose name the monastery is associated, was an important saint of Bidar, and his tomb is still visited by the people of this town and its suburbs. The tomb is situated on the Bidar–Chhidrī road, at a short distance from the Kālī Masjid towards the west.[3] The full name of the saint was Makhdūm Shaikh Muḥī-ud-Dīn Qādirī, and he was the eldest son of Multānī Pādshāh[4] and lived in the tenth century Hijra (sixteenth century A.D.).

[1] The text has been deciphered as follows:

Text

محمدّ

بانيء اين مسجد

احمد خان خيشگي

سنه يك

هزار

شصت

و نه من هجرة النبويه

Translation

The builder of this mosque is Aḥmad Khān Kheshgī in the year 1069 H. (A.D. 1658–9) from the flight of the Prophet. *Epig. Ind. Mosl.*, 1931–2, pp. 27–8, Pl. XVIII *a–b*.

[2] There is an inscription dated 1318 H. (A.D. 1900) inside the hall, which shows that it has been repaired in recent times.

[3] For the description of the building see *infra*, pp. 200–2, Pl. CXXV.

[4] For Multānī Pādshāh see *supra*, pp. 107–9.

The Khānqāh of Ḥaḍrat Minnat-Ullāh Bī Ṣāḥiba

Close by the last *Khānqāh*, towards the north-west, is another monastery, styled the *Khānqāh* of Minnat-Ullāh Bī. She, according to local tradition, was the sister of Ḥaḍrat Abū'l-Faiḍ, and the association of her name with the Khānqāh shows that she took an active interest in the propagation of the religious doctrine of the Chishtīya order of *sūfīs*. Some parts of the enclosure of the monastery are old, and inside there is a room the arched façade of which is carved in the Baihmanī style. In the back wall of the room is fixed a black stone tablet with an inscription carved on it. The inscription records that the original monastery was built by Yad-Ullāh Shāh, but it was later renovated by Min-Allāh Shāh, the son of Walī-Ullāh Shāh, in 1108 H. (A.D. 1696), which date falls in Aurangzeb's reign. Yad-Ullāh Shāh, the founder of the monastery, was the spiritual guide of Sulṭān ʿAlā-ud-Dīn Aḥmad Baihmanī (A.D. 1436–58), and the saint went over to Bidar from Gulbarga at the special request of this king. The monastery must therefore have been first established sometime in the middle of the fifteenth century.[1]

The Mosque of Khalīl-Ullāh

Mīr Khalīl-Ullāh, entitled Khān Zamān, was appointed the Governor of Bidar by Aurangzeb in 1071 H. (A.D. 1660), and he held charge of this office for little more than two years.[2] The mosque built by him shows distinctly the influence of the later Mughal architecture in the form of the kiosks of its minarets, having an arched opening on each of its four sides and being crowned by a fluted dome (Pl. LXVI). But the parapet of the mosque, which has a trefoil design, indicates that the masons did not quickly give up the architectural devices with which they had become familiar during the reigns of the Barīdī kings, or of their predecessors the Baihmanīs.

The mosque is, however, of small dimensions, comprising a court, the western part of which is paved, and a prayer-hall with three arched openings towards the east. The unpaved part of the court has a lower level than the pavement, and measures 37 feet 2 inches by 25 feet. The pavement has the same length but its

[1] The text of the inscription is given below:

Text

از ید الله شاه دین تعمیر یافت   در نخست از فضل حق این خانقاه

پس من اللہ شاه تجدیدش نمود   قرة العین ولي الله شاه

سال تاریخش چو جستم از خرد   گفت دایم منزل فیض اله

۱۱۰۸ ھ

Translation

In the beginning this monastery by the grace of God was built by Yad-Ullāh, the king of faith.

Afterwards it was renovated by Min-Allāh Shāh, the son (lit. the apple of the eye) of Walī-Ullāh Shāh.

When I enquired of Wisdom regarding the chronogram, it said (that it was contained in the phrase), '*the everlasting abode of divine grace*'.

This phrase according to the *Abjad* system gives the date 1108 H. (A.D. 1696) which falls in Aurangzeb's reign.

[2] *Supra*, p. 15.

width is a little less, namely, 18 feet 10 inches only. The dimensions of the hall are: length 31 feet 3 inches, width 16 feet. The arched openings look small when we compare the height of the façade (Pl. LXVI), the span of these arches being 5 feet and their height up to the apex 7 feet 8 inches.

The façade was originally decorated lavishly with plaster-work, the traces of which may still be seen. Above the central opening an inscriptional tablet fixed into the wall forms a decorative feature of the building. The inscription contains a quotation from the *Qur'ān*.

BAIHMANĪ TOMBS

The entire group of these monuments is situated at Āsh̲ṭūr, a small village in the lowlands at a distance of one mile and six furlongs towards the east from Bidar town. The main route is from the Dulhan Darwāza, whence a Local Fund road passing by the village, Agrār, enables the visitor to reach these mausolea. The road is motorable in fair weather, but during the rains on account of its steep gradient and the waterflow of the neighbouring hillock of Ḥabs̲h̲ī Koṭ it is badly cut and sometimes entirely washed away.[1] At the time of the establishment of the Department these monuments were in a ruinous condition, being overgrown with grass and trees and their interiors choked with debris and silt, the latter deposited by rain-water. A systematic scheme has, however, been carried out since to save these precious gems of medieval Muslim architecture from further deterioration, and as a result of this not only have the majority of them been thoroughly conserved but measures have also been adopted to give them a suitable setting by clearing their environment. The land around the tombs has been levelled and tidied up, and the huts and other modern buildings which had sprung up in the vicinity have been demolished.[2]

There are eight tombs of the kings of the Baihmanī dynasty in this area, and their comparative dimensions and style of architecture demonstrate in the clearest manner the gradual deterioration of the political power of the dynasty. The tombs are described below in chronological order.

Tomb of Aḥmad S̲h̲āh al-Walī Baihmanī

Aḥmad S̲h̲āh was the ninth king of the Baihmanī dynasty and ruled for thirteen years (A.D. 1422–36) with considerable pomp and glory. He was a religiously inclined prince, and accordingly fond of the company of saintly personages. During the early part of his reign he was devoted to the renowned saint, Sayyid Muḥammad, popularly known as Ḥaḍrat Banda Nawāz Gesū Darāz of Gulbarga, but after

[1] It has been proposed to His Exalted Highness' Government to build a metalled road with an easy gradient, which would enable visitors to motor to these tombs with convenience in all seasons. The proposal is receiving the sympathetic consideration of the Roads Committee and it is hoped that it will be sanctioned soon.

[2] Three small houses in front of 'Alā-ud-Dīn Aḥmad's tomb are still an eyesore, which, however, may soon be removed, thanks to the enlightened policy of His Exalted Highness' Government who are planning the acquisition of these houses also.

the demise of this famous devotee he joined the order of Shāh Niʿmat-Ullāh of Kirmān and invited their founder to Bidar.[1] The saint did not come himself but sent his grandson Nūr-Ullāh with a green crown of twelve facets and a letter in which he addressed Aḥmad Shāh as Walī.[2] The title Walī and the green crown appealed much to the imagination of the king, and he honoured not only Nūr-Ullāh but other descendants of Niʿmat-Ullāh who subsequently migrated to Bidar on hearing of the king's regard for their family. Some scholars are of opinion that Aḥmad Shāh, in following the teachings of Niʿmat-Ullāh, embraced the Shīʿite creed, but there are also strong reasons which contradict this view. First there are no saints (*walīs*) among the Shīʿites, who believe only in the twelve *Imāms*; secondly, there are two *shajrās*, tables of succession,[3] painted on the vaulted ceiling of the tomb of Aḥmad Shāh, and according to one of them the saint Niʿmat Ullāh belonged to the Qādirīya order of dervishes, while according to the other he belonged to another order which sprang from Junaid of Baghdad through his illustrious disciple Abū ʿAlī Rūdbārī. Niʿmat-Ullāh was no doubt a descendant of the fifth Shīʿite Imām, Ḥaḍrat Bāqir, but during his pilgrimage to Mecca he became a disciple and afterwards *khalīfa*[4] of the famous Shaikh ʿAbd-Ullāh Yāfiʿī.[5] Niʿmat-Ullāh subsequently wrote a large number of tracts on different aspects of Ṣūfī doctrine, and one of them is inscribed *in extenso* on the walls of Aḥmad Shāh al-Walī's tomb (*infra*, pp. 119–24, note). The descendants of Niʿmat-Ullāh, evidently as a result of their lineage, had Shīʿa tendencies in their faith which Aḥmad Shāh, inspired

[1] For Niʿmat-Ullāh Walī see *Encyclopaedia of Islam*, No. 51, p. 21, and Rieu, *Catalogue*, pp. 43*a*, 629*a*, 634*b*, 641*b*, 774*b*, 831*b*, and 869*b*.

[2] *Firishta* (Persian text, vol. i, p. 634 Bombay ed.) writes that the title *Walī* was used by order of the king in the religious address from the pulpit (*khuṭba*) and was also engraved on coins, but no specimen of Aḥmad Shāh's reign bearing the title *Walī* has yet been found, although this title appears with his name on the coins of his son and grandson. And *Firishta* himself gives a different story of the origin of the title in another part of his work, wherein he writes that at the time of a severe drought Aḥmad Shāh went outside the city of Bidar to pray for rains and that he had hardly finished his prayer when a copious shower fell. The people were so much impressed by the quick acceptance of his prayer that they styled him *Walī* (Persian text, vol. i, pp. 621–31). The title may indeed have been used in the *khuṭba*, but on the coin-dies it was probably engraved for the first time during the reign of ʿAlā-ud-Dīn Aḥmad.

[3] One of the *shajrās* is as follows:

محمد المصطفىٰ، علي المرتضىٰ، حسن البصري، حبيب العجمي، داوٗد الطائي، معروف الكرخي، سري السقطي، جنيد البغدادي، الشبلي (ابو بكر)، ابو الفضل التيمي، ابو الفرح زنگاني، علي الهكّاري، ابو سعيد المحزمي (المحزومي ؟)، عبد القادر الجيلاني، يونس التيمي، محي الدين العربي، احمد الواسطي، مجير . . . . ني، ابراهيم المكي، عبد اللّٰه (يافعي)، نعمت اللّٰه الولي.

The second *shajrā* is given in this order:

محمد رسول اللّٰه، علي المرتضىٰ، حسن البصري، حبيب العجمي، داوٗد الطائي، معروف الكرخي، سري السقطي، جنيد البغدادي، ابو علي روذباري، ابو علي الكاتب، ابو عثمان المغربي، الشيخ ابو القاسم، ابو بكر النسّاج، احمد الغزالي، ابو الفضل البغدادي، ابو البركات ابو سعيد الاندلسي، ابو مدين المغربي، ابو الفتوح السعيد، كمال الدين الكوفي، صالح التبريزي، عبد اللّٰه يافعي، نعمت اللّٰه الحسينى.

(Pl. LXXIV)

[4] *Khalīfa*, an authorized successor of a Shaikh.

[5] For Yāfiʿī see *Encyc. Isl.* Fasc. S, pp. 1144–5.

by his liberal views, may have respected, just in the same way as he respected the doctrine of the *lingāyats*, a religious order of the Deccan.[1] The devotion of the followers of the latter sect to Aḥmad Shāh continues to this day, and at the time of the 'Urs[2] their chief priest (*Jangam*) comes from Gulbarga to Bidar with a large retinue to make offerings and perform ceremonies according to their own ritual (Pl. LXXV).[3] It should also be added that, along with the two *shajrās*, the names of the twelve Shī'ite Imāms which are generally inscribed on the tombs of the votaries of that sect are painted on the ceiling (Pl. LXXIV). Further, above the small arch to the left of the eastern door of the tomb the following verse is painted:

پرسند اگر کہ شیخ در این خانقاه کیست
مهدي هاديست بگو شيخ خانقاه

Translation

If people inquire of thee, 'Who is the Shaikh of this monastery';
Tell them that Mahdī, the Leader, is our Shaikh.

The author of the verse is Ni'mat-Ullāh, and it shows that the saint, although a disciple of 'Abd-Ullāh Yāfi'ī, maintained the Shī'ite views which he had inherited from his forebears; Aḥmad Shāh also, who succeeded him, had no fixed doctrine to follow, and his religious vagaries made him swing between the Sunnī and Shī'a faiths on the one hand and Ṣūfīism and corresponding schools of Indian thought on the other. He perhaps resembled Akbar or Dārā Shukoh, who appeared on the scene after him in the pageant of Indian history.

The architecture of the tomb, as indicated by its external features, shows strength combined with majesty, although except for the stucco-work in the spandrels of arches there is no decoration on the walls of the building. It has a square plan measuring 77 feet 1 inch on each side externally. The walls are most massively built, their thickness being 12 feet 6 inches. To add further strength the architect has given them a batter, since they rise 57 feet above the floor and are surmounted by a parapet the height of which is 4 feet 9 inches above the top of the walls. The

[1] The Lingāyat form of worship seems to have had its origin in the Deccan previous to the present Brahmanical form, and its great apostle was Basava who died in A.D. 1168–9. Basava was born of Brahman parents in Bagewadi in the Kaladghi district, but refused to be invested with the sacrificial thread, affirming that he was a worshipper of Śiva, and that he did not belong to the generation of Brahma. After settling at Kalyāṇa he promulgated his new doctrine. His followers, who according to the last census number 97,836, abound in Southern India, and perform their worship in the Mahādeva temples which have a distinct and separate apotheosis of the *linga*. They dislike the Brahmans, neglect Brahmanical rules about purification for dead bodies, &c., and wear a little linga, called *Ishta Linga*, on their bodies. The ceremonies of their religion are conducted by Bairāgīs called *Jangams*, who are believed to be the offspring of the god, and are enjoined to be constantly on the move and to be unmarried and poorly dressed, begging their food from place to place. Their numbers are recruited by barren women addressing themselves to the deity, and if they be blessed with children, they devote one to the god which, if a male, becomes a Lingāyat priest. *Hist. and Descript. Sketch* by Syed Husain Bilgrami and C. Willmott, vol. i, pp. 350–1.

[2] *'Urs*, the annual celebrations of the death of a Muslim saint.

[3] A representative of the *lingāyats* is always in attendance at the tomb, and he marks the foreheads of votaries with sandal-paste. The conch is blown frequently when the votaries perform the ritual.

latter are pierced by three doors, towards the north, the south, and the east, and in front have arches in the form of recesses (Pl. LXIX).[1] These arches are constructed on a large scale, the span of each of them being 19 feet 7 inches and the height up to the apex 29 feet 9 inches. The surface of the walls on the outside is further divided by arched niches of varying dimensions, but all showing a pleasing sense of proportion in their shape. A feature common to all of them is the stilt at their apexes. Some of the niches have small arched openings in their backs, these being filled up with trellis-work which admits light and air to the interior of the tomb and also relieves to a certain extent the heaviness of the exterior of the building. The parapet has a plain design of arch-heads, but the turrets at the corners are quite ornate and their tiny niches give them a picturesque appearance.

The dome of the building is three-fourths of an orb in shape and resembles the domes of the Lodhī kings at Delhi both in its own design and in that of its finial. Aḥmad S̲h̲āh al-Walī was a contemporary of the first Lodhī king, Bahlol (A.D. 1451–89), and the similarity of the architecture of the Deccan to that of Delhi at this period is not limited to the form of the dome but extends also to the patterns of the stucco decoration around the arch-heads and in the spandrels. The dome of Aḥmad S̲h̲āh al-Walī's tomb has an octagonal base at the roof level, measuring 214 feet 8 inches in girth, each side of the octagon being 26 feet 10 inches in length. The walls of the base have a parapet of trefoil design at the top (Pl. LXIX), and they rise 16 feet 6 inches above the roof level. The dome at its springing-point has a circumference of 196 feet, and its height up to the top of its finial is 54 feet from the roof and 38 feet from its springing-point, close to the parapet above the walls of its octagonal base. The finial by itself measures 11 feet 7 inches in height. The total height of the dome including the finial is 107 feet 9 inches measured from ground level.

The inner plan of the tomb comprises a square hall, 52 feet 2 inches long on each side. There is a lofty arch in the middle of each of the four sides of the hall, and the hall itself is flanked by a deeply recessed niche both on its right side and on its left (Pl. LXVIII). The plan of the interior of the tomb on account of these features looks pleasing to the eye, but the architect has further ornamented it by building squinches at the four corners of the hall, the plan of the building thus becoming octagonal at the top of the squinches. Above this level there is another change in the plan of the building which becomes 24-sided owing to the pendentives constructed below the circular base of the dome.

The interior of the tomb, although somewhat dark, is artistically relieved by splashes of most brilliant colours which have been used in the paintings of the walls and the vault. Among these gold and vermilion are prominent, but almost every tint in the colour-box of the painter has been used, there being several shades of cobalt and terra-verde, and also such mixtures as buff, grey, and russet (Pls. LXX–LXXIII). The excellence of the paintings, however, does not consist in the variety of tints but in the lovely contrasts which have been shown in the colour schemes of the different panels. For instance, in the spandrels of the large arch of the southern

[1] Above the northern door the *Āyat al-Kursī* (Throne verse, *Qur'ān*, ch. ii, verse 256) is inscribed in relief in stucco-work.

wall the artist, in order to show with effect the brilliance of the gold of the creeper design, has used an extremely dark colour for the background, and with the same object in view he has painted the circular design in the middle of the spandrel in bright vermilion and gold with the contrast of dark brown shown in the loops of the pattern (Pl. LXX).[1] Again, on the same wall, above the niche to the right of the door, is a square panel painted in the style of a book-cover with floral designs in the margin, geometric patterns in the middle, and an intricate *Ṭughra* device at the centre.[2] The tints used in this panel (Pl. LXXI) show the skill of the artist in blending colours with a view to producing an effect suitable to the subtle drawing of the subject. The refined taste of the artist in the choice of colours can be better appreciated in the band of *Kūfic* and *Thulth* inscriptions in gold and white over a light blue background (Pl. LXXII). As the colours of the middle part of this panel are soft, the painter for purpose of contrast has used deep bright tints of vermilion and gold in the margin.[3]

The practice of giving a white outline to the drawing with the view of suggesting an idea of depth to the subject and also of enlivening the colours, which was frequently resorted to by the artists of Ajanta during the fifth and sixth centuries A.D., may be seen with very happy results in the painting on the thickness of the main arch towards the east (Pl. LXXIII). The designs here as well as in other places possess considerable artistic merit, but the connoisseur may consider these to be of a stereotyped character on account of their being frequently used in the illumination of manuscripts, the embroidery work on wearing apparel, and the decorative patterns on carpets. By religious restrictions the artist was prohibited from portraying living beings in the interior of tombs, and his imagination was therefore employed either in inventing new designs for religious texts or in adding further delicacy and subtleness to the geometric and floral devices by making the drawing more and more intricate.

The designs of the vault can best be appreciated from Pl. LXXIV which, although in monotone, represents faithfully the various creeper and floral patterns, the numerous geometric devices, and several calligraphic styles. The last-named are exhibited in four concentric bands with a circular panel in the middle at the apex of the vault. The first band is divided into eight oval panels by small hexagons containing the name of ʿAlī written thrice in the *Kūfic* script. The background of the eight oval panels is bright red and on it the *durūd*, comprising benedictions on the souls of Muḥammad, his descendants, and other prophets and holy personages, is inscribed in letters of gold in the *Thulth* style of an intricate pattern.[4] The next

[1] The design, which is in the form of a medallion, contains the phrase توکّلت علی خالقي 'I trusted in my Creator' arranged in the *Ṭughra* style.

[2] The *Ṭughra* device contains the names of الله , محمّد and علي written in *Kūfic* script.

[3] The text in gold contains the epithets of God such as are used in the *Holy Qur'ān*, and the writing in white the second hemistich of a verse by Niʿmat-Ullāh—هفت دریارا چو سیلی دیده ام.

[4] The text of the *durūd* is as follows:

(۱) بسم الله الرحمٰن الرحيم. اللّهم صلّ علی محمّد (2) امّا اختلف الملوان والتعاقب العصران وتكرر الجديدان (3) واضاء القمران بلّغ منّا روح محمّد تحيّةً وسلاماً و (4) اللّهم صلّ علی محمّد عبدك ورسولك النبي الامّي (5) وعلی آل محمّد و سلّم

band has a clear azure background, and the table of succession which connects Niʿmat-Ullāh Walī with the founder of the Qādirīya group of saints is inscribed in a continuous lace-like pattern of closely interwoven letters.[1] The background of the third band is vermilion, and it is divided into twenty-one panels, the heads of which are in the form of a semicircular arch. Each of these panels contains the name of a saint, and the whole table gives the connexion of Niʿmat-Ullāh with Junaid al-Baghdādī through his disciple ʿAlī Rūdbārī.[2] The fourth or last band represents an intricate scroll delineated in gold on a green background. The scroll contains the Shīʿite *durūd*, invoking blessings on Muḥammad, and on his descendants, styled the twelve Imāms. The panel at the apex has a *Tughra* device in bold gold letters representing the name of Allāh and Panjatan, the five holy personages, that is Muḥammad, ʿAlī, Fāṭima, Ḥasan, and Ḥusain. To brighten these names the architect has fixed a shining crystal at the apex of the vault, and the effulgence of the stone is enhanced by pious visitors, who throw the light of the sun on it by reflection through a mirror. In the gloom of the vault this display of gold and other brilliant colours represents admirably the 'mystery' and 'glory' of the Ṣūfic doctrine, the texts of which are inscribed in great profusion on the walls of this shrine.

The paintings of dadoes, being within easy reach of the hands of the pious visitors, have completely perished, and the modern renovations in cheap colours and tinsel look extremely inartistic. A dark coloured band, deep blue or black, immediately above the dadoes, is preserved in some places, and it contains the text of a Ṣūfic tract by Niʿmat-Ullāh, referred to above (*supra*, p. 115).[3] The text, wherever

(*text continued on p. 124*)

اللّهم صلّ على محمّد سيّد الاوّلين (6) وصلّ على محمّد سيّد الآخرين اللّهم صلّ على محمّد وعلى (7) آل محمّد و سلّم وبارك وصلّ على جميع الانبياء و المرسلين و (8) الملائكة المقربين وعبادك الصالحين والحمد للّه ربّ العالمين .

Translation

In the name of God the Most Merciful and the Most Compassionate. O God bless Muḥammad, (2) until the day and night differ, and the two periods ('Past' and 'Present') come one in reverse succession to the other, and the day and night follow one another, (3) and the two luminaries (sun and moon) shine. Convey from us to the soul of Muḥammad benedictions and salutations. And (4) O God, bless Muḥammad, Thy servant and apostle, the illiterate Prophet, (5) and the progeny of Muḥammad and assoil them. O God bless Muḥammad, the lord of the early nations, (6) and bless Muḥammad, the lord of the coming nations. O God bless Muḥammad and (7) his descendants and assoil them. And bless and grant benediction to all prophets and apostles sent by Thee, (8) all angels who are in close attendance on Thee, and all servants of Thine who are pious: and all praise unto God, the Cherisher of all the worlds.

[1] The table of succession has already been given in footnote 3, p. 115.

[2] This table also has been given in footnote 3, p. 115.

[3] Beginning from the left side of the *miḥrāb* in the western wall the text has been deciphered as follows:

(١) اول چو. . . . . شد   قطره درياست چون بدريا شد

(٢) قطره و بحر و موج چو آبند   عين مارا بعين ما يابند

(٣) نقد گنجينه . . . .

(٤) گرنه آنست اصل گوهر چيست   جوهر گوهر منوّر چيست

(*continued overleaf*)

(note 3, p. 119, continued)

(٥) همه . . . . دریا   . . . . جوهرت دریا

(٦) آن حقیقت که اول همه اوست   صورتش عالمست و معنی دوست

(٧) گنج و گنجینه و طلا . . . . و صفا . . . . .

(٨) . . . . . . احد آشکار شد . . .   .

(٩) او احدیٔ در عدد هو . . . .

(١٠) . . . . . وحدتست در هر باب   مجملاً و مفصلاً دریاب

(١١) کثرتش چون حباب دان دایم   وحدتش بحر و بن (؟) بآن قایم

(١٢) وحدت و کثرت اعتباري دان   نسخهٔ عقل‌را چنین مي خوان

(١٣) نقش عالم خیال مي بینم   در خیال آن جمال مي بینم

(١٤) او لطیفست در همه ساري   آب حیوان بجوی ما جاري

(١٥) نه حلولست حلّ حال منست   سخنی از من و کمال منست

(١٦) هر که در معرفت سخن راند   وصف خود مي کند اگر داند

(١٧) تو مني من تو ام دوئي بگذار   من نماند هم تو من توئي بگذار

(١٨) انت لا انت و انا ما هو   هو لا الٰه الّا هو

(١٩) لیس فی الدار غیره باق   غیره عندنا که قزاّق

(٢٠) هر چه دایم جماه وجود ویست   جود او نزد ما وجود ویست

(٢١) ور تو گوئي که غیر او باشد   بد نه باشد بگو نکو باشد

(٢٢) تن بود سایه‌بان و جان خورشید   این یکی چتردان و آن جمشید

(٢٣) سایه و شخص مي نماید دو   بحقیقت دو یکیست بی من و تو

(٢٤) . . . . . جان . . . . سوز . . . . و سوزم . . . . . سوزنین

---

(٢٥) یا حبیبي و قرة العین انا عینك   و عینك عیني حقیقت یکی بود بی شك

(٢٦) درْ ظهور این دوئی نمود از یك   احول است نگهٔ دو یك

---

(٢٧) مي بیند چون دو بیند   یگانه صوت نشنید

(٢٨) صادق بود صدا کاذب   راز صادق مگوئے با کاذب

---

(٢٩) صفت و ذات واحدش خوانند   بی صفت ذات را احد خوانند

(٣٠) بصفت ذات‌را توان دانست   هر که دانست آنچنان دانست

(٣١) آنکه دانیم . . . . بکشوفست

(٣٢) گنج با گنج نزد او گنجد   گنج او در دلم نکو گنجد

(٣٣) عاشقانی که عین هم دگرند   عین خودرا بعین هم نگرند

(٣٤) بتعیّن اگرچه اشخاصند   بحقیقت نه عام و نه خاصند

(٣٥) همه همدرد هم دگر باشند   هر چه باشند بپائے هم باشند

(٣٦) هر که همدرد دردمندان نیست   گوئیا از قبیل مردان نیست

(٣٧) درد دل دارم و دوا اینست   درد مي نوشم و صفا اینست

(note 3, p. 119, continued)

(۳۸) ذوق رندي را	. . . .
(۳۹) . . . . سرّ وجود آگاهم	محرم راز نعمة الله هم

---

(٤٠) عشق مجنون و خوبی لیلی	گفته اند و شنوده خیلی
(٤١) سخن عاشقان بیا بشنو	مشنو از ما تو از خدا بشنو
(٤٢) خوش حیوتي روان شده در جو	عین دریا بجو و از ما جو
(٤٣) حمد آن حامدی که محمود است	بخشش اوست هر چه موجود است
(٤٤) فرض عینست حمد حضرت او	بر همه خلق خاصّه بر من و تو
(٤٥) حمد او از کلام او گویم	لا جرم حمد او نکو گویم
(٤١) شکّر شکر او چو شیرین است	شکر گویم که شکّر من ایست
(٤٧) مدح صنعت که مدح صانع اوست	مدح جمله بگو که آن نکوست
(٤٨) هر چه مخلوق حضرت اویند	همه تسبیح حضرتش گویند
(٤٩) صد هزاران درود در هر دم	بر روان خلاصهٔ عالم
(٥٠) عالم از	. . . . . او باشد
(٥١) عارف سرّ عین عالم اوست	واقف راز اسم اعظم اوست
(٥٢) عقل اول وزیر آن شاهست	باطناً شمس و ظاهرا ماهست

---

(٥٣) در الف نقطه ایست بنهفته	اول و آخر الف نقطه
(٥٤) در نقطه الف جمال نموده	الفی حروف در خیال بسته
(٥٥) نے نے الف و الف نے نے	نے الف بے نقطه بود نے نے
(٥٦) قطب عالم چو نقطهٔ پرکار است	. . . .
(٥٧)	. . . .
(٥٨)	. . . .
(٥٩) گنج و طلسم	. . . .
(٦٠)	. . . .
(٦١) عین وحدت چون ظهور فرمود	بحر در قطره بما رو بنمود
(٦٢) گر من از اوست گر هزار هزار	اولی او بود یکی بشمار
(٦٣) آئینه گر هزار مي بینم	در همه روی یار مي بینم
(٦٤)	. . . .
(٦٥) عین عینی بعینه عیني	. . . .
(٦٦)	. . . .
(٦٧)	. . . .
(٦٨)	. . . .
(٦٩)	. . . .
(٧٠)	. . . .
(٧١) آب از آفتاب گرمي یافت	گرمیش بر وجود کوزه بتافت
(٧٢) آب شد بکوزه کوزه شد بآب	اسم و . . . . . . ز اسم . . . . دریاب

(*note 3, p. 119, continued*)

Translation

(1) In the beginning . . . was . . .
The drop is the ocean when the former has entered it.
(2) The drop, the ocean, the wave are (all various aspects of) water,
They (people) will perceive the reality of water from its entity.
(3) The cash of the treasury . . . .
. . . .
(4) If He is not that; what is the origin of the pearl?
What is the effulgence in the lustrous pearl?
(5) All . . . . the ocean,
Thy radiance . . . from the ocean.
(6) This (hypothesis) is reality, that the beginning (origin) of all is He;
The universe is His appearance, and the reality (lit. meaning) the Friend (God).
(7) The treasure, the treasury and . . . . . .
. . . . and purity . . . . . .
(8) . . . . . the One revealed Himself . . .
. . . .
(9) He and the One (both) signify Him . . .
. . . .
(10) . . . . . there is unity in every aspect;
Thou shouldst ascertain that individually or collectively.
(11) Thou shouldst consider His multiplicity always like the bubble transitory,
His unity like the ocean, and the source thus established.
(12) Thou shouldst regard Unity and Multiplicity as hypothetical,
And read the book of wisdom in that way.
(13) I notice the picture of the universe as imaginary,
And in that imaginary picture I see His Beauty.
(14) He is the quintessence, pervading all;
The water of Life flowing in our stream (existence).
(15) He is not embodied, but is the solution of (the problem of) my existence,
He is the word explaining my entity, and the exaltedness of my entity.
(16) Whoever talks of knowledge (Truth),
He speaks of himself, if he were to understand that.
(17) 'Thou art I, and I am Thou', thou shouldst leave duality;
Ego does not survive, hence give up (the idea of separate entities of) 'me' and 'thee'
(18) Thou; and not 'thou and I' except He;
He, and there is no god but He.
(19) None remains in the house but He;
According to me, any one but He is the thief (deception).
(20) That which is everlasting is all His existence;
His bounty according to us is His existence.
(21) If thou sayest that that which is not-God exists;
That not-God cannot be evil; say that it is 'good'.
(22) The body is the canopy and the soul the sun,
The former may be regarded as the umbrella and the latter as Jam<u>sh</u>id.
(23) The shadow and the person appear two;
But really they are one, without 'I' and 'thou'.
(24) . . . . the soul . . . . . anguish . . .
. . . . my grief . . . . . burning pain . . .

(25) O my Friend and the apple of my eye, I am Thy vision,
And (to say that) Thy existence is my existence undoubtedly means the same.
(26) In manifestation duality emanated from unity,
The eye which sees one as two is squint.

(*note 3, p. 119, continued*)

(27) The (squint) eyed perceives two when he perceives;
He does not hear the single note.
(28) The false echo is true;
Thou shouldst not communicate the secret truth to the liar.
(29) The (wise people) consider God and His attributes (both united) as one;
They call the Divine Being without His attributes single.
(30) The Divine Being can be ascertained through His attributes:
Whoever has perceived Him, he has perceived Him thus.
(31) Whatsoever we know . . . .
. . . . is by dispersion (of the one reality into a variety of appearances).
(32) Treasures and treasures can be accommodated in Him,
His treasures are well accommodated in my heart.
(33) Lovers who represent each other's existence,
They perceive their own existence from the existence of each other.
(34) Apparently, although they are several in number;
But in reality they are (one), neither of them being a commoner or distinguished.
(35) They are all sympathetic to each other;
Whatever happens, they stand by each other.
(36) Whoever is not sympathetic to the afflicted,
Thou mightst say that he is not from the group of manly (persons).
(37) I have pain in my heart and the cure is with me (lit. this);
I drink the dregs although the clear wine is with me.
(38) The inclination to drunkenness . . . .
. . . .
(39) . . . . as I am initiated into the secret of Existence,
I know the secret of Niʿmat-Ullāh also.
(40) The love of Majnūn and the beauty of Laila;
Have been described amply and heard of amply.
(41) The conversation of lovers, come and listen;
Do not listen to 'We and Thou', but listen to God.
(42) Delightful life is flowing in the stream,
Thou shouldst seek the source of the stream and seek it from the waters.
(43) Praise be unto (God) Who is the Praiser and the Praised,
All that which exists is His gift.
(44) To praise Him is a compulsory duty,
For all mankind, and particularly for me and thee.
(45) I praise Him from His own Words;
Hence I praise Him well.
(46) As the 'sugar' of his gratitude has a sweet taste;
I thank Him, for that is the 'sugar' which I possess.
(47) The praise of 'creation' which is the praise of the Creator,
Thou shouldst praise *all*, for that would be more appropriate.
(48) All those who have been created by His Providence,
They all praise His Providence.
(49) May hundreds of thousands of blessings every moment,
Be upon the soul of the most chosen one in the universe (Muḥammad).
(50) The universe . . . . . by . . . .
. . . . he . . . . . . is . . .
(51) He is the knower of the secret of the existence of the world,
He is initiated into the mystery of 'the Most Exalted Name'.
(52) The First Reason (Gabriel) is the minister of that king,
In reality he is the sun although apparently he is the moon.

(*text continued from p. 119*)

intact, represents the similes used by the metaphysicians of those days in explaining their abstruse views regarding the unity of God and all creation emanating from Him.

There are also inscriptions above the *miḥrāb* in the western wall and above the three entrance arches towards the north, east, and south.[1] They comprise benedic-

(*note 3, p. 119, concluded*)

(53) (In the letter) *alif* (Allāh) the 'vowel' (creation) is concealed,
The beginning and end of *alif* indicates the 'vowel' (creation).

(54) The *alif* manifested Himself in the 'vowel',
And the *alif* of the alphabet (universe) assumed shape in imagination.

(55) Nay, nay the latter is not the real *alif*, nor can that be so, nay, nay;
Nor can the *alif* (Allāh) be (perceived) without vowels (creation); never, never!

(56) The axis of the universe (God) is like the point of the pair of compasses,
. . . .

(57) . . . .
. . . .

(58) . . . .
. . . .

(59) The treasure . . . and the talisman . . . .
. . . .

(60) . . . .
. . . .

(61) The Divine Unity (the One God), when He manifested Himself,
The ocean as if in the form of a drop showed itself to us.

(62) If ego (creation or universe) has emanated from Him, although it has thousands and thousands of forms;
Since He is the beginning the (multifarious forms of creation) represent the Divine Unity.

(63) Although I see a thousand mirrors,
In all of them I notice the countenance of the Beloved.

(64) . . . .
. . . .

(65) The quintessence of my entity is identically His entity . . .
. . . .

(66) . . . .
. . . .

(67) . . . .
. . . .

(68) . . . .
. . . .

(69) . . . .
. . . .

(70) . . . .
. . . .

(71) The water received heat from the sun,
The heat of the sun caused the formation of material bodies (lit. cup).

(72) The water entered the cup, or the cup dipped in the water;
(Different) terms . . . . and from the terms determine . . . .

[1] The full text of the inscriptions, beginning from the *miḥrāb* in the western wall is as follows:

(1) *Above the miḥrāb*

لا خوف عليكم ولا انتم تحزنون. امّا فهذه البقعة المباركة كعبة الحاجات وقبلہ . . . جنّة الفردوس طاب نعيمها من روضة الرضوان

عمل العبد شكر اللّه
القزويني نقّاش

. . . فيہ

tory verses and also the name of the king, and the dates of his accession to the throne and demise. The full name of the king with his titles as given in the inscription above the southern arch is as follows:

السلطان السلاطين افضل خليفه (خليقة ؟) الآله في العالم الواثق بتائيد اللّه القوي
ابو المغازي شهاب الدنيا والدين احمد شاه الولي البهمني

In this inscription it is also stated that the affairs of government were entrusted to Aḥmad Shāh in 825 H. (A.D. 1422), and he expired on the night of Tuesday, the 29th of Ramaḍān, 839 H. (A.D. 17th April 1436). Another important feature of these inscriptions is that one of them contains the name of the painter with a reference to his native place:

عمل العبد شكر اللّه القزويني نقّاش

(*note 1, p. 124, concluded*)

(2) *Over the southern arch*

روضة شريفة لسلطان السلاطين افضل خليفة (خليقة ؟) اللّه فى العالمين. الواثق بتائيد اللّه القوي ابو المغازي شهاب الدنيا والدين احمد شاه الولي البهمني قدّس اللّه روحه ونوّر ضريحه. ثمّ انّه فوّض اليه امر الامارة في سنه خمس و عشرين وثمانماية.

(3) *Over the eastern door*

فعاش في دنياه حميدا ورجع الى ربّه سعيدا في ليلة الاثنين ليلة المباركة التاسع والعشرين من شهر الملك العلّام سنه تسع و ثلاثين و ثمانماية من هجرة النبي عليه السلم (السلام). اللّهم اجعل له شفاعة شاملة و اكرمه على الخلق فايضة دايمة بحق النبي و عترته الاخيار.

(4) *Over the northern door*

[سبحان من اعلى منزله] و اولياه في الدنيا والدين ورفّع مكانهم في اعلى عليّين وجعلهم في الغرفات آمنين في مقعد صدق عند الملايك فايزين فهم في روضة يُحبرون وبما اٰتهم اللّه من فضله فرحون.

Translation

(1) '*There shall come no fear on you, neither shall ye be grieved.*' (*Qur'ān*, vii. 47). But this holy place, the *Ka'ba* of the fulfilment of desires, and the *Qibla* of . . . the garden of Paradise, the delights of which are agreeable, from the meadow of Heaven . . . therein . . . [The work of the servant Shukr-Ullāh of Qazwīn, the painter.]

(2) The sacred tomb of the king of kings, the most distinguished vicegerent of God in all the worlds, trustful of the help of God the Powerful, the victorious in religious wars, Shihāb-ud-Dunyā wad-Dīn Aḥmad Shāh al-Walī al-Baihmanī, may God sanctify his soul and illuminate his grave! And the affairs of government were entrusted to him in the year 825 H. (A.D. 1422).

(3) He lived in the world to be praised, and returned to his God to be blessed, on the auspicious night of Monday the 29th of the month of the Omniscient God in the year 839 from the flight of the Prophet, may God's peace be upon him! (Tuesday, 17th April, A.D. 1436).* O God, grant him complete forgiveness and distinguish him among people by everlasting success through the grace of the Prophet and his holy progeny!

(4) [Holy is God the Most Exalted] And his friends in the world and in Faith; And (O God) raise their abode to the highest heaven, and accommodate them comfortably in the alcoves (of Paradise), resting on seats of 'truth' and distinguished among the company of angels! May *they take their pleasure in a delightful meadow*†, and enjoy what God has provided for them through his bounty!

* According to Firishta the date of Aḥmad Shāh's death is 28th Rajab 838 H., corresponding to Sunday, 27th February, A.D. 1435, which is apparently wrong. *Persian Text*, Bombay ed., vol. i, p. 633.

† *Qur'ān*, xxx. 14.

Translation

The work of the servant, Shukr-Ullāh al-Qazvīnī, the painter.

This inscription, combined with the record on the façade of the Madrasa Maḥmūd Gāwān,[1] and the emblem of the rising sun and the tiger in the spandrels of the arch at the Takht Maḥall (Pl. XXXVII), clearly suggests that the kings of Baihmanī dynasty employed Persian architects and artists to design and decorate their buildings.

The arch-heads of the eight niches built in the walls of this tomb are decorated with calligraphic bands containing verses by Niʿmat-Ullāh, written in gold on a dark background.[2] The art of calligraphy is, however, best represented in the panels

[1] *Supra*, pp. 91–6.

[2] These verses have been deciphered as follows:

(1) *Above the niche to the right of the southern entrance*

با تحفهای معرفت و هدیهای علم　　هر لحظه ام ز غیب مسافر رسید ز راه

(2) *Above the niche to the left of the southern entrance*

روز و شبند بسته میانرا بخدمتم　　یك خادم سفید و دگر خادم سیاه

(3) *Above the niche to the right of the eastern doorway*

ز آن متّکای مهر بود زیر دست من　　کز چاربالش فلکم هست تکیه گاه

(4) *Above the niche to the left of the eastern doorway*

پرسند اگر که شیخ درین خانقاه کیست　　مهدي هاديست بگو شيخ خانقاه

(5) *Above the niche to the right of the northern doorway*

این گنبد رفیع مرا خانقاه هست　　قندیل خانقاه ببینید آفتاب و ماه

(6) *Above the niche to the left of the northern doorway*

فرش زمرّدین بزمین بین بساط او　　پر نقش و پرنگار از گل و گیاه

(7) *Above the niche to the right of the miḥrāb*

بحر محیط برکه و سقّا بود سحاب　　فرّاش این رواق بود باد صبحگاه

(8) *Above the niche to the left of the miḥrāb*

خوانی کشیده است خدا شرق تا بغرب　　وقفست بر شهان و گدا نعمت الله

Translation

(i) Travellers from the path of the Unknown arrive here bearing presents of knowledge and offerings of Truth.

(ii) Day and night have girded up their loins to serve me; one of them has a fair complexion and the other a dark.

(iii) For this reason the resting place of the sun is under me, that the throne of heaven is my sofa.

(iv) If people inquire of you, 'Who is the Shaikh (preceptor) of the monastery?' Tell them that (Imām) Mahdī, the Leader, is the preceptor of the monastery.

(v) This lofty vault is my monastery, you will notice the sun and the moon (serving) as the lamps of this monastery.

(vi) Thou wilt see the green verdure of earth as the carpet (of the monastery), decorated with patterns and designs of natural flowers and creepers.

(vii) The ocean is the fountain (of the monastery) and the cloud the water-carrier, and the morning breeze is the sweeper of the lofty porch.

(viii) God has spread the table from the east to the west, and Divine fare is offered to the king and the beggar alike.

arranged higher up on the walls above the three entrance arches. They contain religious texts in the *Kūfic* script and verses by Niʿmat-Ullāh in <u>Thulth</u> characters, the styles of both being most elegant (Pl. LXXII).[1] The surface of the walls and the ceiling is further decorated with sacred texts and the names of God, Muḥammad, ʿAlī, and his descendants arranged in the form of talismans. In the ceiling besides the four concentric bands, alluded to above (*supra*, pp. 118–19), there is another along the rim of the dome, a little above its springing line. This latter band contains some writing in prose and verse on the *Ṣūfic* doctrine.[2] The text is apparently a quotation

[1] Of these inscriptions the writing on the northern and western walls has been completely effaced by the percolation of water which continued for a considerable time through a crack in the dome. The leakage of water has also disfigured the paintings on the north-western parts of the dome and the walls adjoining it. This crack has indeed been thoroughly repaired, but it has proved difficult to make good the damage which has been caused to the paintings since the now general use of modern European pigments by Indian artists has led to the complete disappearance of the indigenous industry of making colours which kept their freshness for centuries. The verses inscribed on the southern and eastern walls are intact, and have been deciphered as follows:

(1) *On the eastern wall*

غير معشوقم نيامد در نظر   عاشقان را گرچه خيلے ديده ام

تا محيط ديده برزد موج عشق   هفت دريا را چو سيلے ديده ام

Translation

Except the beloved I do not notice anyone, although I have looked much for lovers.
When through love the ocean of my eye broke into waves,
I found the seven seas dwindling to a stream.

(2) *On the southern wall*

نعمت اللّه يافتم در هر وجود   با همه عشقى و ميلى ديده ام

نعمة اللّه در همه عالم يكيست   لا تجد مثلى و مثلي لا تجد

Translation

I have found Niʿmat-Ullāh (Divine bounty) in every form of existence, for I have noticed love and infatuation in all.

Niʿmat-Ullāh (Divine bounty) is One in the entire universe; thou shalt not find any one like me, nor one like me can be found (by others).

The first three verses ending in ديده ام are included in the *Dīvān* of <u>Sh</u>āh Niʿmat-Ullāh Walī, Tehran ed., p. 459. The fourth line is also printed in this *Dīvān* on p. 710.

[2] The inscription has been considerably damaged by the percolation of rain-water, but such portions of it as are intact have been deciphered with the help of binoculars as follows:

Text

.... بديديم همه خوش بود آن چنان نيست — و آن در نظر ما هست تا چنين باشد — و بود تا چنين بود — سيد قدح باده بمن داد — بخودم داري چه كنم — مصلحت بنده در آن بود

ما شاه جهانيم گدائي چه بود   و بخدا اصل ......

Translation

... Whatsoever we observed is good, but really the Truth is not that. And we shall continue to observe in that manner as long as the mystery of existence is not solved. It (the false view) will last as long as the mystery lasts. The Master offered the wine-cup to me, how shall I restrain myself: the wise course for the servant was to restrain himself.

Verse

We are the lord of the world, what is indigence?
And with God . . . . the origin . . . .

from some work of Niʿmat-Ullāh, who was a prolific writer and is described as having been the author of more than five hundred books and tracts.

The various features of this tomb, such as its vast dimensions, solid architecture, choice colour schemes, and subtle decorative patterns, show the lofty ideals of the builder on the one hand and his exquisite taste and religious spirit on the other. This last-mentioned quality is amply demonstrated by the holy texts inscribed on the building, as also by the ritual which is still observed by the votaries of the tomb, who, although professing different faiths and belonging to different nationalities, all join together in paying their homage to the memory of the saintly king (Pl. LXXV).[1]

The Tomb of Sulṭān Aḥmad Shāh's Wife (?)

To the east of Aḥmad Shāh's mausoleum, but at a lower level, is a tomb which is assigned to the wife of the king. There is no inscription on the tomb, and as in comparatively recent times it has been used for dwellings and for other purposes by the villagers, much of its internal decoration has perished. It is still surrounded by mud huts, although the Archaeological Department has repaired and cleaned the tomb.[2] Its architecture is almost the same as that of Aḥmad Shāh's tomb, but it is considerably smaller in dimensions than the latter. The base of this building measures 48 feet 3 inches square externally in contrast to the 77 feet 1 inch of the

[1] During one of my visits to the Baihmanī tombs in A.D. 1927 a black stone tablet which is inscribed on both sides was brought to my notice. It was lying loose in Aḥmad Shāh al-Walī's shrine, but belongs to another tomb which was probably situated in the vicinity of this. The tablet was picked up and preserved in Aḥmad Shāh al-Walī's tomb apparently on account of its beautiful writing. It is arch-shaped, and on the face of it the Throne verse (*Qur'ān*, ii. 256) and the following date are inscribed:

في شهر رجب احدىٰ و عشرين سنه خمس و خمسين و تسعمأة

Translation

On the 21st of the month of Rajab, 955 H., corresponding to Sunday the 26th of August, A.D. 1548. On the back of the tablet there are first the words—

هو اللّه الباقي

Translation

He is the Everlasting God

and afterwards a quotation from the *Qur'ān* (ix, 21), and below that the following words—

. . . . المرحوم نتيجة (نخبة؟) الخوانين خواجه محمّد شاه بن خطّاط خان جعل اللّه الجنّة ماواه

Translation

. . . the deceased, the best of Khāns, Khwāja Muḥammad Shāh, son of Khaṭṭāṭ Khān, may God make Paradise his resting place!

The date 26th August A.D. 1548 falls within the reign of ʿAlī Barīd (A.D. 1542–80), or within the reign of the Quṭb Shāhī king, Subḥān Qulī (A.D. 1543–50). In the Patancheru inscription of Ibrāhīm Quṭb Shāh, dated A.D. 1558, the name of one Khaṭṭāṭ Khān is mentioned who may be the same person as is referred to in the Bidar record. Khaṭṭāṭ Khān may have outlived his son Khwāja Muḥammad Shāh, who died in A.D. 1548. But this is only a surmise, and the Khaṭṭāṭ Khān of the Bidar inscription may have been a different person from the Khaṭṭāṭ Khān of the Patancheru epigraph.

[2] On the representation of the Archaeological Department, the Revenue authorities are kindly planning the evacuation of the entire area occupied by the Baihmanī tombs and the shifting of the village population to an appropriate site some distance away from the tombs.

tomb of Aḥmad Shāh. It must at one time, nevertheless, have been quite imposing, because it is built on a platform 4 feet 2 inches high, and the walls of the tomb rise 28 feet 8 inches above the Sulṭān's own tomb.[1] The walls have a slight batter to counteract the thrust of the vault of the dome which has a circumference of 129 feet at the roof level.

The tomb is entered by a doorway from the south, the arch of which shows a stilt at the apex. The interior of the building has a square plan, measuring 31 feet 7 inches on each side. But squinches at the corners, and above them clusters of triangular abutments projecting from the walls, have converted the square plan first into an octagon and afterwards into a 24-sided figure. There are traces of painting on the ceiling of the vault, but owing to the neglect of centuries the colours and the designs have almost completely perished. There are five graves in the sepulchral hall, of which the one at the extreme left is said to be that of Aḥmad Shāh's wife.

The Tomb of Aḥmad Shāh's Son (?)

There is another tomb to the south of Aḥmad Shāh Walī's mausoleum which is reported to be that of the king's son, Ḥasan Khān. But as Ḥasan Khān was really the nephew of Aḥmad Shāh Walī, and after the latter's succession to the throne he was first kept under surveillance at Fīrozābād and subsequently was blinded and died in captivity at the same place, it appears improbable that the corpse of a rival prince would have been brought to the capital for burial in the royal cemetery.[2] The king himself had four sons, including ʿAlā-ud-Dīn, who was the eldest and succeeded Aḥmad Shāh in A.D. 1436. Of the other three sons Maḥmūd Khān was appointed the governor of Rāmgaṛh, Māhūr and Kallam, Dā'ūd Khān the governor of Telingāna, and Muḥammad Khān was associated with the eldest ʿAlā-ud-Dīn in learning the methods and principles of administration.[3] Maḥmūd Khān and Dā'ūd Khān apparently died during their father's reign, for Firishta mentions the name of Prince Muḥammad Khān only. This prince contested the right of sovereignty with ʿAlā-ud-Dīn, and after some warfare had ensued between the two, he was pardoned by ʿAlā-ud-Dīn and granted the territory of Raichur, included in the Telingāna province, since Prince Dā'ūd Khān had died.[4] The tomb, in view of the above facts, probably contains the grave of one of the two princes Maḥmūd Khān and Dā'ūd Khān, or perhaps of both, for there are eight graves inside the tomb, and it may have been the family vault of the descendants of Sulṭān Aḥmad Shāh.[5]

At the time of the establishment of the Department in A.D. 1914 several large trees were growing on the dome of the tomb whose roots had forced large cracks in

[1] This height includes that of the parapet which is 3 feet 2 inches; thus the height of the wall without the parapet is 25 feet 6 inches.

[2] *Firishta*, Persian Text (Bombay ed.), vol. i, p. 616.

[3] Ibid., p. 630.

[4] Ibid., pp. 636–7.

[5] There was another prince in the royal family who bore the name Ḥasan. He was the son of Sulṭān ʿAlā-ud-Dīn and the grandson of Sulṭān Aḥmad Shāh. But as he rebelled at the beginning of Humāyūn Shāh's reign, the latter threw him to his tigers to be devoured by them. A tomb therefore could not have been built over his last remains. *Burhān-i-Ma'āthir* (Hyderabad ed.), pp. 93–4.

its masonry. The trees have since been cut down and the apertures grouted with cement, but as the cracks have disturbed the masonry courses of the dome the present conservation is only a stopgap arrangement, and it is desirable that the damaged parts of the building should be pulled down and rebuilt as soon as adequate funds shall be available. From an architectural point of view the building is not of much importance, for its style, both externally and internally, is the same as that of the tomb of Aḥmad Shāh's wife, and in dimensions it is even a little smaller than the latter, the square base measuring 45 feet 7 inches on each side externally, and 31 feet 1 inch internally, the height of the walls being 23 feet 3 inches, and the circumference of the dome at the springing-point 122 feet 7 inches. The interior of the tomb was originally decorated with stucco-work representing floral designs and religious texts, the remnants of which may be noticed at the tops and the spandrels of the arches, notably in the *miḥrāb*. The latter is built in the form of an arched niche in the western wall and has a semi-decagonal plan at the base. The ceiling was adorned with paintings in the style of Aḥmad Shāh al-Walī's tomb.

The Tomb of Sulṭān 'Alā-ud-Dīn Shāh II

As explained above,[1] 'Alā-ud-Dīn was the eldest son of Aḥmad Shāh al-Walī, whom he succeeded after the death of the latter in A.D. 1436. He was a cultured prince, fond of literary pursuits and benevolent in his attitude towards the distressed, but at the same time a little weak in administration; and as a result of this there were revolts both in the capital itself and in different parts of his kingdom during his reign. He built a large hospital at Bidar and endowed lands from the income of which medicines, food, and drink were provided for the sick. He also appointed physicians, both Hindu and Muslim, to treat the patients.[2] He was an orator and sometimes went over to the Masjid-i-Jāmi' (the Assembly Mosque) to deliver the Friday sermon (*khuṭba*) himself.[3]

The tomb of 'Alā-ud-Dīn, which was perhaps built by him during his lifetime, must have been a magnificent building when intact, for such features of it as have survived show a great improvement in its decoration compared with that of Aḥmad Shāh's mausoleum. The tile panels and the carving on the black stone margins of arches attract the eye at once by their colour schemes and delightful designs. To the tiles much damage has been done by the inclemencies of the weather and by the vandalism of curious visitors who have torn out the tiles from the panels up to the height their hands could reach on the walls. The specimens which are intact show pleasing devices, comprising floral scrolls, geometric patterns, and calligraphic motifs. The principal colours represented are blue, green, and yellow shown on a white background. Yellow has been used as a contrast to deep blue and green. The technique is the same as that of the tiles of the Audience Hall in the Fort, and it is not unlikely that the craftsmen who designed and manufactured the tile-panels of the dadoes of the Audience Hall were also employed for the decoration of the tomb (Pls. XXVII–XXIX). Maḥmūd Gāwān, who was familiar with the artisans and craftsmen of Persia, acquired much influence during the reign of 'Alā-ud-Dīn, being honoured by

[1] *Supra*, p. 129. [2] *Firishta*, Persian Text, vol. i, p. 634. [3] Ibid., p. 653.

the rank of one thousand retainers (*hazārī*), and he may have arranged to bring out some clever designers and manufacturers from that country to embellish the buildings at Bidar.

The black stone margins along the decorative panels and the architectural features of the building are also distinctive characteristics of this tomb, showing a refined colour sense combined with well-developed skill in the art of carving (Pl. LXXVII). For example, the slender black stone bands at the four corners of the tomb, where its walls join one another, are not only pleasing to the eye on account of their architectural elegance and fine polish, but their ingenious carving, which comprises an elaborate form of the key-pattern design, also arrests the attention. Some of these stone margins are plain but beautifully polished, and some have rope-pattern and geometric devices carved on them.

Further, the arches of the tomb display an air of majesty in their large dimensions and perfect taste in their fine proportions. The three entrance arches in the middle of the walls towards the south, east, and north, have each a span of 16 feet 9 inches in contrast to a height of 35 feet 6 inches from the floor to the apex. They have no stilt at the top and are more or less like the pointed arches of the Mughals in North India, or the four-centred Tudor arch of England (Pl. LXXVII). The exterior of the building on each side, beside the lofty arches in the middle, has a pair of comparatively smaller arches flanking the latter towards both the right and the left. The pairs of smaller arches differ in dimensions for the sake of variety, but their shapes are uniform. They have also alcove-like recesses behind them which originally were lavishly decorated with encaustic tiles. The ornamentation of the exterior of the tomb may perhaps at one time have given the same impression of splendour and glory as is produced by the tile-decorated walls of the Dome of the Rock at Jerusalem. The name of the king with his title was given in the band of tiles above the southern doorway, but except the word *as-Sulṭān* the rest of the inscription has perished.[1]

[1] The name of ʿAlā-ud-Dīn with his titles is, however, preserved in an inscription on a tomb at Naubād which is described elsewhere in this book. As it is a contemporary inscription, being dated Shahūr san 847 (A.D. 1446), the importance of the information contained therein regarding the titles must not be underrated. A quotation from the inscription is therefore given below:

. . . . المجتهد في نصب سرادق الامن والامان المستمسك بالنص اللّه يامر بالعدل والاحسان ابو المظفر علاء الدنيا والدين احمد شاه بن احمد شاه البهمني السلطان ابن السلطان . . . .

Translation

The holy warrior in setting up the canopies of peace and safety, the abider by the Divine text in administering justice and benevolence, *Abū-'l-Muẓaffar ʿAlā-ud-Dunya wad-Dīn Aḥmad Shāh son of Aḥmad Shāh al-Baihmanī, the Sulṭān son of the Sulṭān* . . . . *Infra*, p. 206, and *Epig. Ind. Mosl.*, 1935–6, pp. 35–6.

Firishta (Persian text, vol. i, p. 653) has given the titles which the king himself used in the *khuṭba*:

السلطان العادل الكريم الحليم الرّؤف على عباد اللّه الغني علاء الدنيا والدين علاء الدين ابن اعظم السلاطين احمد شاه ولي البهمني.

Translation

The just, benevolent and clement Sulṭān, the merciful to the servants of the Bountiful God, the exalter of the world and the faith, ʿAlā-ud-Dīn son of the greatest of the Sulṭāns, Aḥmad Shāh Walī Baihmanī.

(*note continued on p. 132*)

The dimensions of the square base of the building and the dome surmounting it are practically the same as those of the mausoleum of Aḥmad S͟hāh, but the parapet above the walls is of the trefoil pattern, differing from that of the latter building, which is arch-shaped. Of the two designs the trefoil pattern has a better artistic effect and it is more appropriate to the other decorative features of ʿAlā-ud-Dīn's tomb. The inner arrangement of the building can be best understood by comparing the plan given on Pl. LXXVI. It comprises a square hall with deeply recessed arches and niches built on all its four sides. The hall itself measures 51 feet 2 inches on each side. The niches have openings at their backs for light and air, and originally they were filled with tracery of different pleasing designs. The tracery was subsequently destroyed through various causes, and the openings were filled with substitutes which betray poor taste. These are now being gradually replaced by the trellis-work of the original design.

The ceiling of the dome was originally painted, and a few fragments of the paintings may be traced here and there. The interior of the tomb seems to have been very roughly used at one time by some uncultured people, causing damage not only to the paintings of the ceiling, or to the plaster of the walls, but destroying completely the sarcophagus over the grave; this has been rebuilt by the Archaeological Department in order to let ignorant folk know that the building is a tomb. The whirligig of time occasionally takes strange turns to mock the glory of the mightiest kings.

The Tomb of Sulṭān Humāyūn

It is situated next to the tomb of his father, Sulṭān ʿAlā-ud-Dīn, but having been struck by lightning in comparatively recent times, the larger part of its dome and walls have fallen down.[1] However, such parts of the building as are intact show some features which may be of interest to the student of Baihmanī architecture. In the description of the tombs of Sulṭān Aḥmad S͟hāh and Sulṭan ʿAlā-ud-Dīn it has

(*note continued from p. 131*)

The name and title of the king as given on his coins are as follows:

(*a*) السلطان الحليم الكريم الرؤف علا عباد اللّه الغني

ابو المظفر علاء الدنيا و الدين احمد شاه بن احمد شاه الولي البهمني

(*b*) المعتصم باللّه المنّان سمي خليل الرحمٰن ابو المظفر

علاء الدنيا و الدين احمد شاه بن احمد شاه السلطان

Vide *Cat. Brit. Mus.*, *Indian Coins*, *Muhdn. States*, 150–1, xi.

(*c*) السلطان القوي للاسلام مع الفضل والعدل والاحسان

ابو المظفر علاء الدنيا والدين احمد شاه بن احمد شاه السلطان

Vide *Cat. Coins Ind. Mus.*, vol. ii, pp. 201–2.

On the copper issues the titles . . . المتوكل على اللّه الغني : المستوثق باللّه الحنّان المنان الغني and الواثق بتائيد الملك الالٰه are also noticed.

[1] In the chapter on 'History' it has been noted already that the debris of the dome were lying on the site until A.D. 1917 when the Archaeological Department removed them and covered the open masonry of the walls and the other parts of the building with lime plaster with a view to protecting them from the destructive effect of the rain-water.

been pointed out that the arches of the former show a stilt at the apex,[1] while those of the latter resemble the pointed Mug͟hal arch of North India or the four-centred Tudor arch of England.[2] The architect of Humāyūn's tomb with a view to offering a contrast to the above-mentioned two kinds of arches has chosen a different shape for the arches of this building, which he has arranged by giving a wide span and low imposts to the arches. This shape is seen first in the outer corridor of the Great Mosque in the Fort at Gulbarga which was built in A.D. 1367. From the artistic point of view the effect is not very pleasing to the eye, the arch looking somewhat squat in its proportions,[3] but it is good for the purpose of variety, and also stronger in construction, for the voussoirs being carried down to low altitudes, towards the ground level, the force of the thrust is considerably diminished. This shape of the arch has, however, been used more frequently in the buildings of the ʿĀdil S͟hāhī kings at Bījāpur and also of Barīdī kings at Bidar itself. The dimensions of the large arches of this style in Humāyūn's tomb are: span 12 feet 10 inches, height of the imposts 9 feet 6 inches, and height of the arch from ground level up to the apex, 18 feet 2 inches. The face of the walls internally has another series of arches in its upper part; they are smaller in dimensions than the lower ones but more squat in proportions than the latter (Pl. LXXVIII). Above the smaller arches the architect has built triangular corbels arranged in clusters, and placed above them heavy stone slabs which make the plan of the building 24-sided at that level, while the weight of the corbels and the stone slabs which project inwardly also assists in counteracting the thrust of the dome.

The tomb at its base measures 77 feet 5 inches on each side externally and 52 feet 4 inches internally, the thickness of the walls thus being 13 feet 6 inches approximately. There are, however, steps built in the thickness of the walls which lead to the roof. The tomb is entirely built of black trap masonry laid in lime, but the upper courses of the dome are of light spongy bricks[4] which float in water, and are similar in composition to those used by the Kākatīya kings in building the spires of their temples, notably those at Pālampeṭ in the Warangal district. It is apparent that the majority of the masons employed for building these tombs would have been Hindus, and they must have recommended the use of light bricks in the construction of the upper part of the dome in order to avoid the unnecessary load.

As the interior of the dome is not plastered, and further its masonry has been split

[1] *Supra*, p. 117. [2] *Supra*, p. 131.

[3] The contrast between the narrow- and wide-span arches is shown with considerable effect in the Gagaṇ Maḥall, Ānand Maḥall, and Sangat Maḥall at Bījāpur. *Vide* Henry Cousen's *Bījāpūr Architecture*, Pls. XVI, LV, and LXIII.

[4] Some bricks of the Rāmappa temple and Humāyūn's tomb were sent for examination to Dr. Habib Hasan, Chief Chemist of Government Industrial Laboratory, Hyderabad, Dn. He has kindly reported as follows: 'The samples of floating bricks from Bidar are similar to those from Warangal as far as the method of manufacture is concerned. The material used to make the brick spongy was apparently saw-dust. The weight of the specimens is $\frac{1}{3}$ to $\frac{1}{4}$ of the ordinary bricks of the same size. The Bidar specimens show better quality as regards homogeneous mixing and uniform burning than their prototypes from Rāmappa, as a result of which the porosity is well-maintained in the body of bricks from Bidar and they float well in water.' The bricks used in Humāyūn's tomb vary in size, the largest being 10 in. × 7 in. × 2 in.; some of them are wedge-shaped.

by lightning, the student can see that the construction of the dome comprises concentric belts of masonry which decrease in thickness upwardly; in other words, the thickness of the crust of the dome near its springing point is 6 feet while at the top it has decreased to 3 feet 4 inches only.

Another distinctive feature of the interior of this tomb is the trabeate style of the frames of its niches, while those of the tombs of Aḥmad S͟hāh and ʿAlā-ud-Dīn, alluded to above, are arch-shaped. The change shows the influence of Hindu architecture, for niches with carved rectangular openings are a distinguishing feature of the medieval temples of the Deccan, in which the images of different gods and goddesses are installed. In this building the niches when fitted with wooden doors may have been utilized for keeping sacred texts and other articles, such as tomb-covers, canopies, and censers, connected with the ritual of the tomb.

The Tomb of Sulṭān Niẓām S͟hāh

It is situated to the west of Humāyūn's tomb, and as Niẓām S͟hāh was a boy of only eight years old when his father abdicated the throne in his favour, and he ruled for only two years, the idea of building a tomb would not have occurred to him at such an early age. His mother, who acted as Regent, may have ordered the building of the tomb, but it remained incomplete, apparently through her demise also on a subsequent date. The enclosure walls of the tomb are massively built of trap masonry and still rise to a height of 25 feet from the ground level. The external dimensions of the tomb at the base are the same as those of the other royal tombs, that is, 77 feet on each side. The sepulchral hall, which is square in plan, measures 50 feet 4 inches in each direction. It is very likely that the architect had planned to build a dome identical in height and circumference with the domes raised over the tombs of the forebears of Niẓām S͟hāh, for the thickness of the walls, 13 feet 2 inches approximately, indicates that they could easily well support the weight of a structure of that magnitude.

There are openings in the southern, eastern, and northern walls which show that the tomb was entered from these directions, while in the western wall is a semi-decagonal niche in the form of a *miḥrāb*, whence sacred texts were probably recited at the time of the ritual. In the thickness of the eastern wall there are steps which apparently would have led to the roof.

The exterior of the tomb towards the south has a large arch in the middle which forms the entrance, and two arches outlined on the wall on each side of the former. The shape of the large arch does not look very pleasing to the eye owing to its irregular dimensions, which are span 13 feet, height of the imposts 9 feet, and the total height from the floor to the apex 17 feet 8 inches. The pairs of arches which flank it on either side of the entrance arch show a better sense of proportion, as the span of each of them is 9 feet 1 inch, the height of the imposts 8 feet 1 inch, and the height up to the apex 15 feet 10 inches.

The Tomb of Sulṭān Muḥammad S͟hāh III, entitled Las͟hkarī

This tomb is also incomplete, for although Muḥammad S͟hāh ruled nineteen years, yet when he was placed on the throne he was only a lad of nine years old, and for a considerable time a puppet in the hands of the queen-mother, or the two ministers, Khwāja Jahān Turk and Maḥmūd Gāwān, the three together constituting the Council of Regency.[1] The tomb is almost a replica, both in the methods of construction and the general appearance, of the tomb of Niẓām Shāh, and was perhaps designed by the architect of the latter. The only difference is that the dimensions of the arches vary slightly, for instance, the difference between the middle arches of the two tombs is as follows:

Name of building	*Span*	*Height of imposts*	*Height up to the apex*
Tomb of Muḥammad Shāh	14 ft. 8 in.	8 ft. 8 in.	16 ft. 8 in.
Tomb of Niẓām Shāh	13 ft.	9 ft.	17 ft. 8 in.

The construction of the southern wall of Muḥammad Shāh's tomb was carried to a stage where squinches are to be seen now, the height of the latter being 34 feet 6 inches from the level of the floor, while the walls of the tomb of Niẓām Shāh could be built only to a height of 25 feet. Inside the enclosure there are three graves, the middle one of which is probably that of Muḥammad Shāh, while to the right of it is that of his wife.

The Tomb of Malika-i-Jahān

The title Malika-i-Jahān, meaning the 'Queen of the World', was enjoyed by the queen-consorts of the Baihmanī dynasty and subsequent ruling families of the Deccan, but here it refers to the wife of Sulṭān Humāyūn, who played an important role in the history of the Deccan during the reigns of her minor sons Niẓām Shāh and Muḥammad Shāh.[2] She retired from State affairs and devoted herself to the religious life when Muḥammad Shāh was of age and could perform his kingly duties independently.[3] She is mentioned in contemporary history under the title Makhdūma-i-Jahān also, meaning 'Mistress of the World'.[4] Her tomb is situated to the south-west of that of her royal husband, Humāyūn, and to the south-east of the incomplete tombs of her two sons, Niẓām Shāh and Muḥammad Shāh.

The Malika's tomb is a little smaller in dimensions than those of her husband and of her two sons, and measures 46 feet 5 inches on each side externally. The walls have three arches of pleasing proportions in each direction, and the middle arch in the southern wall forms the entrance to the interior of the tomb. The dimensions of these arches are uniform, their span being 8 feet 3 inches, springing-point 12 feet above the level of the ground, and height up to the apex 19 feet 2 inches. The spandrels of the arches are decorated with medallions of stucco-work exhibiting neat workmanship. The height of the walls on each side is 30 feet 10 inches from the ground level, and at the top they have a parapet which rises 4 feet 2 inches higher still.

The tomb is surmounted by a dome the circumference of which is 124 feet

[1] For further information regarding Muḥammad Shāh see the chapter on 'History', *supra*, pp. 9–10.

[2] *Firishta*, Persian text, vol. i, pp. 662 ff.

[3] Ibid., p. 673.

[4] Ibid., p. 672.

externally. There are four graves below the vault, and the second of these, which is in the middle of the hall, is pointed out as that of the queen. The *miḥrāb* in the western wall of the tomb has some ornamental plaster-work.

The Tomb of Maḥmūd S͟hāh Baihmanī

This king also ascended the throne at the early age of twelve years. The government at that time was *de facto* the government of the ministers, who formed cliques to undermine the influence of their rivals, and there were constant murders—sometimes the puppet kings were made responsible for these crimes. As a result of such a state of affairs some of the governors felt afraid to attend the court, and ultimately became independent during the reign of Maḥmūd S͟hāh (A.D. 1482–1518), although they did not assume regal titles until after his death. Maḥmūd S͟hāh, however, ruled for thirty-six years and probably had his tomb built during his lifetime, for he would have seen the incomplete tombs of his father Muḥammad S͟hāh and uncle Niẓām S͟hāh, both of whom had died young. The tomb of Maḥmūd S͟hāh (Pls. LXXIX–LXXX) possesses all the solid dignity of the tombs of the earlier Baihmanī kings, but it looks somewhat austere in architectural effect, for neither is its exterior lavishly decorated with encaustic tiles like the tomb of ʿAlā-ud-Dīn, nor is its interior embellished with paintings like the mausoleum of Aḥmad S͟hāh al-Walī. The walls, which rise to a height of 45 feet 10 inches from the floor, indicate a clear batter which the architect has purposely arranged with a view to ensuring the safety of the high walls on the one hand and counteracting the thrust of the gigantic dome on the other. The walls are crowned with a parapet of plain design representing arch-heads, the latter rising 5 feet above the top of the walls.

The enclosure walls at their base measure 77 feet on each side, and their face in each direction has an arch of massive proportions in the middle and smaller arches built both above its top and in its sides. These smaller arches are arranged in three rows, having been built one above the other. The shapes and dimensions of the arches of the three rows differ, those at the bottom being the largest and those at the top the smallest. The arches of the middle row have a wide span in proportion to their height and look thick and clumsy (Pl. LXXIX). The large arch in the middle has a span of 18 feet, while the height of its apex from the floor is 26 feet 4 inches. The device of decorating the walls with arched niches arranged one above the other is seen more frequently in the post-Baihmanī tombs of the Deccan, the idea of the architect being twofold: to remove the monotony of the uniform surface of the wall, and to produce an effect of depth and volume by means of the recessed niches.

The dome has an octagonal base on the roof and its walls rise 13 feet 4 inches above this. The circumference of the dome at its springing-point is 206 feet. The interior of the tomb is somewhat sombre, the light entering either through the small door, or through the windows filled with trellis-work. There is no decoration on the walls of the building except an ornamental parapet of trefoil design built below the rim of the vault of the ceiling and the miniature arches in the depth of the squinches. The sepulchral hall is square in plan and measures 51 feet on each side. The walls, as usual with the Baihmanī architecture, are most massively built, their thickness being 12 feet 10 inches on each side.

Two Anonymous Tombs (The Sepulchres of Sulṭān Aḥmad Shāh and Sulṭān 'Alā-ud-Dīn?)

To the south of Sulṭān Maḥmūd Shāh's tomb there are two sepulchres of small dimensions wherein may have been interred the last remains of the two puppet kings, Aḥmad Shāh and 'Alā-ud-Dīn, who were placed on the throne by the all-powerful minister, Amīr Barīd, in A.D. 1518 and 1521 respectively. Aḥmad Shāh was a son of Maḥmūd Shāh Baihmanī, and although virtually a prisoner he was shown to the chiefs of the neighbourhood as the ruler of the Baihmanī kingdom. He held this position for a little over two years, and either died a natural death or was disposed of by poisoning in the year 927 H. (A.D. 1521). After his demise Amīr Barīd placed 'Alā-ud-Dīn, another son of Maḥmūd Shāh, on the throne; but as this prince proved himself to be of a stubborn nature, Amīr Barīd removed him after a period of two years and three months following his accession and confined him in a prison.[1]

Of these two sepulchres, one has a conical dome with eight facets, which are marked by plaster ribs. The interior of the tomb is square at the base, measuring 15 feet 3 inches each way, but the squinches at the corners and overlapping arches have made it necessary that the plan near the rim of the vault should become octagonal so that it may fit in with the plan of the vault. The walls of the sepulchre have an arch on each side, and they rise to a height of 12 feet above the ground level and are crowned with a parapet which rises 2 feet 2 inches higher still. There is only one grave below the vault, which may be that of Aḥmad Shāh.

On the west of the above tomb there is another sepulchre which is incomplete. The walls of this building have not been plastered, but the traces of a tomb were noticed by the Archaeological Department in 1915, and it has since been restored by them. This sepulchre may belong to 'Alā-ud-Dīn who, like his brother Aḥmad Shāh, fell a victim to the cruelty of the minister Amīr Barīd in A.D. 1521.[2]

The Tomb of Sulṭān Walī-Ullāh

This king also was maltreated by the wicked minister Amīr Barīd, and after his nominal sovereignty of three years when he endeavoured to extricate himself from the clutches of the tyrant, the latter first had him under surveillance in the royal palace and ultimately arranged for his murder. The lustful minister afterwards married the wife of Walī-Ullāh.[3]

The tomb of this king is situated in the main group of the Baihmanī tombs, to the west of Maḥmūd Shāh's mausoleum. It is an insignificant structure compared with the majestic tombs of his forebears, and consists of a square base crowned with a conical dome (Pl. LXXXI). The walls of the base measure 26 feet 10 inches on each

[1] For further information regarding these two kings see *Firishta*, Persian text, vol. i, pp. 726–8.

[2] To the east of these two sepulchres is a tomb with an underground vault. The walls of the latter have some *Qur'ānic* texts inscribed on them. The grave in this vault is that of a lady.

[3] *Firishta*, Persian text, vol. i, p. 728.

side, and they rise to a height of 16 feet 2 inches above the ground level. On the top of the walls there was originally a parapet, traces of which still exist. The height of the parapet when intact must have been 2 feet 2 inches. Above the roof a conical dome rises which has eight facets. The interior of the sepulchre is entered by a small door from the south, the dimensions of the latter being: width 2 feet 3 inches, height 4 feet 7 inches. The plan of the interior of the tomb is square, but on account of the arches which are built at the corners and which project a little from the lines of those built in the side walls, it has become octagonal, and fits in with the shape of the vault of the ceiling.

The Tomb of Sulṭān Kalīm-Ullāh

He was the last nominal king of the Baihmanī dynasty, whom the minister Amīr Barīd proclaimed in public as the rightful sovereign in A.D. 1525, but in reality kept him under the closest watch and treated him with such indignity that in A.D. 1527 he had to flee for his life, first to Bijāpur and afterwards to Ahmadnagar. The unhappy king did not receive a generous reception from the rulers of either of these two places, and he passed the remaining part of his life virtually as a prisoner. After his demise his body was brought from Ahmadnagar to Bidar and interred in the royal cemetery close to the tomb of his brother Walī-Ullāh.

The tomb built over his remains is similar in style to the tomb of Walī-Ullāh, although slightly larger in dimensions than the latter (Pl. LXXXI). The walls of the tomb measure 28 feet 10 inches on each side at the base externally, and rise 17 feet 5 inches above the ground level. On the top of the walls was originally a parapet, the remains of which may be noticed in a few places. These remains show that the parapet when intact must have been 3 feet 2 inches high. The vault of the tomb has a conical shape externally and is divided into eight facets, but internally the shape is considerably modified and it looks more or less circular with only a slight stilt towards the apex (Pl. LXXXII). The tomb is entered by an arched door from the south, and the internal arrangement of the building can be studied best by comparing the plan and section given on Pl. LXXXII. The sepulchral hall is octagonal in plan with pentagonal projections at the corners. The arrangement of overlapping arches to distribute the weight of the dome, which is seen on a grand scale in the Gol Guṃbad at Bijāpur, may be noticed on a diminutive scale in this tomb. The building is crowned with a pinnacle of cylindrical shape made of black stone (Pl. LXXXI), in contrast to the finial of Aḥmad Sh̲āh al-Walī which is composed of several orbs of copper plated with gold, placed one above the other.

The Mosque

To the south-west of Kalīm-Ullāh's tomb, on the other side of the road, is a mosque which was used for offering prayers before the corpse was interred in the tomb.[1] It

[1] In the royal cemetery at Golconda each tomb has a separate mosque attached to it. These were apparently used by the reciters of the *Qur'ān* who were employed in intercession for the soul of the deceased. In the Baihmanī cemetery besides this mosque there is another between the tombs of Aḥmad Sh̲āh al-Walī and Sulṭān 'Alā-ud-Dīn. The latter mosque is, however, a very small structure.

is a small building comprising a single hall which measures 34 feet 3 inches in length and 13 feet 6 inches in width. The ceiling of the hall is divided into three compartments, each compartment having a shallow vault. In the front of the mosque there are three arched openings of uniform size, the span of the arches being 8 feet 3 inches, the springing-point 4 feet 5 inches above the ground level, and the height of the apex 9 feet 9 inches from the floor. The height of the front wall of the mosque up to the dripstones (*c͟hhajja*) is 14 feet 10 inches, and above that was a parapet which is now in ruins, but which when intact must have risen 4 feet 7 inches above the dripstones of the front wall.

In the western wall the *miḥrāb* is built in the form of an arched niche, the upper part of which is adorned with miniature arches of plaster-work, and the spandrels with medallions.

The Tomb of S͟hāh Ruk͟h K͟hān (?)

To the north of Sulṭān Maḥmūd S͟hāh's mausoleum, at a distance of nearly two furlongs, is a tomb reported to be that of S͟hāh Ruk͟h K͟hān. He was probably a scion of the royal family, for in this area the only tombs are those of the Baihmanī dynasty. Owing to the growth of a tree, which has now been cut down by the Archaeological Department, the plaster of the southern and western parts of the dome had peeled off and the masonry below it was exposed to the weather.

The façade of the tomb is lavishly decorated with plaster-work, comprising floral devices, a chain-and-pendant motif,[1] and calligraphic designs. Over the eastern doorway the *Āyat-al-Kursī* (Throne verse, *Qur'ān*, ii. 256) is inscribed. The walls forming the base of the tomb measure 39 feet 4 inches on each side, and rise to a height of 34 feet 8 inches including the parapet, which by itself measures 3 feet 8 inches above the top of the walls. The circumference of the drum of the dome at the roof level is 108 feet.

The inner plan of the tomb is square, but it has been converted into an octagon by means of arches in the corners which project a little from the lines of the side walls. Higher up, near the dome, the plan becomes sixteen-sided owing to a band of arched niches. The dimensions of the interior of the tomb according to its octagonal plan are 26 feet 8 inches across, from one side of the octagon to the corresponding one in the opposite direction. The arrangement of overlapping arches for the distribution of the weight of the dome is clever architecturally, and pleasing to the eye artistically. The shape of the arches of this tomb also indicates a fine sense of proportion. Inside the building there are two graves with stone sarcophagi which have been damaged by vandals. The floor of the tomb has also been completely destroyed by its rude occupants in comparatively later times.

To the east of S͟hāh Ruk͟h K͟hān's tomb there is another, but it is of smaller dimensions than the first. It was impossible to ascertain who is buried in the small tomb, but he must have been a member of the royal family and was perhaps related to S͟hāh Ruk͟h K͟hān. The walls of the building at their base measure 14 feet 8 inches externally on each side, and they rise to a height of 13 feet 5 inches from the ground

[1] This device is seen more frequently on Barīdī monuments.

level. The parapet originally built on the top of the walls has perished almost completely, but when intact must have been 2 feet high. The interior of the tomb has a square plan at the base, measuring 14 feet 3 inches on each side, but higher it becomes octagonal owing to the squinches which are built at the corners. There is only one grave, the masonry of which has decayed. There is a stone sarcophagus which is lying apart separately in the sepulchral hall.

The Well

The late Mr. Sultan ʿAlī Khān Farūqī, who did some excellent work as the Superintendent of the Archaeological Monuments at Bidar, when repairing the tombs at Āshṭūr traced the site of an old well in the lowlands to the south of Aḥmad Shāh al-Walī's tomb, the distance of the well from the latter being half a furlong. On excavating the site a large well with masonry walls and steps and an arcade built in the south-west corner, a little higher than the water level, was disclosed.

The most important feature of the discovery is that the well has two inscriptions, one of them being in Persian and the other in Marāṭhī, but both mentioning the name of Mirza Walī Amīr Barīd, who as the eighth ruler of the Barīdī dynasty is mentioned by Firishta, but in the *Cambridge History of India* (vol. iii, p. 709) the name of this king has been given as ʿAlī Barīd Shāh. As Firishta's statement regarding the name of the eighth Barīdī king is also supported by the author of *Basātīn*,[1] there remains no doubt that the name of the king was Mirzā Walī Amīr Barīd and not ʿAlī Barīd Shāh as given in the *Cambridge History*.[2]

[1] *Basātīnu-s-Salāṯīn*, Hyderabad lithograph, p. 273.

[2] The text of the Persian inscription is as follows:

باني٭ اين چاه در دور حضرت سليمان جاه اميرزا ولي امير بريد شاه خلد اللّه سلطانه العبد جگتراؤ بن بنچال يكهندو دولتي سنه ١٠١٨

Translation

The builder of this well, during the reign of His Majesty with Solomon's glory, Amirzā Walī Amīr Barīd Shāh, may God perpetuate his sovereignty, was the servant of the state, Jagat Rāo, the son of Banchālīkhandū. In the year 1018 H. (A.D. 1609).

The Marāṭhī record has been deciphered by Mr. R. M. Joshi, M.A., whose reading of the text is given below:

1. अज सळतनत सुळतान अह
2. मद शाह बहमनि बाजद ऊमायुन
3. अकरम बरीद शाहा आठविं पिढी
4. अमीर बरिद शाहाचि पादशाही
5. याचा फर्जंद जगपति राव दौळती वि
6. हीरी बारींविं चौरस बांधविळि
7. असे शुऊर सन अशर अळफ
8. याचि हिंदवि बेरिज १०१० श
9. के १५३१ साम्यनाम संवत्सर (*note 2 continued on p. 141*)

The Chaukhaṇḍī of Haḍrat Khalīl-Ullāh

Chaukhaṇḍī is a compound Hindī word, *chau* meaning four and *khaṇḍ* meaning a storey, thus *chaukhaṇḍī* meaning a four-storeyed building. The term has been applied to this building because it is situated on a high place and approached by several flights of steps, although the building itself is only double-storeyed. Haḍrat Khalīl-Ullāh was the son of Shāh Ni'mat-Ullāh Kirmānī, and the former came over from his native place to Bidar after the death of his revered father in 834 H. (A.D. 1431). The king 'Alā-ud-Dīn, who was ruling at the time, received him with the utmost kindness, and two of his sons, Shāh Ḥabīb-Ullāh and Shāh Muḥibb-Ullāh, were married to the royal princesses.[1] The *Chaukhaṇḍī* has three graves in the main vault and several others in the corridor.

The tomb is approached from the road which goes from the Dulhan Darwāza to the mausolea of the Baihmanī kings, being situated some three furlongs from the latter on the city side. To approach the outer gateway of the tomb the visitor has first to ascend a flight of five steps and walk across a pavement, 39 feet 5 inches by 64 feet 7 inches, at the end of which there is another flight of steps, numbering seven and leading to another pavement which extends to a length of 37 feet 9 inches, up to the steps of the gateway. The latter has a pleasing façade, comprising an arch in the middle and a parapet of trefoil pattern at the top of the wall. The total height of the wall including the parapet is 30 feet 4 inches, while the entrance arch has a height of 21 feet up to its apex, with a span of 13 feet. The arch has a stilt at the top showing Persian influence. There is a panel with two medallions of stucco-work to decorate the arch; the panel contains a religious text and the medallions the names of Allāh, Muḥammad, and 'Alī, written in the *Kūfic* script but arranged in the *Ṭughra* style.

The visitor has to ascend two more steps to enter the gateway, which has a passage in the middle and two halls flanking the latter, one on either side of it. The width of the passage is 11 feet and its length up to the inner arch 39 feet. The ceiling over the passage is divided into three compartments by means of arches

(*note 2 continued from p. 140*)

Transliteration

1. Aja Saḷatanata Suḷatāna Aha
2. Mada Shāha Bahamani bājada Humāyuna
3. Akarama Barīda Shāhā āṭhavin piḍhī
4. Amīr Barida shāhāchi pādashāhī
5. Yāchā pharjanda Jagapati Rao Dauḷati vi
6. Hīrī bāriṅvīṅ chauras bāndhaviḷi
7. Ase Shuhur Sana ashar aḷapha
8. Yāchi hindavi berija 1010 Śa
9. Ke 1531 Sāmyanāma Sanvatsara

Translation

During the period of the reign of the dynasty of Aḥmad Shāh Baihmanī, after whom there was Humāyūn Akram Barīd Shāh, and in the eighth generation there was Amīr Barīd, his son Jagapati Rāo Daulatī constructed a well with steps, the *Shahūr* year was *'ashare alaf* totalling 1010, the Śaka year is 1531 cyclic year Sāmya (Saumya). *Epig. Ind. Mosl.*, 1937–8, pp. 3–4.

[1] *Firishta*, Persian text, vol. i, pp. 634–5.

built across its width, each compartment containing a vault. The halls on both sides of the passage are of uniform dimensions, each measuring 36 feet 7 inches in length and 11 feet 5 inches in depth. They have three arched openings towards the passage and their plinth rises 3 feet 4 inches above the latter.

Passing through the gateway the visitor has to ascend two steps in order to reach the passage, which leads to a terrace eleven steps higher than itself. The length of the passage from the gateway to this terrace is 58 feet and its width 12 feet 5 inches. On either side of the passage at this stage are a large number of graves belonging to the disciples of Shāh Khalīl-Ullāh and his successors. The passage continues after the visitor has ascended the eleven steps referred to above, and extends to a distance of 73 feet with a breadth of 13 feet 6 inches, until another flight of steps is approached. The latter number fourteen and lead to a platform the exact dimensions of which, owing to the tombs which have been built towards the east and west in later times, cannot be determined with precision now. But the distance between the doorway of the *Chaukhaṇḍī* and the steps of the platform is 57 feet 5 inches.

The building appears to have been designed by the same architect who planned the tomb of Sulṭān 'Alā-ud-Dīn, for there is much in common between the architectural features and decorative schemes of the two monuments, although their ground plans differ, the tomb of 'Alā-ud-Dīn being square (Pl. LXXVI) and the *Chaukhaṇḍī* octagonal (Pl. LXXXIII). The walls of the *Chaukhaṇḍī* were originally richly decorated with encaustic tiles, the traces of which exist only in a few places now, but the designs of the arch-shaped, lozenge-shaped, and rectangular panels which contained the tile-work are almost identical with those of 'Alā-ud-Dīn's tomb, and the uniformity is all the more complete because of the black stone borders with their elegant carving, representing a key-pattern, a rope-motif, and other geometrical and floral designs, which are to be seen in both buildings (Pls. LXXVII*b* and LXXXIV–LXXXV). The form of the arches also suggests a striking resemblance, indicating in both monuments a fine sense of proportion. The outer arch of the entrance of the *Chaukhaṇḍī* has a span of 14 feet 8 inches, while its height up to the apex is 30 feet, and the span of 'Alā-ud-Dīn's tomb is 16 feet 9 inches, and the height up to the apex 35 feet 6 inches, the proportions being practically the same, that is, the span being nearly half of the height up to the apex. There are similar arches on all the eight sides of the octagon, and above them another series the spans of which are the same as those of the lower arches, but the height up to the apex has been kept less by the architect in order to avoid monotony in the general appearance of the building. The height of the walls is 51 feet 4 inches, and above them rises a parapet of massive arch-heads which measure 8 feet 8 inches in height above the roof level. The circuit of the walls at the base is 176 feet, each side of the octagon measuring 22 feet. The walls are built of black trap masonry laid in lime and they are very massive in construction, being 15 feet 10 inches thick. They could have easily borne the weight of a dome upon them; but whether the architect had planned to build one is doubtful, for the arrangement of the arches in the upper part of the walls in the interior of the building is such as not to support the view that the building of a dome was part of the original scheme. The walls in the interior of the building have not been plastered over, and the building material and methods can be studied with advantage. There are steps in the thickness of the walls which lead to their top, and as behind the parapet there is a clear space 10 feet 9 inches wide, the visitor can walk with comfort on the top of the walls and enjoy the panorama of the surrounding country. The site of the *Chaukhaṇḍī* is 165 feet higher than that of the Baihmanī tombs, the height of the former being 1,955 feet above sea-level, and that of the latter 1,890 feet.

The interior of the tomb is approached by a covered passage from the arch facing the south, which has a recess 6 feet 4 inches deep to serve the purpose of a portico, and a room built in the thickness of the wall behind it (Pl. LXXXIII). The ceiling of the passage is divided into three compartments by means of arches built across its width, and each compartment has a vault of pleasing design, the middle one being fluted. The tomb of the saint, which is built in the middle of the interior of the *Chaukhaṇḍī*, has a square plan externally and an octagonal plan internally, the latter form arranged by means of semi-decagonal projections at the corners. The external dimensions of the tomb are: the walls at their base on each side, 33 feet 10 inches, their height including the parapet, 24 feet 1 inch, and the circumference of the base of the dome at roof level, 133 feet 4 inches. The walls of the tomb are decorated with stucco-work both internally and externally, and such architectural features as overlapping arches or the ornamental border of trefoil design along the rim, or medallions in the spandrels of arches add further to the beauty of this tomb.

In later times separate vaults have been built for the graves of the descendants of Shāh Khalīl-Ullāh, one of which is attached to the *Chaukhaṇḍī* itself, and may be noticed in the form of a projection to the east of the passage (Pl. LXXXIV). The external dimensions of the projection are 23 feet by 34 feet 11 inches, and the walls rise to a height of 27 feet 1 inch and are crowned with a parapet which rises 3 feet higher still above them. The circumference of the dome at its springing-point is 65 feet. Over the doorway of this vault the *Nād-i-'Alī* and the date 1086 H. (A.D. 1675) are carved, which show that it was built after the conquest of Bidar by Aurangzeb in A.D. 1658.[1] Inside the vault there are nine graves, seven being large and two small. The latter are probably those of the children of the family. Some descendants of the saint are buried in the corridor, four graves being in the apartment to the right of the passage and four in that to the left. There are two more graves in a chamber facing the south-west side of the *Chaukhaṇḍī*. The beautiful inscription in the Thulth style of writing which begins from the main doorway of the *Chaukhaṇḍī* is continued to this side of the octagon. It was designed by a calligraphist of Shiraz called Mughīth.[2]

[1] Some descendants of Shāh Khalīl-Ullāh still live in Bidar.

[2] This inscription is carved in relief on a black stone tablet the face of which is decorated with a floral scroll of delicate design, the letters being superimposed on it. It is not only the subtleness of the design but also the large size of the letters which impress the lover of art. The height of the letters is 15 inches and their thickness over an inch, so that the skill of the calligraphist in writing such bold

(*note continued on p. 144*)

On the western side of the octagon there is a small enclosure with screens of trellis-work projecting from the main building. The designs of the trellis-work are very attractive. The dimensions of the enclosure are: length 15 feet, width 6 feet, height of the screen including the parapet, 11 feet 10 inches. There is only one grave in this enclosure. Outside the main building towards the west there is another enclosure with screens of trellis-work. The screens measure 7 feet 8 inches in height, and the other dimensions of the enclosure are: length 20 feet 7 inches, width 14 feet 5 inches. Inside the enclosure there are only two graves, apparently belonging to the members of the saint's family.

To the east of *Chaukhaṇḍī*, until some twelve years ago, stood a tomb which has since perished completely, but photographs of its exterior and interior were fortunately taken by the Department in A.D. 1917, and they are reproduced as Pls. LXXXVI–LXXXVII. The tomb was not of large dimensions, but it had certain decorative features which made the building very picturesque. The walls of the tomb on each side measured 28 feet 10 inches at their base externally, and they rose to a height of 23 feet 10 inches from the floor. The façade was adorned with arches of elegant proportions and a parapet of trefoil pattern (Pl. LXXXVI). The spandrels of the arches were decorated with medallions of stucco-work, which was also used in the ornamentation of other architectural features. The dome was a little flattish at the top, not showing the stilt of the earlier vaults of the Baihmanī architecture. Its circumference near the base was 81 feet. The plan of the interior of the tomb was octagonal, and the walls were lavishly decorated with plaster-work, the designs being floral, geometrical, and calligraphic. On Pl. LXXXVII the reader will also notice pairs of brackets of Hindu design used as ornamentation on the wall below the inscriptional band. The latter, besides the religious texts, contained also the name of Sulṭān Maḥmūd Shāh, son of Sulṭān Muḥammad, and perhaps also the name of the person who was buried in the tomb. It may be the sepulchre of Shāh Muḥibb-Ullāh[1] who occupied a pre-eminent position at the beginning of Sulṭān Maḥmūd Shāh's reign, being one of the two holy personages who helped the king to ascend the throne during the ceremony of his coronation.[2] The saint appears to have died during Maḥmūd Shāh's reign for, in the great revolt which broke out at the capital in the form of a conspiracy to murder the king in 892 H. (A.D. 1487), a son of Shāh Muḥibb-Ullāh craved mercy for the guilty party.[3]

(*note continued from p. 143*)
characters can be duly appreciated. The text contains a quotation from the *Qur'ān* (xiii. 23), but the name of the artist with his cognomen is given on the southern doorway:

كتب الفقير المحتاج الى الله تعالى مغيث القاري الشيرازي

'*Written by the humble dependant upon the High God, Mughīth al-Qārī al-Shīrāzī.*'

For further information regarding this inscription see *Epig. Ind. Mosl.*, 1927–8, p. 18.

[1] A tomb at Malkāpur also is assigned to Shāh Muḥibb-Ullāh, *supra* pp. 212–13.

[2] According to Firishta two chairs of silver were placed, one on either side of the Turquoise Throne, and Shāh Muḥibb-Ullāh and Sayyid Ḥabīb, who were the two most saintly personages of the time, placed the royal crown of the Baihmanī kings on Maḥmūd Shāh's head, and then, each of them holding one of the king's arms, helped him to ascend the royal throne, and they themselves sat on the silver chairs placed for them on either side of the throne. (Persian text, vol. i, p. 700.)

[3] *Firishta*, Persian text, vol. i, p. 711.

To the south-west of the *Chaukhanḍī* there is another anonymous sepulchre similar in style to the above-mentioned tomb which has now perished. This was also until recently in a dilapidated condition, but it has been thoroughly restored now and saved from further decay. Like the first tomb it has a square base and is crowned with a dome. The walls on each side measure 27 feet at the base and rise to a height of 17 feet 6 inches from the ground level. The parapet has crumbled into ruins and has not been restored, but the dome is intact, and at the roof level it measures 76 feet 7 inches in girth. The interior of the tomb is square in plan, measuring 18 feet 10 inches on each side, and although the arrangement of squinches and overlapping arches is the same as in the last-mentioned tomb, yet the stucco decoration is more profuse than it is in the latter (Pl. LXXXVIII). The ornamentation further does not exhibit a refined taste, and it appears that at that time Hindu architects were freely employed for designing both the architectural features and the decorative schemes of buildings, and that their love of ornamentation often overbalanced the architectural plan. The bracket-motif decoration along the rim of the vault, and in the space between the apexes of the overlapping arches, has a rather tawdry effect. The band of small squares incised in plaster is not so bad, but the best specimens of this motif may be noticed in the sixth and seventh centuries' rock-hewn shrines of the Deccan, notably at Ajanta and Ellora.

To complete the description of Shāh Khalīl-Ullāh's tomb two more buildings may be mentioned. One of them is a two-storeyed structure to the left (west) of the gateway. The lower storey comprises a double hall, measuring 27 feet 8 inches in length and 19 feet 8 inches in depth. This hall has arched openings towards the east which are somewhat squattish in their proportions. The ceiling of the hall is vaulted, but the vaults are rather shallow. The upper storey has only one hall, which measures 27 feet 8 inches in length and 19 feet 8 inches in depth. The hall has arched openings towards the east which are somewhat clumsy in their proportions. The ceiling of the hall is vaulted, but the vaults are rather shallow. The upper storey has only one hall, which measures 27 feet 8 inches in length and 9 feet 10 inches in width. The upper hall of the building was originally used by musicians, who played on trumpets and drums at the four watches to maintain the ceremonial dignity of the shrine.

The other building is a small mosque near the first flight of steps towards the west. It consists of a prayer-hall with a court in front of it. The prayer-hall measures 22 feet 2 inches in length and 8 feet 2 inches in breadth. The ceiling is divided into three compartments, each comprising a vault. There are three arched openings towards the east.

Adjoining the prayer-hall of the mosque towards the south there is another hall measuring 15 feet 4 inches by 8 feet 7 inches. This latter hall has two arched openings towards the east. The building appears to be a later addition to the prayer-hall.

The *Chaukanḍī*, apart from its lofty position, which has made it a prominent feature in the panorama of Bidar, possesses certain architectural merits placing the monument among the best buildings of the Baihmanī period. It is now denuded of much of its pristine splendour, but its stately arches, neat carving, and magnificent calligraphy and tile-work show the high-water mark of the Baihmanī architecture, which was probably reached during the reign of 'Alā-ud-Dīn (A.D. 1436–58), whose own tomb, as observed above,[1] has many architectural and decorative features in common with those of the Chaukhandī.[2]

Tombs on a Platform under a Nīm Tree

Nearly a hundred yards to the south of Shāh Khalīl-Ullāh's shrine there are several tombs built on a platform. At the time of the survey of the site in 1928, a loose inscriptional tablet was found lying on the platform, which had originally belonged either to one of the tombs built on the platform or to some other tomb in the vicinity of the latter. This inscription contains a chronogram, *Jannat al-Firdaus*, which according to the *Abjad* system gives 834 H. (A.D. 1431) as the date of the demise of Shāh Nūr-Ullāh Ḥusainī,[3] who was the grandson of Shāh Ni'mat-Ullāh and was the first descendant of the saint to visit Bidar. Aḥmad Shāh al-Walī, according to Firishta, deputed the princes and the grandees of his court to receive Nūr-Ullāh at a place in the suburbs of Bidar,[4] and when he attended the court the

[1] *Supra*, p. 142.

[2] Inside the main enclosure of Shāh Khalīl-Ullāh's shrine there is a tomb which has the following epitaph carved on a tablet fixed near its head:

Text

بتاريخ پانزدهم شهر ربيع الثاني سنه هزار و هشتاد و يك هجري نبوي اله لقدي بيگ ابن امر اللّه بيگ ساوجي ازين جهان فاني بعالم جاوداني خراميد غفر اللّه له و ستر عيوبه بحق محمّد و اهل بيته.

Translation

'On the 15th of Rabī' II, 1081 years after the Flight of the Prophet (Monday, 22nd August, 1670 A.D.), Ilah Laqdī Beg, son of Amr-Ullāh Beg, Sāwaji, passed from this mortal world to the everlasting sphere. May God pardon him and conceal his shortcomings through Muḥammad and the members of his house!'

The name Laqdī Beg is extraordinary; it may be Taqdī Beg. The cognomen Sāwajī shows that Taqdī Beg was a native of Sāwa (Sāvah) in Persia. He was evidently a disciple of one of the descendants of Shāh Khalīl-Ullāh. The style of writing is *Nasta'līq* of a neat type. *Epig. Ind. Mosl.*, 1927–8. Pl. X (*c*), p. 19.

[3] The full text of the inscription is as follows:

تاريخ وفات

سال تاريخش از خرد جستم — گفت هاتف كه جنت الفردوس

مقبرهٔ شا(ه) نور اللّه حسينى تيار بود در زمان بريدان شكسشد (*sic*) بعده اسد اللّه خان نبيرهٔ شاه مذكور از سر نو در عمل محمد شاه بادشاه در سنه ١١٩٦ باتمام رسانيد.

Translation

Date of demise.

Verse

'I inquired of my intellect the year of his demise,
The inspirer said, (it may be calculated from the phrase) *The Garden of Paradise*.'

'The tomb of Shāh Nūr-Ullāh Ḥusainī was built up, but it fell into ruins during the time of the Barīdī kings. Afterwards his grandson, Asad-Ullāh Khān, constructed it afresh in 1196 H. during the reign of the king Muḥammad Shāh.' *Epig. Ind. Mosl.*, 1927–8, Pl. X (*d*), pp. 19–20.

[4] The place was styled by the king Ni'matābād, after the name of the saint, and this title still survives. Ni'matābād is now a village in the Janwāra ta'alluqa of Bidar, its distance from the latter being some six miles towards the east.

king placed him above all the saintly personages, even above the descendants of Ḥaḍrat Sayyid Muḥammad Gesū Darāz. Aḥmad S͟hāh afterwards gave one of his daughters in marriage to Nūr-Ullāh.[1] The inscription records that the tomb had fallen into ruin during the rule of the Barīdī kings, but that it was subsequently repaired during the reign of the Mug͟hal king, Muḥammad S͟hāh, in 1196 H. (A.D. 1782).

About five hundred yards to the north-west of S͟hāh K͟halīl-Ullāh's shrine another loose inscriptional tablet was found lying in the open in A.D. 1927. It bears a record of Sulṭān 'Alā-ud-Dīn Aḥmad's reign, mentioning that a well was built as an act of charity by Naṣīr K͟hān in A.D. 1446.[2] The most interesting feature of the inscription, however, is that in line 4 it states 'Alā-ud-Dīn to be of the line of Baihman and Isfandyār. The late Sir W. Haig, on the basis of the Gulbarga Mosque inscription which bears the surname Baihman S͟hāh, for 'Alā-ud-Dīn, the founder of the dynasty, had concluded that all the information contained in Persian histories which stated that the king had been a slave of the Brahman Gangū, and had adopted the title Baihmanī, a shortened form of Brāhmaṇī, in memory of his old master, was false.[3] The mention or incorporation of an amusing story is not extraordinary in books on history, but in this case the agreement of all the writers is so unanimous that it will not be fair to contradict them until an absolutely clear record shall have been secured. The mere mention of the title Baihman S͟hāh, or a

[1] *Firis͟hta*, Persian text, vol. i, pp. 634–5.

[2] The full text of the inscription is given below:

(١) تعالی اللّه (؟) کہ این بائین موزون — مرتب شد بوقت سعد و میمون

(٢) ز ھجرت بود ھیصد سال و پنجہ — بهم تاریخ ماه ربّ بیچون

(٣) بعهد بادشاه بو المظفر — علاء الدین شاه ربع مسکون

(٤) شهنشہ احمد ابن شاه احمد — کہ ھست از نسل بهمن و از فریدون

(٥) نیایش کرد مجموع ممالك — کہ قدرش برترست از اوج گردون

(٦) نصیر ابن علا خانشہ کے دارد — فضایل بیحد و خیرات افزون

(٧) قبول حق باد این خیرجاري — بقاء بانیش با خلد مقرون

Translation

(1) God is High! This delightful *Bā'īn* (well) was built in auspicious and happy time.

(2) The Hijrī year was 850 and it was the 9th of the month of Absolute God (Rajab).

(3) During the reign of the victorious King, 'Alā-ud-Dīn, the sovereign of the fourth part of the universe, which is inhabited.

(4) The Emperor Aḥmad, son of King Aḥmad (Walī Baihmanī), who is from the descent of Baihman and Farīdūn.

(5) The whole world has shown humility to him, for his rank is exalted to heaven (lit. higher than heaven).

(6) Naṣīr, son of 'Alā K͟hān S͟hāh, who possesses innumerable virtues and whose charity is (ever) increasing;

(7) May God accept this charitable institution (lit. flowing charity) and may its builder (Naṣīr) ever last!

Epig. Ind. Mosl., 1927-8, Pl. IX (*a*), pp. 20–1.

[3] *J.A.S.B.*, 1904 (Special Number), pp. 1–4.

reference to the descent of Baihmanī kings from Baihman and Farīdūn in some inscriptions of the dynasty, may only be the eulogy of court panegyrists to please their king, and should not be treated seriously. Firishta's opinion on this point is very illuminating and may be quoted here:

'Alla-ood-Deen Hussun being once asked how he contrived without great treasures or armies to attain royalty, he replied, by kindnesses to my friends, generosity to my enemies, and by courtesy and liberality to all mankind. It has been asserted that he was descended from Bahmun, one of the ancient kings of Persia, and I, the author, have even seen a pedigree of him so derived, in the royal library of Ahmudnuggur; but it was probably only framed, after his accession to the throne, by flatterers and poets, for I believe his origin was too obscure to admit of being traced. The appellation of Bahmuny he certainly took out of compliment to his master, Gungoo, the bramin, a word often pronounced bahmun. The King himself was by birth an Afghan.' (Briggs, vol. ii, p. 297.)

The Tomb of Shāh Rājū

The saint was a disciple of Ḥaḍrat Sayyid Muḥammad Gesū Darāz of Gulbarga, and according to tradition he was one of those personages who were deputed by Sulṭān Fīroz Shāh to receive the latter saint when he arrived in Gulbarga from Delhi. Shāh Rājū appears to have lived long, for he went over to Bidar with the next king Aḥmad Shāh al-Walī and died during the reign of his son 'Alā-ud-Dīn. The exact year of the saint's demise is not known, but as his *'Urs* is celebrated on the 15th Dhū-Qa'da, it is not unlikely that he died on that date.[1]

The tomb is situated near a small hamlet called Mirzāpur, to the right of the Bidar–Āshṭūr road. As the village nestles at the foot of the Habshī Koṭ hill towards the north the tomb can also be approached from the hill-side. It is a small structure, comprising a dome built on a square base. The walls of the latter on the ground level measure 31 feet 6 inches externally on each side, and rise to a height of 19 feet 3 inches above the floor. On the top of the walls a parapet is built which is 2 feet 9 inches high. The circumference of the dome at the roof level is 81 feet 2 inches.

The interior of the tomb is square in plan and the walls are decorated with stucco-work arranged in the form of medallions and bands of intricate design. The latter contain religious texts and the ninety-nine names of God as given in the *Qur'ān*. At the corners of the tomb are squinches which have caused the plan of the tomb to become octagonal above them.

BARĪDĪ TOMBS

This group of tombs is situated about ten furlongs to the west of Bidar city and embraces a large area owing to the vast enclosures of the different mausolea. An attractive feature of these monuments is that originally they had pleasant gardens around them the traces of which in the shape of many very ancient mango-trees may still be noticed. As the soil for the gardens had been specially prepared, the avaricious guardians of the tombs in later times used it for growing food grains and did not confine the cultivation to the area marked out for fruit-trees and flowering shrubs, but destroyed the roads and foot-paths by indiscriminate ploughing, and

[1] The annual ceremony of intercession for the soul of a saint.

in some cases damaged also the plinths and steps of the tombs. The sepulchres themselves were neglected and both climatic conditions and the hand of the vandal had caused damage to the masonry. The Archaeological Department since 1918 has not only carried out a systematic programme for the conservation of the monuments, but has also paid large sums to the pseudo-owners of the land in order to obtain possession of the area with a view to making the surroundings of the tombs more picturesque, following as far as practicable the original plans of their gardens and walks.

The tombs of the Barīdī kings are described in this section in their chronological order, but as the sepulchres of several saints are also situated close to the tombs, an account of these is given as well after the description of the royal monuments.

The Tomb of Qāsim Barīd

He was the founder of the dynasty, and although he did not assume royal titles and called himself only the minister, yet he was the *de facto* ruler of Bidar and the neighbouring districts during the reign of Maḥmūd S͟hāh Baihmanī. Qasīm Barīd died in 910 H. (A.D. 1504) and was buried in the suburbs of Bidar by the side of the Bidar–C͟hhidrī road. In contemporary history the place of his burial is not mentioned, but regarding Amīr Barīd it is stated that his corpse was brought from Daulatābād and interred in the enclosure of his father, Qāsim Barīd's tomb.[1] The incomplete mausoleum of Amīr Barīd is well known to tradition, and as he was buried in the enclosure of his father's tomb this must be somewhere on the same site. As there are several sepulchres close to the tomb of Amīr Barīd in the same enclosure, one of them with a conical dome, situated to the east of the latter, may be identified with that of Qāsim Barīd. A pleasant mango-grove still encircles the tomb and originally there must have been a lovely garden at the site, for during the excavation carried out by the Department in recent years traces of well-laid-out walks and octagonal platforms with stone margins have been found. This tomb resembles in general appearance the sepulchres of Walī-Ullāh Baihmanī and Kalīm-Ullāh Baihmanī, but it is built on a platform raised 4 feet 6 inches above the surrounding land, and approached by a flight of steps of neatly chiselled and polished masonry. The platform is square in plan, measuring 26 feet 7 inches on each side, and the tomb is built in the middle of it. The walls of the tomb measure 19 feet 9 inches in each direction at the base and rise to a height of 16 feet, including the parapet, the latter by itself being 2 feet 6 inches high. The dome has a tapering shape and is divided into eight facets, the girth of these facets near the base being 46 feet approximately.

The interior of the tomb is entered through a small door, 5 feet 9 inches in height and 2 feet 9 inches in width. The inner plan comprises a square chamber measuring 12 feet 8 inches on each side. There are two graves, one of them being that of a lady, probably of Qāsim Barīd's wife.[2] The walls of the chamber in each direction

[1] *Firis͟hta*, Persian text, vol. ii, p. 347.

[2] Below the floor of the chamber in which the sarcophagi of the two graves lie there is another chamber containing the real graves wherein the last remains of Qasīm Barīd and his wife were interred.

have an arch the sides of which near their lower ends overlap the sides of the arches in the adjoining walls. The form of the vault is octagonal internally also, and as it is built of brick laid in lime, the courses of the latter gradually decreasing in girth upwards can be easily seen since the vault is not plastered.

The Tomb of Amīr Barīd

Amīr Barīd acquired still greater power than his father over the last four kings of the Baihmanī dynasty, whom he placed one after the other on the royal throne, and poisoned or murdered them as soon as he had any suspicion of their forming an alliance with the nobles of the court with a view to curtailing his authority. The first two puppet kings among these four were Aḥmad Shāh (A.D. 1518–21) and ʿAlā-ud-Dīn (A.D. 1521–2); the third being Walī-Ullāh (A.D. 1522–5), whom he not only had the audacity to put into prison but whose royal dignity he further injured by taking the married wife of this king into his *harem*. The last victim of Amīr Barīd's outrageous behaviour was Kalīm-Ullāh, who in order to save his life first fled towards Bijāpur; but as his maternal uncle Ismāʿīl ʿĀdil Shāh betrayed to him the regent's sinister design of arresting him, he went over to Ahmadnagar to seek redress at the court of Burhān Niẓām Shāh I.

Amīr Barīd, however, was most shrewd in his statecraft, and he established friendly relations with the Bijāpur and Ahmadnagar kings and helped them by leading troops gallantly under his personal command to fight the marauders from Gujarāt and Burhānpur.[1] He seems to have begun the building of his tomb during his own lifetime, but as he died rather suddenly at Daulatābād in A.D. 1542, when leading an expedition to help Burhān Niẓām Shāh I, the tomb has remained incomplete. It is an imposing structure, built on a platform, 5 feet 8 inches above the surrounding land, and having a lofty portal towards the south. The outer arch of the portal is rather wide in proportion to its height, the span being 15 feet 6 inches and the height up to the apex 24 feet 6 inches; but it shows a stilt at the top, such as may be seen in the early Baihmanī monuments of Bidar (Pls: CV *a–b*). The walls of the building have arches of this style in the other directions also, and further they have a double series of niches, built one above the other and arranged on both sides of the large arches. The base of the tomb measures 63 feet 6 inches externally on each side, and the walls, unfinished as they are, rise 30 feet above the platform, or 35 feet 8 inches above the ground level. They are solidly built of rough-tooled trap masonry laid in lime, and although they are not plastered over, yet rectangular and square panels with black stone margins, arranged in the side walls of the outer arch of the portal, and in the back wall of the same, on either side and at the top of the doorway, indicate that the architect had planned to decorate the façade of the building with encaustic tiles as in the tomb of Sulṭān ʿAlā-ud-Dīn at Āshṭūr (*supra*, pp. 130–1). The rope-pattern carving of the marginal stones which is an attractive feature of the latter monument may be observed in this building also.

A door of considerable dimensions, 9 feet 9 inches in height and 5 feet in width,

[1] *Firishta*, Persian text, vol. ii, p. 347.

leads to a spacious hall which is square in plan, measuring 41 feet on each side. It has no roof, but the design of its massive walls with the arrangement of the squinches at the corners clearly shows that the architect had planned to surmount the building with a dome, which owing to the sudden death of the king could not be built. The walls are nearly 11 feet thick and strong enough to support the load of the masonry of a dome. To go up to the roof the architect had planned steps in the thickness of the walls which may be noticed in the south-east corner of the building.

In the middle of the hall, a temporary tomb was erected with an octagonal base and conical dome, but these would have been pulled down if the large dome had been built over the hall. But as the latter, for reasons given above, was never constructed, the temporary tomb still stands. The sepulchral chamber contains three graves, the middle one of which is that of Amīr Barīd and the others those of two of his wives. The sarcophagi of these three graves are of brick and mortar and the surface has been neatly plastered over.

The site seems to have become in subsequent times the cemetery of the descendants of the Barīdī kings, for there are a large number of graves, which had decayed through neglect but have been repaired recently. Two tombs built on platforms to the west of Amīr Barīd's incomplete mausoleum, however, appear to be of the period when this dynasty held sway over Bidar (A.D. 1542–1619). The masonry of the plinth of the platforms has crumbled in some places, but when intact the height of the platforms from the ground level must have been approximately 4 feet.

Of the two tombs the one towards the east is comparatively in a better state of preservation and it is crowned with a shapely dome. The walls of this building rise to a height of 16 feet 9 inches above the platform and are surmounted by a parapet which rises 4 feet 3 inches higher still. The design of the parapet is pleasing to the eye, representing overlapping arches, a device frequently to be seen in Baihmanī monuments. The plan of the tomb is square both externally and internally, the outside measurements being 19 feet 8 inches on each side, and the inside 12 feet 9 inches in each direction. In the middle of the sepulchral chamber there is a stone sarcophagus which is neatly carved and polished. The casket design indicates that it is the tomb of a male member of the family. The interior of the tomb is ornamented with niches and squinches showing a refined taste (Pl. CVI).

The other tomb on an adjoining platform is incomplete, for the dome appears never to have been built. The walls measure 18 feet 2 inches on each side at the base and rise to a height of 14 feet 11 inches above the platform. Inside the sepulchral chamber there is only one sarcophagus, the '*tablet*' design of which indicates that the tomb is that of a lady.

The Tomb of 'Alī Barīd

'Alī Barīd was the third chief of the dynasty and the first to assume the royal titles, which appear in the following form, as inscribed on his palace in the Fort:[1]

المستنصر بنصر الله الملك المالك المجلس المكرم والهمايون الاكرم بريد ممالك علي

[1] *Supra*, p. 14, and *Epig. Ind-Mosl.*, 1927–8, p. 25.

(The king) aided by divine help, the supreme monarch, al-Majlis-al-Mukarram (of exalted seat), the august, the most benevolent, Barīd-i-Mamālik (the messenger of good news to states)[1] *'Alī.*

He was the most powerful of all Barīdī kings, and he also ruled the longest, namely from 949 to 987 H. (A.D. 1542–80). He was fond of architecture and built his own tomb, which according to the chronogram written on the building was completed in 984 H., some three years before his death.[2] As regards the style of the building experts hold different opinions, some consider it to be a great improvement upon the heavy and sombre architecture of the Baihmanī tombs, while others find fault with its top-heavy dome and narrow base. These criticisms although antagonistic are each correct to a large extent, and will be discussed later when a detailed description of the building shall have been given and the reader have become familiar with all its features.

The architect has shown considerable vision in selecting the site of the building between the two main roads which proceed from Bidar towards the Marāṭhā and Carnatic countries so that wayfarers passing on both those roads may easily visit the tomb. Further, he has arranged the site towards the south immediately above the lowlands of Ḥaḍrat Kunj Nis͟hīn's grove, while the major part of the site on the north occupies the high plateau to the west of Bidar; the intention of the architect in this plan was clearly that the building should both be prominent in the panorama of Bidar and also be easily provided with fertile soil for its gardens. The main entrance to the tomb is from the south where a gateway of considerable dimensions and sufficient architectural merit still stands (Pl. XC). But it was also approached from the north, east, and west, for the remains of doors towards the east and west may still be seen, but the entrance towards the north has completely disappeared. The tomb also had an enclosure wall, traces of which still exist, and some portions of it towards the south have been rebuilt in recent times by the Archaeological Department of Hyderabad.

The façade of the southern entrance is decorated with a number of architectural motifs which, beginning from the top, comprise first a parapet of trefoil pattern, below which is a band of twelve star-shaped panels, sunk in the wall. Below the latter again there are plain bands which form the margins of two series of arches outlined on the wall for the purpose of ornamentation. These arches have wide spans and low imposts, and the fillet-like arrangement along their openings has a pleasing artistic effect. The middle arch in the upper series has three windows of elegant design which open on the hall in the upper storey of the building and by their position remind one of the balconies of the Moorish buildings in Spain. These small windows have a carved band at their top, and above that the *c͟hhajja* supported on brackets. The designs of the brackets and of the carved band are copied from the Hindu temples of the eleventh and twelfth centuries. Above the *c͟hhajja*

[1] *Barīd*, a courier or messenger. The office was probably held by the forebears of 'Alī Barīd, and it became part of the title of the rulers of the dynasty when they assumed regal powers.

[2] The phrase نام گنبد قبّة الانوار گو, according to the *Abjad* system, contains the date 984 H. The date of the demise of the king inscribed on the tomb is 987 H.

is an ornamented parapet of overlapping arches, the design of which is delicate, but the parapet looks superfluous when viewed in relation to the general appearance of the building.

In contrast to the wide-spanned ornamental arches of the façade, the entrance arch of the gateway has very fine proportions resembling those of the gateway of the Takht Maḥall in the Fort[1] (Pl. XC). Beyond the entrance arch a covered passage 28 feet 8 inches long and 8 feet 10 inches wide leads to another arch which opens on the court of the tomb. The roof of the passage is vaulted, being divided into two compartments. On either side of the passage towards the east and west is a rectangular hall, measuring 24 feet 5 inches in length and 14 feet in depth. The roof of each of these two halls is vaulted, being divided into two compartments by wide-spanned arches built in the middle of each hall across its depth. The arches of these halls opening towards the passage are also wide-spanned, their dimensions being: span 9 feet 6 inches, height of the columns 4 feet 5 inches, and height of the apex from the floor 10 feet 5 inches.

The vaults of the ceiling are lavishly decorated with plaster-work, the designs being floral or geometric, or copied from woodwork such as ribbed partitions. The columns have receding fillets of plaster-work from bottom to top along their shafts and also on their heads, and in this feature they resemble the Hindu columns of the twelfth and thirteenth centuries.

A staircase, comprising fifteen rather high uncomfortable steps, is built in the western side of the building and leads to the upper storey of the gateway. The plan at this stage consists of an open court and a hall at its back towards the south. The court measures 34 feet 4 inches in length and 15 feet 4 inches in width, and has two small closets in its eastern wall, one in the form of a lavatory and the other intended for use as a small bathroom. The hall has three arched openings towards the court (north), five windows in its southern wall, and one each in the eastern and western walls respectively. The openings towards the court are in the shape of wide-spanned arches with low imposts, their dimensions being: span 8 feet 8 inches, height of the imposts 3 feet 9 inches, and height of the apex from the floor 8 feet 10 inches. The arches appear squat and clumsy in their proportions, and there was perhaps a craze for wide-spanned low arches in the fifteenth and sixteenth centuries in the Deccan, for they are seen in great abundance in the Barīdī, ʿĀdil Shāhī, and Quṭb Shāhī buildings of the period. The hall measures 37 feet 9 inches in length and 14 feet 2 inches in breadth and has a vaulted ceiling, which is divided into three compartments by means of wide-spanned arches built across the depth of the interior structure. The ceiling, walls, and columns of the hall are elaborately ornamented with stucco-work, but the striking feature of the decorative scheme is the large number of small niches which were apparently intended as receptacles for articles of food and toilet requisites (Pl. XCI). In the beginning such niches may have been designed to supply the need met by modern cupboards, but in later times they seem to have become a regular decorative feature of apartments used for residence, being filled with dainty china and glass-ware such as would nowadays be arranged

[1] *Supra*, p. 66, Pl. XXXII.

by a lady on her dressing-table or in the drawing-room cabinet. Niches of this type are to be seen also in contemporary Mughal buildings, and contemporary court painters have shown them filled with wine flagons and decanters and dessert dishes of exquisite designs. This apartment, although styled the *Naqqār Khāna*, Music Gallery, may well have been used as a residence by the Keeper of the tomb.

Returning to the lower floor of the gateway the visitor enters through its inner arch, which stands at the northern end of the covered passage, a spacious court which is divided into walks and flower-beds and contains the tomb in its centre. The arrangement of the flower-beds is such that there are two, one on each side of the path which leads from each of the entrances to the steps built on the four sides of the platform of the tomb. The court including the platform on which the tomb is built is square in plan, measuring 140 yards on each side (Pl. LXXXIX). Owing to neglect, and the indiscriminate use of the land adjoining the platform of the tomb in later times by the descendants of the original Keeper of the tomb, the walks and the flower-beds had been completely effaced, and they have only just lately been restored by the Archaeological Department.

The platform on which the tomb is built rises 5 feet 10 inches above the ground and its plinth is faced with finely dressed trap masonry having two ornamented bands, one near the top and the other at the lower end of the plinth. This latter band has a leaf pattern on it. The platform measures 154 feet 6 inches on each side, and at the top has a lime-concrete pavement. Above this pavement, leaving a margin 36 feet wide all round, there is another platform which encloses the walls of the tomb. The height of this is only 1 foot 1 inch above the pavement, but it has a length of 82 feet 10 inches and a width of 12 feet 10 inches on each side. The enclosure walls of the tomb rise to a height of 61 feet 8 inches above the second platform, but this height includes the parapet, which by itself measures 3 feet 10 inches. The side walls have each a lofty arch halfway along, the span of each arch being 20 feet 7 inches and its height up to the apex 30 feet 1 inch. The exterior of the tomb is decorated with carved dadoes up to a height of 6 feet 9 inches, and higher up the walls have ornamental arches which are arranged in pairs on each side of the big arches. The space above the apexes of the latter has been divided into five panels by the insertion of stone bands arranged horizontally. This arrangement has been resorted to by the architect apparently to divert the attention of the observer from the disproportionate height (61 feet 8 inches) of the building in regard to its width (57 feet 2 inches). The carving of the dadoes comprises flowers with eight petals of a plain design. The spandrels of both the big and the small arches are decorated with medallions containing calligraphic and floral patterns. Originally they must have been emblazoned with encaustic tiles, for traces of these may be noticed in a few places. The parapet at the top is of stone, neatly carved, the design being a trefoil.

The tomb is crowned with a large dome resting on a circular base which rises 15 feet 6 inches above the roof and is decorated with niches and mouldings. The circumference of the base of the dome at the roof level is 155 feet 6 inches, and it remains practically the same at the springing-point of the dome. The shape of the latter is that of a globe, and near its base it is adorned with a railing of plaster-work representing posts of fancy designs (Pl. XCII). The finial at the top of the dome is of copper, plated with gold, and has a beautiful design, comprising an octagonal disk in the middle with several orbs of different sizes arranged at its bottom and top and the whole crowned with a flower with eight petals and a circular shoot in the middle.

The dome does not show the stilt of the earlier Baihmanī domes and its shape is quite pleasing to the eye, but its size is undoubtedly much too large in proportion to the dimensions of the building and the whole looks top-heavy, particularly when seen from some distance (Pls. XCII–XCIII). The architect has, however, made the walls of the base extremely massive in order to strengthen the building, these being actually 9 feet in thickness, and has further secured them by the two platforms which encircle the structure at its feet.

The interior of the tomb, owing to the four lofty open arches facing the four points of the compass, is very bright and airy and presents an appreciable contrast to the sombre but mysterious sepulchral halls of most Baihmanī tombs. The presence of doors in three directions, north, east, and south, is a feature not unusual in Muslim tombs, but such doors are generally of small size and only subdued light is admitted into the interior of a shrine through them. The object of this arrangement is that the votaries may have a tranquil mental atmosphere for their prayers. Further, the western side of a tomb is always kept closed where a *miḥrāb* is built for saying prayers and chanting holy texts. The utter disregard of these religious conventionalities shows that the architect of the building was probably a non-Muslim, who, according to his lights, preferred an open to a secluded interior; and who, further to display his engineering skill, chose new proportions for the dome and the base of the tomb.

The stone dadoes of the exterior of the tomb with eight-petalled rosettes carved on them are continued to the interior of the building (Pl. XCIV), and their grey hue matches well with the colour of the stone flooring wherein hexagonal slabs are inserted in a diaper design. The interior of the tomb, which measures 37 feet 5 inches square, has a low pavement with polished black stone margins in its middle. This pavement is 4½ inches higher than the floor of the interior of the tomb, and its other dimensions are: length 23 feet 6 inches and breadth 8 feet. On this pavement there are five sarcophagi, three of which are built of brick and lime and two of stone, one of the latter being of highly polished black basalt. This sarcophagus has a casket shape at the top, but lower down it has the usual box-like rectangular form, with well-finished carving on its sides which comprises simple geometric and floral patterns and also a chain design with a pentagonal pendant. The Islāmic creed and the dates of the completion of the building and the demise of ʿAlī Barīd are also carved on the tomb.[1]

[1] The dates are inscribed in the following words:

Translation

تعمیر گنبد سنہ ۹۸٤ هـ

وفات سنہ ۹۸۷ هـ

Date of the building of the tomb 984 H. (A.D. 1576–7)

Demise 987 H. (A.D. 1580).

On the walls above the dadoes there are arch-shaped ornamental panels which are arranged in pairs on either side of the four main arches of the tomb. The spandrels of these arches are decorated with medallions containing religious texts reproduced in brilliant tile-work.[1] A better display of tile-work is seen in the rectangular panels arranged on the walls above the lower series of ornamental arches. The colour schemes of these panels may be appreciated from Pl. XCV. They contain some well-known verses from the Persian poet ʿAṯṯār, the subject being the transitoriness of worldly glory, which seems a very appropriate theme for the tomb of a king.[2] One of these panels built in the eastern wall contains the chrono-

[1] The medallions of the small arches contain the names of God, يا حيّ يا قيّوم, *O (God) the Living, the Self-subsisting*, and those of the lofty arches the *Qur'ānic* text, كلّ من عليها فان الخ (ch. lv, ver. 26).

[2] Beginning from the western side of the northern arch the verses may be read as follows:

Panel I

ای هم‌نفسان تا اجل آمد بسر من　　　از پای در افتادم و خون شد جگر من

دي تازه گلی بودم و اندر چمن باغ *　　　امروز فرو ریخت همه بال و پر من

* This hemistich has another reading in the Hyderabad State Library MS. *Dīwān-i-ʿAṯṯār*, No. 503, folio 36:

دي تازه و خوش روی بود در چمن عشق

Panel II

یاران و عزیزان بسر خاك من آیند　　　وز خاك بپرسند نشان و خبر من

گر خاك جهان جمله بغربال بپیزند　　　حقّا که نیابند نشان و اثر من

Panel III

رفتم بچنان جای که باز آمدنم نیست　　　هم نیست امیدم که کس آید بسر من

عطّار دلی دارم از درد بخون غرق　　　حقّا که نیاید دو جهان در نظر من†

† Hyderabad MS. contains a different reading of these two lines:

عطّار دلی دارم و آن نیز بخون غرق　　　تا بنگرد این درد دلم دادگر من

گر حق بدلم یك نظر لطف برساند　　　حقّا که نیاید دو جهان در نظر من

Panel IV

دریغا که بی‌ما بسی روزگار　　　بروید گل و بشگفد نوبهار

کسانی که از ما بغیب اندرند　　　بیایند و بر خاك ما بگذرند

· *Panel V*

تفرّج کنان در هوا و هوس　　　گذشتیم بر خاك بسیار کس

کرا جاودان ماندن امید ماند　　　چو کس را نه بیني که جاوید ماند

Panel VI

دامن کشان که میرود امروز بر زمین　　　فردا غبار کالبدش بر هوا زود

خاکت در استخوان رود ای نفس خیره چشم　　　مانند سرمادان که درو توتیا رود

Panel VII

بانيء این گنبد گردون مثال　　　شاه فرخنده برید نیك خو

مصرعهٔ آخر که تاریخ بناست　　　نام گنبد قبّة الانوار گو

٩٨٤ هـ

(*note 2 continued on p. 157*)

gram of the building according to the *Abjad* system, and also the name of the calligraphist, Khwājagī of Shirwān. Another panel built in the northern wall

(*note 2 continued from p. 156*)

Panel VIII

شاه سریر مملکت دین علي برید   چون تنگنای فاني، دنیای دون بهشت
آسوده در بهشت شده از ورای غیب   تاریخ فوتش آمده آسوده در بهشت

۹۸۷ هـ

Translation

Panel I

'O companions! when Death knocked at my head,
I fell down and my heart became gory:
Yesterday I was as a rose blooming in the garden (of Existence),
To-day I am shorn of all my plumes and feathers.'*

* This is a case of 'confusion of metaphors' in the original.

Panel II

'Friends and relatives will come to visit my remains,
And inquire of my remains of my destination and whereabouts:
If they sift the earth of the whole world,
By Truth! they will not find any trace or sign of me.'

Panel III

'I have passed to a world whence I cannot return,
Nor do I cherish this hope that anyone will come to the place where I lie:
O 'Aṭṭār! through grief (lit. pain) my heart is weltering in blood;
By God! both the worlds have lost all significance in my eyes.'

Panel IV

'Alas! without us for a long time,
The rose will blossom and the spring will bloom,
Those who are in secrecy with us,
They will come and visit (lit. pass by) our remains.'

Panel V

'Rambling about in ambition and lust,
We passed by the remains of many a pěrson;
Canst thou cherish the desire of living for ever,
When thou hast not seen anyone living eternally?'

Panel VI

'One who goes trailing his long skirts on the earth to-day,
To-morrow the dust of his earthly remains will be scattered to the winds;
O doltard! thy ashes will move about in thy bones,
In the same way as eye-powder moves about in the collyrium-pot.'

Panel VII

'The builder of this heavenly dome,
Is the good-natured king, Barīd, of blessed memory.
The last hemistich contains the date of the building,
Style the dome the vault of Divine light (984 H.—A.D. 1577).'

Written by Khwājagī Shirwānī.

Panel VIII

'The sovereign presiding over the throne of the kingdom of Faith, 'Alī Barīd,
When he passed away from the narrow street of the frail world,
Found rest in Paradise, and these words were heard from Heaven,
Date of his death is contained in—"Found rest in heaven".' 987 H.—A.D. 1580.

Epig. Ind.-Mosl. Ind., 1927–8, pp. 28–9.

records the name of the king and the date of his death according to the above-mentioned system of calculation.

The tile decoration continues in the upper parts of the walls, and there are bands of *Qur'ānic* texts written in the *Thulth* style by a master calligraphist, 'Abdu'l-Fattāḥ, and reproduced in tile-work.[1] It has been observed elsewhere in this book that the kings of Bidar employed Persian artists for the decoration of their edifices, and the two calligraphists Khwājagī of Shirwān and 'Abdul'l-Fattāḥ, who designed the inscriptions of this tomb, may have also been adepts in manufacturing tiles, for no name of any expert craftsman of the latter industry is to be found in the building. The tile-work of the tomb is of a very superior order and the craftsmen have displayed exquisite taste in the choice of colours. In the *Qur'ānic* bands the background is bluish-green of the colour of a turquoise, and the letters are inscribed in white, which makes them stand out well so that they are easy to read.

The architectural features of the interior of the tomb are almost the same as those of the Baihmanī tombs, for example there are squinches at the corners which have changed the square plan of the floor into an octagonal one, and higher up by the construction of overlapping arch-heads it has become 24-sided (Pl. XCVI). Still further above is a band of encaustic tiles, divided into forty-eight panels, the plan thus gradually becoming more suitable for the circular base of the dome. Above the tile-panels there are two bands of rosettes worked out in plaster, and between these two bands there is a series of niches again decorated with tiles arranged in floral patterns. At the top of all these bands is a rail pattern stretching lace-like along the lower end of the vault. The design has been worked out in encaustic tiles.

A special feature of the decorative scheme of this tomb is that there is no exaggerated embellishment, and this fact indicates considerable restraint on the part of the architect in designing the ornamentation. The work as regards technique and skill is, however, of a high order, whether represented in the carving on stone, or the plaster decoration, or the tile-panels. Who would not admire the chaste simplicity of the hexagonal diaper of the flooring, or the plain designs of the rosettes of the dadoes, or the magnificence of the tile-panels which the architect has judiciously inserted only here and there in the vast spaces of the walls and the dome of the building ? The spacious platform with its high plinth adds to the dignity of the building, while the vast court, originally divided into flower-beds and planted with fruit-trees, must have lent further charm to the monument. These delightful features in some way compensate for the lack of religious atmosphere to be noticed in the Baihmanī tombs, but one incongruity which strikes the connoisseur at once is the disproportionately large size of the dome which has given an air of top-heaviness

[1] The arrangements of the *Qur'ānic* texts on the walls is as given below:

North wall	*Qur'ān*, ii. 285–6.
East wall	*Qur'ān*, iii. 25.
South wall	*Qur'ān*, xviii. 107–10, and xxxvii. 180–2.
West wall	*Qur'ān*, ii. 256.

to the building. In this part of the design the judgement and taste of the architect were unquestionably at fault.

On the platform to the south-west of the main tomb there are sixty-seven tombs of the concubines of 'Alī Barīd about whose death a number of scandalous stories are current which illustrate the lust and cruelty of the king. These may have no basis in actual occurrences; but at least there lies behind them the undoubted fact that the kings of the Deccan did possess large *harems*, and contemporary history shows that slave-girls were brought from distant countries like Georgia and Circassia, and that the vassal chiefs of the Deccan also made presents of beautiful girls to their overlords.

Attached to the tomb towards the north-west is a mosque the architecture of which is very typical of the Muslim style of the Deccan during the sixteenth and seventeenth centuries A.D. The mosque has a separate entrance from outside the tomb, near its southern gateway, but it can also be approached from the court of the tomb. The plan of the building comprises an open court, a cistern, a prayer-hall, and an arcade (Pl. XCVII). The court has been divided into four flower-beds by foot-paths which run in the middle of the court from east to west and north and south and cross one another near the centre. The prayer-hall is built at the western end of the open court and comprises a single apartment, measuring 41 feet 4 inches in length and 14 feet 11 inches in depth. The front of the building is distinctly imposing, having three arches in the middle and two minarets at the sides (Pl. XCVIII). The arches are quite wide-spanned[1] and decorated with medallions and wreaths of stucco-work. Above the arches is the row of brackets supporting the dripstones and at the top a parapet of elegant design representing arches overlapping one another. The minarets are slender in form, although resembling in certain features the minarets of the Madrasa of Maḥmūd Gāwān (Pl. LII). The lower part of the minarets of this mosque is, however, octagonal and not round like that of the minarets of the Madrasa (Pl. XCVIII). The ceiling of the prayer-hall is vaulted, being divided into three compartments by arches built across the width of the hall. There are three niches in the western walls and one in each of the northern and western. The middle niche of the western wall is deeper than the other two in its sides, and it projects from the main wall of the building both internally and externally (Pls. XCVII–C) and has a double vault, the lower forming the ceiling of the niche and the upper rising above the roof like a chimney with a square base and a domical top. The walls and ceiling of the prayer-hall are richly decorated with mouldings and floral designs worked out in stucco, and this pretty detail offers a pleasing contrast to the spacious dimensions of the arches which are built across the hall (Pl. XCIX).

The arcade built at the southern end of the court measures 69 feet 10 inches in length and 15 feet 6 inches in width. It has five arches towards the court, the general appearance of which is the same as that of the arches of the prayer-hall, although their dimensions differ slightly, the span of the prayer-hall arches being 11 feet 1 inch and the height up to their apex 11 feet 6 inches. The arcade may well have been used for the recital of the *Qur'ān* or for feeding the poor. The façade

[1] The span of these arches is 10 feet 9 inches and height of the apex from the floor 11 feet 2 inches.

of the arcade has not been plastered over and it appears to have been built after the mosque was finished.[1]

On the northern side of the court of the mosque is a cistern of considerable dimensions, measuring 36 feet 3 inches square at the top. It is 6 feet 3 inches deep; but 3 feet 5 inches below its mouth there is a broad step, 2 feet 8 inches wide, running all along the walls, for the convenience of those bathers who did not know how to swim. The cistern has a spacious margin round its mouth, measuring 6 feet 6 inches in breadth. The water for the cistern was supplied from a well which is built at a short distance towards the west. Traces of the old aqueduct, extending from the well to the cistern, still exist. The water of the well is sweet and it is used for drinking purposes by the people of the locality. There are two more wells, situated towards the north-west and the east of the main building, which were probably dug for the gardens of the tomb. The water of these two wells has dried up owing to neglect, the springs being now choked with silt and rank vegetation.

The Tomb of Ibrāhīm Barīd

Adjoining the western wall of the enclosure of ʿAlī Barīd's mausoleum is the tomb of his son Ibrāhīm Barīd who ruled from A.D. 1580 to 1587. This building as regards some of its features is a replica of the tomb of his father, being situated in an extensive court with fruit-trees and flower shrubs planted in it and foot-paths and platforms artistically arranged. The garden, except for a few mango and tamarind trees, has perished, and the foot-paths also have only recently been restored. The tomb having been built on a high platform presents an imposing appearance; but as it is a little smaller in dimensions than the tomb of ʿAlī Barīd, and further as it has not been finished, it suffers by comparison with the latter. The court of Ibrāhīm Barīd's tomb measures nearly a furlong from north to south and a furlong and 15 yards from east to west.

The platform on which the tomb is built rises 6 feet above the ground and is approached by flights of steps from all four directions, north, south, east, and west. There are nine steps on each side which are built of neatly dressed trap masonry. Similar masonry has also been used for the plinth of the platform. The latter measures 103 feet in length on each side and has a width of 21 feet 10 inches, beyond which another platform is built encircling the tomb. The dimensions of the second platform are: length on each side 60 feet 1 inch, breadth 9 feet, and height above the first platform 1 foot. The floor of the tomb is raised 1 foot above the second platform, and the plinth as well as the walls, up to a height of 5 feet 8 inches, are built of ashlar masonry. At the corners of the building there are slender octagonal pillars the capitals and pedestals of which besides floral and star-shaped patterns have a vase-like decorative motif. On the body of the vase an ornamental disk (*chakram*) is carved. The work seems to have been done by Hindu sculptors (Pl. CIII). Higher up the walls are built of roughly-tooled masonry laid in lime,

[1] There are some rooms on the roof of the arcade which are approached by a staircase built at the western end of the latter. They were evidently meant for the residence of the *Imām* of the mosque.

and as the building has not been plastered over, the methods of construction and the material can be studied to advantage.

The tomb has a large arch in the middle on each side, and there are small ornamental arches arranged in pairs on either side of the large arches (Pl. CI). The latter have each a span of 15 feet 7 inches and rise to a height of 24 feet above the floor. The spandrels of both the large and small arches are adorned with rosettes of stone, the carving of which shows exquisitely careful workmanship. Above the apexes of the arches on either side there are three horizontal panels one above the other, apparently meant for tile or stucco decoration, which was, however, never done. At the top of the walls is a parapet of trefoil design, measuring 3 feet 8 inches in height, while the total height of the walls including the parapet is 41 feet 3 inches above the floor. As the walls at their base measure 41 feet 10 inches in length on each side, which is also nearly their height from the floor, the building up to the top of the walls looks like a cube (Pl. CI). Above the roof the dome of the tomb has a circular base which is decorated with mouldings and a band of niches arranged below the dripstones. The height of the circular base from the roof up to the dripstones is 12 feet 6 inches. The dome has a stilt at the top and it is more like the earlier Baihmanī domes in shape than like a copy of the orb of ʿAlī Barīd's tomb. The circumference of Ibrāhīm Barīd's dome near its springing-point is 115 feet 6 inches. The rim of the dome is decorated externally with a leaf pattern, and the dome rises in the form of a colossal bud from its midst. As the building was not finished the usual gold-plated finial, comprising orbs and disks, is not fixed at the top of the dome, but the rod which would have formed the core of the finial is attached to the building and its cadaverous look has given the tomb the ridiculous name—*Sabbal Barīd kā Guṃbad*, or the Tomb of the Crow-bar Barīd.[1]

The walls of the tomb are 7 feet thick and the interior measures 27 feet 11 inches in each direction, the plan being square. There are three graves, the middle one of which is that of Ibrāhīm Barīd and the other two those of his wives. The sarcophagi of these graves are built of brick and mortar. The walls and the ceiling of the tomb have not been plastered over, and the horizontal courses of the masonry of the walls and the concentric bands of the brickwork of the dome can be clearly seen (Pl. CII). The arrangement of squinches, overlapping arches, and bands of panels and mouldings shows that the tomb when finished would have resembled the tomb of ʿAlī Barīd in its architectural scheme.

There are several graves in the court of the tomb towards the south which are shaded by age-worn mango-trees, the remnants of the old garden of the monument. These graves are apparently those of the members of Ibrāhīm Barīd's family. There is another tomb built on a small platform to the east of Ibrāhīm Barīd's mausoleum. The sarcophagus of this tomb is of polished black basalt, and it is similar in design and finish to the sarcophagus of ʿAlī Barīd's tomb (*supra* p. 155). It is not unlikely that this is the tomb of a later king of the dynasty. There is also a lady's grave on the eastern side of the latter.

[1] The inhabitants of Bidar have given bizarre names to the tombs of Barīdī kings, for instance the tomb of Amīr Barīd I is called *Haṭhīle Barīd kā Guṃbad*, or the Tomb of the Obstinate Barīd.

Raṇ Khamb or Polo Posts

A road from Ibrāhīm Barīd's tomb goes due north to Qāsim Barīd II's tomb, and crosses on the way first the old polo ground and afterwards the Bidar–Udgīr road. Among military sports chaugān, polo or horse-shinty, has been a great favourite with Muslim kings, but a game similar to it was played in India prior to the advent of the Muslims in the Deccan, and a reference to the game has recently been traced in a Deccanese inscription in Canarese. At Bidar four heavy stone pillars, two at each end of the playing-area, are fixed firmly into the ground. The distance between the two pairs of pillars is 591 yards and the spacing between the pillars themselves at each end is 11 feet 9 inches. The pillars are carved of single blocks of pinkish granite, and they rise from heavy circular pedestals in the form of round shafts (Pl. CVII). The circumference of the pedestal of each pillar is 16 feet 2 inches, while the pillar itself is 8 feet in girth and rises 7 feet above the ground. *Raṇ Khamb* means literally the post marking the site of a combat, but here the name must have been used figuratively, signifying the post marking the ground wherein sporting events took place. Some Muslim scholars have expressed the view that the posts mark the eastern and western limits of the sacred grounds in which the Barīdī kings are buried, and, indeed, as they stand close to the old Udgīr road they can hardly be polo-posts. Masonry pillars marking the boundary of the sacred area of the Ka'ba exist in the suburbs of Mecca, and if the opinion of the scholars in question is to be accepted, then the posts at Bidar must have been set up with a similar religious purpose in view.

The Tomb of Qāsīm Barīd II

This tomb is situated to the north of the Udgīr road and faces the tomb of Ibrāhīm Barīd towards the south. The building was originally enclosed by a wall and had a garden in its court. Traces of the enclosure still exist, and its northern and western walls have recently been restored by the Archaeological Department of Hyderabad. The original gateway of the tomb is intact, and it has an arched entrance of modest dimensions towards the south.[1] A passage 22 feet in length and 8 feet 8 inches in width leads the visitor to another arch which gives access to the court of the tomb. The passage has a vaulted ceiling which is divided into two compartments. On either side of the passage is a room, 19 feet 8 inches in length and 10 feet 9 inches in depth, for the accommodation of guards. The court is now crowded with tombs and of the old garden only a few mango-trees have survived. An idea of the spaciousness of the court may be formed from the large dimensions of the area enclosed within the walls, which measures 320 yards from east to west and 108 yards from north to south.

The tomb of Qāsim Barīd II is built on a large platform square in plan and measuring 91 feet 9 inches on each side. The height of the platform above the surrounding land is 5 feet 6 inches and a flight of seven steps leads to its top. The steps are built of neatly chiselled trap masonry which has been used for the plinth

[1] The span of the arch at the entrance is 4 feet 11 inches and its height up to the apex 8 feet 4 inches.

of the platform also. The latter is further embellished with mouldings and a design representing a leaf pattern. There are also elegantly carved pillars of basalt of a dark hue fixed at appropriate places for the support of the masonry of the platform.

The tomb, although of modest dimensions, shows a fine sense of proportion as regards the height of its walls and the circumference of its dome. The former measure 30 feet 9 inches on each side at the base and rise to a height of 25 feet 4 inches above the floor. The circumference of the dome is 82 feet 2 inches at its base, and it has a hemispherical form with a slight stilt at the top. The walls on each side have a large arch in the middle externally and two small arches, arranged one above the other, on either side of the former (Pl. CVIII). Above the middle arches there is an ornamental design comprising a lozenge-shaped panel in the middle and two smaller panels, one on either side of the large panel. At the top of the walls is a parapet of trefoil pattern and small pillars crowned with orbs at the four corners. The dome near its springing-point is decorated with mouldings and floral and geometrical patterns, among which a band of stars incised in plaster is particularly attractive.

The tomb is entered by a single door which faces the south. The frame of this door is of black stone, and above it the spandrels of the arch are embellished with rosettes. The arch-head of the door is carved with spirals, a design which is frequently to be seen in the buildings of the Baihmanī period. The interior of the tomb is square in plan on the floor level and measures 20 feet 6 inches on each side. There are two graves, one of Qāsim Barīd II and the other of his wife. The sarcophagi over these graves are built of brick and mortar and the surface is plastered over. The walls have squinches at the corners and also stalactites which serve as ornaments for the interior of the building. There are also small decorative niches in the middle of which the chain and pendant device worked out in plaster is prominent.

On the platform of Qasīm Barīd's tomb there are some more tombs all of them being those of women. The ornamental plaster-work of these tombs is worthy of notice.

Close to the tomb of Qasīm Barīd II in the same enclosure is another tomb built on a platform to the west of it. This tomb is a little smaller in size than its earlier prototype, and the platform on which it is built measures 42 feet 6 inches on each side and rises 3 feet 9 inches above the ground level. A flight of seven steps leads to the top of the platform, and the building of the tomb thereon measures 23 feet 9 inches on each side externally and 15 feet 6 inches internally. A low-arched door gives access to the interior which has two graves, one that of a ruler or a scion of the family and the other that of his wife. The marginal mouldings of the overlapping arches at the corners of the sepulchral room have produced a sort of network which looks very artistic. The walls are further embellished with niches, and there is also a decorative band of stucco-work along the lower end of the vault of the ceiling. The arches of this tomb have no stilts, and in shape they resemble the Mughal arches of Northern India.

The court of Qāsim Barīd II's tomb seems to have become in later times the cemetery of the family, since beside a large number of graves built on the ground there are four which have domes over them and probably belong to distinguished members of the clan. They are all situated to the east of the main tomb, and the one nearest the latter is built on a platform 38 feet square and 3 feet high. The tomb itself measures 19 feet 6 inches on each side externally and 13 feet 6 inches internally. It is open on three sides now, but originally it had only one door towards the south and was closed in other directions. There are two graves in the interior of the building, of which one in the middle of the chamber is that of a lady. Some parts of the tomb have decayed, and the parapet which was originally built on the top of the walls is missing.

The next tomb is crowned with a pyramidal vault the plaster ribs and the ornamental floral designs of which are interesting (Pl. CIX). It is built on a square platform, 3 feet 4 inches high and measuring 27 feet 4 inches in each direction. The enclosure walls of the tomb measure 17 feet on each side externally and 11 feet internally. The walls at their top have a dentated moulding above which a parapet of trefoil design was constructed. A large part of this parapet has now perished. The walls of this tomb on each side have an ornamental arch, and one of them facing the south contains the door which gives access to the interior of the tomb. In the sepulchral chamber there are two graves.

Close to the pyramidal tomb is a platform, the neatly chiselled masonry of which has been torn away and sold for some modern building by the vandalic keeper of the tomb in comparatively recent times. The platform is square in plan, measuring 23 feet 6 inches on each side, and rising 4 feet 6 inches above the ground. On this platform there were originally three graves, but now the plaster sarcophagi of only two are intact, and one of them on account of the tablet (*ta<u>kh</u>tī*) design may be identified as the tomb of a lady.

Near this platform towards the south-east is a well which originally supplied water to the garden of the tomb. The well is still in good condition. To the north-east of the well is another tomb which on account of the crescent of its finial is popularly called the sepulchre of <u>Ch</u>ānd Sulṭāna, the moon-faced queen, although in contemporary history there is no mention of any lady of this name in the Barīdī family. The tomb is, however, very solidly built and its large dome and artistically carved sarcophagus clearly indicate that it is the tomb of a distinguished lady of the family who might have had any title (Pl. CX–XI). It is built of rough-tooled masonry, and as the walls have not been plastered over it looks somewhat incomplete. The building has a high plinth, the floor being 4 feet 6 inches above the ground level, and the walls rising 31 feet 6 inches still higher. The latter measure 28 feet 6 inches at their base on each side, and near the top they have several mouldings and also a band of carving representing the dentated parapet of the early Buddhist shrines.[1] Higher up the walls are crowned with a parapet of the trefoil pattern and the building is ultimately surmounted by a dome, the circumference of which is 114 feet 6 inches at the roof level. The finial fixed at the

[1] Parapets of this design as described elsewhere in this book have been found at ʿŪr; and they are also to be noticed frequently on Arab buildings in North Africa and Spain.

apex of the dome is probably of copper but plated with gold, and comprises several orbs and disks which are crowned with an eight-petalled flower over which a crescent rises.

The inner plan of the building is square at the floor level,[1] but higher it becomes octagonal owing to the squinches built at the corners, and still higher, near the base of the dome, it turns into a sixteen-sided figure as a result of the arched niches built along the walls. The sarcophagus over the grave is of a close-grained stone greyish in colour (basalt ?). It has excellent polish and also neat carving, both indicating clever workmanship and refined taste (Pl. CXI).

Farther towards the east there is another tomb which is built on a platform rising 4 feet 6 inches above the ground level. A flight of five steps leads to the top of the platform which has a square plan and measures 31 feet 11 inches on each side. The walls of this tomb rise to a height of 20 feet 9 inches and are crowned with a parapet which by itself is 2 feet 9 inches in height. The dome of the tomb is small, but it matches well with the size of its base, and shows a balanced judgement on the part of the architect. The interior of the tomb is square in plan, measuring 13 feet 11 inches on each side. The walls and the dome are plastered over, and the mouldings and other decorative designs show careful workmanship.

While returning to the gateway of the court the visitor will notice a cistern built towards the south-west of the main tomb. It is 3 feet 4 inches deep and measures 25 feet 6 inches on each side at its mouth. The water for the cistern was supplied through a channel from a well built towards the west.

Outside the enclosure of Qāsim Barīd II's tomb near the gateway there is a mosque, the roof of which has fallen down, and the walls of the prayer-hall also, until a few years back, were in a dilapidated condition, but now they have been thoroughly restored. The hall measures 34 feet 4 inches in length and 16 feet 6 inches in depth, and towards the east it has a screen of three wide-spanned arches. The span of each of these arches is 9 feet 11 inches and the height up to the apex 9 feet 6 inches. The plaster carvings on the façade and on the interior of the building show elegant designs.

The ʿĪdgāh

At its eastern end the court of Qāsim Barīd II's tomb adjoins the back wall of the ʿĪdgāh. This latter is situated due north of ʿAlī Barīd's tomb and a motorable road has recently been constructed from the latter monument to it.[2] This building has no inscription, but as *ʿĪdgāhs* are always constructed outside the town in Muslim countries, and as there are no level lands outside Bidar except towards the west, this ʿĪdgāh, which is the only place of worship of its kind outside the town of Bidar, may well have been built by Baihmanī kings. The building comprises a wall facing the *Kaʿba* with a court in front, 175 feet 6 inches from north to south and 169 feet from east to west. A low enclosure wall has been built in modern times on

[1] The tomb inwardly measures 28 feet 6 inches on each side.

[2] It can also be approached with convenience from the road which has been constructed in front of the southern wall of Qāsim Barīd II's tomb.

three sides of the court, towards the north, east, and south. The old wall facing the *Ka'ba* has seven arched niches, the middle one of them being the *miḥrāb* in front of which the *Imām* stands when conducting public prayers. Close by there is also a pulpit which possesses no architectural or artistic merit.[1] The only architectural features of the building worthy of notice are the cylindrical pillars, one at each end of the back wall of the 'Īdgāh. They are reminiscent of the cylindrical *mā'dhanas* of the mosque at Sammarra, but pillars and towers of this shape are frequently to be seen in the monuments of the early Sulṭāns of Delhi, and in the Deccan they were first built by the masons who came with Muḥammad Tughluq from Delhi, and a typical example of them may be noticed in the mosque of Mubārak Khaljī in the Daulatābād Fort. In the 'Īdgāh at Bidar as well as in the mosque at Daulatābād they serve more or less the purpose of buttresses, standing as they do at the ends of walls which have a series of arches each with an outward thrust.

The Barber's Tomb

Along the road which goes from the 'Īdgāh to the northern verge of the plateau there is a tomb on the left of the road, called the Barber's tomb or *Nā'ī kā Maqbara*. Whether this designation is correct or not cannot be ascertained from contemporary history. The tomb is a small structure, but architecturally it has certain features which are worthy of notice. The most prominent among them is the design of its masonry finial which resembles the finials of the Tughluq tombs at Delhi (Pl. CXV). Further, the shape of its dome also resembles that of the domes of the early Sulṭāns of Delhi, looking rather squat and flattened. The tomb is in the form of a pavilion or *chhatrī* and is open on all four sides. It is built on a square platform which is 2 feet 4 inches high from the ground level and measures 25 feet 10 inches on each side at the top. The arches on all four sides of the tombs have receding facets along their openings and are further decorated with a frill-like design near the top of their columns, and a spiral motif along the arch-head (Pl. CXV). The span of these arches is 9 feet 2 inches. The dimensions of the tomb are 17 feet 6 inches on each side externally and 11 feet 9 inches internally. There are three graves in the interior of the building, one of which is that of a male and the other two those of women. The sarcophagi of these graves, which were of brick and mortar, have decayed considerably. The parapet along the edge of the roof of the building has completely perished.[2]

Close by to the south-west of the tomb is a small mosque which apparently is connected with the former and was constructed for funeral services and the recital of the *Qur'ān* for the peace of the soul of the deceased.[3] It has three arched openings

[1] The pulpits of mosques in India are generally of very plain design compared to the magnificent pulpits of the Islāmic countries in the Near East and North Africa, notably those of Egypt, which, whether built of wood or stone, exhibit much artistic skill.

[2] The tomb was in a neglected condition, but it has recently been thoroughly cleaned and restored by the Archaeological Department.

[3] This mosque also had fallen into a sad state of disrepair, the walls were overgrown by wild plants, the roof leaked, and the interior was filled with all kinds of rubbish. These blemishes have been completely removed and the mosque thoroughly cleaned.

towards the east, the span of the arches being 7 feet 5 inches and the height up to the apex 9 feet 7 inches. Owing to these dimensions the arches appear very symmetrical. The prayer-hall, which is divided into two apartments, measures 27 feet 5 inches in length and 19 feet 4 inches in depth. The parapet representing overlapping arches built at the top of the walls has a graceful effect, but unfortunately the small turrets at the corners have suffered much damage from weathering and two of them have completely perished (Pl. CXV). The ceiling of the prayer-hall is divided into vaulted compartments, which are decorated with plaster ribs.

The Tomb of ʿAbdullāh Maghribī

Proceeding some 200 yards from the Barber's Tomb in a westerly direction there is a shrine associated with the name of ʿAbdullāh Maghribī. He was a local saint who lived during the reign of a Barīdī king.[1] The tomb has a large enclosure, but the gate which faces the south has been much damaged by the growth of a banyan tree which stands in front of it. The tree is of colossal size and presents an impressive sight, although its branches have wrought tremendous havoc with the masonry of the enclosure. The area within the enclosure measures 178 yards from north to south, and 141 yards from east to west. The entrance to the court was originally through a lofty arch, the upper part of which has been filled up in comparatively recent times, and the door now measures 9 feet in height and 4 feet 8 inches in width. The façade of the entrance is decorated with arched niches and rosettes, the latter showing traces of blue tile-work.

The tomb of the saint is built on a platform and crowned by a dome which looks rather heavy for its base (Pl. CXVI). The walls of the tomb at their base measure 29 feet 8 inches on each side externally and 18 feet 10 inches internally.

To the left of ʿAbdullāh Maghribī's tomb on the same platform there is another tomb the major part of the dome of which has fallen down (Pl. CXVI). The walls also had developed cracks, but recently they have been carefully grouted with lime-mortar. Below the platform the court is now littered over with graves, but the mango-trees which are to be seen at the back of the tomb and at various places in the court indicate that there was once a well-laid-out garden within the enclosure of the tomb.

The Tomb of Khān Jahān Barīd

Jahān Barīd was the son of Qāsim Barīd the founder of the dynasty, and affectionately attached to his brother Amīr Barīd I, whose corpse on the latter's demise he brought from the precincts of Daulatābād for interment in Bidar.[2] The tomb was perhaps built by him during his lifetime since it is complete architecturally and in addition to the usual adjuncts of a Barīdī tomb, such as the mosque, the *khānqāh* (the rest-house), and the court with a garden, it has a moat around its enclosure,

[1] He is popularly known as *Gūdaṛ-bīnī*, the saint with 'cotton nose', or 'dressed in rags'. Some whimsical *faqīrs* adopt strange masks and dresses.

[2] *Firishta*, Persian text, vol. ii, p. 347.

which is cut in solid rock like the moat of the Fort.[1] This moat is 14 feet wide and 10 feet deep. Inside the enclosure the court has a well-laid-out plan, being divided into flower-beds by foot-paths and octagonal platforms, the arrangement of which can be best understood by looking at Pl. CXII. A few mango-trees growing here and there are now the only remnants of the garden, and a masonry-built aqueduct shows that the water for the garden was supplied from a well which is situated to the south of the tomb. The entire court measures 278 feet from north to south and 279 feet from east to west.

This tomb is constructed on a platform, 6 feet 6 inches in height, and 102 feet square at the top. It is built of neatly chiselled masonry and has flights of steps on all its four sides, each flight comprising seven steps. Around the walls of the tomb there is another platform which rises 9 inches above the main platform and measures 56 feet 4 inches on each side. The walls of the tomb are adorned externally with arches which are arranged in two rows, one above the other (Pls. CXIII–CXIV). In the band which divides the lower series of arches from the upper there are small lozenge-shaped panels filled with religious texts written in *Kūfic* style of an ornamental design. The spandrels of the arches are decorated with medallions worked out in plaster, whilst on the walls at the back of the niches the pendant and chain design is prominent, which, as mentioned above, was the special emblem of the Barīdī kings, for it is always found carved on the sarcophagi of the royal tombs. The walls are crowned with a parapet of trefoil design, which rises 3 feet 3 inches above the walls, while the height of the latter from the floor is 20 feet 6 inches. The dome rests on a circular drum built above the roof and has mouldings and a decorative band carved in plaster around its base. The circumference of the dome near its springing-point is 67 feet 9 inches.

The tomb at its base is square in plan and measures 25 feet 6 inches on each side externally and 17 feet 6 inches internally. The squinches built at the corners in the interior of the tomb have plaster ribs which form a pleasing addition. There are five graves, four of which are those of ladies and the fifth of Khān Jahān himself. There are also two tombs of the male members of the family, and one of a woman, on the main platform.

As this tomb is built on the brink of the plateau, it commands lovely views of the green valley immediately below and of the distant plains chequered with cultivated fields and grassy plots of rocky soil.

The mosque connected with the tomb of Khān Jahān is situated in its forecourt towards the west, and it has also a *khānqāh* (rest-house) attached to it. The prayer-hall of the mosque has three arched openings towards the east, the shape of the arches being somewhat flattened, their span uniformly 7 feet 9 inches, and their height up to the apex 8 feet 6 inches. The hall measures 29 feet 8 inches in length and 18 feet 10 inches in depth, and has a casket-shaped ceiling divided into three compartments. The middle opening of the prayer-hall has a spiral design carved along its arch-head.

[1] The tomb is situated to the north-west of Qāsim Barīd II's tomb, but it can be easily approached by the 'Īdgāh road which skirts round the tomb of the Barber and after passing by the shrine of 'Abdullāh Maghribī touches the forecourt of this tomb towards the south.

The *khānqāh* has an L-shaped plan comprising a single hall at its bottom and a double suite of rooms in its upper part. The single hall measures 37 feet 6 inches from north to south and 13 feet 4 inches from east to west. The ceiling of this hall is vaulted, being divided into three compartments. The suite of rooms in the other part of the building comprises a hall in front facing the south, and three apartments at its back. The front hall measures 39 feet in length and 17 feet in depth. Of the three apartments at the back of the hall, the one towards the east measures 14 feet by 9 feet 3 inches, the middle one 10 feet 3 inches by 9 feet 3 inches, and the third on the western side 13 feet 2 inches by 9 feet 3 inches. The ceilings of these three apartments are vaulted. The front hall also has a vaulted ceiling which is divided into three compartments.

To the south of the mosque is a cistern for ablutions, which is square in plan and has a margin 5 feet 2 inches wide on all its four sides. The dimensions of the cistern itself are 25 feet 5 inches on each side with a depth of 2 feet 9 inches.

The Tomb of Ḥaḍrat Bībī Bandagī Ḥusainī

The road which has been built by the Archaeological Department for the convenience of visitors divides into two behind the western side of Khān Jahān's tomb, and one branch goes in a westerly direction towards the tomb of Ḥaḍrat Walī-Ullāh Ḥusainī, which will be described later, whilst the other is laid out in a north-westerly direction and leads to the tomb of Ḥaḍrat Bībī Bandagī Ḥusainī. The visitor before approaching the tomb will notice a mosque to his left, which until quite recently was in a very neglected condition. Five of the six vaults of the prayer-hall had fallen down and the front court and the interior of the mosque were thickly covered with prickly shrubs and rank vegetation. The mosque has been thoroughly cleaned now and such parts of it as were intact grouted with lime mortar. The prayer-hall has two apartments which together measure 25 feet 6 inches in length and 20 feet 3 inches in width. The eastern wall of the mosque has three arched openings with pillars of Hindu design supporting the arch-heads. The shafts of these pillars are carved, representing concave fluting, and the abacusi, which are square in design, bear the images of the lion-headed god, Narasiṁha. These pillars although possessing considerable girth are rather low in height, each measuring 3 feet 2 inches, and the arches which they support are also not symmetrically graceful, their span being 7 feet 4 inches and their height up to the apex 8 feet 6 inches.

The mosque stands close to the tomb, which is built on a platform about 2 feet high. The shrine was originally enclosed by a low wall which has now fallen into ruins. On the platform there are many tombs, but only two of them have domes over them, and the principal tomb is enclosed on all four sides by walls which indicate a batter as they rise upwards. The height of the walls is 18 feet from the floor, and at their top they are crowned with a parapet 2 feet 6 inches high. The sepulchral chamber is entered by a low door, 5 feet 3 inches high and 2 feet 8 inches wide, which is built in the middle of the southern wall of the tomb. Inside there are three graves, one in the middle and another on the right being those of ladies, and the third, which is on the left, being that of a male member of the family. Bībī Bandagī was a descendant of Ḥaḍrat Banda Nawāz Gesū Darāz of Gulbarga.

The other tomb is crowned by a small dome, and the walls of its base have open arches in all four directions, towards the east, west, north, and south. The base of the tomb is square in plan and measures 17 feet on each side. The walls of this building also indicate a batter. They rise 15 feet above the floor and are surmounted with a parapet which is 2 feet 6 inches high.

The Tomb of Ḥaḍrat Shāh Walī-Ullāh Muḥammad al-Ḥusainī

The main approach to this tomb is from the Bid–Udgīr road, near the eighty-seventh milestone.[1] The tomb stands to the right of the road at some distance, but the Archaeological Department has constructed a motorable path which first leads to the entrance of the tomb and then turning towards the east goes towards the tomb of Khān Jahān Barīd and joins the road which comes from the shrine of Bībī Bandagī Ḥusainī. The tomb can therefore also be reached by proceeding along the latter road.[2] Shāh Walī-Ullāh Ḥusainī was a descendant of the well-known saint of Gulbarga, Ḥaḍrat Banda Nawāz Gesū Darāz,[3] and the son-in-law of the brother of Malik Marjān, who held the governorship of Bidar under the Bijāpur king when the town with its fort fell to Aurangzeb in A.D. 1656.

The enclosure wall and the main gate of the tomb are modern, and the shrine itself, although built in the middle of an extensive court, is also of not much importance from an architectural point of view.[4] The building is square in plan and measures 22 feet 5 inches on each side externally. The walls rise 18 feet 5 inches above the platform on which the tomb is built, and are surmounted by a parapet of trefoil design. The height of the parapet above the walls is 3 feet. The dome of the tomb is semicircular in shape, but there is a bulge near its lower end. The circumference of the dome is 56 feet at its springing-point. The sepulchral room is entered by a small door, measuring 2 feet 10 inches in width and 5 feet 9 inches in height, but the arch above the door is a little larger in dimensions,[5] and it has a carved stone margin along its opening. The posts bear the vase and *chakram* designs as carved on the pillars of Barīdī tombs, while the arch-head has a spiral motif.

Behind the tomb of the saint there is an enclosure which looks modern. Inside

[1] The milestones indicate the distance from Hyderabad.

[2] Near the junction of the two roads the visitor will notice an incomplete tomb built of roughly tooled masonry. It has not been plastered over, and as the parapet on the top of its walls has not been built, the structure looks somewhat cadaverous in its present condition. The building has a square plan, measuring 12 feet on each side with a plinth 2 feet 7 inches high above the ground level. There is an arch in each of the four sides of the building and at the top it is crowned by a dome. The dimensions of the arches are: span 6 feet 9 inches and height up to the apex 7 feet 7 inches. Attached to this tomb there is another built on a platform, but without any dome over it. The shape of the sarcophagus of this tomb indicates that it is that of a lady, probably the wife of the nobleman who is buried in the tomb with the dome.

[3] The *Khānqāh* of Shāh Walī-Ullāh, situated in the town, has already been described, *supra*, p. 110.

[4] The court measures 142 yards from north to south and 114 yards from east to west.

[5] The span of this arch is 6 feet 8 inches and its height up to the apex 10 feet 6 inches.

the enclosure there are three graves apparently of descendants of the saint. There are, however, some old tombs to the east of the main shrine amongst which two are prominent because they are built on platforms. The first of these has a square plan measuring 13 feet 9 inches on each side and having open arches towards the east, west, and south.[1] The northern side of the tomb is closed, and an inscriptional tablet is fixed into the wall on its outer face.[2] The inscription contains two chronograms: one of them gives the date of the demise of a lady, who may be the wife of Shāh Walī-Ullāh and the niece of Malik Marjān, and the other the year of the completion of the tomb. The walls of the shrine rise 13 feet 3 inches above the platform, and at their top they have a parapet which rises 2 feet 6 inches higher still. The ceiling is vaulted, but there is no dome on the roof of the building.

The second platform has the tombs of two more ladies who are buried in a single enclosure. This platform is larger in dimensions than the first, since it measures 38 feet 6 inches in length and 26 feet in width, and has a height of 2 feet 5 inches from the ground level. The enclosure, containing the two graves, is almost square in plan, measuring 15 feet 2 inches by 16 feet 8 inches. The walls of the enclosure have three arches on each side which are filled with trellis-work. The height of the enclosure, including the parapet built on the top of its walls, is 8 feet 3 inches. The two tombs inside the enclosure are built of brick and mortar and they have no roof over them.

The Tomb of the Dog

Proceeding some three furlongs from the eighty-seventh milestone of the Udgīr road, the visitor will notice on his left, near the railway track, a small tomb built of trap masonry with no plaster over it. As regards the shape of its dome and the four open arches built in its sides facing the four cardinal points, it resembles the tomb of ʿAlī Barīd (Pls. XCII and CXVII). The building is called locally *Kutte kī Qabr*, or the tomb of the dog. Among Muslims the dog is considered to be an unclean

[1] The platform on which this tomb is built has a plinth 1 foot 3 inches high from the ground level and at the top it measures 21 feet on each side.

[2] The inscription comprises three lines of Persian verse written in *Nastaʿlīq* characters:

Text

(۱) خاتون زمانه آسوده شد این جا تعالی الله کهست از نکهت فردوس بوی مرقدش به به

(۲) مرتّب گشت چون این روضهٔ عالی بخوبی که رشك روضهٔ خلدست بر روی زمین خه خه

(۳) ز اتمام و بنایش باز جو تاریخ این مصراع بنای قصر خلد اتمام نکو یافته زه زه

۱۰۸۷ هـ ۱۰۸۸ هـ

Translation

(1) The lady of the age is resting here; God be exalted! the sweet smell of her resting-place surpasses the fine odours of Paradise.

(2) When this noble shrine was finished with elegance it became on the surface of the Earth the envy of the gardens of Paradise; how wonderful!

(3) The dates of its completion and foundation may be known from (the two phrases in) this hemistich—(1) '*The foundation of the palace of Heaven,* (2) *reached completion beautifully; how nice!*'

According to the *Abjad* system the first phrase gives the date 1087 H. (A.D. 1676), and the second 1088 H. (A.D. 1677). *Epig. Ind.-Mosl. Ind.*, 1927–8, p. 30.

animal, apparently because of its tendency to become rabid, but Firishta in the account of Aḥmad Shāh al-Walī describes the story of a dog which through its characteristic instinct of devotion saved the life of a person, while its master, suspecting the animal to be disloyal, killed it.[1] The master when he was apprised of the courage of the dog much regretted his hasty judgement and built a dome over its grave outside the town of Bidar. Firishta further writes that the tomb still exists, but except for the popular tradition mentioned there is no evidence whatever that the present structure is the tomb to which Firishta refers in his work.[2] The building, indeed, appears from its style to be of the Barīdī period, so that it may be the tomb of one of the scions of the royal family or of some distinguished official.

Through neglect this monument has been considerably damaged by weathering, but it is still an important landmark in the panorama of Bidar when looking towards the west from the platform of 'Alī Barīd's mausoleum. The tomb was originally enclosed by a wall, traces of which may be seen in a line of debris. The platform on which the tomb is built has also crumbled away in several places, but the walls and the dome are intact and the grass and wild plants which were growing on them have been cleared away by the Archaeological Department. The base of the building, which is square in plan, measures 13 feet 3 inches on each side externally and 7 feet 9 inches internally. The walls rise to a height of 16 feet 6 inches above the floor, and as the parapet at their top is missing, the walls may have risen originally to a height of 19 feet, including the said parapet. This height appears to the eye to be out of proportion to the width of the building which is 13 feet 3 inches only. The excessive height of the building is still more conspicuous owing to the high and narrow base of the dome which projects like a neck from the roof (Pl. CXVII*a*). The dome is globular in form and at its base measures 32 feet 6 inches in circumference.

The arches built on all the four sides of the building are elegant in shape, the span of each of them being 5 feet 3 inches and height up to the apex 10 feet 10 inches. The black stone bands arranged on the façade of the building indicate that the panels formed thereby were to be decorated with tile-work, which, however, was never done, for the building has no plaster over it which could make the bed for the insertion of tiles.

The Tomb of Ḥaḍrat Niẓām-ud-Dīn

Proceeding farther on the Bidar–Udgīr road, the visitor will notice on his left, almost by the side of the road, a tomb which is associated with the name of Ḥaḍrat Niẓām-ud-Dīn. He was a saint of considerable influence and flourished during the reign of the later Baihmanī kings who endowed four villages for the maintenance of his tomb. He is also reported to have held several high offices of state, including the Ministership of the Royal Treasury, but with the decline of the Baihmanīs he was deprived of this latter office, and after his death 'Alī Barīd made an attempt to dismantle the saint's tomb besides attaching to the crown lands the four villages which were granted by the Baihmanīs for religious ceremonies and the repair of his shrine.

[1] *Firishta*, Persian text, vol. ii, pp. 635–6. [2] Ibid., p. 636.

The building is constructed of large blocks of masonry and has a square plan, the walls measuring 31 feet 5 inches at floor level and rising to a height of 23 feet 4 inches above it. At their top the walls have an arch-shaped parapet, 3 feet 2 inches high. The tomb is crowned by a dome which has a circumference of 82 feet 3 inches at its base. The shape of the dome suggests a massive style of architecture, an impression which is confirmed by the batter of the walls as they rise upwards.

The tomb is closed on three sides, and the only entrance is through a small door built in the middle of the southern wall of the shrine.[1] In the interior of the building there are three graves; the sarcophagi of two of them are of black stone and that of the third is of brick and mortar.

Two Anonymous Tombs

At a distance of some two furlongs to the south of Ḥaḍrat Niẓām ud Dīn's shrine there are two tombs of the Barīdī period. They bear no inscription, nor do the local people know anything about the history of the persons who are interred there. The style of one of them (Pl. CXVII*b*) is an imitation of the architecture of ʿAlī Barīd's tomb, and it is not unlikely that it is the burial-place of one of the dignitaries of the Barīdī court. This tomb is incomplete, for it has no plaster over its masonry; and further the dome which was evidently to have been constructed on the top of the building has only two courses of stonework above its duodecagonal base.

The tomb is built on a platform and has an open arch on each of its four sides, facing the four cardinal points. The shape of these arches shows a fine sense of proportion, since each of them has a span of 6 feet 11 inches with a height of 11 feet 3 inches. The façade of the building is adorned with pairs of small arches built on either side of the large arches (Pl. CXVII*b*). The tomb has a square plan, measuring 18 feet 9 inches on each side externally and 11 feet 10 inches internally. The walls of the building rise to a height of 15 feet 3 inches above the floor of the tomb. The interior of the building has a vaulted ceiling which is divided into twelve concave facets by ribs of brick which have not been plastered over. There are many graves below the platform of the main tomb, and these apparently belong to the family of the person who is interred in the latter.

The other of the two principal tombs is situated close by and has a pyramidal roof with eight facets. This tomb is square in plan at its base and measures 19 feet on each side externally. The walls of the building, which are built of trap masonry, rise to a height of 15 feet 5 inches above the floor, and as the parapet has now completely crumbled away, the walls may well have risen a couple of feet higher still when it was intact. The interior of the tomb has been used as a store-room in recent times by the cultivators of the surrounding land and as a result of their ignorant vandalism the tombstone has been completely destroyed.

Some Anonymous Barīdī Tombs

On coming out from the southern gateway of ʿAlī Barīd's mausoleum the visitor will notice almost in front of him a group of tombs built on platforms the masonry of which has been very much damaged by the roots of several *nīm* (*Melia azedirachta*)

[1] The width of the door is 2 feet 6 inches and its height 5 feet 6 inches.

and tamarind trees, which until a few years back grew close by. These trees have been recently cut down by the Archaeological Department and the tombs strengthened and measures taken to prevent further deterioration. To the north-east of this group there are some more tombs which are built on two platforms and are comparatively in a better state of preservation. These platforms are attached to one another, but one of them is smaller than the other and built on the south of the larger one. The plinth of the small platform is faced with neatly dressed trap masonry and has a height of 3 feet 8 inches above the ground. The platform has flights of steps towards the east, west, and south, there being four steps of well-chiselled stone in each flight. At its top the platform measures 48 feet 2 inches by 29 feet 6 inches, and it has a strong lime concrete flooring the margins of which are again of smoothly dressed masonry. On the platform there were originally fourteen tombs, but the sarcophagi of ten of them are now missing.

The large platform is 1 foot 6 inches higher than the small one, and at its top has a square plan measuring 49 feet 10 inches on each side. The platform has a stone flooring comprising well-dressed slabs of trap which have also been used for the facing of the plinth. The height of the flooring is 5 feet above the ground. In the middle of the large platform there is another, rising 1 foot 10 inches higher than the first and measuring 23 feet 8 inches on each side, the plan being square. There are three tombs built on a pavement on this latter platform,[1] the sarcophagi of two of these being of brick and mortar, but of the third the sarcophagus is of a highly polished black stone (basalt ?). The large dimensions and the neat carving of this third sarcophagus, which among other motifs contains the chain and pendant design, would support the surmise that the tomb belongs to a member of the royal family.

The Tomb of Ḥaḍrat Shāh Zain-ud-Dīn Kunj Nishīn

The shrine is situated at a distance of about two furlongs to the south-west of the tomb of ʿAlī Barīd, and is held in considerable reverence by the religiously minded people of Bidar, who visit it frequently. Ḥaḍrat Shāh Zain-ud-Dīn was a descendant of the famous saint Junaid of Baghdād, and he migrated to Bidar during the reign of ʿAlā-ud-Dīn Baihmanī (A.D. 1436–58). The king is reported to have welcomed him with much kindness on his arrival, and when he died ʿAlā-ud-Dīn built a dome over his tomb. According to the information kindly supplied by the Sajjāda Ṣāḥib of the shrine Ḥaḍrat Zain-ud-Dīn was born in 767 H. (A.D. 1365–6) and breathed his last on the 29th of Rabīʿ II (Friday), 861 H. (25th March A.D. 1457). The title *Kunj-Nishīn* ordinarily signifies a person who has retired from the worldly life and taken up his residence in a secluded place, but *kunj* also means a grove and the locality wherein the last remains of the saint are interred and where he had lived is the most delightful mango grove in the suburbs of Bidar.[2] It is not unlikely that he got this title on account of his taking up his abode in the grove.

[1] The pavement has a square plan measuring 15 feet 5 inches on each side with a plinth of only 5 inches.

[2] Owing to the construction of the new aerodrome at Bidar several roads have been laid out in the middle of the grove and numerous huts built which have robbed this beauty spot of much of its natural charm and also caused the destruction of a large number of mango-trees.

The enclosure wall and the gate of the tomb appear to be modern and the tomb itself has undergone considerable alteration in later times, for the cusped arches above the door and the small turrets at the corners of the roof are not of the Baihmanī period. The tomb has a square plan, measuring 36 feet 2 inches on each side externally and 23 feet 5 inches internally. The walls rise to a height of 25 feet 11 inches from the floor and at their top are crowned with a parapet composed of arch-shaped masonry blocks which each measure 3 feet 1 inch in height. The dome has an irregular shape and looks too heavy for the building.

In the interior of the structure there are three graves, the middle one being that of the saint himself, that on the right the tomb of his son, Shāh Jamāl-ud-Dīn, and the third on the left the grave of his grandson, Shāh Niẓām-ud-Dīn. There are traces of painting on the ceiling, but the work does not appear to be original, while the painting above the doorway is absolutely modern and shows poor taste in the choice of colours. The court around the tomb extends 170 feet from east to west and 231 feet from north to south, but a portion measuring 85 feet in length and 22 feet in breadth has been taken away from its eastern side. The court is planted with mango-trees which besides yielding fruit and shade have given a setting to the building.

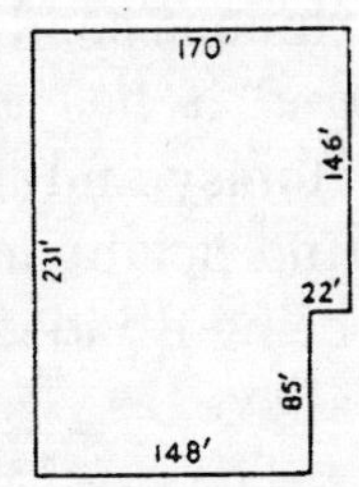

At the back of the saint's tomb towards the south there is another sepulchre containing the graves of three ladies. One of them is reported to be that of the wife of the saint. This building has not undergone much alteration, for the shape of the arches above the doorway is in the Baihmanī style and the small turrets at the corners of the roof follow this same fashion of architecture. The tomb has a square plan and measures 23 feet on each side externally and 18 feet 9 inches internally. The walls measure 17 feet 6 inches in height, and at the top they are surmounted by an arch-shaped parapet which rises 2 feet 6 inches above them.

Two Mosques in the Grove of Ḥaḍrat Zain-ud-Dīn

The grove encircling the shrine of Ḥaḍrat-Zain ud-Dīn extends to a distance of four to five furlongs on each side, and in the midst of the grove faint traces of several old structures may be seen, which have otherwise completely crumbled away, apparently through weathering and not by active vandalism. Two mosques, however, have escaped destruction, one of them being situated to the south-west of the saint's shrine at a distance of some four furlongs from the latter. This mosque is insignificant both in consideration of its dimensions and of the style of its architecture, but it has an inscriptional tablet built into the wall above the middle arch of its façade. The inscription gives the name Fatḥ Shāh as that of the builder of the mosque and also the date, the year 1080 H. (A.D. 1669), when the building was constructed.[1] The design of the mosque includes a prayer-hall with three arched

[1] The inscription consists of three Persian couplets and has been deciphered as follows:

Text

(۱) بنا از فتح شه این بیت سبحان   شده با زیب مسجد بهر انسان

(*note continued on p. 176*)

openings towards the east and a platform in front. The platform measures 44 feet 9 inches lengthwise and 17 feet 9 inches breadthwise, whilst its height above the surrounding land is 2 feet 3 inches. The prayer-hall consists of a single apartment, 20 feet 8 inches in length and 12 feet 3 inches in depth. The arches of the three openings of the hall towards the court are small and they have a flattened and rather clumsy appearance, owing to the span of each of them being 5 feet 6 inches and their height up to the apex 6 feet 9 inches. The ceiling of the hall is vaulted and is divided into three compartments.

The other mosque is to the south-east of the saint's shrine, being situated near an old tank which has now silted up, but at one time must have formed a pleasing feature of the grove.[1] The mosque comprises a single hall, measuring 30 feet 9 inches in length and 15 feet in depth. The western wall of the hall facing the *Kaʿba* is in a ruinous condition, but the eastern is comparatively in a better state of preservation and it has three arched openings. The arches of these openings are somewhat clumsy and flattened in appearance, the span of each of them being 8 feet 6 inches and height up to the apex 9 feet 6 inches. The ceiling of the building is vaulted, being divided into three apartments just as is the ceiling of the mosque described above.

MONUMENTS OF THE SUBURBS

This group embraces all such monuments as are situated within an ambit of six miles from the town of Bidar. They present considerable variety, comprising as they do gardens, tanks, water-channels, tombs, and places of worship of different faiths. It is difficult to observe the chronological order in describing these monuments, for their geographical positions do not indicate any dynastic influence, and the choice of site has been more or less a matter of individual taste, in some cases led by religious associations. In such circumstances for the convenience of the visitor it has been thought best to follow the roads which emerge from Bidar, and proceed in different directions, and to make a divergence from the road whenever any monument is situated away from the former.

Farḥ Bāgh

The name *Farḥ Bāgh*, garden of joy, was given to a beauty spot of Bidar where

(*note continued from p. 175*)

(۲) پدر را نام رکن الدین مي خوان　　که نام مادرش عایشه سلطان

(۳) ز حرف غین و ف اعداد بشمر　　بجو تاریخ . . . . عرفان

۱۰۰۰　۸۰

Translation

(1) This abode of Holy God has been built by Faṭh Shāh: it is a beautiful mosque for mankind.

(2) Read Rukn-ud-Dīn as the name of (Fath Shāh's) father and ʿĀyisha Sulṭān the name of his mother.

(3) Calculate the numerical value of the letters *ghain* and *fa* and (thus) ascertain the date . . . of knowledge.

The numerical value of the letters *ghain* and *fa* gives the year 1080 H. (A.D. 1669). *Epig. Ind.-Mosl.*, 1931–2, p. 29.

[1] The distance of the mosque from the shrine is nearly 2 furlongs.

water oozes out from the bosom of the rock and the valley below is divided into natural terraces and clothed with luxuriant verdure. The Hindu hermits for their meditations have always been in search of such places, and the site long before the advent of Muslims in the Deccan had become sacred to the votaries of the former faith and images of some gods were installed near the fissure whence water flows. The place is situated about a mile and a half to the south-east of Bidar, and a road practicable for motors from the Mangalpeṭ Darwāza has been constructed by the district authorities of Bidar for the convenience of the pilgrim and the ordinary visitor.

The garden laid out by the Mughal governor, Mukhtār Khān,[1] in 1082 H. (A.D. 1671) has fallen into complete ruin, but traces of some of the cisterns and artificial cascades built at appropriate places in the various stages of the garden may still be noticed. Among these cascades the most prominent is the one below the Hindu monastery (*dharamśāla*), the latter having been built in comparatively recent times (Pl. CXVIII). The cascade at its back has a number of niches built in the wall, in which lamps were placed to add to the beauty of the spray during the night. The valley still has some magnificent trees, which besides affording shade to the votaries present a picturesque view, and a lover of nature will enjoy in all seasons the splendour of these trees and also the assemblage of motley groups of votaries who come over partly in religious and partly in holiday mood, and bathe and worship their gods and finally have a meal which is cooked by them at the place.

To describe the monument in some detail: the visitor at the end of his drive, or trek on foot, will notice a flight of broad but abrupt steps, which may always be found in a state of disrepair, being damaged by the rain-water on the one hand,[2] and by the ponies and the cattle of the votaries on the other, the latter feeling no scruple in going down the steps mounted on their beasts of burden. Near the foot of the steps towards the right is a mosque, built, according to an inscription, by Mukhtār Khān who held the governorship of Bidar under the orders of Aurangzeb during the years A.D. 1671–2. The inscription, except for some benedictory words which are in Arabic, comprises a Persian record mentioning the building of a mosque and the laying out of a garden in this delightful place by Mukhtār Khān, the governor of Ẓafarābād,[3] and the bestowal of the garden by Mukhtār Khān upon his grandson, Mirzā Najm-ud-Dīn Muḥammad.[4] The style of writing is *Nasta'līq*,

[1] For Mukhtār Khān see *supra*, p. 15.

[2] The steps have been repaired by the Archaeological Department several times, and side drains and culverts constructed at suitable places, but the force of the water flowing down the plateau is tremendous during the monsoon, and periodical repairs are necessary to make good the damage.

[3] Ẓafarābād was the name given to Bidar by Aurangzeb after his conquest of the place in A.D. 1656.

[4] The full text of the inscription is as follows:

اللّه ولا سواه ولا نعبد الّا ايّاه

بنا کرد مسجد بجای کنشت　　　بر ابوابش انّا فتحنا نوشت

چون همّت والا نهمت خديو دين پناه مويّد من عند اللّه ابو الظفر محي الدين محمد اورنگ‌زيب بهادر عالمگير بادشاه غازي بر انهدام بنيان کفر و ظلام و تاسيس اساس دين اسلام مصروف و معطوف است کمترين بندگان مختار خان الحسيني السبزواري ناظم صوبهٔ ظفرآباد بتخريب بتخانه و ترتيب اين مسجد و باغ پرداخت و بتاريخ بيست و پنجم شهر ربيع الاول

(*note continued on p. 178*)

and the Persian verse given in the beginning of the inscription is a masterpiece of the art of calligraphy which has always been held in great esteem by the Muslim kings.[1] The mosque itself is a small structure comprising a prayer-hall with a terrace in front of it.[2] The prayer-hall measures 21 feet 2 inches in length and 18 feet 10 inches in width, and it has three arched openings towards the east. The middle one of these openings is larger than the two side ones, the span of the middle arch being 7 feet, and its height up to the apex 8 feet 9 inches. The ceiling of the building is vaulted, being divided into three compartments by arches which are built across the depth of the hall.

The garden with its buildings seems to have been made over by the Āṣaf Jāhī dynasty at the time of their establishment in the Deccan to the keepers of the adjacent Hindu shrine, apparently as a mark of their policy with regard to freedom of religious worship, because except for the mosque the whole site is now in the possession of the *pujārīs* of the temple. Almost in front of the mosque the visitor will notice coco-nuts, spices, flowers, and other offerings for worship, arranged on pieces of cloth spread on the ground, and ready for sale to the votaries who come to worship the icons in the temple. Along the southern wall of the mosque steps are built which lead to a cistern, with a pavement and an enclosure wall around it. The enclosure wall has arches outlined on its surface for the purpose of ornamentation which betray a Muslim style of architecture. The cistern is square in plan and measures 16 feet 6 inches on each side and has a depth of 4 feet 6 inches. The water in this cistern is supplied from a channel which is cut in the rock and extends

(*note continued from p. 177*)

سنه ١٤ جلوس همیون موافق سنه ١٠٨٢ هجري نبوي مطابق اين مصرع تاريخ كه ◆ بتكده مسجد شده از لطف حق ◆ بعنايت ملك علّام صورت اتمام يافت و از غايت خوبي و دلنشيني مكان بباغ فرح موسوم گردانيده بفرزند دلبند از عمر و دولت برخوردار ميرزا نجم الدين محمّد خلف فرزند سعادتمند ميرزا قمر الدين محمّد متعلّق ساخت. كتبه قمر الدين محمّد ابن مختار خان الحسيني

Translation

God, there is none but He and we worship not anyone except Him.

Verse

'(He) built a mosque in place of the temple,
And wrote over its door the *Qur'ānic* verse—"Verily We conquered" (ch. xlviii, ver. 1).'

As the exalted mind of the Khedive, the refuge of religion, supported by Divine Grace, Abū'ẓ-Ẓafar Muḥī-ud-Dīn Muḥammad Aurangzeb Bahādur 'Ālamgīr, the victorious, was inclined to, and occupied in, destroying the base of infidelity and darkness, and strengthening the foundation of the Islāmic religion, the most humble servant Mukhtār Khān al-Ḥusainī as-Sabzwārī, the governor of the province of Ẓafarābād, demolished the temple and built a mosque, and laid out a garden, which by the Grace of the Omniscient God were completed on the 25th of Rabī'-ul-Awwal in the 14th year of the auspicious reign (1082 H.) corresponding with the date contained in this hemistich—

'*By the Grace of God this temple became a mosque.*'

As the place was extremely beautiful and charming he (the most humble servant) styled it Farḥ Bāgh (the garden of Bliss), and entrusted it to the charge of his beloved child, blessed by long life and prosperity, Mirzā Najm-ud-Dīn Muḥammad, the worthy son of Mirzā Qamr-ud-Dīn Muḥammad.

'Written by Qamr-ud-Dīn Muḥammad, son of Mukhtār Khān al-Ḥusainī.' Vide *Epig. Ind. Mosl.*, 1927–8, p. 33.

[1] Ibid., Pl. XVII.

[2] The dimensions of the terrace are: length 23 feet 4 inches, width 19 feet 4 inches.

to the natural fissure whence the spring issues. The cistern is at present used by the votaries of the temple for washing their dirty linen, which is revolting in view of its close vicinity to both the temple and the mosque.

Close by, towards the west, adjoining the southern wall of the mosque, is the doorway of the temple. Its iron gate and cusped arch-head have a modern appearance. Passing through the door the visitor enters a passage, which is hewn in the solid rock which forms the walls and the ceiling. The length of the passage is 27 feet 10 inches and its breadth 9 feet 3 inches. Near the end of the passage is a *chhatrī*, or small pavilion with cusped arches, containing a *linga* with a *yonī* and a pair of snakes which are intertwined. Close by, two cells may also be noticed which are cut in the rock and which are used by the votaries for changing clothes. Beyond this stage the passage becomes narrow, measuring 5 feet 9 inches in width; six steps lead down to the water-channel, which in an irregular manner goes towards the spring from which it receives its water-supply. Pilgrims generally bathe near the steps, but those who are both devout and adventurous wade through the channel and proceed until the spring is reached.

The flow of water in the channel is continuous, but as offerings brought by the votaries are often thrown in the channel and the *pujārīs* in attendance at the temple are not very active in cleaning the water, one notices the foulness of the air, and is further annoyed by the swarms of insects which, disturbed by the light of the torch,[1] come out from their dark abodes in the cracks of the rock and fly around the intruders. The water in the channel in fair weather is generally 4 feet 6 inches deep, but during the rainy season it rises and the current becomes rapid, and much impurity is cleansed by Nature. The length of the channel, from the steps to the mouth of the spring, is 298 feet, and at the end some chambers are cut in the rock which also have a landing in front of them, the length of the landing being 18 feet and its width 5 feet 7 inches. A *pancha-linga*, and the images of the lion incarnation of Śiva and of his favourite vehicle, the bull, are installed in the chambers, and lamps are kept burning there night and day to glorify the gods.

Returning to the terrace in front of the mosque where the sweets and spices are sold, the visitor will notice another flight of steps, towards the east, which descend to the second stage of the garden. Originally there were neatly built cisterns, also an artificial cascade with niches for lamps at its back, the remains of which may still be seen in the south-western part of the terrace. But in recent times, owing to the scarcity of running water in Bidar, the washermen of the locality have built small tanks on this terrace for laundry purposes, and on a sunny day the southern hill of the valley is entirely covered with clothes which are spread there for drying. Pilgrims cook their food also on this terrace.

The third stage of the garden is reached from the second by another flight of steps which are built along the basement of the latter towards the east. This terrace is more spacious than the first two and has several *samādhs* (समाधे)[2] in the middle

[1] *Pujāris* who accompany the votaries take torches with them in order to light up the passage as there is danger of the votaries striking their heads against the rock-walls in the darkness.

[2] *Samādh*, the tomb of a *yogī*.

and an arcade along its southern side. The arcade measures 34 feet in length and 12 feet 10 inches in depth, and has seven openings towards the court. Originally the arcade appears to have been continued along the eastern side of this stage, but since the reoccupation of the garden by the *pujārīs* of the temple two shrines have been built in an irregular manner. The one at the south-east end of the terrace has a double hall in front and a cell with two side chambers at the back, the inner dimensions of the entire building being 32 feet 3 inches by 21 feet 7 inches. In front of the cell is an octagonal fire-place with a margin of floral design. This seems to be the ornamental basin of a fountain of the Mughal style, for the large artificial cascade, referred to above, is built below this temple, and the streamlet issuing from the spring and falling down in sprays at the various cascades would have passed through this fountain and finally discharged itself with picturesque effect in the valley below immediately behind the temple.

The portion of the arcade on the north of the shrine has fallen down (Pl. CXVIII), and the district authorities have contributed money for its reconstruction. It is hoped that the new work, at least so far as the façade is concerned, will match the old arcade in appearance and present no incongruity. Beyond this hiatus on the left another temple has been built in comparatively modern times, but the façade of the old arcade has been maintained in the wing towards the court. This temple comprises a hall with a corridor all round it and a shrine at one end. The hall is square in plan, measuring 22 feet 11 inches each way. The corridor is 6 feet 9 inches wide, and the shrine measures 10 feet on each side externally. The temple is dedicated to Śaivite worship and a *linga* is installed therein. The images of Gaṇeśa and the *nandī*, the sacred bull of Śiva, are carved on the building.

This stage of the garden is generally occupied by the *yogīs* and other wandering mendicants; and on entering the temples, built in the eastern wing, fumes of incense, the chanting of hymns, and the dark atmosphere of the interior of the cells have a mysterious effect upon a religious-minded person, although these features may not appear to be of any special significance to an ordinary visitor.

The soil of the valley below the temples is extremely fertile, and originally both fruit-trees and flowering shrubs were planted there, but now it is chiefly used for the cultivation of food grains.

Ḥabshi Koṭ

Ḥabshi Koṭ, or the fortress of the Abyssinians, is a hillock situated close to the town of Bidar towards the east, being separated from the latter by a narrow gorge. The hillock has on its top some tombs of the Abyssinian nobles who were employed at the court of the Baihmanī and Barīdī kings, and who revolted several times against their masters and the Persian and Arab dignitaries in their service.[1] The hillock has a plateau of an irregular shape, which is important from the point of view of military strategy, covering as it does the Dulhan Darwāza, the Mangalpeṭ Darwāza, and the fortifications between, in its section north to south. The best approach to the plateau is from the road going to the Farḥ Bāgh, where at a suitable point steps

[1] Briggs, vol. ii, pp. 427–8, n. 1.

with convenient landings have been built for visitors, the other sides of the hillock being rather steep.[1] Some amusing stories regarding buried treasures guarded by genii on this hillock are current in Bidar, and the *Sajjāda Ṣāḥib* of the Dargāh of Ḥaḍrat S͟hāh Kunj Nis͟hīn told me with great confidence that he knew of a young man who was very fond of resorting to the Koṭ and reciting the holy *Qur'ān* at the tombs there. Suddenly he became very rich, and when people asked him the source of his wealth he told them not to press him on that point. But when the curiosity of the people increased and they forced him to disclose the secret of his wealth, he suddenly became insane. Another story is prevalent that the people of Bidar see occasionally a gigantic Abyssinian rolling and baking cakes of enormous size on the roof of a ruined building, which, owing to the absence of a dome and a parapet, resembles an Indian *c̱hūla* and *tava* (a pan placed on the fire). There is no doubt that the place was at one time occupied by Abyssinians, and as they were severely punished for their misconduct, it is likely that strange stories would have been set afloat about their fabulous wealth and their atrocious character.

On ascending the steps of the plateau the first monument to attract attention is a cemetery enclosed by arched screens on all four sides (Pl. CXIX). These screens measure 99 feet 8 inches in length towards the east and west and 65 feet 6 inches towards the north and south. The eastern and western screens have six arched openings on either side of the entrances built in their middle, while the northern and southern screens have only four arched openings flanking the entrances on those sides. The screens, including the basement which is 3 feet 10 inches high, rise 13 feet 8 inches above the ground now, and when the parapet was intact they may have risen some 3 feet higher still.

The interior of the cemetery is approached by five steps, and on ascending them the visitor will notice a domed tomb in the middle and a large number of graves with brick and mortar sarcophagi around the former. The domed tomb has an open arch on each of its four sides in the style of 'Alī Barīd's mausoleum, and the interior of the building is decorated with plaster-work in which the chain-and-pendant motif and calligraphic specimens are prominent. The tombstone is missing,[2] and it is not unlikely that it was of polished black stone, and hence stolen and sold for use over another tomb built subsequently.[3] The structure is square in plan at the base and measures 14 feet 7 inches on each side externally. The arches have a uniform span of 7 feet 3 inches, and the height of their apexes from the floor is 9 feet 9 inches. The walls on each side measure 13 feet 9 inches in height up to the drip-stones (*c̱hhajjā*), but they rise farther above the latter and are surmounted by a parapet. The dome of the building rests on an octagonal base which is adorned

[1] These steps are on the western side of the road from the Mangalpeṭ Darwāza to the Farḥ Bāg͟h, their distance from the former being nearly a mile and from the latter about four furlongs.

[2] The Archaeological Department have built a brick and mortar sarcophagus over the grave in order to protect it from further decay.

[3] This evil practice is still prevalent in Delhi and Agra, where beautifully carved sarcophagi exist in great abundance, and the keepers of old cemeteries have no scruple in pulling them out and selling them to such customers as may have faith in the piety of the keepers and entrust the building of the tombs of their relatives to those gentlemen.

with bands and posts. The shape of the dome is of the Baihmanī style (Pl. CXIX), and though there is no inscription to fix the exact date of the building, it may be assigned to the late Baihmanī or early Barīdī period. According to local tradition the tomb is reported to be of one Ẓafar-ul-Mulk ʿAlawī.

Close by, towards the north of the arched enclosure of this tomb, is a mosque, apparently connected with the latter. It is a small structure, but shows a certain massiveness in its style of architecture. The mosque is built of trap masonry and has a wide spanned arch as the entrance to its prayer-hall. The span of this arch is 9 feet, while its height to the apex is 8 feet 9 inches only. The prayer-room measures 14 feet 7 inches in length and 11 feet 7 inches in width. Near the mosque there is also a well which was originally used for ablutions by visitors to the tomb. The well is now choked up by the growth of rank vegetation.

About 180 yards from the last tomb,[1] in a north-easterly direction towards the brink of the plateau, another tomb may be noticed which has suffered much through the inclemencies of weather and other causes. As it has neither a dome nor any parapet above its walls the roof of the building appears like a pan (*tava*), hence the origin of the story of the Abyssinian ghost which is described above (p. 181). The base of the building measures 18 feet 5 inches north to south and 13 feet east to west. There are arches on all four sides of this structure, the span of each arch being 8 feet 6 inches and height up to the apex 7 feet 3 inches. From the roof of the building excellent views are obtained of the country around, the Malkāpūr tank being towards the east, the Baihmanī tombs towards the north-east, and a long stretch of lowlands towards the north, in which the river Mānjra may also be seen as a shining streak.

To the north-west of the building, at a distance of 140 yards, is another tomb the dome of which is intact, but the plaster of the walls and the parapet above them have much decayed. The building has an arch on each of its four sides, the span of these being uniformly 7 feet 9 inches and height up to the apex 9 feet 4 inches. The walls rise to a height of 13 feet 4 inches from the floor, and when the parapet above them was entire they may have risen a couple of feet higher still. The shape of the dome resembles that of Qāsim Barīd II's tomb, and some other features of the building, such as an open arch in each of its side walls, also suggest that it belongs to the Barīdī period. This tomb can also be approached from that with the arched enclosure, the distance from the latter being 132 yards (Sketch-plan on opposite page).

Another tomb is situated at a distance of 72 feet towards the south-west from the last-mentioned monument. This is built on a platform which rises 7 feet 2 inches above the surrounding land and measures 52 feet 3 inches north to south and 65 feet 11 inches east to west at its top. The tomb itself is square in plan and measures 15 feet 3 inches on each side externally. The walls of the building have an open arch in the middle on each side, and at their top they are crowned with a parapet of trefoil pattern.[2] The height of the walls including the parapet is 17 feet from the

[1] The exact distance between these two monuments is 176 yards.

[2] The parapet by itself measures 2 feet 6 inches in height.

floor level. The arches in shape are very characteristic of the Barīdī style of architecture, the span of each of them being 7 feet and height up to the apex 8 feet 9 inches. Inside the building there are three tombs, the middle one being of a man and that on the right of a woman. The tomb on the left is much ruined, hence the difficulty in determining whether it is that of a woman or of a man. The real graves are built in a vault below the floor of the monument. The building has some delicate

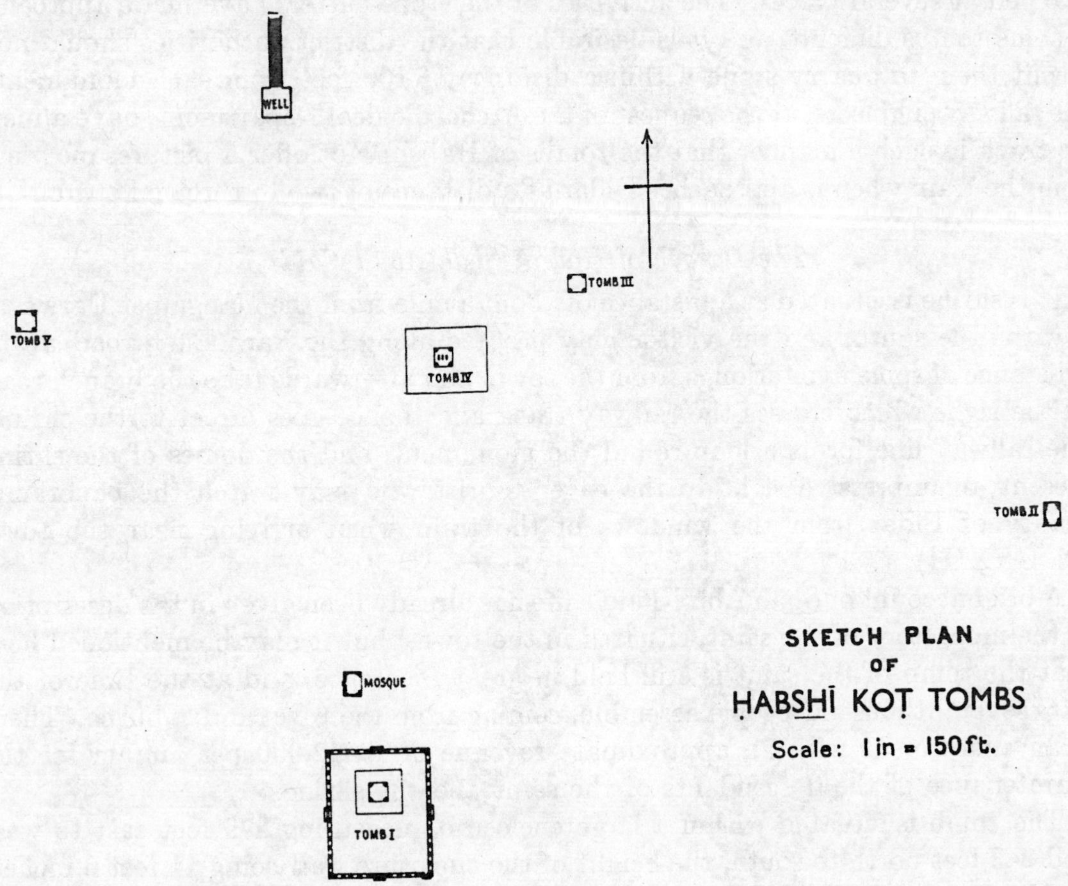

SKETCH PLAN
OF
HABSHĪ KOṬ TOMBS
Scale: 1 in = 150 ft.

plaster-work on both its exterior and interior, and from the style of the latter and also from the shapes of its dome and arches there remains no doubt that the tomb was built some time during the rule of the Barīdī kings.

To the north-west of this tomb is a deep well in which the water-level was 74 feet below the surface of the plateau at the time of the survey of the area in 1935. There is a passage with a flight of steps cut into the rock on the northern side of the well. The steps go down to the level of the water, and the dimensions of the well there are 23 feet 2 inches on each side.

Proceeding 102 yards farther west from the last tomb (Sketch-plan) the visitor will come across another which is incomplete and is larger in dimensions and more massive in construction than the others described above. This tomb also has an open arch on each of its four sides, the span of the arches being uniformly 8 feet 10 inches and height up to the apex 11 feet 5 inches. The dome of the building seems to have never been built, but there is no doubt that one was included in the original design of the building because the octagonal base from which it would have sprung may still be seen at the top of the building. The base is supported inwardly by squinches built at the corners of the building which have converted the plan from a square into an octagon.

The plateau is still used as a burial ground by Muslims, and laterite stone is also quarried at several places. The activities of the stone-cutters have made approach to some tombs difficult, and it is desirable that the district authorities should not permit them to quarry stone within a distance of 100 feet from each monument. The railway engineers, at the request of the Archaeological Department, have alined the track in such a manner that the tombs of Ḥabshī Koṭ offer a picturesque view from the train when it approaches Bidar at a distance of two to three miles from it.

The Dargāh of Ḥaḍrat Shah Abū'l-Faiḍ

This shrine is situated at a distance of about a mile from the Mangalpeṭ Darwāza, towards the south, and the visitor may proceed along the Farḥ Bāgh road up to a distance of some five furlongs from the town, and afterwards take the branch road on the right which crosses the railway track and thence goes direct to the shrine. The railway line forms a loop round the monument, and the domes of the shrine present an impressive sight to the eager tourist who may watch the panoramic beauty of Bidar from the windows of the train when arriving near the town (Pl. CXXIII).

A brief account of Shāh Abū'l-Faiḍ's life has already been given in the description of the monastery of the saint, situated in the town,[1] but it may be mentioned here that the tomb of the saint is still held in great reverence, and at the time of the *'Urs* several thousand people assemble, coming from the town and suburbs. There is an endowment with an approximate revenue of Rs.12,000 per annum for the maintenance of the descendants of the saint and the shrine.

The tomb is situated within a large enclosure, measuring 279 feet east to west and 243 feet north to south, the height of the enclosure wall being 11 feet 6 inches. Inside the area is divided into several courts by means of neat *muram* paths, and evergreen leafy trees are planted at appropriate places, the long-living *maulsarī* (*Mimusops elengi*) being prominent among them. The tomb architecturally has all the characteristics of a Baihmanī building, for the saint died during the reign of Muḥammad Shāh III, and as this king and his forebears had great respect for Shāh Abū'l-Faiḍ, the tomb was perhaps built at his instance. It is a massive structure, comprising a square hall with walls nearly 6 feet in thickness on each side, and crowned with a majestic dome. The walls at their base measure 51 feet 6 inches on each side externally, and they rise to a height of 34 feet 8 inches above the floor, and at their top are surmounted by a parapet which rises 5 feet 2 inches above the roof level. The dome rises from a circular base above the roof, the circumference of the base being 142 feet 3 inches.

The annual coats of whitewash on the exterior of the building have effaced to

[1] *Supra*, pp. 109–10.

a considerable extent the delicate plaster-work of the medallions arranged in the spandrels of the arches; and similarly the continuous burning of incense in the interior of the shrine during the last five centuries has covered the painting of the ceiling with a thick pall of smoke. Religion is sometimes fanatically antagonistic to artistic feeling, and it is difficult either to persuade the votaries of the shrine to give up the practice of burning incense at the time of the ritual, or to stop them from white-washing the building in an indiscriminate manner at the time of the *'Urs* every year. Besides the stucco decoration the walls are adorned with arches arranged one above the other in series; but all these features do not detract from the solid and massive character of the building.

The access to the interior of the shrine is through an arch which has a door in the post-and-lintel style at its back (Pl. CXXIV). The spandrels and the side walls of the arch are decorated with tile-work representing chiefly floral designs. The work has been spoiled by careless whitewashing, for the corrosive effect of lime has not only destroyed the glaze but made the surface of the tiles rough, thus ruining their artistic beauty. The arch, along its margin, has a black stone frame, comprising two neatly carved columns and a border with a spiral design at the top. This motif is frequently noticed on Baihmanī monuments. The carving above the door of the shrine shows Hindu workmanship.

The inner hall is square in plan at the floor level and measures 39 feet on each side. There are three graves, the middle one of the saint himself, whose full name was Shāh Amīn-ud-Dīn Abū'l-Faiḍ, and who died on the 6th Rabī' I, 879 H. (Thursday, 26th July A.D. 1474), in the evening. The grave on the right is of Sayyid Shāh Kalīm-Ullāh Ḥusainī, who was the second son of the saint, and who died in 892 H. (A.D. 1487). The grave on the left is of Sayyid Shāh Abū'l-Ḥasan, who was the grandson of Shāh Abū'l-Faiḍ and succeeded his father, Shāh Kalīm-Ullāh as *sajjāda*, on the latter's death. Shāh Abū'l-Ḥasan expired in 903 H. (A.D. 1498).

In front of the tomb of the saint is an enclosure built of black stone, wherein the remains of two sons of Mīr Niẓām 'Alī Khān Āṣaf Jāh (A.D. 1763–1803), are interred. The names of these two sons are Mīr Riḍā 'Alī Khān and Mīr Ḥusām-ud-Dīn 'Alī Khān. The enclosure has a screen of cusped arches on each of its four sides.

To the west of Shāh Abū'l-Faiḍ's tomb is the family vault of the saint, which comprises a hall crowned with a dome in the middle and a rectangular apartment on each side. The walls of the middle hall measure 32 feet 5 inches at their base externally from south to north, and rise to a height of 24 feet 2 inches above the pavement. At their top the walls were surmounted by a parapet which has largely crumbled away, yet its height above the roof can be determined from such remains as still exist. This is 2 feet 9 inches approximately. The circumference of the dome of the tomb at the roof level is 36 feet 2 inches.

The two apartments, one on each side of the central hall, communicate with the latter by means of massive arches which have a span of 20 feet 7 inches, and walls 4 feet 8 inches thick on either side of them for support. The height of each of these arches up to their apexes is 20 feet 4 inches from the floor level. The central hall is square in plan and measures 24 feet 5 inches on each side, while the two flanking apartments which are rectangular in plan measure 28 feet 9 inches north to south and 14 feet 5 inches east to west. The ceilings of these apartments are vaulted, but have no domes above their roofs.

In the central hall stand two tombs; that on the right is of Sayyid S͟hāh ʿAbd-ul-Qādir Muḥammad al-Ḥusainī, and that on the left of Sayyid S͟hāh ʿAbd-ul-Minallāh Muḥammad al-Ḥusainī. The latter died in 939 H. (A.D. 1533). Below the arch on the right of the hall is another grave which is reported to be that of Sayyid S͟hāh Yamīn-Ullāh. The rectangular apartment on the right contains only one grave, wherein according to the *Sajjāda Ṣāḥib* S͟hāh Yamīn-ur-Raḥmān is buried. The arch on the right has also a tomb below it in which Sayyid S͟hāh Luṭf-Ullāh is buried. There are two more tombs in the apartment adjoining the latter arch, towards the west. Of these tombs one on the right is of Sayyid S͟hāh ʿAtīq-Ullāh and the other, on the left, of Sayyid S͟hāh ʿAbdullāh Muḥammad.

Almost in front of the family vault of the saint is the tomb of ʿĀs͟hūrī Begam, wife of Nawāb Niẕām ʿAlī K͟hān. The tomb is built in the open, but it has a stone enclosure around it. The enclosure has panels of jālī-work which is quite artistic.[1] Close to the tomb of ʿĀs͟hūrī Begam, towards the south, is a small cistern for ablutions. It is square in plan, measuring 9 feet 2 inches on each side and 3 feet 6 inches in depth. The cistern has a polished black stone margin around it and a fountain in the middle from which water shoots forth. For the maintenance of ʿĀs͟hūrī Begam's tomb there is an endowment comprising two villages from the revenues of which food is distributed daily to the poor, and a certain sum is set apart for the daily and annual rites and the cost of lighting, incense-burning, and offering of flowers. To the south of ʿĀs͟hūrī Begam's tomb is a *langar-k͟hāna*[2] which comprises a hall with five arched openings.

Along the southern wall of the enclosure of S͟hāh Abū'l-Faiḍ's shrine there is a hall for the recital of the *Qur'ān* which has arched openings towards the court. To the north-west of the *dargāh* there is a small mosque with a single hall, measuring 24 feet 5 inches in length and 12 feet in depth. The hall has three arched openings towards the court, the dimensions of the latter being insignificant. The span of each of these arches is 6 feet 3 inches and height up to the apex 7 feet 10 inches.

Adjoining the enclosure wall of the shrine towards the south is a *samʿa-k͟hāna* or Music Hall which, although a separate building, forms an important adjunct to the shrine. The plan of the *samʿa-k͟hāna* consists of an open court, 178 feet by 72 feet, a platform 65 feet 10 inches by 22 feet, and a double hall with rooms on either side of it. The double hall measures 65 feet 10 inches in length, east to west, and 26 feet in width, north to south. It has five arched openings towards the court. The hall is used for *qawwālī* (singing) for dervishes and the general public on ceremonial occasions.

Leaving by the main gateway of the *dargāh* a visitor who walked towards the south along the western wall of the enclosure would notice a deep well which has been the main source of the supply of water for the multifarious requirements of

[1] The interior of the enclosure is square in plan, measuring 11 feet 6 inches on each side.

[2] A place for distributing food to the poor.

the *dargāh*. The well has an octagonal plan at its top, measuring 15 feet across, and on one side it has a covered passage with a long flight of steps which extend to the surface of the water some 80 feet below the ground. The traces of a water-channel laid out from the well may also be seen.

The Shrines of Ḥaḍrat Shāh ʿAlī and Ḥaḍrat Shāh Abū'l-Ḥasan

Ḥaḍrat Shāh ʿAlī was the great-grandson of Ḥaḍrat Shāh Abū'l-Faiḍ in the direct line,[1] and the tomb of the former is a replica on a slightly smaller scale of his ancestor's mausoleum. The tomb is built on a platform, measuring 153 feet north to south and 144 feet east to west. The base of the building, which is square in plan, measures 51 feet 10 inches on each side externally, and the walls rise to a height of 39 feet 8 inches and at their top are surmounted by a parapet 4 feet 9 inches high. The circumference of the dome, which is 142 feet 6 inches above the roof level, shows a fine sense of proportion, as the dome does not look top-heavy in relation to the dimensions of its base. The façade of the building is decorated with medallions and floral designs carved in plaster and arranged in the spandrels of the arches. The doorway is adorned with encaustic tiles, their colours being yellow, green, and blue.

The interior of the building has a square plan at the floor level,[2] but higher it becomes first octagonal owing to the squinches built at the corners, and afterwards sixteen-sided on account of niches constructed below the circular rim of the dome. The walls of the interior of the tomb are decorated with stucco-work representing various motifs, among which the chain-and-pendant design may also be noticed. In the middle of the hall there are three graves, the central one being that of Shāh ʿAlī himself with that of his son on the right, while the grave on the left is that of his grandson. Over the doorway of the tomb an inscribed tablet is fixed into the wall which gives 992 H. (A.D. 1584) as the date of the demise of Shāh ʿAlī and the building of the sepulchre wherein he 'rests in peace'.[3] The general architectural

[1] Ḥaḍrat Shāh ʿAlī is popularly called Ḥaḍrat Kāle Ṣāḥib; the name was probably given to him on account of his dark complexion.

[2] It measures 34 feet 11 inches on each side.

[3] The full text of the inscription has been deciphered as follows:

سنہ اثنی تسعین　　تاریخ عمارت گنبد مبارك　　تسعمائة

(۱) حبّذا گنبدی عالي کہ شد آسوده در او　　شاه فردوس مکان شاه علي رهبر دین

(۲) سال تاریخ بالین ز خرد جستم و گفت　　هاتف از غیب کہ شد گنبد فردوس برین

۹۹۲ هـ

Translation

The chronogram of the building of the auspicious dome: 992 H. (A.D. 1584).

Verse

(1) 'How felicitous is this high dome, wherein Shāh ʿAlī, the king of heavenly abode, the leader of the faith, is enjoying rest?'

(2) 'I inquired of Wisdom the chronogram of this shrine; the unknown voice said, "the heavenly dome has been built".'

The numerical value of the last phrase according to the *Abjad* system gives the figure 992, which tallies with the date given in the first line of the inscription. *Epig. Ind. Mosl.*, 1927-8, p. 31, Pl. XIV.

effect of the building is one of massiveness in the structural parts combined with a love of detail in its decorative features.

At the south-east end of the platform the tomb of another saint, called Shāh Abū-'l-Ḥasan, is built. He, like Shāh Abū'l-Faiḍ, belonged to the Chishtīyya order of Ṣūfīs, and died in 1089 H. (A.D. 1678). The building is comparatively small; its base measures 24 feet 6 inches on each side externally. The walls rise to a height of 19 feet 2 inches above the platform, and at their top they have a parapet which is 2 feet 9 inches high. The façade of the building is adorned with stucco-work and arches outlined on the walls. An inscription is carved above the doorway of the tomb, which consists of three lines of Persian verse written in *Naskh* characters of an ornamental type.[1] The interior of the tomb is square in plan and measures 16 feet 5 inches on each side. There are three graves, one of which is that of Shāh Abū'l-Ḥasan and the other two are of members of his family. The building is crowned by a shapely dome which has a circumference of 62 feet immediately above the roof level.

There are several tombs of the descendants and disciples of Shāh ʿAlī and Shāh Abū'l-Ḥasan on the platform and also a large graveyard at the back of the shrine of the latter saint. Below the platform, towards the north-west of Ḥaḍrat Shāh ʿAlī's tomb, is an enclosure containing four graves wherein the principal successors of the saint are buried. Farther westward is a mosque which was apparently built for prayers as an adjunct to Shāh ʿAlī's tomb. The building comprises a double hall, measuring 29 feet in length and 21 feet 1 inch in width. The hall has three arches opening on the court in front, the span of each of these arches being uniformly 7 feet 8 inches and their height up to the apex 9 feet 2 inches. The ceiling of the hall is vaulted, being divided into six compartments by arches built across the inner and outer apartments of the hall. The front wall of the mosque rises 13 feet 7 inches above the floor and is surmounted by a parapet the height of which above the dripstones (*chhajjā*) is 4 feet 3 inches. Close by is a cistern for ablutions which is square in plan, measuring 28 feet on each side and being 5 feet 3 inches deep. The

[1] The full text of the inscription is given below:

سنہ تسع   تاریخ عمارت گنبد مبارك   ثمانين و الف

(۱) بو الحسن شاه دین و عارف حق   کہ ولیّ نبي سرشت آمد

(۲) حبّذا گنبدی کہ مرکز او   خاتم خواجگان چشت آمد

(۳) هاتف از غیب گفت تاریخش   کوی نور یا دل بهشت آمد

۱۰۸۹ هـ

Translation

The chronogram of the building of the holy dome: 1089 H. (A.D. 1678).

Verse

(1) 'Abū'l-Ḥasan, the lord of the faith, and the knower of God; who is a saint possessing the qualities of a prophet.'

(2) 'How auspicious is this dome below which the last of the Chishtīyya saints rests!'

(3) 'The unknown inspirer suggested its chronogram, "the avenue of (divine) light, or the heart of Paradise has appeared".' *Epig. Ind. Mosl.*, 1927–8, pp. 31–2, Pl. XIV.

water for the cistern was supplied from the well built towards the east (*supra*, pp. 186–7), and the remains of the old aqueduct may still be seen.

The tomb of S͟hāh ʿAlī and the other sepulchres described above can easily be visited from the road of S͟hāh Abū'l-Faiḍ's Dargāh, because they stand near the latter shrine towards the south and south-west.

The Tomb of Ḥaḍrat Sayyid Amīr Ḥamza Qādirī

Proceeding about 100 yards farther west from the last group of tombs we come on the shrine of Ḥaḍrat Amīr Ḥamza Qādirī, who is reported to be the twenty-second S͟haik͟h in descent from Ḥaḍrat Muḥī-ud-Dīn ʿAbdu'l-Qādir al-Jīlānī. He arrived in Bidar from Bag͟hdād some time during the reign of Aurangzeb, apparently after the conquest of the town by the emperor in A.D. 1656, and was treated with respect by him and his governor on account of the saint's strict observance of the tenets of Islām. A *sanad* of Aurangzeb is in possession of the descendants of the saint who still survive in Bidar, and who celebrate the anniversary of the demise of the saint regularly on the 9th of Ramaḍān.

The tomb of the saint is built on a platform on which are three other tombs, but the former is easily distinguished from them by the screen built near it. Close by is another platform with two tombs, the latter belonging to the descendants or disciples of the saint. There is also a small mosque near the tomb which comprises a single hall, and has three arched openings towards the east. The hall measures 21 feet 3 inches in length and 13 feet in width, while the arches of the openings have a uniform span of 5 feet 8 inches and height up to the apex 7 feet 5 inches. The ceiling of the hall is vaulted but divided into three compartments. The mosque being small, the wall of its façade rises to a height of 12 feet only up to the drip-stones (*c͟hhajjā*), above which is an ornamental parapet measuring 3 feet 4 inches in height.

To the north of Ḥaḍrat Amīr Ḥamza's tomb is the C͟haukhaṇḍī of Dūlāh Mīyān and the tomb of a courtesan. All these monuments may be visited from the Hyderabad–Bidar road, near the eighty-third milestone.

Hanūmān's Temple

This shrine is situated on the right of the main road from Hyderabad to Bidar, and it attracts the notice of visitors by its white spire and walls painted with red ochre. The building does not appear to be old, and it comprises a chamber for the icon, a pillared hall (*mandap*) for the assemblage of the votaries and the performance of the ritual (*pūja*), and a *dharamśāla* for the accommodation of visitors. The *dharamśāla* is of considerable dimensions; it has arched openings towards the court and a double hall at the back. There are also rooms at the western end of the court near the doorway. The spire of the temple has receding bands of masonry as it rises upwards, and at the top is crowned with a finial. Near the road under a tamarind tree is the *samādh* of a hermit, which may be approached with convenience from the court of the temple.

The shrine is dedicated to the worship of the monkey-god *Hanūmān* who, according to the Hindu legend, led the forces of Rāma against Rāvaṇa. Hanūmān is the most popular deity in Indian villages, and his figure carved on slabs, or even on boulders, and daubed with red paint, is frequently to be seen in rural areas.

The Dargāh of Banda 'Alī Shāh Majdhūb, the Chaukhaṇḍī of Mīr Kalān Khān and the Tomb of Khāṣṣ Maḥall

These monuments are situated in the vicinity of Bidar, on the right side of the road, and the visitor notices them when coming from Hyderabad, either in a private motor-car or by the omnibus service. The tomb of Banda 'Alī Shāh is built on a platform situated within an enclosure. The court around the platform measures 79 feet 7 inches north to south and 59 feet 9 inches east to west. The wall of the enclosure rises 9 feet 8 inches above the ground level and is surmounted by a parapet representing arch-heads. *Majdhūb*, according to the Ṣūfī terminology, is a dervish so absorbed in divine love as to forget all worldly concerns. Some charlatans pretend this attitude to deceive the credulous votaries who are fleeced by the agents of such pseudo-dervishes.

Mīr Kalān Khān was the governor of Bidar for a long time, first under the Mughal emperor of Delhi and afterwards under Āṣaf Jāh I, when he declared his independence in A.D. 1724. The Chaukhaṇḍī, to be described presently, is associated with the name of Mīr Kalān Khān, but according to tradition his last remains were interred in the shrine of Multānī Pādshāh.[1] It is likely that Mīr Kalān Khān built the Chaukhaṇḍī for such members of his family as died before him, while his own body, owing to his special devotion to Multānī Pādshāh, was buried within the enclosure of the saint's tomb. In the Chaukhaṇḍī there are three graves.[2] The building is small, measuring 18 feet in length and 15 feet in width at its base. The ceiling is vaulted, and the monument has an arch on each of its four sides. Of these arches two facing the north and south are of uniform dimensions, but a little larger than those towards the east and west. The span of the former two arches is 6 feet 3 inches with a height of 7 feet 5 inches, in contrast to the span of the eastern and western arches which is only 4 feet 2 inches with a height of 6 feet 9 inches. The exterior of the building is richly decorated with stucco-work. The Chaukhaṇḍī has also a platform in front of it.

Farther on is the *Takīya*, or the cemetery of Nadīm-Ullāh Shāh, which has a door facing the road and several platforms with tombs thereon. It has also a small sepulchral chamber, square in plan.

At a short distance from the latter cemetery is the tomb of Khāṣṣ Maḥall, the daughter of Ḥaḍrat Abū'l-Faiḍ who was married to Amīr Barīd. The title Khāṣṣ Maḥall signifies a lady of special rank. The tomb is enclosed by a wall, and the court inside has foot-paths with stone margins. The gateway of the enclosure is intact, and may be seen near the south-west end of the court.

[1] *Supra*, pp. 107–9.

[2] It is also possible that the Chaukhaṇḍī may have been built over the grave of Mīr Kalān Khān II, who was also the governor of Bidar from A.D. 1766–7 (*supra*, p. 18).

The plan of the main building comprises a double platform with one stage above the other, the lower being only 1 foot above the ground and measuring 48 feet 2 inches on each side, and the upper rising 4 feet 6 inches above the former and measuring 39 feet at its top in each direction. The tomb is built in the middle of the upper platform, and at its base, which is square in plan, measures 18 feet 3 inches on each side externally. The building has an arch in the middle of each of its four sides, and the walls rise to a height of 14 feet 5 inches above the floor. The tomb is built of trap masonry, and in the interior of the building the square plan has been converted by squinches and arched niches into a twelve-sided figure with a view to fitting in with the circular base of the dome. The monument has a sepulchral chamber below its upper floor which can be reached through an arched opening. Seven steps lead down to this chamber, which is rather small in dimensions, measuring 9 feet 6 inches on each side. The ceiling of the chamber is vaulted.

The Tomb of Ghālib Khān alias *Miṭṭhū Khān*

Near the tomb of Khaṣṣ Maḥall there is another the dome of which rises into view with that of the former as one comes to Bidar from Hyderabad by road. The building is associated with the name of Ghālib Khān, *alias* Miṭṭhū Khān,[1] who was probably an officer employed by some Mughal governor of Bidar. The tomb is built on a platform 3 feet high and measuring 36 feet 6 inches on each side at the top. The plan of the base of the tomb is also square, and it measures 15 feet on each side. The walls rise to a height of 12 feet 3 inches above the platform, and at the top have a parapet which is 2 feet 2 inches high.

The tomb is crowned with a dome which has a circumference of 40 feet 5 inches at the roof level. The architectural arrangement of the squinches and overlapping arches is almost the same in this building as in the late Barīdī tombs, and it has also an open arch in each of its four side walls.[2] The sarcophagus has decayed, but the plaster-work on the exterior of the building is more or less intact, and in the decorative motifs figures of birds may be seen, which show that the masons employed for building the tomb were Hindu.

Attached to the platform of the tomb towards the north there is another with several graves. There are also two wells and a mosque connected with the monument, situated close by. The mosque comprises a single hall with three arched openings towards the east. The inner dimensions of the hall are: length 23 feet 9 inches, width 14 feet 9 inches. The ceiling is vaulted, being divided into three compartments by arches built across the width of the hall. The ornamental parapet above the walls of the mosque and the turrets at the corners have almost completely crumbled away, and the present height is only 12 feet.

The Tomb of Ḥaḍrat Nūr Samnānī

This tomb is situated at a distance of about 2 miles south-east of Bidar, on the

[1] *Miṭṭhū* in Hindī means 'sweet', Miṭṭhū Khān, the sweet Khān. The epithet is also applied to the parrot, which is called *Mīyān Miṭṭhū*.

[2] These arches show a fine sense of proportion, their span being 4 feet 5 inches and their height up to the apex 8 feet 3 inches.

verge of the plateau, and thus commands excellent views of the valley below and the lowlands beyond. It is an ideal place for a picnic; visitors should drive to the second railway crossing and then turn to the left and leave their vehicles where the land has been furrowed by rain-water and other climatic causes. The distance of the tomb from the second railway crossing is about half a mile.

Shāh Nūr came from Samnān[1] to Bidar during the Baihmanī period, and must have exercised considerable influence, for his *'Urs* is still celebrated on the 20th of Jumādi I by his descendants who live in Bidar and impart the teachings of the saint and initiate others into the special religious practices of their order.

The tomb of the saint is built in the open on a long platform which is shaded by two stately banyan trees. Towards the south-west is another platform with several tombs wherein the descendants of the saint are enjoying their final peaceful rest.[2]

The Tomb of Maḥmūd Gāwān

This is situated two and a half miles to the south of Bidar, of which the first two miles are traversed by the Hyderabad road. From near the eighty-second milestone a special road leads to the monument, which first goes in a westerly direction until the Sharbat Bāgh is reached, then turns towards the south and, skirting the tank still associated with the name of Maḥmūd Gāwān, climbs up the hillock on which the tomb is built. Owing to the tragic circumstances in which this great statesman was executed no monument worthy of his rank could be erected, and his remains rest under the shade of some *nīm* trees.[3]

The tomb is built on a platform square in plan measuring 56 feet 6 inches on each side. The masonry of the platform had decayed considerably, but the Archaeological Department has not only repaired it thoroughly but also fixed a railing along the margins of the platform to stop the trespass of stray cattle which caused injury to the masonry of the tomb and made the pavement untidy. As there are several other tombs on the platform, the Archaeological Department, in order to distinguish Maḥmūd Gāwān's grave from others, has set up an inscriptional tablet at the head of the tomb under the orders of the late Mahārāja Sir Kishan Parshad, when he was President of His Exalted Highness the Nizam's Executive Council.

Besides the platform of Maḥmūd Gāwān's tomb there is another, but of smaller dimensions, on which several tombs are built. The latter are probably those of the relatives of the great vizier, or of the professors of the college founded by him at Bidar, for the latter might have expressed a desire to be buried near his tomb. The grove of *nīm* trees and the solitude of the hillock offer a peaceful environment for the rest of the soul of a warrior-statesman like Maḥmūd Gāwān, whose life was mainly spent in leading strenuous expeditions or in solving the knotty problems of the State which generally arose from party intrigue.

[1] A town in Persia between Damaghāṇ and Khwār, 35° 29′ N., 53° 20′ E.

[2] Below the cliff whereon the tomb of the saint is built there is also a natural spring of sweet water, but as it is at a considerable distance from Bidar, the water which flows from the spring is used chiefly for agricultural purposes.

[3] An account of the execution of Maḥmūd Gāwān is given elsewhere in this book, *supra*, pp. 9–10.

The Mosque at Gornallī

About four furlongs to the south-west of the tomb of Maḥmūd Gāwān, and three furlongs to the south of Sharbat Bāgh, is the small village of Gornallī, which has a mosque bearing an inscription of Amīr Barīd II, dated 1019 H. The name of this king as the eighth ruler of the dynasty is given by the author of *Basātīn*,[1] and also confirmed by the inscription on the well at Āshṭūr, quoted already in this book.[2] The epigraph is in Persian and consists of four lines, the first two of which contain the *Bismillah* and the Islamic creed. The script is Thulth of an elegant type.[3]

The mosque is a small building, comprising a single hall with a court in front. The hall measures 22 feet 5 inches in length and 14 feet in width, and has three arches opening on the court. The span of the arches is uniformly 5 feet 5 inches, and the height up to the apex 7 feet 3 inches. The height of the front wall up to the dripstones is 12 feet 4 inches, and above that a parapet is built which has a trefoil design at its top. The arches of the façade of the mosque are flanked with a pier on each side which has a square section in its lower part and at the top is crowned with an ornamental turret rising 6 feet 4 inches above the row of dripstones.

The court of the mosque is rectangular in plan and measures 32 feet north to south and 15 feet east to west. It has a plinth one foot above the surrounding land. At the southern end of the court is a room with two arched openings towards the north. It measures 14 feet in length and 10 feet in width, and has a vaulted ceiling which is divided into two compartments. The room was apparently meant for the recital of the *Qur'ān*, for there are two tombs built on a platform at the northern end of the court of the mosque. The tombs seem to be those of important personages, for the plinth of the platform is lined with neatly chiselled masonry. The platform rises 3 feet 6 inches above the floor of the court and has a square plan, measuring 14 feet 6 inches on each side. The tombs are those of a man and a woman, but one of the sarcophagi, which were originally of polished black stone, has been stolen.

The Kālī Masjid of Aurangzeb

The name *Kālī* (black) appears to be a misnomer now, for the masonry of the building is covered with plaster which, in spite of being weather-stained, has a

[1] *Basātīn-us-Salāṯīn*, Hyderabad lithograph, p. 273.

[2] *Supra*, pp. 140–1.

[3] The full text of the inscription has been deciphered as follows:

بسم اللّٰه الرحمٰن الرحيم

لا اله الا اللّٰه محمد رسول اللّٰه

بناء هذا المسجد في زمان السلطاني امير بريد شاه

ثاني وباني اين مسجد خواجه بوستان سنه ١٠١٩

كتبه احمد (؟)

Translation

In the name of God the Merciful and Compassionate!

'There is no god but God and Muḥammad is the apostle of God.'

This mosque was built during the sovereignty of Amīr Barīd Shāh II, and the builder of this mosque was Khwaja Bostān in 1019 H. (A.D. 1610). Aḥmad (?) wrote this. *Epig. Ind. Mosl.*, 1937–8, p. 4.

yellowish-white tint. The mosque is situated at a distance of about four furlongs from the Fatḥ Darwāza in the low land towards the south-west. It has a long inscription in Persian verse carved on its façade, which records the building of the mosque by one ʻAbd-ur-Raḥīm in 1106 H. (A.D. 1695), during the thirty-eighth regnal year of Aurangzeb, whose sense of justice, benevolent temperament, and strict observance of the Islāmic law are also mentioned in the inscription.[1] The building

[1] The style of writing is *Nastaʻlīq* and the text of the inscription has been deciphered as follows:

بسم اللّه الرّحمٰن الرّحيم

(١) ز لطف و عنايات پروردگار — مرتّب شد اين مسجد با وقار

(٢) چنان دارد اميد از كردگار — كه ماند ز من اين نشان يادگار

(٣) بعهد شهنشاه اورنگ‌زيب — كزو يافت دوران و عالم نصيب

(٤) عجب بادشاهی بعدل و بخير — كه ثانيش خاقان نيامد بدير

(٥) بشرع نبي از دل و جان مطيع — زهی شاه دين‌دار عمرش وسيع

(٦) كريما عطا كن تو عمر مزيد — بفرزند و اولاد شاه رشيد

(٧) بنا كرد مسجد براه كريم — گنهگار شرمنده عبد الرّحيم

(٨) گذشته معيشت بفعل لئيم — آلهي كرم كن بر عبد الرّحيم

(٩) بيامرز يا رب مرا از گناه — بحقّ محمّد شفاعت پناه

(١٠) بروز قيامت مرا كن قبول — بر انگيز در خاك راه رسول

(١١) غلام علي از دل و جان بود — ز كمتر غلامان بايمان بود

(١٢) هر آنكس نگاهی برين جا كند — مگر از كرم آفرينها كند

(١٣) بتاريخ مسجد و چاه زلال — چنين گفت هاتف بعزّ و جلال

(١٤) بفضل خدا شد روا كام خلق — بود مسجد و چاه آرام خلق

١١٠٦ هـ

سنه ٣٨ جلوس عالمگير شاهي

Translation

In the name of God the most Merciful and Compassionate.

(1) By the grace and beneficence of God this stately mosque was built.
(2) This is my prayer to God that this mosque may remain a memorial of me.
(3) During the reign of the Emperor Aurangzeb, which has been a boon to Time and the world.
(4) An extraordinary king as regards benevolence and administration of justice; his rival will not be born in the world.
(5) He observes with his heart and soul the law of the Prophet; what a religious king, may he be blessed with long life!
(6) O Benevolent God, bless the son and progeny of this righteous king with long lives.
(7) In the path of the Benevolent (God), the remorseful sinner, ʻAbd-ur-Raḥīm, built the mosque.
(8) He has spent his life in evil pursuits, O God, show mercy to ʻAbd-ur-Raḥīm.
(9) O God, forgive my sins through the kind intercession of Muḥammad.
(10) Accept my prayer on the day of judgement; revive me as the dust of the path of the Prophet.
(11) (My humble self) is the slave of ʻAlī with heart and soul; may this humble self rank as one of ʻAlī's devoted servants.

(note continued on p. 195)

is, however, insignificant from the architectural point of view because it comprises a single hall for prayers and a small platform in front of the same, towards the east. The prayer-hall measures 20 feet 9 inches in length and 13 feet 6 inches in width, while the dimensions of the platform are, length 24 feet 6 inches, breadth 19 feet 11 inches. Below the platform is a court with a cistern for ablutions, the measurements of the latter being: length 25 feet 8 inches, breadth 19 feet 11 inches, and depth 2 feet 3 inches. The ceiling of the prayer-hall is vaulted and divided into three compartments. The building has three openings towards the east, the span of each of these arched openings being uniformly 5 feet 6 inches and the height up to the apex 7 feet 5 inches. The front wall rises to a height of 12 feet 2 inches up to the dripstones, above which is an ornamental parapet 3 feet 8 inches high. The parapet has a screen of four cusped arches in the middle and small turrets crowned with fluted orbs at the corners. The cusped arches and the kiosks with fluted domes represent two typical features of the Mughal architecture.

The Tomb of Ḥaḍrat Shaikh Muḥammad Ḥusain Imām-ul-Mudarrisīn

The title, Imām-ul-Mudarrisīn, 'the head of teachers', was enjoyed by the Principal of the College founded by Maḥmūd Gāwān at Bidar.[1] During his lifetime the Madrasa was staffed by some of the greatest savants of the Islāmic world, the names of some of them are preserved in the *Riyāḍ-ul-Inshā*, a collection of the letters of Maḥmūd Gāwān which was preserved in manuscript, but the Hyderabad Persian MSS. Society is shortly issuing a printed edition of the work. Shaikh Muḥammad Ḥusain, according to his descendants who still live in Bidar, was born in Bijāpur, and he held the office of Principal of the College during the reign of Aurangzeb, who had great respect for his learning and piety.

The tomb is situated to the north of the Kālī Masjid, close to the fencing of the railway yard of Bidar station. It has an enclosure of its own, measuring 122 feet 7 inches east to west and 80 feet 7 inches north to south. The tomb is built in the open on a platform 3 feet 5 inches high, and has a length of 37 feet 11 inches with a width of 31 feet 8 inches at the top. Besides the tomb of the Shaikh there are ten other graves on the platform. A mosque with a single arched opening may also be noticed within the enclosure of the tomb.

Another enclosure near the doorway to the tomb of Shaikh Muḥammad Ḥusain has two graves within it. One of these graves is that of a woman and the other that of a man. In front of the enclosure is a platform with a large number of tombs built on it. These tombs, and the graves within the two enclosures, apparently belong to the disciples and the descendants of Shaikh Muḥammad Ḥusain.

(*note continued from p. 194*)

(12) Those who look at this building, may perchance through their noble-mindedness praise it.

(13) As regards the date of the building of this mosque and this sweet-water well, the Inspirer spoke graciously—

(14) 'By the grace of God the need of people has been fulfilled, *may this mosque and well be the source of comfort to them.*' 1106 H. (A.D. 1694) 38th year of the reign of Aurangzeb.

Epig. Ind. Mosl., 1927–8, pp. 33–5, Pl. XIX.

[1] For a description of the building see *supra*, pp. 91–100.

The Kālī Masjid

This monument is situated on a side of the old Chhidrī road, about two furlongs to the south-west of Bidar railway station. It is built of trap masonry of a dark colour, hence the name Kālī Masjid, or 'the Black Mosque'. The monument represents a style of architecture which came into vogue in the Deccan by the fusion of Muslim and Hindu principles of building, and though quaint and meaningless in certain aspects, on the whole it is pleasing. The building has three massive wide-spanned arches in its front flanked by two slender minarets, one at each end. Minarets in the architectural scheme of a mosque have generally a threefold significance: to serve the purpose of a tower (*ma'dhana*) to call the *faithful* to prayer; to show the high ideals of religion by their soaring dimensions; and lastly to serve as buttresses to hold the thrust of the arches built in the front of mosques in India. The minarets of this mosque serve none of these three purposes, but at the same time their neatly dressed masonry, graceful carving, and slim form captivate the eye of even a connoisseur (Pl. CXXI).

The arches of the mosque are of considerable dimensions, each having a span of 11 feet 10 inches and a height up to the apex of 15 feet 3 inches. The arch-heads rest on masonry columns which are strongly built and rise to a height of 7 feet above the floor of the mosque. The general appearance of the arches shows a fine sense of proportion. Above the arches the façade of the building has two bands of polished hornblende which project from the surface of the wall and form a sort of frieze. The latter in the original design of the building may have borne religious texts or inscriptions mentioning the date and name of the builder of the mosque. Higher up is a row of brackets which support the dripstones. These have weathered badly, but the brackets are intact and their carving exhibits considerable skill. Between the brackets are arch-shaped panels decorated with the chain-and-pendant motif and other designs carved in relief. The height of the mosque is 25 feet 5 inches up to the dripstones, but it may have risen a few feet higher still when the original parapet, which has perished completely, was intact.[1] In comparatively recent times a low wall has been built at the top of the old masonry, apparently with a view to stop the percolation of rain-water into the open joints of the stone-work.[2]

The minarets, octagonal in form, rise from large stone pedestals which comprise a series of bands arranged one above the other but each decreasing in girth compared with the one below it. The bands are neatly carved, their general design representing the base and the feet of a wooden casket. The influence of the carpenter's craft is also apparent in the thin neat bands of masonry placed round the shafts of the minarets, which would have been more appropriate to wooden columns in order to keep together their component parts. The minarets are incomplete, and their upper parts were either never built or have been destroyed by vandals during the political upheavals which took place after their construction. Their total height

[1] The parapet on the back and side walls of the mosque still exists and has a trefoil design.

[2] The wall is an eyesore, and the sooner it is demolished the better. The holes and cracks in the masonry at the top can easily be grouted with cement, and a slope given towards the roof to guard against the accumulation of water on the old masonry.

is 38 feet 2 inches at present, and the girth of the octagonal shaft is 10 feet, each facet measuring 1 foot 3 inches in width. The architect had also designed two balconies round each minaret; the remains of one of them may be seen above the row of brackets and the other about 8 feet higher (Pl. CXXI).

The interior of the building measures 45 feet 10 inches by 35 feet, and is divided into six bays by the insertion of massive columns. The ceilings of all the six bays are vaulted, five being in the form of shallow domes, while the sixth, adjacent to the *miḥrāb*, has the form of a casket decorated with stone bands which project from the surface of the ceiling (Pl. CXX).

The *miḥrāb* has a decagonal plan at the base internally, three sides being covered by the entrance arch. The roof of the *miḥrāb* is double, the lower roof being on a level with the roof of the prayer-hall, and the upper rising in the form of a dome above it. The dome rests on a high square base with an open arch in each of its four sides in the style of Barīdī tombs (Pl. CXXII). The chimney-like effect of this arrangement is similar to a certain extent to the chimney-shaped domes of the prayer-chambers of the Jāmiʿ Zaitūnīya of Tunis and of several other mosques in North Africa. The back view of the mosque shows a neat style of building, and the thin round pillars, with bands round their girth at the joints of walls, are again reminiscent of the influence of the carpenter's workmanship (Pl. CXXII).

The building has no inscription to give its exact date,[1] but from the style of its architecture it may be assigned to the early Barīdī period, that is, the first half of the sixteenth century A.D. The mosque has also a large well towards the west.

The Tomb of Shāh ʿAlī son of Khalīl-Ullāh and the Mosque of Barkhwurdār Beg

About 150 yards in a westerly direction from the Kālī Masjid, the tomb of Shāh ʿAlī may be visited. It is situated on the left side of the Chhidrī road. The tomb is incomplete; it stands in a large enclosure with an arched entrance over which an inscriptional tablet is fixed into the wall.[2] The inscription contains the name of

[1] On the wall of a well which is situated to the west of the Kālī Masjid, and is away from the cart-track going to Chhidrī, a Persian inscription has been noticed which gives the name of the builder of the well and the date of its digging. The text of the inscription has been deciphered as follows:

بعنایت آلهی بیاد حضرت حسین شهید

حفر این چاه نموده و موسوم بحسین بائین ساخت

کمترین خلق خدا محمّد مومن طباطبا بتاریخ غرّه

شهر محرم الحرام سنه ۱۰۸٤ دم آبی بکش بیاد حسین

Translation

By the grace of God this well dug and called Ḥusain Bā'īn in memory of His Holiness Ḥusain, the Martyr, by the humblest creature of God, Muḥammad Momin Ṭabāṭabā, on the first of the sacred month of Muḥarram in the year 1084 H. (A.D. 1673). Drink a mouthful of water in memory of Ḥusain.

Epig. Ind. Mosl., 1931–3, p. 29, Pl. XIX *b*.

This well has no connexion with the Kālī Masjid, and according to the inscription carved on its wall it is of a much later date than the Kālī Masjid.

[2] The access to the interior of the enclosure is through a door, measuring 4 feet 2 inches in width and 7 feet 8 inches in height. The total height of the entrance up to the top of the parapet is 21 feet.

Shāh ʿAlī and also the Hijrī date 1104 (A.D. 1692), in which year he probably passed into the mercy of God.[1] Shāh ʿAlī may have been the son of Mīr Khalīl-Ullāh who was appointed governor of Bidar by Aurangzeb in 1068 H. (A.D. 1658).[2] The tomb of Shāh ʿAlī is built in the middle of a mango-grove which, although at present much ruined through neglect, yet in its palmy days would have given an attractive setting to the tomb.

The base of the tomb is 1 foot 5 inches high from the surrounding land, and above that the incomplete walls rise to a height of 5 feet 5 inches and end abruptly. The building is square in plan, and measures 28 feet 4 inches externally and 20 feet 10 inches internally. The sepulchral hall, which has no roof, contains six graves, one of them being that of Shāh ʿAlī and the other five those of his relatives. In the court of the tomb there is also a platform which has nine graves.

Within the enclosure of Shāh ʿAlī's tomb, at the western end of the court, is a mosque associated with the name of Barkhwurdār Beg, whose name is also mentioned in the inscription carved on the building.[3] It is a small structure, comprising a prayer-hall flanked with a minaret on either side, and a paved court in front. The prayer-hall measures 26 feet 7 inches by 15 feet 2 inches, and has three arches opening on the court. The span of each of these arches is 7 feet 3 inches and its height up to the apex 8 feet 5 inches, hence they look rather squat. The ceiling is divided into three shallow vaults by arches built across the width of the hall. The minarets are slender in form and crowned with orbs. They rise only 25 feet above the floor. The height of the façade of the building, including the parapet, is 17 feet

[1] The text of the inscription is given below:

بندهٔ درگاه رسول الله

شاه علي ابن شاه خليل الله

سنه ١١٠٤ هـ

Translation

'The slave of the court of the Prophet of God,
Shāh ʿAlī, son of Shāh Khalīl-Ullāh.'
1104 H. (A.D. 1692).

The style of writing is *Naskh* and the language Persian. *Epig. Ind. Mosl.*, 1927–8, p. 35, Pl. XVIII *b*.

[2] *Supra*, p. 15.

[3] The inscription has been deciphered as follows:

(١) شد بنای این مکان فیض بخش — در زمان عدل عالم‌گیر شاه

(٢) گشت برخوردار بیگ از روی صدق — باني مسجد بتوفيق آله

(٣) سال تاریخش همین جستم ز عقل — گفت هاتف معدن فیض آله

١٠٩٠ هـ

Translation

(1) 'This felicitous building was erected during the just reign of King ʿĀlamgīr.
(2) 'By a sincere motive through the grace of God Barkhwurdār Beg built this mosque.
(3) 'I inquired of Wisdom the chronogram of its erection: the Inspirer said, "the mine of divine grace".'

The phrase gives the date 1090 H. (A.D. 1679) according to the *Abjad* system.

Epig. Ind. Mosl., 1927–8, pp. 35–6, Pl. XVIII *b*.

1 inch.[1] The mosque makes no pretension to architectural merit, and it seems to have been constructed during the régime of Mughal governors in the last quarter of the seventeenth century A.D.

The paved court in front of the mosque measures 41 feet 6 inches north to south and 30 feet 6 inches east to west. It has a cistern for ablutions in its middle, the plan of the latter being square, measuring 20 feet on each side and being 2 feet 10 inches deep.

The Tomb of Shaikh Badr-ud-Dīn Qādirī

He was the fourth son of Ḥaḍrat Multānī Pādshāh, and like his revered father was held in great veneration for his piety and religious devotion during his lifetime and afterwards. The gateway of Shaikh Badr-ud-Dīn's tomb is situated on the northern side of the Chhidrī road, close to Barkhwurdār Beg's mosque. The gateway is in a ruinous condition now, but on entering through it the visitor will notice a cemetery with a large number of graves among which the tomb of Shaikh Badr-ud-Dīn is prominent. It is built on a square platform, measuring 42 feet 5 inches on each side and rising 5 feet 2 inches above the surrounding land. The tomb has no roof over it, but it is enclosed by a low wall with a parapet at its top, the height of the wall and the parapet together being only 4 feet 8 inches above the platform. Inside the enclosure there are five graves, one of the saint himself and four of his family. Among the latter two graves are women's.

Close to Shaikh Badr-ud-Dīn's tomb towards the west there is another, the gateway and enclosure of which have almost perished, but their plan can be traced from the line of debris lying at the site. The tomb is built on a square platform which measures 47 feet 8 inches on each side and rises 3 feet 3 inches above the ground. The margined stones of the platform are neatly dressed. The building of the tomb also has a square plan, measuring 24 feet 8 inches on each side externally and 17 feet 11 inches internally. The floor of the interior of the tomb is of stone, the slabs being smoothly dressed. A sarcophagus of polished black stone (basalt ?) with the *takhtī* design shows that the tomb is that of a woman.[2]

The building has an open arch in each of its four sides. The dimensions of these arches are insignificant, their spans being uniformly 3 feet 6 inches and heights up to the apex 6 feet 7 inches. The walls rise to a height of 16 feet 6 inches up to the dripstones, but above them is a parapet of the trefoil pattern which rises 3 feet 6 inches higher still. The building possesses certain features of Barīdī architecture, but the design of panels carved in plaster on the exterior of the building leaves no room to doubt that the tomb, like others in the vicinity, belongs to the Mughal period, in the latter half of the seventeenth century A.D.

A mosque connected with the tomb is situated to the west of the latter. The plan of the mosque comprises a prayer-hall with a platform in front of it. The platform measures 27 feet 10 inches north to south and 11 feet 10 inches east to west, and rises 1 foot 10 inches above the surrounding land. The floor of the prayer-hall

[1] The parapet by itself is 2 feet 9 inches high, and it has a trefoil design.

[2] Recently an inscriptional tablet of Shāhbād stone has been fixed into the wall above the doorway stating the name of the lady, بي بي فاطمہ, buried in the tomb.

is 1 foot higher still, and the inner dimensions are: length 22 feet 5 inches, width 20 feet 6 inches, the plan being almost square. The ceiling is vaulted, comprising a single dome with stalactites of cut plaster-work at the corners. The front wall of the mosque has three arches opening on the platform. The middle arch is larger in dimensions than the two at the sides. The span of the middle arch is 8 feet 5 inches and the height up to the apex 8 feet 9 inches, while the span of the side arches is only 3 feet 2 inches, with a height of 5 feet 10 inches. The front wall of the mosque rises to a height of 15 feet 9 inches up to the *chhajjā*, and above that is a parapet 3 feet high. The latter is modern and does not match with the general architectural style of the building.

The Tomb of Ḥaḍrat Makhdūm Qādirī

The full name of the saint is Shaikh Ibrāhīm Muḥī-ud-Dīn al-Qādirī, and he was the eldest son of Ḥaḍrat Multānī Pādshāh and died in 970 H. (A.D. 1563). The tomb is situated on the old Chhidrī road about three furlongs to the west of Barkhwurdār Beg's mosque. The shrine has a double enclosure, the outer having a large gateway facing the south. The covered passage of the gateway measures 27 feet 5 inches in length and 8 feet 6 inches in width, and has a vaulted ceiling which is decorated with stucco-work. On either side of the passage there is a room for guards, the floor of the latter being 2 feet 10 inches above the passage. The gateway has a hall in its upper storey with three arched openings towards the north.[1]

The tomb of the saint is built on a platform which is approached by four steps and has a plinth 3 feet high above the ground. The platform extends both towards the front and the back of the tomb, and its dimensions in the front are: length 110 feet 6 inches, width 78 feet. The general design of the tomb is of the Baihmanī style, but the tile-work above the doorway, the small niches arranged in the upper arches of the façade, and the cusped design of the panel over the entrance arch all seem to be later additions, and they have disturbed the simple dignity of the building to a considerable extent. The plan of the tomb at its base is square both externally and internally, measuring 42 feet 2 inches on each side outwardly and 28 feet 3 inches inwardly. The walls rise to a height of 31 feet 1 inch and are surmounted by a parapet, comprising trefoil arch-heads and posts crowned with orbs (Pl. CXXV). The height of the parapet is 3 feet 6 inches above the walls. The base of the dome is decorated with several ornamental bands, among which one representing a trefoil pattern is prominent. The circumference of the dome above the roof level is 110 feet 6 inches.

The sepulchral hall is entered by only one door which is arch-shaped and has a width of 5 feet with a height of 8 feet 6 inches. Inside the hall there are five graves, one of the saint himself which has a wooden canopy over it, and four of his family; two of these have the *takhtī* design which is the symbol on the grave of a woman. The walls of the hall are decorated with plaster-work representing various

[1] There are rooms for the dwelling of the guards of the shrine on either side of the gateway towards the east and the west. There are five on each side, and they have arches above their doors which open onto the outer court of the shrine.

designs, while the corners of the building have pairs of squinches, which convert the square plan of the hall first into an octagon and afterwards into a sixteen-sided figure. Higher up on the walls a band of niches may also be noticed, which have made the plan twenty-four-sided in order to adapt it to the circular base of the dome.

Adjoining the sepulchre of the saint towards the east is another tomb, much smaller in dimensions than the former. The façade of the building is adorned by two rows of arches, arranged one above the other, and at the top of the walls there is a parapet of the trefoil pattern. The walls rise to a height of 18 feet 4 inches above the floor, while the parapet rises 2 feet 2 inches higher still. The plan of the building at the base is rectangular both externally and internally, measuring 26 feet 6 inches by 19 feet 4 inches, and 19 feet 7 inches by 15 feet 8 inches, respectively. The architect has, however, in the interior of the hall designed two massive arches towards the north and south in order to provide the rectangular plan of the hall with a square in the middle. There are six graves, of which two have decayed badly. Of the remaining four the symbols carved on two show them to be tombs of women and the other two of men.

There is another tomb towards the left of the main tomb which, like the two described above, is crowned with a dome. The building has a square plan at its base, measuring 23 feet on each side externally and 16 feet 10 inches internally. The walls rise to a height of 18 feet 5 inches above the floor and are surmounted by a parapet which is 2 feet 2 inches high. The drum of the dome at the roof level measures 57 feet 7 inches in circumference. The interior of the building is plain and has only squinches at the corners.

To the north-east of Ḥaḍrat Makhdūm Qādirī's tomb, and close to it, is a mosque the façade of which is lavishly decorated with stucco-work (Pl. CXXVI). In general appearance this building resembles very much the Bukhārī Masjid and the Rangīn Masjid at Bijāpur,[1] and represents a style of architecture which grew up in the Deccan when Hindu masons had the upper hand both in designing and decorating the buildings. The plan of the mosque comprises a prayer-hall with three arches facing the east and a low platform in front. The platform measures 43 feet 6 inches north to south and 32 feet 7 inches east to west. The floor of the prayer-hall is 1 foot 4 inches higher than the platform, and measures 31 feet 5 inches in length and 19 feet 10 inches in width. The ceiling of the hall is vaulted, and divided into three compartments, the middle one of which has a dome rising above the roof of the building (Pl. CXXVI). The vaults of the two side compartments are shallow and concealed in the thickness of the roof. The openings of the arches are adorned with receding bands in the style of the doors of medieval Hindu temples. The arches are of uniform size, each with a span of 7 feet 10 inches and height up to the apex of 10 feet 8 inches. The spandrels of the arches and the portion of the wall below the *chhajjā* are richly decorated with medallions and floral designs worked out in plaster. The parapet above the front wall of the mosque is considerably damaged through climatic conditions, but when intact it must have been

[1] *Bījāpūr Architecture*, by H. Cousens, Pls. XIII and XLII.

a pleasing feature of the monument. The height of the wall including the parapet is 21 feet 4 inches.

The minarets of the mosque have a graceful form, and they rise 36 feet 5 inches above the base of their pedestals. The galleries which project from the body of the shafts have crumbled very much, and the plaster of the minarets has also peeled off in several places, but the portions of the decorative work which are intact give a fair idea of its pristine beauty (Pl. CXXVI). In the forecourt of the mosque there are three platforms carrying tombs and also a large number of ordinary graves.

There was also a cistern in front of the mosque the remains of which may still be seen. The mosque was apparently built during the régime of the Bijāpur governors of Bidar in the middle of the seventeenth century A.D.

The Tomb and the Mosque of Shāh ʿAlī Qādirī

Farther along the cart-track which skirts the tomb of Ḥaḍrat Makhdūm Qādirī and goes to the village of Chhidrī, the tomb of Shāh ʿAlī Qādirī may be visited.[1] The tomb has a mosque attached to it which, according to the inscription carved on the façade of the mosque, was built by Rustam Dil Khān in A.D. 1695. Rustam Dil Khān was the son of Jān Sipār Khān, the governor of Bidar under Aurangzeb, and when the father was promoted to the governorship of Golconda by the Emperor, Rustam Dil Khān was appointed in his place.[2] According to local records Rustam Dil Khān retained the governorship of Bidar until 1099 H. (A.D. 1688), but from the wording of this inscription it appears that he was in power until 1107 H. (A.D. 1695) when the mosque was built by him.[3]

Shāh ʿAlī Qādirī was a descendant of Ḥaḍrat Multānī Pādshāh, and as the majority of monuments built by the governors of Bidar during the reign of Aurang-

[1] Between the tombs of Makhdūm Qādirī and Shāh ʿAlī Qādirī there is another tomb the dome of which is built of laterite masonry. The dimensions of the latter tomb at its base are 17 feet 5 inches by 13 feet 3 inches externally, and 14 feet by 8 feet 8 inches internally. This tomb has also a mosque attached to it, which has a single opening in the form of a wide-spanned arch towards the east. The prayer-hall of the mosque measures 15 feet 2 inches by 14 feet externally.

[2] *Supra*, p. 16.

[3] The text of the inscription has been deciphered as follows:

(۱) چو در روضهٔ شه علي قادري — که بن بوترابست رحمت پناه

(۲) ز رستم دل او خان والا نشان — بنای بر آمد که شد سجده‌گاه

(۳) ز تاریخ مسجد شده این ندا — منوّر شده همچو بیت الله

۱۱۰۷ هـ

Translation

(1) 'In the shrine of Shāh ʿAlī Qādirī, who is a descendant of Abū Turāb (ʿAlī) and the refuge of mercy.

(2) By Rustam Dil, the Khān of exalted rank, this building was erected which became a place of worship.

(3) Regarding the chronogram of the mosque this was heard—"*It became resplendent like the Abode of God* (*the sacred Kaʿba*)".'

The last hemistich gives the date 1107 H. (A.D. 1695) according to the *Abjad* system. *Epig. Ind. Mosl.*, 1927-8, p. 36, Pl. XVIII *c*.

zeb are associated with the names of the holy personages of the saint's family, it appears that the Mughal governors had special reverence for the progeny and the followers of Multānī Pādshāh. The tomb of Shāh 'Alī has a plinth 3 feet high, and above that the plan of the building is square both externally and internally, measuring on each side 24 feet 10 inches and 17 feet 9 inches respectively. The walls rise 18 feet above the floor of the building, and inside there are three graves, of which one is that of the saint himself. Of the remaining two graves one is that of a man and the other that of a woman. The tomb in its present condition looks somewhat incomplete.

The mosque comprises a prayer-hall with three arches opening towards the east. The arches do not show a happy sense of proportion, the span of each of them being uniformly 7 feet 4 inches and height up to the apex 8 feet 8 inches. The prayer-hall measures 26 feet 7 inches north to south and 15 feet east to west, and has a vaulted ceiling. The front wall of the building rises 13 feet 8 inches above the floor and at the top is surmounted by a parapet which rises 3 feet 2 inches higher still. At each end of the parapet, towards the north and south, there is a short minaret which rises 8 feet 2 inches above the dripstones.[1]

The Tank at Kamthāna

Prior to the advent of the Muslims in the Deccan the Hindu engineers had built some colossal dams to develop the agricultural output of the country, and thus add to the prosperity and general uplift of the people. The most notable examples of these irrigation works are the tanks at Pākhāl, Rāmappa, and Lakhṇarām, all situated in the Warangal district which was the seat of the Kākatīya kings for nearly two hundred years, from the eleventh to the beginning of the thirteenth century A.D. As the sway of the Kākatīya kings in their palmy days extended to almost the entire plateau of the Deccan, it is most probable that the tank at Kamthāna with its massive dike was also built during their rule. Kamthāna is now a village some six miles to the south-west of Bidar, nestling below the western expanse of the plateau which stretches from Chhidrī to the Mailūr village. As the lowlands above Kamthāna, towards the north, get all the water of this part of the plateau during the monsoons, the engineers of the eleventh century A.D. built a large embankment extending over a mile in length for the storage of water for purposes of cultivation. The embankment once rose 30 to 40 feet above the water surface, and it had several sluices for the exit of water, but it appears that they were not judiciously used because the dike seemed to have been breached by the pressure of water in the pre-Barīdī period. A Marāṭhī inscription carved on the masonry of a sluice built in the western part of the embankment warns the people that the water of the tank should not be allowed to rise high enough to overflow the embankment,

[1] At a short distance from the tomb of Shāh 'Alī, towards the west, there is another enclosure with a tomb built on a platform in the open. It has also a mosque attached to it which has a single arched opening towards the east. The prayer-chamber of the mosque is square in plan, measuring 11 feet on each side.

for there was danger of its being washed away.[1] The inscription further records that the dam was breached and subsequently repaired by the order of Ibrāhīm Barīd Shāh in A.D. 1579. The earthwork of the dam is nearly 100 feet wide at its top and much wider at its base, while on the water side it is strongly protected by masonry work in which very large blocks have been used, the style of construction being Cyclopean.

The Muslim historians of the medieval period have given glowing descriptions of the fertility of the soil and the abundance of fruit in the vicinity of Bidar, which are difficult to believe when looking at the rocky and bare character of the lands surrounding Bidar town.[2] There are some rich spots immediately below the plateau towards the north, like the Sayyid-us-Sādāt, or Pāpnās groves, but none of them touches Kamthāna in the luxuriance of flora or the grandeur of trees. The bed of the tank owing to the breaches made in the embankment through neglect at various times has silted up, but the visitor will notice many acres of land below the embankment planted with sugar-cane, while along the embankment itself are rich groves of stately mango-trees and date-palms. The engineers of the Muslim period, who apparently hailed from Persia, have constructed an underground masonry channel, like the *kārez* of their own country, from the tank to a large reservoir built near the village towards the north. This reservoir is square in plan and measures 260 feet on each side. The margins of the reservoir are of neatly dressed black stone, and its bed is paved; thus the reservoir when filled with water would have offered a clean supply to the people of the village for drinking purposes. It is not unlikely that this reservoir was originally situated in the middle

[1] The full text of the inscription has been deciphered by Mr. R. M. Joshi, Superintendent of Monuments at Bidar, and it is given below:

Text

1 चंड कोळा करितां हौजाचा तुंब नुकसान जा-
2 ळा होता हजरत बरिद शाहाने अजम मनसुर खां
3 नाचे हातिं तुंब बांधविळा पाणि उचळन नेतां हौ-
4 जास मजरत आहे ऐसे न करणे माहे मोहरम स-
5 न सबा समानिन सुह्र सन तिसा सबैन व
6 तिसा मेया

Transliteration

(1) chaṇḍa koḷā karitâṅ haujāchā tumba nuksān jā-
(2) ḷā hotā Hajarata Barida Shāhāne Ajama Manasura Khân
(3) nāche hâtiṅ tumba bândhaviḷâ pâṇi uchaḷan netâṅ hau-
(4) jâsa majrat âhe aise na karaṇe mâhe Moharam sa-
(5) na sabâ samânin suhur sana tisâ sabaina va
(6) tisâ meyâ

Translation

The *bund* built for the great reservoir was damaged. It was constructed for Ḥaḍrat Barīd Shāh by Aʿẓam Manṣūr Khān. If water is carried over the *bund*, there is likelihood of its being damaged. Do not do so! The month of Muḥarram in the year 87 (*Hijrī*) corresponding with *Shahūr San* 979 (A.D. 1579). *Epig. Ind. Mosl.*, 1937–8, pp. 1–2.

[2] *Supra*, p. 2.

of a garden, for a large number of old mango and tamarind trees are still to be seen in its vicinity. The mouth of the covered channel (*kārez*) may be seen in the middle of the northern side of the reservoir. The depth of the reservoir from the masonry margin, which is built all round it, is only 4 feet, but the water of the reservoir may have risen 1 or 2 feet above that because the side walls rise 2 feet 10 inches above the margin. The width of the margin is 4 feet. Walking from the embankment of the tank towards the reservoir the visitor will notice on the way the remains of an old bridge. It was supported by arches, two of which are still intact.[1]

The Subterranean Canals of Naubād and Bidar

Naubād is a pleasant village some four miles to the west of Bidar, situated on the left of the Udgīr road. In the Baihmanī period there was probably a scheme for the development of the village, for as a preliminary measure it was equipped with an adequate supply of clean water which is essential in a country where the soil is rocky and the successful digging of wells is problematic. The Muslim kings of Bidar, apparently under the expert advice of Persian engineers, have followed the *kārez* system, and laid out subterranean canals in the heart of the rock by widening the natural rift which starts from the different cavities in the trappean bed over which the upper laterite crust of the plateau of Bidar rests. As to trace these cavities from the surface of the plateau is a difficult task, the engineers of those days thought it easier to commence the building of the canal from the mouth of a natural spring, and follow the rift in the rock which had been caused by physical phenomena, as far as the main cavity in the trappean bed where the rain-water percolating through the laterite crust had accumulated. For air and light the engineers have constructed square manholes at suitable points, varying from 30 to 75 yards apart from each other. The subterranean canal of Naubād has twenty-one such manholes, starting from the ʿAlīābād spring and continuing to the large sugar-cane field in the south-west of the village wherein a press for extracting juice and a large iron pan for preparing molasses are installed. The distance between these two places is a little over a mile. The crust of the laterite rock above the subterranean channel being 60 to 80 feet in thickness, the depth of the manholes, where they have not silted up owing to the growth of rank vegetation or other causes, is the same, and one hears the sound of the water flowing in the canal from the top of the plateau. The manholes are lined with ashlar masonry, and their average dimensions at the top are 9 feet by 7 feet.

The development of Naubād was given up owing to the death of a king or some other cause, but the subterranean canal still exists and may profitably be used to carry out some modern scheme in this area.

A similar *kārez* was laid out for the water-supply of Bidar town and fort, and a line of manholes extending from the Fatḥ Darwāza to the moat of the fort may still be traced. They are shown in the map of the town attached to this volume. Among the people of Bidar the channel is known as the Jumna Morī; it is, however,

[1] The village of Kamthāna has now 700 houses and comprises a population of 4,000 persons, the majority of whom are agriculturists.

not a drain but a *kārez* for the supply of drinking-water to the inhabitants of the town and the garrison of the fort.

The Tomb at Naubād

To the south-east of the village in the midst of a mango-grove is a tomb wherein, according to tradition, the last remains of Qāḍī Shams-ud-Dīn are interred. He was the Chief Qāḍī of Bidar during the reign of Sulṭān ʿAlā-ud-Dīn Baihmanī, and according to an inscription carved on the building he built the dome during his lifetime. Through neglect the building had fallen into a sad state of disrepair, but the Archaeological Department have now thoroughly restored it. It is, however, a small structure, and except for the inscriptional tablet it is not of any outstanding significance.[1]

[1] The inscription consists of five lines of Persian prose written in *Thulth* characters of an intricate type. As the stone of the slab on which the inscription is carved is not close-grained, it has suffered considerably from the weather, and the letters have been abraded in several places. The text of the inscription, however, has been deciphered in full and is given below:

Line 1 حمد بیحد پروردگاری را کہ طاق نہ ایوان گردون برآوردۂ معمار قدرت اوست و بساط شش جهت زمین گستردۂ فراش حکمت اوست و صلوات نامتناهي

Line 2 بروضۂ مطهر و قالب معطر مقصود آفرینش و مقصد اهل بینش ختم یسین رحمة العالمین سلطان رسل سراج ملّت هادي سبل شفیع امت و بر آل و اصحاب او

Line 3 رضوان اللّه علیهم اجمعین و بعد تمام شد این قبّۂ مروحہ در دور عدل بادشاه عالي تبار کیخسرو و جمشید مدار المجتهد في نصب سرادق الامن و الامان

Line 4 المستمسك بالنّص اللّه یامر بالعدل و الاحسان ابو المظفر علاء الدنیا و الدین احمد شاه بن احمد شاه البهمني السلطان ابن السلطان بفرمایش و اهتمام اقضی قضاة الاسلام

Line 5 مولانا امام شمس الدنیا و الدین بن مولانا سعد الدین النعماني الاحسنابادي النامي (؟) دیوان القضا بدار الملك محمد آباد المشتهر بقاضي مهین في شهور سنہ سبع و اربعین | ثمانمایة ⊙ یا مفتح الابواب ⊙

Translation

'Unlimited praise is due to God, the architect of Whose providence built the vault of nine apartments of heaven, and the chamberlain of Whose wisdom spread the carpet of the six directions of the earth; and uncounted blessings be upon the holy mausoleum and the scented body (of Muḥammad) who is the purpose of the creation, and the ideal of men of wisdom, the last of the prophets, the "Mercy of Both Worlds", the prince of apostles, the lamp of faith, the leader of the paths (of Truth), the intercessor of the community, and upon his descendants and companions—with all of whom God be pleased! After that (be it known) that this delightful vault was built (lit. completed) during the just reign of the king of exalted rank, possessing Kaikhusrau and Jamshīd's majesty, (who is) endeavouring to pitch the tents of peace and safety, taking inspiration from the Word of God, "*administers with justice and benevolence*" (*Qur'ān*, xvi. 92), Abū'l-Muẓaffar ʿAlā-ud-Dunya wad-Dīn Aḥmad Shāh, son of Aḥmad Shāh, al-Baihmanī, the Sulṭān son of Sulṭān, at the instance and under the superintendence of the most sagacious of the Qāḍīs of Islām, Maulāna Imām Muḥammad Shams-ud-Dunya wad-Dīn, son of Maulāna Sa'd-ud-Dīn an-Nuʿmānī al-Aḥsanābādī the chief Qāḍī, at the capital, Muḥammadābād (Bidar), known also as the Great Qāḍī, in the *Shahūr san* 847 (A.D. 1446). O Opener of gates!'

Epig. Ind. Mosl., 1935–6, pp. 35–6.

The tomb is built on a platform which rises 2 feet above the surrounding land, and measures 32 feet 4 inches east to west and 41 feet 9 inches north to south. The tomb has a square plan, and measures 16 feet 6 inches on each side externally, and 9 feet 8 inches internally. The walls rise to a height of 11 feet 4 inches above the floor, and are surmounted by a parapet which rises 2 feet higher still. The circumference of the dome at the roof level is 42 feet. In the interior of the building the square plan has been converted into an octagon by the insertion of corbels at the corners. There is only one grave, and the entrance to the sepulchral room is through a small rectangular door measuring 4 feet 8 inches by 2 feet 6 inches. The door is, however, inserted in an arch which also has small dimensions, its span being 4 feet and its height up to the apex 7 feet 5 inches.

Pāpnās Spring

The spring is still sacred to the Hindus, and as its name Pāpnās,[1] 'annihilator of sins', signifies, it is much resorted to as a place of pilgrimage by the people of the locality and even by those of distant places. It may be approached by the Hyderabad–Udgīr road by taking a transverse course towards the edge of the plateau from near the eighty-seventh milestone, and afterwards following the cart-track which goes down to the valley below and has many abrupt turns and is generally unfit for vehicular traffic owing to being cut up by rain. The cart-track leads to a pleasant grove in which mango and guava trees abound (Pl. CXXVII). The visitor on arriving will notice a *linga* fixed to a *yonī* on a mound under a stately mango-tree. These symbols, representing the god Śiva and his wife Parvatī, are made of polished black stone. On the mound circular masonry work may also be seen, and in the niches formed thereby small images of Gaṇeśa and some other gods of the Hindu pantheon are installed. Close by a sculpture, representing two intertwined snakes, is placed under a tree. This symbolizes fecundity, and is worshipped particularly by those women who desire children. In front of this same sculpture is the image of a bull carved in stone, and towards its left a small enclosure within which three *lingas* fixed to *yonīs* may be observed.[2] At the foot of the scarp is a cistern measuring 16 feet by 14 feet. On descending five steps the water-level is reached, but as people bathe there in large numbers with their *dhotīs* on, which generally are not clean, the water of the cistern is unsavoury, although it has a continuous flow and is replenished by a fresh supply from the natural spring in the bosom of the rock. At a short distance from the cistern are the remains of a hall where pilgrims take rest and also perform certain rites. The hall measures 27 feet by 19 feet and was originally divided into six bays, of which only two towards the south-east are intact. In front of the hall is a pool without any masonry margins. People bathe in this pool also.

Southwards along the water-channel the end of the valley is reached where the

[1] *Pāp* (पाप), in Sanskrit means sin, and *nāś* (नाश) annihilation and death.

[2] A temple has been built on the slope of the hill in recent times and all the religious images, referred to above, have been installed therein. This temple comprises a temple hall measuring 35 feet 8 inches in length and 33 feet 5 inches in depth. The hall has three arches in its front, the design of the arches being one with cusps.

scarp has a semicircular form. There is a natural spring in the rock-bed, and near by some cells are hewn which have irregular plans. There is a double cell facing the west; the outer apartment measures 7 feet 9 inches by 6 feet, while the inner is more commodious, measuring 12 feet 9 inches by 7 feet 6 inches. The cells cut in the northern projection of the scarp are even more irregular in plan; one of them is L-shaped, while another in the western side of the hill has more or less a square form.

Towards the north of the glen, as the slopes of the hill afford an abundant supply of water during the monsoons, the engineers of former days have taken advantage of the natural features and built a massive dike for the storage of water. The dike is 691 feet in length and has a sluice in its north-western part. The level of the water is generally 23 feet below the top of the dike, but during the monsoons it rises considerably, and for the exit of the water the sluice is opened. The water of the tank is utilized for irrigating crops. In the cold weather, November to February, ducks and other aquatic birds gather in large swarms around the tank and offer a tempting opportunity for shooting.

The tank with its dike most probably dates back to pre-Muslim times; first on account of its association with the antiquities of Pāpnās, and secondly because the Hindu rulers of the Deccan in the eleventh and twelfth centuries A.D. built tanks at many places, and their dikes show a highly developed skill in this branch of engineering.

The Tomb of Ḥaḍrat Sayyid-us-Sādāt

The real name of this saint was Muḥammad Ḥanīf, and he got the title Sayyid-us-Sādāt, 'the chief of chiefs', either through his descent from the Prophet Muḥammad or through his noble character. He is reported to have been a native of Gīlān, and to have migrated to the Deccan some time during the reign of Aḥmad Shāh al-Walī, who was fond of the company of saintly personages and invited them to his capital from distant lands.[1] The tomb of Ḥaḍrat Sayyid Muḥammad Ḥanīf is still held in great reverence, and in the interior of the shrine the visitor will notice hundreds of petitions hung by the votaries for the fulfilment of their requirements. The tomb is situated in a mango-garden below the brink of the plateau near the tombs of later Barīdī kings. The Archaeological Department have constructed a motor road which passes by the ʿĪdgāh and the Barber's Tomb and ends at a point of the cliff which offers an excellent view of the tomb and its charming surroundings (Pl. CXXVIII). The Department have also constructed steps with landings at spaced intervals, with a view to enabling the visitor to reach the garden and the shrine below with convenience. The tomb may also be approached by the road which branches from the Udgīr road a little beyond the District Jail and goes down the hill with a steep gradient direct to the shrine.

There are two tombs, in one of which the saint himself is buried, and in the other his wife, daughter, and one of his sons rest. The name of this son was Sayyid Yaḥyā. Both the buildings are of uniform size, and as they are also close together, they

[1] Aḥmad Shāh al-Walī also invited Niʿmat-Ullāh of Kirmān to Bidar, but the saint instead of going himself sent his grandson Mīr Nūr-Ullāh. *Firishta* (Persian text), vol. i, p. 634.

look almost like twins in the panorama when seen from the plateau (Pl. CXXVIII). The tomb of the saint is built on the right towards the east, and is approached by a paved walk from the place where vehicles halt. The building has a square plan at its base, measuring 39 feet 7 inches on each side externally and 26 feet 11 inches internally. The walls are adorned with a double series of arches arranged one above the other, and at their top the walls have a parapet comprising arch-heads. The height of the walls is 34 feet above the floor, and the parapet rises 3 feet 6 inches higher still. The height of the walls in relation to their width at the base of the building has given the latter the form of a cube which is crowned by a circular dome (Pl. CXXVIII). The circumference of the dome at the roof level is 104 feet 10 inches. The entire building attests the architect's fine sense of proportion.

The interior of the tomb has squinches at the corners, and above them niches which convert the square plan of the building into a polygon with a view to fitting in with the circular base of the dome. The walls are further decorated with stucco-work representing medallions and floral designs. There are three graves, the middle one being that of the saint himself, which is distinguished by a wooden canopy built over it, and the two on the sides are those of the saint's sons. The saint died on the 15th of Rajab, 901 H. (Wednesday, 30th March, A.D. 1496).

The other tomb is built on a slightly lower level, although the dimensions of the building are almost identical, the walls including the parapet rising to a height of 38 feet and measuring at their base 39 feet 9 inches on each side, the circumference of the dome at the roof level being 105 feet. Inside the sepulchral hall are three graves, one being that of the wife of the saint and the other two those of his daughter and son. The grave of the daughter is on the right of her mother's. The inner features of this tomb bear considerable resemblance to the fourteenth- and fifteenth-century tombs of Delhi, built during the reigns of the early Sulṭāns.

Towards the south-west of the saint's tomb is a mosque which is connected with the shrine. It comprises a single hall, measuring 22 feet 9 inches by 13 feet 2 inches. The mosque has three arched openings of uniform size towards the east. The span of these arches is 5 feet and their height up to the apex 7 feet 8 inches. The ceiling is vaulted, but divided into three dish-shaped compartments by arches built across the width of the prayer-hall.

At a short distance from the saint's tomb towards the south-east there is another tomb, which is, however, much smaller in dimensions than the former. The building has a square plan at the base, measuring 15 feet on each side externally and 9 feet internally. The walls rise to a height of 12 feet above the floor and are surmounted by a parapet which rises 2 feet higher still. The dome of the building has a leaf-pattern decorative band round its drum, and the circumference of the dome at that point is 38 feet 9 inches. Inside the building is the grave of a lady, and the tomb is visited particularly by women.

To the west of these tombs, which are all built on a natural eminence, a pavilion may be noticed which once overlooked a tank. The building measures 21 feet 5 inches by 15 feet externally. The arches of the pavilion are somewhat squat in proportions, their span being 7 feet 7 inches and height up to the apex the same.

The masonry base of the pavilion shows that the water surface of the tank was originally 5 feet below the floor of the pavilion.[1]

The road goes farther westward from the shrine of Ḥaḍrat Sayyid Muḥammad Ḥanīf, and after passing through a mango-garden reaches the spring which is associated with the name of the saint owing to an inscriptional tablet fixed into the wall above the mouth of the spring.[2] The water of the spring is believed to possess certain healing properties, and people suffering from skin diseases come from distant places hoping to be cured by taking a bath in the cistern immediately in front of the orifice in the rock-wall, whence the water gushes out. Credulous women who desire children also assemble there in large numbers, and bathe near the inscriptional tablet, which according to them has some miraculous power to bless them with fertility. The water of the spring has been examined chemically, and it is reported to contain sulphur and iron, but found wholesome for drinking purposes. The well-to-do people of Bidar get their drinking-water from this spring, but care must be observed to obtain the water from the interior of the cavity in the rock, for the water of the cistern in front is generally fouled by the frequent bathing of the votaries in the cistern. There is an enclosure wall and several steps descend to the water level,

[1] On the slope of the hill a little higher than the pavilion, towards the north-east, there are remains of some old structures among which a cistern is more or less intact. It has a square plan, measuring 29 feet on each side, with a depth of 2 feet 8 inches.

[2] The inscriptional tablet is of polished black stone and measures 2 feet 5 inches by 11 inches. The inscription is carved in three lines in the <u>*Thulth*</u> style of an intricate type. The language is a mixture of Persian and Arabic, and the text has been deciphered as follows:

(۱) بنا کرد عمارة این چشمۀ حیات درین مقام شریف و روضۀ مطهر لحضرت سیّد السادات المخدوم السیّد حنیف نور اللّه مرقده

(۲) في زمان السلطان الاعظم المتوكّل على اللّه القوي الغني ابو المغازي شهاب الدنيا والدين محمود شاه بن محمّد شاه الولي البهمني

(۳) اقل عباد اللّه درویش حسیني مشهدي المخاطب من الحضرت العالیه بسفا (*sic*) بسیف خان غفر اللّه له ولوالدیه ⊙ في سابع من شعبان سنه عشر تسعمایة الهجریّه النبویه.

Translation

(1) 'The building of this fountain of life was constructed at this holy spot, (and) the sacred garden of His Holiness Sayyid-us-Sādāt, al-Makhdūm, as-Sayyid Ḥanīf—may God illumine his grave;

(2) during the reign of the great king al-Mutawakkil 'alā'llāhi'l Qawī'l-Ghanī Abū'l-Mughāzī Shihābu'd-Dunya wad-Dīn Maḥmūd Shāh bin Muḥammad Shāh al-Walī'l-Baihmanī;

(3) by the humblest of the servants of God, Darwesh Ḥusainī Mashhadī, styled Safā (sic) Khān by the exalted court—May God pardon him and his parents; on the 7th Sha'bān in the year 910 H. (Monday, 13th January, A.D. 1505).

Three names are mentioned in this inscription, the first being of Sayyid-us-Sādāt Sayyid Muḥammad Ḥanīf. The influence wielded by him at the court is manifest from the fact that at the accession of Maḥmūd Shāh Baihmanī the saint was asked to place the crown on the king's head. The second name is of Maḥmūd Shāh the fourteenth king of the Baihmanī dynasty, who ruled from A.D. 1482 to 1518. The third name is of one Darwesh Ḥusaini Mashhadī who may have been a relative of Sayyid Mirzā Mashhadī, who saved the life of Maḥmūd Shāh in the rebellion of 896 H. *Epig. Ind. Mosl.*, 1925–6, p. 19, Pl. IX.

but the dimensions of the cistern being very small, the water of the spring is carried down by means of a covered channel to another cistern, which is built in the garden at a short distance from the former, and measures 81 feet 10 inches north to south and 61 feet 10 inches east to west. People bathe in the latter cistern as well, but as they also wash their clothes there the surface of the water is always covered with a scum of soap. The surplus water flows down to a pool farther northwards in the lowlands, and the 'untouchables' use its water for purposes similar to those specified above. On the slope of the hill above the spring a house is built where women can change their dress after their bath and also take rest. The house has a double hall, measuring 40 feet 10 inches in length and 21 feet 4 inches in width, with five arches opening on to a court in front. On festive occasions the votaries assemble in large crowds, when booths are set up and seats slung by ropes from the trunks of trees. Both men and women bathe and swing and sing in hilarious mood, and present an attractive spectacle to the onlooker.

The Tomb of Fakhr-ul-Mulk at Fatḥpūr

Fatḥpūr is a village in the Janwāḍa *ta'alluqa* of Bidar, its distance being six miles as the crow flies from the latter town, but as the lands immediately below the plateau of Bidar are cut up by gullies, the route is circuitous and extends to some eight miles. Fakhr-ul-Mulk was one of the dignitaries of the Baihmanī court, and he came to Bidar from Gīlān. The tomb bears a striking resemblance in the shape of its dome to the pre-Mughal tombs in the vicinity of the shrines of Niẓām-ud-Dīn Aulīya and Ḥaḍrat Naṣīr-ud-Dīn Raushan Chirāgh in Old Delhi. The shape marks an intermediate stage between the hemispherical dome of the early Sulṭāns of Delhi and the stilted turnip-shaped dome of the Mughals (Pl. CXXX). The finial at the top of this dome is also reminiscent of the *guldastas* of the domes of the early Sulṭāns of Delhi.

The tomb has a high basement, and there are flights of long steps on all its four sides. The base of the building at the ground level measures 188 feet in each direction, but at the top of nineteen steps, where the first landing is reached, its size is reduced to 155 feet 3 inches. This landing is 2 feet 9 inches wide, and at its inner end it has a sort of retaining wall which is built of neatly dressed masonry and rises 4 feet 6 inches above the first landing. There is another landing which is broader than the first, being 5 feet wide and running round the basement on all four sides. At the end of the second landing there is another retaining wall which is built of large blocks of masonry and is 8 feet thick. The coping of this wall is decorated with knobs and lobes in the style of the plinths of Hindu temples. The basement of the building at the foot of this wall measures 150 feet on each side.

From the second landing steps lead to the court of the tomb, which has a platform 16 feet 9 inches wide built along the upper retaining wall on all four sides. The lower part of the court, below the platform, is square in plan and measures 97 feet on each side. The tomb is built in the middle of this part of the court, where its base rises 3 feet 6 inches above the floor and has two masonry bands, each 1 foot 9 inches high, arranged around it (Pl. CXXIX). The walls of the building are decorated with a double series of arches, built one above the other, and at the top they have a parapet, comprising arch-heads and little pillars crowned with orbs. The total height of the wall on each side above the floor of the building is 38 feet 6 inches, of which 4 feet 7 inches are included in the parapet. The base of the building measures 51 feet in each direction, externally. The sepulchral hall is entered by a door which is built in the middle of the southern wall. The door measures 8 feet 9 inches by 4 feet 2 inches. In the hall there are two tombs, but the real graves are in the vault below, which is approached by a flight of steps descending from an opening in the floor of the hall towards the west.

There are traces of paintings on the vaulted ceiling of the building, but owing to percolation of rain-water through cracks in the masonry of the dome, developed by the growth of plants on it, the colours have faded badly. The entire building, although the income from an *in'ām* land is available for its maintenance, had fallen into a ruinous condition, but it has now been repaired by the Archaeological Department. The lofty plinth of the building, divided into several stages, is very reminiscent of the basements of the medieval Hindu temples, but the style of architecture of the tomb itself is purely Muslim, and the great affinity in the shape of its dome and the decoration of its walls to the contemporary tombs at Delhi clearly show that for designing important buildings in both the north and the south architects from Persia were employed, while for actual building work and decoration the services of Hindu masons were utilized.

The Tomb of Shāh Muḥibb-Ullāh al-Ḥusainī (?)

Near the village of Malkāpur in the *ta'alluqa* of Janwāḍa there are two tombs, one of which is assigned to Sayyid Shāh Muḥibb-Ullāh. He was the grandson of Ḥaḍrat Shāh Ni'mat-Ullāh Kirmānī and migrated to Bidar with his elder brother, Shāh Ḥabīb-Ullāh, after the saint's death. Shāh Muḥibb-Ullāh was apparently much junior in age to his brother Shāh Ḥabīb-Ullāh, for the latter on his arrival in the Deccan was married to the daughter of Aḥmad Shāh al-Walī, while Shāh Muḥibb-Ullāh was wedded to the daughter of 'Alā-ud-Dīn, the son of the king. Firishta writes that as Shāh Ḥabīb-Ullāh possessed soldierly habits he took part in the administrative affairs of the Baihmanī kingdom, and appointed his younger brother Shāh Muḥibb-Ullāh as the spiritual successor (*sajjāda*) of his holy forebears.[1] Firishta further mentions the name of Shāh Muḥibb-Ullāh in connexion with the enthronement of Maḥmūd Shāh Baihmanī in A.D. 1482, and states that he was one of the two holy personages who placed the royal crown on Maḥmūd Shāh's head and afterwards, holding his arms as an indication of their religious support, led him to the throne.[2] Shāh Muḥibb-Ullāh must have been at that time quite advanced in age, because if we place his arrival in the Deccan near the close of Aḥmad Shāh's reign, that is, A.D. 1432–6, and consider his age as about twenty-five at that time, then he would have been nearly seventy-five years old at the time of the accession of Maḥmūd Shāh.

The tomb can be easily approached in fair weather by walking cross-country nearly a mile to the east of Aḥmad Shāh al-Walī's tomb at Āshṭūr. The building is

[1] *Firishta* (Persian Text), vol. i, pp. 635–53.

[2] Ibid., p. 700.

more or less in the same style as the contemporary tombs of the Baihmanī kings, but owing to its being away from the beaten track it has not been looked after properly and has fallen into a sad state of disrepair. The walls of the tomb at their base measure 50 feet 8 inches on each side externally and 33 feet 2 inches internally. They rise to a height of 36 feet above the floor and are surmounted by a parapet which rises 4 feet higher still. The base of the dome at the roof level measures 139 feet 10 inches in circumference. The face of the walls on each side of the building is adorned with arches arranged in a double series, placed one above the other. The floor of the sepulchral hall has decayed through neglect, but the arches in the interior of the building are intact and show a refined sense of proportion.

The other tomb which is situated close by is considerably smaller in dimensions than the above. It measures 37 feet 3 inches on each side externally and 25 feet 3 inches internally. The building has doors towards the north, east, and south, the western side being occupied by the *miḥrāb*. The arches of the exterior of the building show a distinct stilt near their apexes. The walls of the tomb rise to a height of 21 feet 5 inches above the floor and were originally surmounted by a parapet which has almost completely perished. The base of the dome at the roof level measures 97 feet 4 inches in circumference. In the interior of the building there is some plaster decoration on the walls, and *Qur'ānic* verses are carved on the arch-heads and the alcove of the *miḥrāb*. The squinches at the corners have receding facets of plaster-work along their arch-heads. This tomb is now also in a neglected condition.

ARABIC, PERSIAN, AND URDŪ INDEX

ت

تاریخ 36 n. 1
تاریخِ وفات 146 n. 3
تاسیس اساس دینِ اسلام 177, n. 4
تعاقت المصران 118 n. 4
تفرّج در هوا و هوس 156 n. 2
تفنگچی 30 n. 5
تن بود سایـبان 120
تنک و تمن 66 n. 1
تنگهی فانیٔ دنیای دون 156 n. 2
توپ الٰهی 36 n. 1
توپی پر آشوبی 85–6 n. 1
توتیا در سرمادان 156 n. 2
توفیق الله 49 n. 2
توکّلت علیٰ خالقی 118 n. 1
تو منی من تو ام 120

ج

جانفراز دل پسند 106 n. 2
جاودان ماندان 156 n. 2
جلوس میمنت مانوس 87 n. 1; 89 n. 2
جم جاه ملائک 84 n. 2; 87 n. 1; 89 n. 2
جمشید 42 n. 2; 206 n. 1
جنّة الفردوس 124; 146 n. 3
جنت الماویٰ 66 n. 1
جنید البغدادي 115 n. 2

اوج گردن 147 n. 2
اورثنا الارض 95 n. 3
اورنگ‌زیب 31 n. 3
ایوانِ بارگ 33

ب

بائین 147 n. 2
باخلاص بیا بر در 111 n. 2
باد صبحگاه 126
باز آمدم نیست 156 n. 2
باطناً شمس ظاهراً ماه 121
باغ فرح 177 n. 4
بال و پرِ من 156 n. 2
بُتکدا مسجد شده 178
بحر و موج 119
برخوردار بیگ 198 n. 3
برق فرود 39 n. 1
بساطِ شش جهت زمین 206 n. 1
بسم الله الرحمٰن الرحیم 193 n. 3
بشرع نبی مطیع 194
بنیاد 33
بودِ دریا و کان 54 n. 3
بي‌بي فاطمہ 199 n. 2
بی گنہ محمد گاوان 10

پ

پرکار 121
پروردگار 206
پشنگ 39 n. 1
پیرامون آسمان 66 n. 1
پیشگاهی و قصر 66 & n. 1

آب حیوان 5 n. 6
آب حیوان بجوی 120
ابو المظفر 206 n. 1
ابو المغازي 125
ابو تراب رحمت پناه 202 n. 3
اتمام و بنایش 171 n. 2
احمد بهمن 66 n. 1
آذري 66 n. 1
ارحم الراحمین 85–6, n. 1
ارکانِ دین 33 n. 1
اژدها 39 n. 1
اسمِ اعظم 121
آسمان 33 n. 1
آسمان از پایۂ درگاه 6
اصلِ گوهر 119
اضاء القمران 118 n. 4
اطیب عیش 36 n. 1
اعلیٰ علیین 125
آفتاب دستِ جودش 54 n. 3
الاوا 106
آل طٰہٰ و یٰسین 109 n. 3
آلِ محمد 118 n. 4
آل و اصحابِ او 206 n. 1
الف ـــ الله 121
الله ولا سواه 177 n. 4
امر الامارة 125
انّا فتحنا 177 n. 4
اندر بهشت سید ولي 107 n. 3
اندهام کفر و ظلام 177 n. 4

جود و وجود 120
جهان فانی 146

چ

چاربال 126
چاه نموده و موسوم 197 n. 1
چترداِن جمشید 120
چراغ لالہ 5 n. 6
چشمۂ حیات 210
چون، حباب دائم 120

ح

حامدی کہ محمود 121
حسین بائین 197 n. 1
حضور پر نور 88 n. 1
حق النبي وعترته 125
حقیقت 120
حلِّ حالِ من 120
حلقۂ درگاه جاه 33 n. 1
حمد بیحد پروردگاری 206 n. 1
حوراِن بهشت 66 n. 1
حیّي و قیوم 156

خ

خاتم خواجگان چشت 188 n. 1
خاتون زمانہ 171 n. 2
خادم سفید و خادم سیاه 126
خاطر ناسك پسند 87 n. 3
خاك بغربال بپیزند 156 n. 2
خاكِ راه رسول 194
خاكِ ما 156 n. 2
خاكت در اُستُخوان 156 n. 2
خالدین 95 n. 3
خراب شد 92 n. 6
خسرو کیوان غلام 66 n. 1
خشت کبود 66 n. 1; 71
خصماِن شہ 85-6 n. 1
خطم یٰسین 206 n. 1
خلاصۂ عالم 121
خلد اللّہ ملکہ 87 n. 1
خلوتگۂ دل 47
خلیفہ یزدانی 54
خواجہ محمد ثناه بن حطّاط خان 128 n. 1
خوانی کشیده 126
خورشید ضیا گستر 66 n. 1
خوش حیوٰتی روان 121
خیال و جمال 120
خیرات افزون 147
خیرجاري 147 n. 2
خیر حافظا 85-6 n. 1

د

دار الامارة 28
داؤد الطائي 115 n. 2
درّ ثمین 47
در و بام 47
دل بخون غرق 156 n. 2
دم آبي بکش 197 n. 1
دوا و صفا 120
دو جهان نیاید در نظر 156 n. 2
دوران و عالم نصیب 194
دو سہ دل و دل یکدلہ 111 n. 2
دوئی از یك 120
دوئي بگذار 120
دهن بکشوده است 85-6 n. 1
دیباچۂ نورس 87 n. 3
دي تازه گلی بودم 156

ذ

ذراع دور و ارتفاع 30 n. 5
ذوق رندي 121
ذو قعده 89 n. 2; 148

ر

راِز صادق 120
راه کریم 194
ربّ بیچون 147
رخت بربست 107 n. 3
رکن الدین و عایشہ سلطان 175 n. 1
رواق منظر چشم 46
رواقی 54 n. 3
روز قیامت 194
روضۂ مطهّر 210 n. 1
روضۂ مطهّر و قالبِ مطهّر 206 n. 1
روضۂ عالی 171 n. 2
روی صدق 198 n. 3

ز

ز اسم . . . درياب 119 n. 3; 121
ز خاك پرسند نشان 156 n. 2

ژ

ژرفائی 30 n. 5

س

سالِ سلطان 66 n. 1
سایہ و شخص 120

[ال]غرفات آمين 125
غفر الله لـ ولوالديه 210

ف

فرّاش رواق 126
فرزند و اولاد شاه رشيد 194
فرش زمرّدين زمين 126
فرّاق 120
فصيح گو 87 n. 3
فضايل بيحد 147
فلس نورس 87 n. 3
فنّ موسيقي 87 n. 3
فيروزه منظر 54 n. 3
في روضة يُحبرون 125

ق

قبة الانوار 156 n. 2
قبة النور 152 n. 2
قبلي سلطاني 54
قبۀ مروحه 206 n. 1
قبيلِ مردان 120
قدح باده 127
قدر قدرت 84 n. 2
قرّة العين 120
قصر مشيّد 66 n. 1; 6
قصر و پيشگاهى 66 & n. 1
قصۀ قتل بناحق 10
قطرۀ دريا 119
قلعۀ محمدآباد 66 n. 1
قنديل خانقاه 126

ك

كشوف 120
"كلّ من عليها فان" 156 n. 1

ط

طاقِ درگاه 33 n. 1
طاقِ نۀ ايمان گردون 206 n. 1
طغرا 33 n. 1
طلسم 121

ظ

ظاهراً ماه 121; 119 n. 3
ظهور اين دوئي 120; 119 n. 3

ع

عاشقان 120
عالم جاوداني 146
عالم‌گير شاه 198 n. 3
عام و خاصّ 120
عبادت با اطاعت 106 n. 2
عبد القادر نورسي 87 n. 3
عتبۀ عالى 102 n. 1
عشق مجنون و خوبى ليلى 121
عقلِ اوّل [جبرئيل] 121
علم از هند رفت 109
علمِ نورس 87 n. 2
علوى [مسجد] 106 n. 2
عنايت ملك علّام 177 n. 4
عيدِ نورس 87 n. 3
عينِ دريا 121
عين عيني بعينهٔ عيني 121
عينِ ما 119

غ

غايت خوبي و دلنشين 178
غبار كالبدش بر هوا 156 n. 2

ستارهاى فلك 66 n. 1
سجدۀ ريختن بار سر 106 n. 2
سجده‌گاه 202 n. 3
سخنِ عاشقان 121
سراجِ ملت 206 n. 1
سرادق الامن والامان 131 n. 1; 206 n. 1
سكۀ نورس 87 n. 3
سليمان 42 n. 2
سيّد السادات 210 n. 1
سيد حنيف 210 n. 1
سيد ولي 107 n. 3

ش

شاخ زمرّد 5 n. 6
شاه نشين چشم 46
شاهي همايون اكرم 36 n. 1
شب سياه فروغ 66 n. 1
شفا سحاب 126
شفاعت پناه 194
شقايق 5 n. 6
شكّرِ شكر شيرين 121
شمسِ فلك 109 n. 3
شهاب الدنيا والدين 125
شهان و گدا 126

ص

صدا كاذب 120
صدر رفيع 33 n. 1
صدفِ درّ 47
صفت و ذات واحد 120

ض

ضريحۀ [نور الله] 125

كمال الدين الكوفي 115 n. 2
كوى نور يا بهشت 188 n. 1
كيخسرو 206 n. 1

گ

گذشتـه معيشت بفعل لئيم 194
گرمىء آفتاب 121
گل و نوبهار 156 n. 2
گنبد رفيع 126
گنبد فردوس برين 187 n. 2
گنج در دل 120
گوشوارۀ عز و جاه 33 n. 1
گوشِ فلك 85-6 n. 1
گوكهرو 73 n. 1

ل

لا الـه الا الله 193 n. 2
لا الـه الا هو 120
لا انت و انا ما هو 120
لا خوف عليكم 124
لا نعبد الا ايّاه 177 n. 4
لطف و عنايت 194
لطيف در همـه 120
ليس فى الدار غيره 120

م

متكاى مهر 126
[ال]مجلس المكرم 151
مجملاً و مفصلاً 120
محلها و ايوان 49 n. 2
محمّد شاه الولي (titles of) 210 n. 1
محمّد مؤمن طاطبا 197 n. 1
محيط بركـه 126
محيطِ ديده 127
مخلوقِ حضرتش 121
مدحِ صنعت و صانع 121
مدرسهٔ رفيع 92 n. 2
مستنصر بنصر الله 47 n. 2
مسجد علوى 106 n. 2
مسجد و كوت 49 n. 2
مشيّد 66 (strongly defended) n. 1; 68
مطالع شمس و قمر 66 n. 1
معدن فيض الـه 198
مقام شريف 210 n. 1
مقام محمد مرضى 45
[ال]ملائكة المقربين 118 n. 4
من توئى بگذار 120
منوّر شده همچو بيت الـه 202 n. 3
مهدي هادي 126; 116
مهندسان اقليدس شعار و طرّاحان الخ 29 n. 1
ميان يادگار 106 n. 2

ن

[ال]نبي الامّي 118 n. 4
نخست بارگـه 66 n. 1
نسخهٔ عقل 120
نسل بهمن و فريدون 147 n. 2
نسيم صبح 5 n. 6
نشانِ نورس 87 n. 3
نشان و اثر 156 n. 2
نشان يادگار 194
نصر من الله 85-6 n. 1
نعم اجر العالمين 95 n. 3
نعمت الله 127
نقدِ گنج 119
نقشِ عالم 120
نقشِ و پرنگار از گا، و گياه 126
نكهت فردوس 171 n. 2
نگاهٔ احول 120
نورسامـه 87 n. 3

و

وجودِ وى 120
وحدت و كثرت 120
وصفِ خود 120
وقت سعد و ميمون 147

ه

هادي سبل شفيع امت 206 n. 1
هاديهاى علم 126
هر چـه موجود 121
همدرد هم ديگر 120
هند و سند 85 n. 1
هو الله الباقى 128 n. 1

ي

يادگارى 54 n. 3
ياران و عزيزان 156 n. 2
يامر بالعدل والاحسان 206 n. 1
يا مفتح الابواب 206 n. 1
يگانـه صوت 120

MARĀṬHĪ AND SANSKRIT INDEX

अजम मनसुर खां 204 n. 1
अलाओ 106
गगण 60
चंड कोळा तुंब 204 n. 1
तुंब बांधविळा पाणि उचळून 204 n. 1
नाश 207 n. 1
पाप 207 n. 1
माहे मोहरम सत सबा सामानिन 204 n. 1
समाधि 179
सुरूर तिसा सबैन व तिसा 204 n. 1
हजरत बरिद शाहा 204 n. 1
हीरी बारी'विं चौरस 140 n. 2

GENERAL INDEX

A

abacusi, 169.
Abban Ṣāḥib, 88 & n. 1.
'Abbās Pansālī kī Ta'līm, 20 n. 2.
'Abd-ul-Fattāḥ, 158.
'Abd-ul-Ḥanīf, 11.
'Abdullāh Khān, an Abyssinian, 19.
— Maghribī, 167; — —, tomb of, 168 n. 1.
— Minallāh Muḥ. al-Ḥusainī, 186.
— Muḥammad, 186.
'Abd-ul-Qādir Gīlānī, 107 & n. 1; 111.
— Muḥammad al-Ḥusainī, 186.
'Abd-ur-Raḥīm, 194.
abjad, 113 n. 1; 152 n. 2; 187 n. 2; 198 n. 3.
— system, 92 nn. 2 & 6; 146.
ablution-cistern, 169; 188; 195; 199.
ablution-well, 182.
abrupt turns in passage, 38.
absorption in divine love, 190.
Abū 'Alī Rūdbārī, 115.
Abū-'l-Faiḍ, 113; 184; 190.
Abū-'l-Fatḥ, Shams-ud-Dīn, 107.
Abū-'l-Ḥasan, 16; 185; 188.
Abyssinian, 11; 44; — officers, 14; — general, 49; — giant, 181.
— occupation of Bidar, 181.
accommodation for guards, 40 n. 5.
— of Madrasa, 98–9.
acrobatic performances, 40.
Ādharī, vi, 6; 23; 66 n. 1; 68; —, couplets by, 66 n. 1.
'Ādil Shāhī buildings, 153.
— — dynasty, 11.
— — kingdom, 14.
— — kings, 133.
— — territories, 27.
adoration of icons, 178.
Afḍalī, 85–6 n. 1.
Afghan king, 148.
Africa, North, 103.
—, North-West, 91.
Agra, 27; 73; 181 n. 2.
agricultural produce, 203.
Aḥmad Baihman Shāh, 6–7.
— Khān Kheshgī, 112 & n. 1.
Aḥmadnagar, 11; 14; 82; 138.
Aḥmad Shāh, 116; 125; 132; 134; 150.
— — and 'Alā-ud-Dīn, 137.
— — II, 12.
— —, Niẓām Shāh, 9 n. 1.
— —'s tomb, 128 & n. 1; 129.
— Walī, al-Baihmanī, vi; 4; 6; 23–4; 28; 29 & n. 4; 34; 44; 55; 66 & n. 1; 67; 70; 82; 90; 100; 109; 117; 130; 146–8; 172; 208; 212.
—, writer of inscription, 193 n. 2.
'Ahmudnuggur', 148.
aḥshām, 34 n. 1.
Ā'īna-i-Bidar, 82 n. 4.
aisles, 61–2; 110.
Ajanta, 116; 118; 145.
'Alā Khān Shāh, 147 n. 2.
'Ālamgīr, 107 n. 3; 198 n. 3.
'alams, 102 n. 1.
alāo, 106.
'Alā-ud-Daula Dilīr Jang, 18.
'Alā-ud-Dīn, 4 n. 5; 5–7; 129; 131 n. 1; 132; 134; 136; 142; 146; 148; 206 n. 1; 212.
—, tomb of, 24.
— Aḥmad, 109; 147.
— Baihmanī, 105; 113; 114 n. 2; 137; 174; 206.
— 'Imād Shāh, 13.
— Shāh III, 12.
alāvā, 105.
alcove, 213; — recesses, 131.
'Alī, 64; 110; 119; — (protective power of his symbol), 32.
'Alīābād, 1 n. 3; 205.
'Alī 'Ādil Shāh, 13.
— as-Ṣūfī, calligraphist, 95 n. 3; 96.
— Bāgh, 104–5.
— Barīd, 13; 30; 43–4; 46; 48; 82 n. 4; 85–6 n. 2; 128 n. 1; 155; 160; 165; 171.
— —, his mausoleum, 25–6; 172–4.
— —, his gun, 35.
'Alī Barīd Shāh', 140.
alif (Allāh), 124.

ʻAlī Ḥusain, Shāh, 111.
— Rūdbārī, 119.
— the tiger (lion), 101 n. 3.
ʻĀlī Jāh Bahādur, 18, 19.
Allāh, Muḥammad and ʻAlī, 141.
ʻAmal-i-Ṣāliḥ, 30 n. 5; 54 n. 1.
Amīn-ud-Dīn Abū-'l-Faiḍ, 185.
Amīn-ul-Mulk Bahādur, 18.
Amīr Barīd, 12–13; 42; 137; 149; 151; 190.
— — I ('the obstinate Barīd'), 161 n. 1.
— — II, 27.
Amīr Ḥamza Qādirī, 189.
Amīr-i-Jumla, 11.
Amīr-Ullāh Beg, 146 n. 2.
Ānand Maḥall, 133 n. 3.
Āndhra rājas, 3.
animal fights, 61.
Annual Report, Arch. Dept., Hyderabad, 8 n. 3; *1925–6*, 16 n. 3; *1928–9*, 16 nn. 7–8; *1930–1*, 14 n. 5.
Anonymous Tombs, 132; 173–4.
Antiquities of Bidar, The, v n. 1; vii; 15 n. 1.
antiquity of temple, 80.
Anūp Singh Bundelā, 17.
apartments below bastion, 40.
— of prayer-hall, 55. *See also* prayer-hall.
apex, apexes, of domes, 41, 56.
— of arches, 176.
— of parlour, 209.
apotropaic tiger symbols, 32.
appearance and reality, 122.
aqueduct, 168; —, traces of, 160.
Arab art, 24.
— buildings in N. Africa and Spain, 164 n. 1.
arabesque and geometric, 71; 73.
Arab guards, 59; 61.
Arabic and Persian texts, 73.
— texts, 98.
— words, 177.
arcade, 43; 60; 159; — in ramparts, 34 n. 3; —, machicolated, 37.
Archaeological Dept., Hyderabad, v; 3; 6 n. 1; 12 n. 1; 14; 16; 23; 38; 43–4; 46; 50–2; 54 & n. 3; 56; 59; 62; 66–7; 68 & n. 1; 91; 93; 98; 128 & n. 2; 132 & n. 2; 137; 140; 144; 149; 152; 154; 162; 166 n. 2; 172; 174; 177 n. 2; 184; 192; 206; 208; 212.
Archaeological Museum, 73.
arched niches, 136.
— openings, 49–50; 106; 176; 200.
— windows, 55.
arches, 38; 65; 69; 96; 203.
— and arch-heads, 117.
—, large and small, 161.
—, lofty, 89.
— of mosque, 196.
—, Persian, 34.
arch-head parapet, 190.
arch-heads, 103.
architects, Persian, 46.
architecture in Deccan, XIIth–XIIIth centuries, 21.
architraves, 21.
arch of pavilion, 23.
arch-shaped niches, 134.
— panels, 156.
— parapet, 173.
arch under ramparts, 43.
armour, 73 n. 1.
arrangement of arches, 142.
Art and Crafts School, 104–5.
art-critics, 97.
articles made of Bīdrī-ware, 20 n. 1.
Asad ʻAlī Khān, 19.
— al-Ghālib, 32.
— Khān, 146 n. 3.
Asad-Ullāh, 12 n. 3; 101 n. 3.
Āṣaf Jāh, 88 n. 1; 185.
— — I, 190.
— —, his independence, 27.
Āṣaf Jāhī, 178; — — dynasty, 17; — — rulers, 83.
Āṣaf-ud-Daula Nuṣrat Jang, 18 n. 2.
ashlar masonry, 160; 205.
Āshṭūr, 7; 10; 12; 28; 105; 114; 137; 140; 148; 150; 212.
Āshṭūr, well at, 193.
ʻĀshūrī Begam, 186.
ʻĀshūr Khāna, 102 & n. 1; 103–6; 110.
A.S.I., Imperial Series, 64 n. 1.
Assembly Mosque, 103; 130.
assimilation of Hindu and Muslim practices, 26.
Āthār Maḥall, 64.
ʻAtīq-Ullāh, 186.
atrocious character of Abyssinians, 181.
ʻAṭṭār, 156.
attractive designs, 144.
attributes, 123.
audience hall, 64; 67; 130.
audiences, public, 63.
Aurangābād, 14.
Aurang Khān, 16.
Aurangzeb, 14; 15 & n. 5; 17; 30; 54; 74 n. 1; 84 n. 2; 87 & nn. 1–2; 89 n. 2; 113 & n. 1; 170; 177; 189; 194–5; 198; 202.
Ausa, 11; 25.
axis of universe, 124.
Āyat-ul-Kursī, 36; 117; 139.
Aʻẓam-i-Humāyūn, 4–5.
Aʻẓam Mansūr Khān, 204 n. 1.
azure background, 119.
'azure window of heaven', 54 n. 3.

B

Bagewadi, 116 n. 1.
Baghdād, 189.
Bahlol, 117.
'Bahmuny', 148.
Baihman and Isfandyār, 4 n. 5; 147.
Baihmanī architecture, 24; 104; 145.
— family, 13.
— jewels, 13.
— kings, 44; 52; 57; 60; 64; 69; 141; 145; 165; 172; 213.

Baihmanī kings, tombs of, 22.
— palace, 70.
— period, 45–6; 141.
— style, 200.
— tombs, 26; 114; 128; 158; 183.
— tombs, architecture, 152.
Baihman Shāh, 147.
baits by Ādharī, 66 n. 1.
baked clay pipes, 77.
baking cakes, 181.
balconies, 44; 94; 152; — on minaret, 197.
balcony-like apartments, 65.
Banda 'Alī Shāh, 190.
Banda Nawāz Gesū Darāz, 110; 114; 170.
band, dark-coloured, 119.
bands around towers, 26.
—, calligraphic, 96.
—, carved, 59; 94; 196.
— of masonry, 99; 211.
— of stucco-work, 163.
—, stone, 154. *See also* bands, carved &c., *above*.
Bangle-sellers' School, 102–3.
banyan trees, 35; 49; 167; 192.
bāṛā, 90.
Barber's Tomb, 166–7, 208.
barbican, 32; 36; 85; 88.
barīd (courier), 152 n. 1.
Barīdī and Baihmanī, 110–11; 113.
— architecture, 59; 104; 199.
— building, 153.
— court, 173.
— dynasty, 52.
— kings, 19; 57; 60; 82; 101 n. 1; 133; 147; 208.
Barīd-i-Mamālik, 152.
Barīdī period, 27; 45–6; 197.
— pillars, 170.
— tombs, 28; 42; 148 ff.; 183.
Barīd Shāh, 39 n. 1.
— Shāhī building, 26.
— — territory, 13.
— — tombstones, 57 n. 2.
Barī Khānqāh, 111.
Barkhwurdār Beg, 198–200.
barracks, cavalry, 92 n. 6.
barrel ceiling, 76.
barrel-shaped bastion, 35.
barrel-type, 52.
bārūt in *Firishta*, 29.
basalt, black, 155.
— pillars, 163.
— sarcophagus, 199.
Basātīn-us-Salāṭīn, 14 & n. 6; 87 n. 3; 140 n. 1; 193 & n. 1.
Basava, 116 n. 1.
basement, 91.
basin of fountain, 58.
bastions, 23; 31; 34; 68; 85; 90.
— and ramparts, 81.
—, rounded, 79.
bath attendants, 51.
bathing pool, 207.
— ritual, 177; 179; 200.
bathrooms, 74.
Bath, Royal, 64; 73.
batter on walls, 87; 129; 136.
battery, 87 n. 3.
battlements, 83.
bays of hall, 51; 55.
beasts of burden, 177.
beauty of form, 95.
Belgām, 29.
Berar, 11.
Bhāgavata, 3 n. 1.
Bhīma Rāja, 3.
Bhongīr, 82 n. 3.
Bībī Fāṭima, 199 n. 2.
— Bandagī Ḥusainī, 169.
Bidar, 19; 22–3; 27–31; 44; 82; 130–1; 133; 143; 145; 146 n. 4; 148; 152; 165; 170; 172; 274; 177; 190 & n. 2; 195; 198; 212 *et passim*.
— city, 55; — fort, 15, — people, 102; — town and fort, 205.
Bidar-Āshṭūr road, 148.
Bidar-Chhidrī road, 112; 149.
Bidar-Udgīr road, 162; 172.
Bīdrī-ware, manufacture of, 20 & n. 1.
Bijāpur, 11–14; 22; 27; 57; 82; 110 n. 4; 133; 138; 150; 195; 201.
'*Bījāpūr Architecture*', 201 n. 1.
Bijāpur governors, 202.
— kingdom, 49.
— kings, 170.
Binyon, Laurence, 13 n. 4.
birds, aquatic, 208.
— at fort, 35.
bird-carvings on gun, 80.
bird-figures in decoration, 191.
Bismi'llāh, 39 n. 1; 193.
black basalt, polished, 161.
'Black Mosque', 196.
black stone, 204.
— — bands, 172.
— — (basalt ?), 174.
— — (hornblende ?), 163.
— — frame, 185.
— — margins, 64; 130; 150.
— — pillars, 105.
— — sarcophagi, 193.
— — with inscription, 32.
— trap masonry, 79; 91; 142.
blocks, eastern and western, 81.
— of carved stone, 62.
blue, green and yellow, 130. *See also* colours, green, yellow.
— tiles, 45; 63; 71.
— tile-work, 167.
— ware, Persian, 73.
bombardment, 88.
Bombay ed. of *Firishta*, 125.
bounty of the Divine, 122.
box-like form, 155.
brackets, 196.
— absence of, 94.
— of Hindu design, 144.

Brahman Gangū, 147.
Brahmanical buildings, 63.
Brahmans and Brahmanical rules, 116 n. 1.
breaches in embankment, 204.
bread and sweets, 107 n. 3.
brick and lime channels, 77.
— — — graves, 155.
— — mortar graves, 151.
— — — sarcophagi, 161; 163; 166; 173–4; 181.
— — — tombs, 171.
bricks and brick-architecture, 21.
—, spongy, 133.
bridge over moat, 85.
— with arches, 205.
Briggs's *Firishta*, 4 nn. 2, 4, 6; 5 nn. 1–3; 10 n. 1; 25 n. 3; 64 n. 2; 73 n. 2; 82 n. 2; 92 nn. 4–6; 100 n. 1; 148.
brilliant tile-work, 156.
British Museum, 63.
broad steps, 177.
Brown, Mr. Percy, 95 & n. 1.
Buddhist buildings, 63; — shrines, 164.
Bukhārī masjid, 27; 201.
bull carved in stone, 207.
bullets, 81.
bullock-carts, 89.
bull of Siva, 179–80.
Bulsar, 29 n. 5.
bungalow of District Club, 66.
Burhān-i-Ma'āthir, 5 nn. 4 & 6; 6 nn. 2–5; 7 nn. 2–3; 129 n. 5.
Burhān Niẓām Shāh I, 150.
Burn, Sir Richard, vii.
Butchers' Mosque, 63 n. 3.
buttresses, 100; 196.

C

cactus, 69.
Calicut, 29 n. 5.
caliver, 29 n. 5.
calligraphic designs, 24; 118.
— devices, 45; 47.
— masterpiece, 178.
— motifs, 94; 96; 130.
— patterns, 154.
calligraphist, 158.
Cambridge History of India, 3 n. 2; 14 n. 6; 25 n. 1; 95 n. 1; 140.
canal, subterranean, 205.
Canarese inscription, 162.
cannon, 81.
canopy, wooden, 209.
Carnatic country, 152.
— Darwāza, 31; 43.
carpenter's craft, 196–7.
'carpet of six directions', 206 n. 1.
carpet patterns, 118.
carpets, 107 n. 2.
cart-track, 202; 207.
carved masonry, 94.
— sarcophagus, 164; 174.
— slab, 53.
carved slabs (as building material), 36.
— stones, 40; — — looted, 181 n. 2.
carving, decorative, 21.
— on stone, 158.
cascade, 53.
— and cistern, 65.
— and fountains, 180.
—, artificial, 179.
— in garden, 177.
casket design, 151.
casket-like forms, 52.
casket-shaped ceiling, 168.
casket, wooden, 196–7.
Castanheda, 89 n. 5.
Cat. Brit. Mus., Ind. Coins, Muh. States, 132 n. 1.
cathedrals, European, 104.
cattle-breeding, 20.
cavities, 205.
ceiling designs, 60.
— of corridor, 58.
— of hall, 139.
— of mosque, 97.
— of passage, 67.
ceilings, flat, 21.
—, vaulted, 51; 61.
celadon, 73.
cells, hewn in rock, 208.
cemetery, 181.
— of Barīdī kings, 151.
central apartment, 99.
— hall, 185.
ceramics, Islamic, 73.
'chain-and-pendant' emblem or motif, 57 n. 2; 163; 174; 181; 187; 196.
chain patterns, 73.
chakram designs, 160; 170.
Chālukyas, 3.
'chamber of my heart', 48.
Chamkoṛa Maṛī, 1 n. 3.
Champanir, 29 n. 5.
Chāndnī Chabūtrā, 16.
'Chānd Sulṭāna,' 164.
chantrys of Qur'ān, 104.
charge of big gun, 36.
charlatans, 190.
Chār Minār, 26; 27 n. 1.
chastity of style, 56.
chau, 90.
Chaubārā, The, 90–1; 103; 109.
Chaubārā Mangalpeṭ, 110.
chaugān, 162.
Chaukhaṇḍī, 141–6; 190 & n. 2.
Chaukhaṇḍī of Dulāh Mīyān, 189.
— of Khalīl-Ullāh, 141–6.
— of Mīr Kalān Khān, 190–1.
chauth, 18.
Chemical Laboratory, British Museum, 63.
chhajjā, 139; 152; 181; 188–9; 200–1.
chhatrī, 166; 179.
Chhidrī, 12 n. 6; 203.
— road, 191; 196; 199.
Chhoṭi Khānqāh, 111–12.

'chief of chiefs', 208.
chimney-like effect, 197.
china and glass-ware, 153.
China ware, 73.
Chinese patterns, 64.
chiselled and polished steps, 149.
— masonry, 163; 168; 193.
— stone, 174.
— trap masonry, 162.
Chishtīya ṣūfīs, 113.
Chītā Khāna, 104–5.
chronogram, 92 n. 2; 111 n. 2; 146.
— of 'Alī Barīd, 156 n. 2.
chronograms, 107, 171.
chronological order, 176.
— — of descriptions, 28.
chūla, 181.
Churasanische Baudenkmäler, 92 n. 1.
Circassian beauties, 59; 159.
circuit of fort, 40.
— of ramparts, 83.
circular apertures, 81–2.
— bands, 91; 94.
— base, 90; 154; 184; 191.
— court, 38.
— curtain walls, 36.
— drum, 168.
— masonry, 207.
— — caps, 21.
— shoot, 155.
— staircase, 70.
circumference of cistern, 97.
— of dome, 135; 143; 163; 187; 207; 209.
cistern, 46; 50–1; 53; 73; 103; 112; 159–60; 165; 188; 202; 207; 211.
— in open court, 75.
— with jets, 35 n. 1.
— with pavement, 178.
Civil Court, 51.
clamps, metal, 21.
clan-members, 164.
classical beauty, 56.
clay pipe-lines, 77.
clays, coloured, 73.
cleft in façade, 93.
clerestory, 56.
climate, 1.
climatic conditions, 99.
clock, 91.
coco-nuts, spices, and flowers, 178.
coin cabinet, Hyderabad Museum, 15 n. 4.
— of Shāh Jahān with m.m. Ẓafarābād.
coins of Aḥmad Shāh, 115 n. 2.
— of 'Alā-ud-Dīn, 132 n. 1.
coin-stamping, 100.
coins with royal titles, 132 n. 1.
Collector's headquarters, 20.
collyrium-pot, 157.
colonnade, 110, — with piers, 50.
colonnades, 65; 105.
colossal size of arches, 72.
'Coloured Palace', 44.
coloured tiles, 187.
colour, love of, 28.
— schemes, 156.
colours of parapet, 32.
— of tiles, 63; 71; 94–6.
—, show of, 80.
Commandant's quarters, 35 n. 1.
commoner and aristocrat, 123.
compensation, vi.
Comptroller of Ordnance, 41.
concave compartments of ceiling, 76.
— facets, 173.
— fluting, 169.
concentric bands, 127; 161.
— belts, 134.
conceptions of beauty, 26.
conch-blowing, 116 n. 3.
concubines of 'Alī Barīd, 159.
Condapalli, 9.
cone, facetted, 69.
conical dome, 137–8; 151.
— shape, 76.
— vaults, 75.
connoisseur, 118.
co-operative societies, 20.
coping, 211.
copper coins of 'Alā-ud-Dīn, 132 n. 1.
— — of Amīr Barīd, 14.
copper finial, gilded, 56 n. 1.
— —, gold-plated, 155.
corbels, 133; 207.
— and friezes, 25.
co-relations of parts in building, 26.
corners, NE. and NW. 98.
corps de garde, 34 n. 1.
corridor, 58; — and hall, 180; — on west, 64.
cosmetic boxes, 20 n. 1.
cotton tape, 102.
couch with wooden frame, 101.
countenance of Beloved, 124.
court, 50; —, divided, 43; — of Dīwān, 63; — of mosque, 160; — of temple, 189.
Cousens, H., 201 n. 1.
— —: *Bījāpūr Architecture*, 27 nn. 2 & 4; 64 n. 1; 95 n. 2.
covered channel, 211.
— mosque, 22.
— passage, 60; 79; 143; 153; 187; 200.
crack in dome, 127.
cracks in walls, 56.
craze for low arches, 153.
crescent, finial, 165.
cross-shaped plan, 76.
crosswise streets, 90.
'Crow-bar Barīd', 161.
crystal in vault, 119.
cube-shaped building, 161.
cubicles, 97.
cultivated fields, 168.
culverts, 177 n. 2.
cupola, 48.
cure and clear wine, 123.

curtain walls, 34; 36; 40–1.
curves of plateau edge, 87.
curvilinear form, 94.
cusped arches, 46; 105; 185; 195.
— arch-heads, 179.
— design, 58; 75.
— panel, 200.
cut-plaster-work, 57; 200.
Cyclopean architecture, 21.
— construction, 204.
— masonry, 82 n. 3.
cylindrical bastion, 35.
— tower, 90.

D

dadoes, 47; 52; 71; 74; 119; 130.
—, carved, 154–5.
— with rosettes, 158.
Damaghān, 192 n. 1.
Damayanti (and Nala), 3.
Dārā Shukoh, 116.
dargāh, 186.
Dargāh of Banda, 'Alī Shāh Majdhūb, 190–1.
— of Ḥaḍrat Makhdūm Qādirī, 27.
— of Shāh Abū-'l-Faiḍ, 184–7; 189.
dark basalt, 163.
dark-grey piles of ramparts, 57.
Darogha of Dept., 66.
Dār-ul-Imāra, 28.
Darwesh Ḥusainī Mashhadī, 210 n. 1.
date-palms, 204.
Dā'ūd Khān, 129.
Daulatābād, 8; 13; 16; 91; 149; 167.
debris, 93.
— and silt, 114.
—, heaps of, 72.
— of dome, 132 n. 2.
— of wall, 172.
decagonal plan, 197.
decay and destruction, 93.
Deccan, 91, *et passim.*
Deccanī architecture, 26; 117; 201.
— —, XIIth–XIIIth centuries, 21, 23.
— buildings, Muslim, 101.
— Muslims, 203.
Deccanīs, 44.
Deccanī tombs, 136.
decline of Baihmanī dynasty, 27.
decorative detail, 188.
— features, 103.
— motifs, Hindu, 100.
— niches, 65.
— panels, 131.
— schemes, 76.
— work, 93; 96; 202.
deep well, 183.
deer, 1.
defence of gateway, 90.
defences of Bidar, 83.
Delhi, 11; 73; 117; 209.
— and Agra, 181 n. 2.
— Darwāza, 31; 40–1.
Delhi Sultāns, 68.
— tombs, 212.
delicate patterns, 96; 99.
— plaster-work, 183.
dense population, 84 n. 1.
dentated moulding, 164.
denuded minaret, 25.
Deogiri (Daulatābād), 3; 22.
Dept. of Public Works, 48.
dervishes (and drummers), 107; 186.
'descendants and companions', 206 n. 1.
descendants of saint, 189; 192.
designs, floral and calligraphic, 144. *See also* floral, calligraphic.
detail by Hindus, 100.
deterioration, 26; — of power, 114.
devout pilgrims, 179.
Dhākir-ud-Dīn Khān, 18–19.
dharamśāla, 177; 189.
dhobīs, 179.
Dhū-Qa'da, 89 n. 2; 148.
diaper design, 155.
Ḍia-ud-Dīn Barnī, 3.
Diez, Ernst, 92 n. 1.
dike, 208.
dilapidated condition, 145.
dimensions, 43 nn. 2 & 5; 44 n. 1; 46 n. 1; 106.
— of arch, 40 nn. 1 & 5.
— of Big Gun, 35.
— of gun, 38 n. 3.
— of tomb, 213.
dish-shaped apartments, 52; 209.
disk, octagonal, 155.
—, ornamental, 160.
disloyal retainers, 68.
disrepair, 56; 213.
distribution of food to poor, 186.
District Club Bungalow, 66.
— Jail, 49–50; 208.
— Treasury, 61.
Dīvān of Ni'mat-Ullāh, 127.
Divine Being, 123.
Dīwān-i-'Ām, 62–6; 74.
Dīwān-i-Khāṣṣ, 73.
dodecagonal cistern, 97.
dome, 50; 55.
dome-crowned tomb, 191; 201.
dome-shaped ceiling, 97; 103.
domed ceiling, 45.
— chamber, 51.
— tomb, 181.
dome, in highest fort, 72.
Dome of the Rock, 131.
domes in ceiling, 68.
— in contour, 99.
dome-shaped ceiling, 35.
domical halls, 50.
dormitories, 70.
double arcade, 38.
— hall, 51; 58; 188.
— platform, 191.
— series of arches, 209; 212.

double series of niches, 150.
dowels, 21.
drain, 40 & n. 3.
drawbridge, 31.
dressed slabs, 199.
dressing apartments, 51.
dressing-rooms, 72.
dressing-table and cabinet, 154.
drinking water, 204.
dripstones, 159; 181; 188–9; 193; 195–6; 203.
drop in ocean, 122.
drum of dome, 139; 201; 209.
— of vault, 97.
du'ā, 45.
duality and unity, 122.
ducks, 208.
Dulāh Mīyān, 189.
dulhan, 88 n. 2.
Dulhan Darwāza, 83; 88 & n. 2; 89 & n. 1; 114; 141.
durūd, 118 & n. 4.

E

earthwork of dam, 204.
eastern arcades, 60.
— hall, 69.
— Persia, 25.
— wall, 62.
Education, Primary, Higher, &c., v.
effigies of tiger and rising sun, 70.
effulgence, 122.
ego's non-survival, 122; 124.
egress and ingress, 69.
Egypt, 166 n. 1.
eight-arched openings, 60.
—, sixteen-, and thirty-two-sided openings, 21.
eight facets, 149.
eight-facetted roof, 173.
eight-petalled flowers, 154–5; 165.
eighty steps, 91.
electric pump, 52.
elegance and grandeur, 56.
elegant designs, 60; 97–9.
— proportions, 68.
elephants in warfare, 88.
— on stone carvings, 40 n. 4.
elephant-trunk shape struts, 55.
Elliot, 29 n. 5.
—'s *History of India*, 54 n. 3.
elliptical dome, 100.
Ellora, 23.
— caves, 23.
embankment, 203; 205.
embassies, 64.
emblem, chain and pendant, 57 n. 2.
— of Persia, 70.
embroidery, 118.
eminent personages, 91.
encaustic tiles, 24; 48; 52; 70; 72; 94; 96; 150; 154; 158.
Enclave of Fort, 28.
enclosure walls, 37; 56; 82; 152; 154; 175.
Encycl. of Islam, 107 n. 1; 115 & nn. 1 & 2.
endowment (وقف), 184; 203.
engineering skill, 155.
engineers, Hindu, 203.
entity, 122.
entrance passages, 65.
entrances, 62.
Ephemeris of Swāmikannu Piḷḷai, 85–6 n. 2.
Epigraphia Indo-Moslemica 3 n. 7; 11 n. 2; 15 nn. 1 & 6; 16 nn. 2, 6–7, 9; 30 nn. 1, 3–4; 31 n. 3; 47 n. 2; 49 n. 2; 54 n. 3; 57 n. 1; 83 nn. 1–3; 89 n. 2; 107 n. 3; 109; 112 n. 1; 141; 143 n. 2; 146 n. 3; 147 n. 2; 157; 171 n. 2; 177 n. 4; 187 n. 2; 188 n. 1; 193 n. 2; 194 n. 2; 197 n. 1; 198 nn. 1 & 3; 204 n. 1; 210 n. 1.
epigraphic evidence, 29.
erosion, 192.
European pigments, 127.
evergreen trees, 184.
exaggerated embellishment, 158.
excavations, recent, 62; 64; 68.
Excise Dept., 50.
Executive Council of H.E.H., 192.
explosion of magazine, 92 n. 6; 93.
explosives, 81.
exquisite workmanship, 161.
eye-powder, 157.

F

façade, 56; 67–8; 70; 79; 94; 97; 153; 173; 187; 196; 198.
—, carved, 165.
— of arcade, 159–160; 180.
— of gateway, 87.
— of halls, 44.
— with arcades, 144.
— with niches and rosettes, 167.
— with stucco work, 48.
face of walls, 213.
facets of columns, 100.
— of cone, 69.
'faithful dog' story, 172.
faiths, various, 176.
fallen roofs, 79.
false echo, 123.
family vault, 185.
— — of Aḥmad S͟hāh, 129.
Farḥ Bāg͟h, 1 & n. 3; 176; 181 n. 1.
— — mosque, 15.
Farīd-ud-Dīn S͟hakar Ganj, 110.
Farīdūn and Baihman, 147–8.
Farūqī, 'Alī K͟hān, 140.
'Fat-belly Bastion', 41.
Fatḥ Darwāza, 83; 85; 87–8; 103; 194; 205.
'Fatḥ Las͟hkar', 38.
Fatḥpur, 211.
— Śikrī, 27.
Fatḥ S͟hāh, 175.
Fatḥ-Ullāh 'Imād-ul-Mulk, 11.
Fāṭima, 119.
Faujdārship of C͟hūragarḥ, 15.
fecundity magic, 210.

fecundity symbol, 207.
feeding the poor, 159.
fencing and wrestling, 102.
fertility of soil, 204.
festivals, 211.
Fez, 91.
—, schools of, 24.
Fifth Journey, P. M. Sykes, 92 n. 3.
fillets of plaster-work, 153.
finial, 138; 211; — of temple, 189.
finials, carved, 59; —, gold-plated, 161.
fire-arms, 36–7; 43; 73 n. 1.
fire of garrison, 32; 90.
fire-place, octagonal, 180.
fire-temples, 105.
firing of tiles, 73.
Firishta, 3 & n. 6; 4 n. 5; 5 n. 5; 6 nn. 2–4; 7 nn. 3 & 5; 8 n. 2; 9 n. 5; 10 n. 5; 11; 14 n. 4; 23; 28 & n. 2; 29 nn. 1–3; 30 n. 1; 44 n. 3; 64; 67; 73 n. 2; 82 n. 2; 85–6 n. 2; 92 nn. 4–6; 115 n. 2; 125*; 129 & n. 2; 130 n. 2; 131 n. 1; 135 n. 2; 132 nn. 1–3; 140; 141 n. 1; 144 n. 2; 146; 148; 149 n. 1; 167 n. 2; 172 n. 1; 208 n. 1; 212.
Firishta (Persian text quoted), 167 n. 2; 212 n. 1.
Fīroz Khān, 111.
— Shāh, 5.
— — Baihmanī, 8 n. 3; 22.
— — Koṭla, 91.
Fīrozābād, 129.
first floor, 61.
First Reason, 123.
First Ta'alluqdār, 44 & n. 5; 48.
fissure spring, 177; 179.
five holy personages, 119.
flagons and decanters, 154.
flanked with halls, 68.
flanking apartments, 185; — chambers, 77.
flat ceiling, 101.
fleet against pirates, 29 n. 5.
flight of five steps, 165.
— of long steps, 211.
— of seven steps, 163; 168.
— of steps into well, 183.
— — — to roof, 60 n. 3.
— — — to water, 210.
flights of steps, 45; 78; 160; 177; 187. *See also* landings; staircase; steps.
floor excavated, 93.
— level, 81.
floral and geometrical designs, 153–5; 158.
— — — patterns, 163.
— ceiling and mural decorations, 159.
— designs, 40; 45–7; 59; 98; 101; 126; 130; 185; 187; 201; 209.
— margin, 180.
— patterns, 22.
— scroll, 143 n. 2.
flower-beds, vi; 103 & n. 1; 154; 158–160; 168.
flowering shrubs, 148; 180.
flower vases, 101.
fluted corner turrets, 34.
— dome, 113; 195.
fluted vault, 143.
food grains, 79; 180.
foot-paths, 159–160.
forecourt (peshgāh), 74.
— and palace, 66.
foreign embassies, 64.
fort, v–vi.
— area, 67.
Fort Enclave, 28.
fortifications, 29; 83; 89.
fort-walls, 84.
fosse, 83.
foundations of fort, 34.
foundries, gun-, 39.
fountain, 46; 48; 65.
— on terrace, 58.
—, square in plan, 71 & n. 2.
four-centred arch, 60.
XIVth and XVth centuries, 68.
XIVth- and XVth-century tombs, 209.
fragmentary inscriptions, 28. *See also* inscribed, inscriptions, tablets.
fragment of arch-head, 72.
Friday prayers (Ṣalāt-ul-Juma'), 54.
friezes, 21; 63 n. 1; 196.
frill-like design, 166.
fruit- and flower-gardens, 79.
fruit-trees, 148; 158; 160.
funeral services, 166.
funnels, 72.
fusion of cultures in XVIth-century India. 26.

G

Gagaṇ Maḥall, 57 & n. 1; 59; 60–2; 133 n. 3.
galleries on minarets, 202.
Gaṇeśa, 180; 207.
garden, 53.
— of tomb, 164.
— with buildings, 178.
gardens, fruit- and flower-, 148–9; 152.
garrison, 37.
gates, bossed in iron, 30.
gateway, 85; 97; 100; 199; 200; 152–3; 162.
—, arched, 50.
— of fort, 32; 101 n. 3.
Gateway of Lowlands, 79–80.
gateway of shrine, 107 n. 2.
—, inscribed, 31.
Gāwān Maḥmūd, 10.
geological formation of site, 1.
geometric and flowered designs, 118.
geometrical designs, 65; 144.
— patterns, 55.
Georgia, domicile of Qāsim Barīd, 12.
Georgian women in ḥarīm, 59; 159.
Gesū Darāz, Banda Nawāz, 170.
—, Ḥaḍrat Sayyid Muḥammad, 147.
Ghālib Khān, 191.
Ghauth, Saif-ud-Daula, Muḥammad, 18.
Ghiyāth-ud-Dīn, 3.
ghost, Abyssinian, 182.
Ghulām 'Alī Āzād, 68 n. 2.

Ghulām Maḥmūd Khān, 18 n. 3.
gigantic dome, 136.
Gīlān, 91; 208; 211.
gilded and carved couch, 102.
— copper finial, 56 n. 1. *See also* copper, finial (many such being gilded).
girth of domes, 99.
— of tower, 91.
glacis, 31; 36; 83; 87.
glare of sun, 98.
glass, painted, 55.
glaze of tiles, 63; 185.
globe, 155.
'globe-trotter', v.
globular dome, 172.
Goa, 9.
Golconda, 5; 13; 14; 16; 19; 57; 82 & n. 3; 138 n. 1; 202.
gold and vermilion, 72; 117.
— creeper design, 118.
— designs, 24.
gold-lettered text, 118 n. 3.
gold on green, 119.
gold-plated copper, 155; 165.
— — — orbs, 138.
gold-smith's work, 21.
Gol Gumbad, 27; 138.
Gornallī, 193.
Gothic cathedrals, 56.
Government Industrial Laboratory, Hyderabad. 133 n. 4.
— of India, vi.
governors, 136.
— of Bidar, 19 n. 1; 105.
graceful carving, 196.
grain market, 84 & n. 1.
granite polo posts [?], 162.
grass and overgrowth, 172.
graves in enclosure, 135.
Great Monastery, 111.
— Mosque at Gulbarga, 133.
Greeks in Bactria and India, 23 n. 1.
green tiles, 71.
— valley, 168.
—, yellow, and buff tiles, 63.
grenades & rockets, 74 n. 1.
gridiron town-plan, 90.
Grigson, W. V., 91.
grouting of walls, 167; 169.
Γ-shaped plan, 40.
guards, accommodation for, 67.
— of the fort, 35.
— of the shrine, 200.
guards' lodgings, 101.
— rooms, 33; 43; 50; 79.
guava- and mango-trees, 207.
Gūdaṛ-bīnī, 167 n. 1.
Gujarāt, 6; 29 n. 5.
Gulbarga, 5; 8; 22; 28; 55; 56 & n. 3; 82; 113; 116.
—, mosque inscription, 4 n. 5; 147.
guldastas, 34; 211.
Gumbad Darwāza, 12; 34; 35 n. 1; 44; 81.
'Gungoo', 148.
Gungoo the Brahman, 4 n. 5.
gun, large, 85.
gunners and musketeers, 29 n. 5.
gunpowder, 28; 30.
— in the Deccan, 23.
— storage, 81.
guns, small-size, 83.

H

Ḥabīb-Ullāh, 141; 212.
Ḥabīb Ḥasan, Dr., 133 n. 4.
Ḥabshī Koṭ, 35; 88–9; 114; 148; 180–4.
Ḥaḍrat Barīd Shāh, 204 n. 1.
— Ibrāhīm Multānī, 109.
— Kāle Ṣāḥib, 187 n. 1.
— Khalīl-Ullāh, 24; 100; 141.
— Makhdūm Qādirī, 27; 201; 202 & n. 1.
— Multānī Pādshāh, 109; 199; 202.
— — —, tomb of, 107–9.
— Nūr Samnānī, 106–7.
— Shaikh Ibrāhīm, 107; 109.
Ḥaidar 'Alī's title, 42 n. 1.
'Ḥaidarī Mushtarī' gun, 42 n. 2.
Haig (in *Camb. Hist. Ind.*), 85–6 n. 2.
—, Sir W., 147.
hall above gateway, 200.
—, 'Alī Barīd's, 46.
—, great, 64.
—, principal, 63.
hand-paintings, 72.
Hanūmān, 2; 62; 190.
Hanūmān's temple, 189–90.
harem (*ḥarīm*), 61–2; 72; 150.
harems of Deccanī kings, 159.
Harivamśa, 3 n. 1.
Ḥasan and Ḥusain, 119.
— Khān, 129.
Haṭhīla Barīd, 161 n. 1.
Ḥauḍ Khāṣṣ, 56 n. 2.
havoc caused by explosion, 92 n. 6.
hazārī, 131.
Hazār Koṭhṛī, 77–8.
healing spring, 210.
Heavenly Palace, 60.
H.E. Government, 66; 141 nn. 1 & 2.
height of apex, 159 n. 1.
hemispherical compartment, 52.
— dome, 34; 163; 211.
hermits, Hindu, 177.
hexagonal diaper flooring, 158.
— slabs, 155.
— tiles, 59.
hexagon and star patterns, 64.
high explosives, 81.
High School, 104.
hillock near Purāna Qil'a, 38.
Hindu architects, 25–6; 145.
— carvings, 40 n. 4.
— columns, 153.
— conventions, 26.

Hindu craftsmen, 101.
— designs, 37; 46.
— — in mosque, 169.
— engineers, 203.
— masons, 72; 133; 191; 201; 212.
— masons' work, 25–6.
— offerings on sale near mosque, 178.
— pillars, 169.
— rulers of Deccan, 208.
— sculptors, 160.
— sculpture, 71.
— shrine-keepers, 178.
— styles, 24; 82.
— temples, 211.
— workmanship, 80.
Historical and Descriptive Sketch, 116 n. 1.
historical evidence, 29
honeycombed underground rooms, 77.
horizontal bands of sculpture, 21.
— courses, 161.
— panels, 161.
hornblende, 63; —, dark, 48; —, green and black, 21; 24.
horse-bits, 73 n. 1.
Hoshiyār, 5.
hospital at Bidar, 7.
hot and cold water, 52.
— bath, 75.
hub of town, 90.
Humāyūn, 7–8; 109.
— Shāh, 129 n. 5.
Humāyūn's tomb, 133–4.
Humāyūn az-Zālim, 7.
Humāyūn-i-Akram, 39 n. 1; 47 n. 2.
hunting leopards (cheetahs), 106.
— scenes, 40.
Ḥusain Khān, 18 n. 3.
Ḥusām-ud-Dīn 'Alī Khān, 16–17 & n. 1; 185.
Hydari, Sir Akbar, v.
Hyderabad, 170 n. 1.
— Archaeological Society, v.
— -Bidar road, 189.
— Museum coin cabinet, 15 n. 4.
— Persian MSS. Society, 195.
— -Udgīr road, 207.
hymn-chanting, 180.

I

Ibrāhīm 'Ādil Shāh II, 14; 49 n. 2; 74 n. 1; 82; 87.
— Barīd Shāh, 14; 85–6 n. 2; 160–2; 204.
— kā Rauḍa mosque, 27.
— Quṭb Shāh, 13; 128 n. 1.
— Shaikh, 107.
icons, 81.
'Īdgāh, 165–6; 168 n. 1; 208.
—, Baihmanī, 91.
Iftikhār Khān, 14; 15 & n. 5.
Ilāh Laqdī Beg, 146 n. 2.
illustrated MS. of Khamsa, 46 n. 2.
'Imād Shāhī Dynasty, 11.
'Imād-ul-Mulk, 4.
image-chambers, 21.
image-niches, 21. *See* niches.
imaginary picture, 122.
imām, 56; 98; 104; 107 n. 2.
Imām Mahdī, 126.
— of mosque, 160 n. 1.
Imām-ul-Mudarrisīn, 195.
Imperial Court at Delhi, 24; 27.
imported craftsmen, 73.
imposts, low, 153.
in'ām land, 212.
incense-burning, 180; 184; 186.
— pit (*alāvā*), 105.
incomplete sepulchre, 137.
incongruity of old and new material, 66.
— of pillars, 102.
Indian Architecture, Percy Brown, 95 n. 1.
individually and collectively, 122.
Indo-Muslim style, 71.
inner hall, 62.
inscribed slab, 206 n. 1; — tablet, 108; — texts, 128.
inscription, 187. *See* inscriptions, inscriptional, texts, &c.
— and titles of 'Alā-ud-Dīn, 131 n. 1.
inscriptional band, 144.
— tablet, 146.
— tablet of Fatḥ Shāh, 175.
— tablets and texts, 196–7.
inscription of 'Alī Barīd, 47.
— of Amīr Barīd, 14.
— — — — II, 193.
— on Āshṭūr well, 193.
— on façade, 104.
— on gateway, 31.
— on metal tablet, 31 n. 3.
— on shrine, 171.
inscriptions, 107.
— in Fort, 28.
insect-swarms, 179.
Inspector of Schools, 51.
interior of shrine, 155.
internal diameter of dome, 34.
intertwined snakes, 179.
intrigue of parties, 192.
Iran, 105.
iron doors, 33.
— gate, 179.
— knobs and bands, 84.
iron-plated and bossed doors, 34.
iron-studded door, 88.
irregular foundations, 70.
irregular-shaped dome, 174.
Isfandyār, 147.
Ishta Linga, 116 n. 1.
Islāmic buildings, 91.
— creed (كلمہ), 155; 193.
— law, 194.
— style, 90.
— tombs, 26.
Ismā'īl 'Ādil Shāh, 12–13; 82; 150.

J

Jagapati, Rāo Daulatī, 141.
Jagat Rāo, son of Banchālīkhandū, 140 n. 2.
Jahān Barīd, 167.
Jahāngīr, 57.
Jahān Turk, Khwāja, 7; 8 & n. 3.
Jail, District, vi.
Jālī Maḥall, 62.
jālī screens, 22; 96–9.
jālī-work, 55; 186.
Jamāl-ud-Dīn, 174–5.
jambs of black stone, 71 & n. 1.
Jāmiʿ-az-Zaitūna, (Jāmiʿ Zaitūnīya) of Tunis, 103; 197.
Jāmiʿ Masjid, 103.
— — at Gulbarga, 22.
Jamshīd, 31 n. 3; 84 n. 2; 206 n. 1.
Jangam, 116 & n. 1.
Jannat al-Firdausī, 146.
Jān Niṣār Khān, 15–16.
— Sipār Khān, 102.
— — — Bahādur Dil, 16.
Janwāda taʿalluqa, 211–12.
Janwāṛa, 146 n. 4.
J.A.S.B., 147 n. 2.
Jaswant Singh, 15 n. 5.
Jerusalem, 131.
jest by Ādharī increases his reward, 66 n. 1.
jets, 53.
joints of stone building, 31.
Johnson, Dr. John, vii.
Joshi, R. M., 140 n. 2; 204.
Journ. Hyderabad Arch. Soc., 11 n. 2.
Jumna Morī, 40; 205.
Junaid al-Baghdādī, 115; 119; 174; *also* Junaid of Baghdād.
jungle clearance, vi.

K

Kaʿba, 56; 162; 165; 176.
kachcha man of Deccan, 36.
Kākatīya, 3; 203.
— kings, 133.
Kālā Burj, 43.
Kaladghi, 116 n. 1.
kaleidoscopic effect, 96.
Kālī masjid at Bidar, 26; 195; 196 & n. 1; 197.
— — of Aurangzeb, 193–5.
Kalīm-Ullāh Baihmanī, 138; 149–50.
— Ḥusainī, 185.
Kalinjar, 29 n. 5.
Kallam, 6; 129.
Kalmadgī Gate (Darwāza), 28: 31; 37.
Kalyāṇa, 116 n. 1.
Kalyānī, 3; 13.
— Burj, 31; 38; 40–1; 80.
— Darwāza, 31.
Kambay, 29 n. 5.
Kamkol, 1 n. 1.
Kamthāna, 203–4; 205 n. 1.
Kanchī, 9 n. 5.
kangūras, 31 n. 2; 95 & n. 2.
kārēz, 1 n. 3; 204–6.
Kāshānī craftsmen, 70.
Kashmir, 64.
keep, 35.
Keeper of the Tomb, 154.
key-pattern design, 131; 142.
Khāfī Khān, 11; 54.
— Khān's *Muntakhab-ul-Lubāb*, 4 n. 6.
khalīfa, 115.
Khalīf Ḥasan Basarī, 7.
Khalīl-Ullāh, 102; 141–2; 143 n. 1; 145–7.
— Khān, Sayyid, 19.
—, mosque of, 113–14.
Khamsa, 46.
Khānapūr, 5.
Khāna-zād Khān, 17.
Khandesh, 15.
Khān Jahān, 54; 168.
— — Bahādur, 19.
— — Barīd, 13 n. 2; 167.
Khānqāh, 167–9.
Khānqāh of Ḥaḍrat Shāh Abū-'l-Faiḍ, 109–10.
— of Nūr Samnānī, 106–7.
— of Shāh Walī-Ullāh al-Ḥusainī, 110.
Khān Sāmān, 17.
— Zamān Mīr Khalīl-Ullāh, 15.
Khargird, 92.
Khāṣṣ Maḥall, 104–5; 190.
— — group, 107.
Khaṭṭāṭ Khān, 128 n. 1.
Kherla, 9; 28.
Kheshgī Afghans, 112.
khilʿats, 11.
Khizāna ʿĀmira, 68 n. 2.
Khurasan (Khorasan), 11; 92.
khuṭba, 115 n. 2; 130.
Khwāja Bustān, 193 n. 2.
Khwājagī Shirwānī, calligraphist, 157–8.
Khwāja Jahān Turk, 135.
— Momīn Khān, 17.
— Muḥammad Shāh, 128 n. 1.
— Munʿim Khān, 19.
Khwār, 192 n. 1.
King's Room, 23–4.
kiosks, 195.
—, pillared, 94.
Kirmān, 100.
kitchen, royal, 49.
knobs and lobes, 211.
— on balcony, 59.
knowledge of building principles, 25.
Konkan, 6; 9.
Krishna Prashad, Sir, 192.
Kūfic script, 64; 99; 118 & n. 2; 127; 141; 168. *See* inscriptions, &c.
kunj (*Kunj-Nishīn*), 174.
Kunj Nishīn Ḥaḍrat, 152.
Kutte kī Qabr, 171.

L

labyrinthine underground passages, 23.
lace-like patterns, 158.

ladies' graves, 161; 164; 168–9; 170 n. 2; 171; 174; 209.
ladies of harem, 49.
—, royal, 59.
Lahore, 11; 73.
laid-out court, 168.
Lakhnarām, 203.
Lā'l Bāgh, 72 n. 1.
Lāl Burj, 42; 85.
laminated metal bars, 36.
lamp-lit spring of fountain, 177.
'lamp of faith', 206 n. 1.
lamps of dargāh, 107 n. 3.
—, perpetual, in shrine, 179.
landing, 76; 181; 208; 211. *See* flights of steps, staircase, steps.
of swimming bath, 78
langar-khāna, 186.
langūr (Hanūmān monkey), 2.
lantern cupola, 48.
lantern-like vault, 48.
lantern-shaped projection, 56.
Large Gun Bastion, 35; 37.
laterite, 1; 88.
— crust, 205.
— masonry, 105.
— rock, 31.
lattice-work, 96.
laundrymen (dhobīs), 179.
leaf- and flower-patterns, 73.
leaf- and vase-motif, 71.
leaf-pattern, 154; 209.
leather buckets, 77.
Leopard's House, 104–5.
level, floor-, 81.
levels, various, of landing, 78.
library, 97.
— of Madrasa, 24.
— of 3,000 MSS., 92.
lightning conductor, 93.
—, destruction by, 92.
limonitic surfaces, 1.
linga, 116 n. 1; 180; 207.
— and *yonī*, 179.
lingāyats, 80; 116 & nn. 1 & 3.
lintels, 63 n. 1.
— and door frames, 21.
— and joints, 72.
lion and rising sun, 24; 70.
lion-headed god, 169.
lion incarnation of Śiva, 179.
'Little mosque' between tombs, 138 n. 1.
live coals as defence, 37.
living rock, moat cut in, 168.
Local Fund Office, 48.
lock, primitive, 40 n. 2.
locks, iron, 23 n. 1.
Lodhī kings, 117.
lofty entrance, 95; 98.
long front of buildings, 55.
'Long Gun' Bastion, 80–1.
long gun, carved, 80.
long-range firing, 36.
— gun, 41.
loopholed battlements, 83; 90.
loopholes, 43.
loop in road, 39.
lotus leaf orb, 101.
love of colour, 25.
low-arched door, 163.
lowlands, 68; 79.
—, eastern, 36.
lozenge-shaped panels, 142; 163; 168.
L-shaped block, 81.
— cells, 208.
— plan, 169.
Luṭf-Ullāh, 186.
luxuriant painting, 72.

M

Ma'āthir-ul-Umarā (Bibl. Ind.), 15 nn. 5 & 7; 16 & nn. 1, 4, 8; 17 n. 1.
machicoulis (machicolations), 31, 35–7; 90.
ma'dhana, 196.
Madrasa, v; — at Bidar, 24.
Madrasa–Dulhan Darwāza road, 112.
Madrasa–Fort road, 111.
Madrasa of Maḥmūd Gāwān, 17; 24; 91–100; 126; 159.
magazines, 81.
Mahābhārata, 3 n. 1.
Mahārāja, Sir Kishan Parshad, 192.
Mahārāshtra, 5.
Māh Bāno 8.
Maḥbūb Subḥānī, monastery of, 111.
Maḥmūd Ganj, 83.
— Gāwān Khwāja, 7–8; 9 & n. 5; 29–30; 73; 130; 135; 193; 195.
— Khaljī, of Mālwā, 8–9.
— —, Sulṭān, 29; 24 n. 1.
— Khān, 129.
— Shāh Baihmanī, 33; 44–5; 136; 210 n. 1; 212.
— — — II, 85.
— — of Gujarāt, 8; 29 n. 5.
— —'s Gun, 82.
— —, son of Muḥammad Shāh III, 10.
Māhūr, 6; 129.
Mailūr, 203.
main entrance, 93.
Majdhūb, 190.
majestic dome, 184.
Majlis-i-Mukarram, 47 n. 2.
Majnūn and Laila, 123.
Makhdūma-i-Jahān, 135.
Makhdūm-i-Jahāniyān, Jahān-Gasht, 102 n. 1.
Makhdūm Qādirī, Khānqāh of, 112.
Makkī Darwāza, 84.
Mālavikāgnimitra, 3 n. 1.
Malik Aḥmad Baiḥrī, 11.
— Marjān, 14–15; 27; 30; 49; 74 n. 1; 170–1.
Malkāpūr tank, 183; 212.
Mallū Khān, 8.
Mālwā, 6; 8–9.
mandap, 189.

maṇḍapa, 21.
Maṇḍū Darwāza, 31; 35; 56 & n. 3; 81; 85.
Mangal (Tuesday), 88.
Mangalpeṭ Darwāza, 83; 87–9; 89 n. 1; 109; 110 & n. 1; 177; 181 & n. 1.
mango-trees, 148–9; 160–2; 167–8; 174 n. 2; 125; 204.
mango- and tamarind-trees, 160.
Manhiyār Ta'līm (Bangle-Seller's School), 20 n. 2; 102–3.
manholes, 205.
Mānjra river, battle at, 18; 183.
Marāṭhā army, 18.
— country, 89; 152.
Marāṭhās, 12.
Marāṭhī inscription, 140; 203.
marble decoration, 108.
marginal mouldings, 163.
margins, black stone, 53; 112.
—, masonry, 103.
—, stone, 61; 199.
Marrakesh, 91.
Marshall, Sir John, vii; 23 n. 1; 24; 95.
Masjid-i-Jāmi', 54; 130.
masonry, 40.
— blocks, 173.
—, carved, 59.
—, clumsy, 56.
— of gateways, 62.
massive arch, 136.
— arches and walls, 67–8.
— block, 82.
— building, 37–8.
— masonry, 188.
— structure, 184.
— style of building, 40; 173.
— walls, 155.
matchlocks, muskets, 81.
maulsarī trees, 184.
mausolea, 28.
mausoleum, 187.
— of Jahān Barīd, 110 n. 4.
— of Maḥmūd Shāh, 137.
Māzandarānī, Sharaf-ud-Dīn, 66 n. 1.
measurements of court, 38 n. 1.
Mecca Gate, 84.
medallions, 101; 135; 141; 143; 148; 187; 201; 209.
medieval Deccanī temples, 47, 59.
— Hindu shrines, star-shaped, 25.
— — temples, 72; 100; 201; 212.
— Muslim architecture, 114.
meditation cell, 81.
melā at sacred spring, 177.
melia azedirachta, 173.
Meshhed, 92.
metaphysicians, 124.
middle and side arches, 62.
— hall, 56.
miḥrāb, 26; 56; 97; 103; 119 n. 3; 130; 134; 136; 139; 155; 197; 213.
military prowess, 20.
Mimusops elengi, 184.
Min-Allāh Shāh, 113 n. 1.
minarets, 26; 93–5; 159; 196; 202.
miniature column, 101.
— towers, 26.
ministers' halls and rooms of audience, 65.
Minnat-Ullāh Bī Ṣāḥiba, Khānqāh of, 113.
Mint (Taksāl), 100.
Mīr 'Ālam, 84 n. 1.
— Asad 'Alī Khān, 19.
— Jumla, 14.
— Kalān Khān 17 & n. 2; 190.
— — II, 18.
— Khalīl-Ullāh, 15; 198.
— Lillāhi, 19.
— Niẓām 'Alī Khān, 17.
— — — — Āṣaf Jāh, 185.
— Nūr-Ullāh, 208 n. 1.
— Shams-ud-Dīn Mukhtār Khān, 15.
Mirzā Ibrāhīm Zubairī, 87 n. 3.
— Ḥusain Beg, 19.
Mirzāpur, 148.
Mirzā Walī Amīr Barīd, 140.
missiles, 79.
'Mistress of the World', 135.
Miṭṭhū Khān, 191.
Mīyān Miṭṭhu, 191 n. 1.
— Yādgār, 106 n. 2.
moat, 29–31; 37; 41; 61; 167.
—, gateway to, 44.
molasses-pan, 205.
monastery, 110.
— of Abū-'l-Faiḍ, 184.
— of Maḥbūb Subḥānī, 111.
— of Shāh 'Alī Ḥusain, 110–11.
monkeys at fort, 35.
monotony, 68.
monsoon rains, 41; 80; 208.
monuments of historical, religious, and architectural significance, 28.
'moon-faced queen', 164.
moonlit nights, 49.
Moorish–Spanish buildings, 152.
mortar, use of, 21.
mosaic design, 64.
mosaic-tiles, 48, 76.
mosque, 165.
Mosque at Gornallī, 193.
— at Ḥabshī Koṭ, 182.
mosque, in palace, 74.
Mosque of Shāh 'Alī, 203 n. 1.
—, The, 138–9.
mosque with arched openings, 84 n. 1.
'Most Exalted Name', 123.
mother-of-pearl, 25; 44; 47–8.
mouldings, 24; 163.
— and niches, 154; 161.
—, black stone, 46.
— for tiles, 23.
— in plaster, 165.
— in stucco, 159.
Mubārak Khaljī, 91.

Mubāriz Khān, 17.
Mudgal, 57 n. 1.
Mughal arches, 163; — architecture, 113; — cusped arches, 46; — Empire, 16; 27; — forts, 73; — governors, 83; 191; 199; — inscriptions, 102 n. 1; — kings, 147; — kingdom, 30; — *mīnārs*, 94; — pointed arches, 131; — period, 199; — style, 27; — tombs, 26.
Mughīth al-Qārī ash-Shīrāzī, 143 & n. 2.
Muḥammadābād (Bidar), 29 n. 4; 206 n. 1.
Muḥammad 'Ādil Shāh, 57 n. 1.
— al-Qādirī, 107.
— bin Tughluq, 3 n. 4; 4; 22.
— Ḥanīf, 208; 210.
— ibn Aḥmad Shāh al-Walī al-Baihmanī, 15 n. 3.
— Khān, 129.
— Mu'azzam, 14.
— Qāsim's guns, 41.
— Qulī Quṭb Shāh, 60 n. 1.
— Ṣāliḥ Kambo, 15 n. 2; 30 & n. 5; 54.
— Shāh, 10; 146 n. 3.
— — II, 5; 134–5.
— — III, 9; 73; 184.
— — Baihmanī, 29–30.
— — — I, 22.
— — — III, 12.
— Sulṭān, 82 n. 4.
Muḥarram festival, 20 n. 2; 85; 102 n. 1; 197 n. 1.
Muḥibb-Ullāh, 141; 144; 212.
Muḥī'ud-Dīn Gīlānī Qādirī, 107 n. 3; 189.
Mu'izz-i-Fādil, 49 n. 2.
Mukhtār Khān, 16; 87 n. 1; 177.
— — al-Ḥusainī 84 n. 2; as-Sabzwārī, 30; 31 & n. 3; 89 n. 2.
Mukkā Bī, 107 n. 3.
Multānī Pādshāh, 107; 109 n. 2; 112 & n. 4; 190; 203; — — shrine, 17 n. 2; 18 n. 1.
Muṇḍā Burj, 82; 84–5.
Muntakhabu'l-Lubāb, 54 n. 2.
Muqtada Khān, 17.
muram paths, 184.
murders, 136.
Murtaḍa Khān, 18.
— Niẓām Shāh, 13; 74 n. 1; 82.
Mushir-ul-Mulk, 19.
music at the fort, 34.
Music Gallery, 33; 154.
musicians' hall, 78; 145.
Muslim architecture, styles in, 24; 212.
— buildings, 63.
— craftsmanship, 71.
— designs, 46.
Muslims in the Deccan, 177.
mysterious sepulchral halls, 155.
mystic effect, 97.

N

Nād-i-'Alī, 143.
Nadīm-Ullāh Shāh, 190.
Nagina Maḥall, 57.
Nā'ī kā Maqbara, 166.
Nala and Damayanti, 3.
nandī, 180.
Naqqār Khāna, 33; 154.
Narasiṁha, 169.
narrow arcades and hall, 80.
— passage, 179.
Nāṣir-ud-Daula, 84 & n. 1; 88 & n. 2; 102 n. 1.
— Āṣaf Jāh IV, 83.
Naṣīr-ud-Daula, Bahādur Nawāb, 2.
Nāṣir-ud-Dīn, Ismā'īl, 4.
Naṣīr-ud-Dīn, Raushan Chirāgh, 211.
Naṣīr Khān, 147.
— —, Fāruqī of Asīr, 6.
naskhī characters in handwriting, 188; 198 n. 1.
— and *nasta'līq*, 111.
nasta'līq, 84 n. 2; 107 n. 3; 171 n. 2; 177.
national pride, 20.
natural terraces, 177. *See* terraces.
Naubād, 1 n. 3; 205.
Naubat Khāna, 78, 83.
nauras, 87 & n. 3.
Nauras Darwāza (Fatḥ Darwāza), 87.
Nawāb Āṣaf Jāh, 17.
— Naẓar Bahādur Khān, 19 n. 1.
— of Hyderabad, H.E.H., 20–1.
'Nayres', 29 n. 5.
Near East, 166 n. 1.
neglected ruins, 169.
neglect of buildings, 56.
network of arches, 163.
niches, 56; 101; 117; 159; 161; 200.
—, arched, 90; 191.
—, as cupboards, 153.
—, decorative, 65.
— for statues of gods, 72.
nīm trees, 173; 192.
Ni'matābād (palace at), 5; 7; 146 n. 4. &c.
Ni'mat-Ullāh Walī, 119; 127–8; 146.
— Kirmānī, 115 & n. 1; 116; 118 n. 3; 141; 208 n. 1; 212.
nine domes, 68.
— graves, 143.
ninety-five bays, 55.
'ninety-nine names, the', 148.
Niẓām 'Alī Khān, Nawāb, 18–19; 186.
Niẓāmī, 13 n. 4.
Nizam of Hyderabad, H.E.H., vi.
Niẓām Shāh, 8–9; 134–6.
— — Baihmanī, 29; 109.
— —, tomb of, 9 n. 2.
— Shāhī Dynasty, 11.
Niẓām-ud-Dīn, 173–5.
— Auliya, 211.
Niẓām-ul-Mulk Āṣaf Jāh, 17.
— Baiḥrī, 11.
non-embodiment, 122.
North Africa, 166 n. 1.
Northern India, 59; 68; 163.
northern steps, 77.
— wall, 62.
North Indian buildings, 57.
north-south-east-west doors, 152.
note to H.H. Govnt., v.

not-God and God, 122.
nullahs, 40.
Nūr Khān kī Ta'līm, 20 n. 2.
— Muḥammad Khān, 18–19.
Nūr-Ullāh, 115.
— Ḥusainī, 146–7.

O

'Obstinate Barīd's' tomb, 161 n. 1.
ocean and wave, 122.
octagon, 207; —, star-shaped, 71.
octagonal bases, 94; 99; 117; 136; 151; 159; 181; 184.
— bastions, 35; 90.
— cisterns, 65; 75.
— floor, 93.
— pillars, 160.
— rim, 137–8.
— rooms, 59; 70–1; 74; 76.
— shaft, 197.
— tombs, 142–4; 148.
— towers, 26.
Odeon, or Music Hall, 78.
offerings of Truth, 126 n. 2.
officers of the court, 65.
— of the garrison, 79.
offsets, 79.
ogee arch, 79.
Old Fort bastion, 31.
Oldham, C.E.A.W., vii.
Old Naubat Khāna, 78.
oomara ('umarā), 11.
open-air bath, 75.
open-arched tomb, 183.
open arches, 155; 191.
— court, 75; 153.
'opener of gates', 206 n. 1.
openings, arched, 57 n. 3; 81; 110.
opulence and power of Baihmanī kings, 64.
orb-crowned minarets, 117; 198.
— pillars, 163; 212.
orb, lotus-leaved, 101.
— of tomb, 161.
orbs and disks, 165.
— of gilded copper, 138.
— on turrets, 111.
ordnance, pieces of, 38.
origin of pearl, 122.
— of title 'Baihman', 147.
Orissa, Rāi of, 8–9.
ornament, stucco, 58.
ornamental arch, 164; — bands, 200; — border, 143; — cascade, 65; — parapet, 136; 153; 189; 191.
ornamentation, 65; 94; 145.
ornate turrets, 117.
Osmania University, v.
outer and inner staircases, 90 n. 2.
— court, 62.
outlined arches as ornamentation, 178.
oval form, 63; — panels, 118.
overgrown ruins, 166 n. 3; 169.
overlapping arches, 82; 138–9; 143; 145; 150–1; 153; 158–9; 161; 163; 167.
oxen, to draw water, 77.
Oxford University Press, vii.

P

painted ceilings, 129; 132; 175; 212.
— glass, 55.
— mausoleum, 136.
— names on ceiling, 116.
'painted palace', 13.
painter's name, 125.
paintings, 117; — on dome, 127 n. 1.
pairs of arches, 134.
Paithan, 3.
Pākhāl, 203.
palace, 61.
— and forecourt, 66–7.
—, plan of, 48.
Pālampeṭ, 133.
pancha-linga, 179.
panels, 95–6; — inscribed, 36.
— of guns, inscribed, 42 n. 2.
— of tile-work, 63.
—, ornamental, 85.
Paniya Khandaq, 31 n. 1; 80.
Panjatan, 119.
panorama of country, 143.
—, picturesque, 62.
pantheon, Hindu, 207.
panthers, 70 n. 1.
Pāpnās, 1; — groves, 204; — spring, 207–8.
parade of royal guards, 74.
parallel streets, 90.
parapet, 52; 55; 88–9; 91; 99–100; 110; 135; 138; 171–2; 196; 203; 209; 212–13.
— on walls, 148.
— ruined, 145.
— with coloured tiles, 32.
— with trefoil-pattern design, 101 n. 1; 117; 193.
paraphernalia, royal, 76.
parking of carts, 84 n. 1.
parkoṭa, 37–8; 41.
parrot, 191 n. 1.
Parvatī, 207.
partridges, 1.
Pasand Khān, 11–12.
passage, 85; 89.
— between forts, 41; — from tomb, 162; — hewn through rock, 37; —, covered, 79; — with arches, 67.
paṭa, 102.
Patancheru inscription, 128 n. 1.
path of the Unknown, 126.
paved court, 70; 113; 198–9.
— walk, 107; 209.
pavements, 61; 93.
pavilion, 209–10; —, arcaded, 105; —s of palace, 23; —s, royal, 47–8; 69.
pedestals in pavilion, 76.
—, stone, 63 & n. 3; 196.

'pendant and chain' design, 168. *See also* 'chain and pendant'.
pendentives, 117.
pentagonal pendant, 155.
— projections, 138.
Penth (पन्थ), 88.
percolation of rain-water, 212.
perpendicular fall, 90.
Persia, 6; 91.
Persian architects, 23; 46; 72; 126; 212.
— and Turkish architects, 29.
— artisans, 73.
— couplets (بيت), 111 n. 2.
— craftsmen, 64.
— dames, 59.
— emblems, 70.
— engineers, 205.
— influence (in military architecture), 34.
— inscription, 89 n. 2. *See* inscriptions, tablets, &c.
— inspiration, 24.
— merchants in Deccan, 73.
— record, 177.
— style couch, 102.
— verses, 188; 194.
peshgāh, 68; 74.
petitions, 65; — hung on tomb walls, 208.
Peṭlā Burj, 41–2.
Physical Training School, 110.
physicians, Hindu and Muslim, 7.
picturesque gateway, 89.
picturesqueness, 52.
picturesque view, 177; — — from train, 184.
piers and walls, 68.
—, masonry, 60; 77.
—, massive, 93.
pilgrims to shrine, 179. *See* shrine, bathing &c.
pillar and lintel, 101.
pillared halls and porches, 21.
pillar pedestals, 74.
pillars, 91; —, carved, 37; from elsewhere, 102; — in rows, 63; —, masonry, 110.
pipe-line, 39.
places of worship, 176.
plain bands, 152.
— surfaces, 55.
plan of cistern, 53.
— of Jamāl-ud-Dīn's tomb, 175.
— of Royal Pavilion, 75.
— of subterranean rooms, 77.
plaster decoration, Hindu, 27.
plastered surface, 163.
— walls, 132.
plaster ribs, 137; 168.
— sarcophagi, 164.
plaster-work, 59–60; 78; 114; 163; 191; 200; 213.
— decorations, 100; 153.
— of vaults, 33; 35.
—, ornamental, 101.
Plate XVII, 104; — LVIII, 103; — LX, 104.
plateau, 39; 71; 83; 182; — of Bidar, 30.
platform, 50–1; 53; 100; 108; 211.
platform above reservoir, 154.
— of tombs, 154; 174; 191; 195; 207.
plinth, 93; 96; 105; 108; 149; 203; 211.
—, high, 164.
— of block, 82.
— of hall, 107.
— of platform, 151; 158; 160; 174.
— of steps, 74.
— of tomb, 171.
poems by Quṭb Shāhī kings, 60 n. 1.
— of Niẓāmī, 13 n. 4.
poet and sulṭān, 66 n. 1.
police sawār stables, 104.
— station, 91.
polished black stone, 65–6; 109; 155; 186.
— stone, 131.
— — steps, 149.
polish of stone, 22; 63; 74.
political causes of deterioration, 26.
polo, inscription referring to, 162.
— posts [?], 162.
Polybius, 23 n. 1.
polygonal buildings, 209.
ponies and cattle, 177.
Poona, 19.
porcelain, Chinese, 73.
porch, 76; 99; —, rectangular, 70.
portico, 93; 143.
Portuguese, 29 n. 5.
post-and-lintel style, 21.
post-Baihmanī tombs, 136.
powder and shot, 36; 39.
— magazine, 92 n. 6.
prayer-hall, 22; 55; 103–4; 110–111; 145; 159; 165; 167–9; 176; 178; 195; 197–9; 201; 203; 209.
prayer-niche, 97.
prayer-room, 107 n. 2; 182.
pre-Islāmic forts, 82.
— tower, 90.
pre-Mughal tombs, 211.
prickly shrubs, 169.
principal teacher, 98.
privacy provided, 69.
privy, 75; 78.
professors of college, 192.
professors' rooms, 99.
projection, northern, 64.
projections, 93; —, masonry, 93; —, rectangular, 97 n. 2.
props, carved, 71.
pseudo-dervishes, 190.
pseudo-owners of land, 149.
Public Works Dept., v.
pūjā, 189.
pūjāris of temple, 178; 180.
pulpit (*minbar*) 166 n. 1.
pump, electric, 52.
Punishment Houses, 103.
Punjab Museum Coin Catalogue, 15 n. 4.
puppet kings, 137.
Purāna Qil'a, 37–8; 40–1; 70 n. 1; 80.

Purāna Qil'a bastion, 85.
pyramidal tomb, 164.

Q

Qādirīya, 119.
Qāḍī Shams-ud-Dīn, 206.
Qāḍīs of Islām, 206 n. 1.
Qalandar Khān, 15–16; 54 n. 3.
— Khān's tomb, 16 n. 3.
Qamr-ud-Dīn, 177 n. 4.
Qandhār, 11, 13, 25.
qaṣba, 3.
Qāsim Barīd, 11; 12; 13 n. 2; 25; 149.
— — II, 14; 42 & n. 2; 85 & nn. 1–2; 162–5.
— — II's tomb, 183.
Qassaboñ-kī-Masjid, 63 n. 3.
qawwālī, 816.
qiblah, 26; 92 n. 2; 125.
Qubād Khān, 16.
Qublī Sulṭānī, 54.
queen-mother, 9.
quintessence of entity, 122; 124.
Qur'ān, 95; 148.
Qur'ān vii. 47, 125; — xvi. 92, 206 n. 1; — xxx. 14, 125.
Qur'ān, chapters of, quoted, 85 n. 1; —, in Kūfic, 110; —, quotation, 114; —, recitals, 186, 193; —, reciters, 138 n. 1.
Qur'ānic quotation, 143 n. 2; — —, by Ādharī, 66 n. 1.
— texts, 33 n. 1; 38; 39 n. 1; 137 n. 2; — — on bands, 158 & n. 1.
— verses, 92 n. 2; 213.
Quṭb road, 56 n. 2.
— Muḥammad Multānī, 107 n. 3.
— Shāhī, 153.
Qutlugh Khān, 4.

R

Rabat, 91.
Rafī', Persian architect, 22.
Raghoba, 18.
Raichur, 129.
railing of plaster-work, 155.
rail-pattern, 158.
railway engineers, 184.
—, Hyderabad-Bidar, 20.
— track, 171.
rain-water erosion, 192.
— percolation, 196.
— tunnel, 80.
Rajab, 147 n. 2.
Rāja Chandra Sen, 17.
Rājamundrī, 8–9.
Rāma, 2; — and Rāvaṇa, 190.
Ramaḍān, 42 & n. 2; 125; 189.
Rāmappa temple, 133 n. 4; 203.
Rāmgaṛh, 6; 129.
ramparts, line of, 34 & n. 3; 41; 45; 51.
Rangīn Maḥall, vi; 13; 14 n. 1; 25; 44–49; 91.
— Masjid, 201.
Raṇ Khamb, 162.
Rāvaṇa, 2; 190.
Raymond, Monsieur, 19; 41.
receding arches, 97.
— bands, 189; 201.
— facets, 166; 213.
recessed façades, 101.
— windows, 47.
recital, reciters, reciting, of Qur'ān, 107 n. 3; 138; 159; 166; 181.
Records Office, 58.
rectangular apartments, 77.
— door, 207.
— entrance room, 33.
— halls, 69; 71.
— openings, 37; 134.
— panels, 156.
— plan, 74; 201.
— porch, 70.
— tank, 52.
— windows, 96.
red and gold designs, 71.
Red Bastion, 42.
red flowers, 62.
Regency, Council of, 8–9.
relics, room for, 102.
religious atmosphere, 158.
— buildings, Muslim, 26.
— ceremonies, 172.
— conventionalities, 155; 158.
— expressions, 26.
— learning, 109.
— practices, 192.
— shrines, 80.
— texts in tile-work, 156.
remains of buildings, 80.
remodelling of fortifications, 29.
repair of old fort, 29.
reservoir, 53; 56; 77; 78; 205.
retaining walls, 211.
retinues of nobles, 74.
Revenue authorities, 128 n. 2.
— Department, 66.
— Member, 91.
revolt in capital, 144.
rhomboid-shaped fort, 30.
Rieu, *Catalogue*, 115 n. 1.
ribbed partitions, 153.
ribs of brick, 173.
rich decoration, 57; 64; 190.
Riḍā 'Alī Khān, 185.
ritual at tomb, 128.
Riyāḍ-ul-Inshā, 10; 195.
Roads Committee, 114 n. 1.
roads emerging from Bidar, 176.
Robāh-i-Deccan, 13 n. 1.
rockets and shells, 73 n. 1; 82.
rock-hewn moat, 34 n. 3.
— shrines, 145.
rock- or wood-architecture, 21.
rock-partitions, 30.
rock-wall, 43.
rock tunnel, 80.
rocky soil, 205.

roof-corner turrets, 175.
roof level, 213.
— of fort, 43.
— of hall, 57.
rope motif, 142.
rope-pattern, 46; 131.
— — carving, 150.
rosaries of *rudraksha* beads, 80 n. 2.
rose blossoming in garden, 157.
rosettes in bands, 158; 163.
rough-tooled masonry, 150; 160; 164; 170 n. 2.
— — trap, 100.
rows of arches, 103.
— of columns, 55.
royal apartments blown up, 74 n. 1.
Royal Bath, 64; 73.
royal 'courier', 14 n. 1.
— factory, 36 n. 1.
— family apartments, 70.
— hall, 72.
— tower, 44.
— treasury, 172.
rubbish dumps, 93.
— heaps, 63.
Ruby Gardens, 52–3.
rudrakhsa bead pattern, 80; 100.
Rukn-ud-Dīn Khān, 18 n. 3.
running water, 74.
russet, buff and grey, 117.
Rustam Dil Khān, 16; 202.

S

Sābājī, 12.
Sabbal Barīd kā Gumbad, 161.
Sabzwārī, as-, 84 n. 2.
sacbuts, 29 n. 5.
Sād and Nūn, 85–6 n. 1.
Sadāśiva Reddi, 18–19.
Sadr-i-Jahān, 9.
Ṣadr Ta'alluqdār, 19.
Sa'd-ud-Dīn an-Nu'mānī, 206 n. 1.
safety exits, 23.
Ṣāḥib Khān, 13.
saintly personages, 208.
saints, popular, 107.
saint's sepulchre, 201.
Śaivite devotees, 80 n. 2.
— emblem, 80.
— worship, 180.
Sajjādas, 106; 109–10; 212.
Sajjāda Ṣāḥib, the, 181; 186.
Saif Jang Najm-ud-Daula, 18.
— Khān Kotwālbek, 33.
Ṣalābat Jang, Nawāb, 17–18.
salts in earth, 63.
sam'a-khāna, 186.
samādh, 179; 189.
samādhī, 80.
Samarqand, 92.
Samarra, Great Mosque, 90.
Samnān, 192.
Samūgaṛh, battle of, 15 n. 5.
sanad of Aurangzeb, 189.
sanads, 109.
Sangat Maḥall, 133 n. 3.
Sanskrit words, 60 n. 1.
Sarā'ī of Mīr 'Ālam, 84 n. 1.
sarcophagus (sarcophagi), 132; 149 n. 2; 151; 155; 168; 173.
Sardār-ul-Mulk Ghānsī Mīyān, 19.
sāt gazī gun, 18.
Sāvah (Sāwa), Sāwajī, 146 n. 2.
sawārs, 104.
Sayyid 'Alī Ṭabaṭaba, 66 & n. 1; 67; 71.
— Ḥabīb, 144 n. 1.
— Ḥanīf, 1 n. 4.
— Khalīl-Ullāh, 19.
— Mīrān, 102 n. 1.
— Mirzā Mashhadī, 210 n. 1.
— Muḥammad, 114.
— Murtaḍa, 102 n. 1.
— -us-Sādāt, 1& n. 3; 204; 210 n. 1.
— Walī, 107 n. 3.
— Yaḥyā, 208.
Sazāwār Khān, 17 & n. 1.
scalloped arches, 46.
scarp, 31, 83, 207–8.
— of Daulatābād fort, 23.
'scented body', 206 n. 1.
school built by Maḥmūd Gāwān, 10.
schools for physical training, 20 n. 2.
scientists and philosophers, 92.
scions of royal family, 172.
screens, arched, 181.
— of trellis-work, 144.
sea route from China, 73.
secret passages, 77.
— truth, 123.
semicircular dome, 170.
semi-decagonal projections, 98–9; 143.
separate vaults, 143.
sepulchral chamber, 107 n. 3; 108; 151; 169; 190–1.
— hall, 134; 136; 138; 140; 198; 200; 209; 212.
— room, 207.
seraglio, royal, 51.
seven-step flight, 163.
XVIIth century, 202.
seven vaults, 81.
shade of mango-grove, 175.
shadow of reality, 122.
Shāh 'Abd-ur-Razzāq, 18 n. 3.
— Abū-'l-Faiḍ, 184.
— 'Ālamgir, 54 n. 3.
— 'Alī, 188–9; 198; 203.
— — Qādirī, 202 n. 1.
Shāhbād stone, 199 n. 2.
Shāh Burj, 12; 44.
— Ganj, 17 n. 3.
— — Darwāza, 83–4; 87 & n. 1; 90; 104.
— — grain market, 84.
Shāhī Ḥammām, 51–2.
— Maṭbakh, 49–51; 58.
Shāh Isḥāq, 108.

Shāh Jahān, 14–15; 30; 54; 57.
— Khalīl-Ullāh, tomb of, 7.
— Kunj Nishīn, 181.
'Shah Mohib Oolla', 11.
Shāh Muḥibb-Ullāh, 141; 144 & n. 1.
— Ni'mat-Ullāh Kirmānī, 141.
— Nishīn, 46; 48.
Shāh-nishīn, 110.
Shāh Nishīn, 'royal chamber', 25.
— Nūr, 192.
— Rājū, 148.
Shāhur year, 141.
Shaikh, 106.
— Badr-ud-Dīn, 199.
— Bāwī, 107 n. 3.
— Muḥammad Ḥusain, 195.
— Nūr Samnānī, 192.
shajrās, 115 n. 2; 116.
Shakar Khelda, 17.
Shams-ud-Dīn, 5; 88 n. 1.
— Mukhtār Khān, 15.
Shankar Rāi, 7.
Sharf-ud-Dīn Māzandarānī, 66 n. 1.
Sharbat Bāgh, 192–3.
Sharza Darwāza, 12; 32; 34.
shells, artillery, 73 n. 1.
—, manufacture of, 29 n. 5.
Sher Shāh, 29 n. 5.
Shī'a tendencies, 115.
Shihāb-ud-Dīn, 4.
—, Khwāja 'Alī Yazdī, 12.
Shī'ite creed, 115.
— *durūd*, 119.
— faith, 102 n. 1.
— Imāms, 116.
Shīrāzī calligrapher, 143.
shot and powder, 36; 39.
shrines, 80.
— in garden, 180.
Shrines of Ḥ. Sh. 'Alī and Ḥ. Sh. Abū-'l-Ḥasan, 187.
Shukr-Ullāh of Qazwīn, 125–6.
Ṣiddīq Shāh, 105.
— — kī Ta'līm, 20 n. 2.
side-walls, 96.
Sīdī Marjān, 83; 110 n. 4.
siege, 61; — defences, 34.
sifting the earth, 157.
sikhara (spire), 80.
silhouette, architectural, 95.
silted-up tank, 176.
silver chairs, 11; 144 n. 1.
— devices on inlaid ware, 20 n. 1.
single-hall mosque, 191.
Sirka, Konkan chief, 7.
Sītā, 2.
situation of Bidar town, 1.
six compartments, 188.
sixteen-sided building, 187.
— figure, 201.
— plan, 139.
sixty stages, 29.
Śiva, 116 n. 1; 207.
Siyādat Khān, 18.
sketch plan of Ḥabshī Koṭ, 182.
skilled technique, 158.
skin diseases, 210.
slab, carved, 53.
slabs, marginal, 97.
slender apices, 94.
slim proportions, 68.
sluices, 203; 208.
Small Monastery of Maḥbūb Subḥānī, 111–12.
small squares in plaster, 145.
smoke covering paintings, 185.
smooth glazed tiles, 73.
smoothly dressed masonry, 174.
snakes, intertwined, 179; 207.
social purposes, 52.
Solah Khamb mosque, 16; 54; 57; 60 & n. 3.
solidarity of architecture, 58.
solids and voids, 95.
Solomon, 140 n. 2.
sombre architecture, 152.
source of stream, 123.
southern and northern parts of court, 63.
— apartments, 51.
— side of court, 60.
— wing, 61.
— — of court, 50.
— — of palace, 59.
south gate of tomb, 167.
— rooms, 79.
Spain and North Africa, 164.
spandrels, 46; 68; 70; 96; 107; 116; 118; 156; 161; 163; 201.
— of arches, 143.
— with medallions, 154; 168.
Spanish Moors, 152.
Span of arch, 34 n. 2; 57 n. 4; 69; 80; 89; 162 n. 1; 183.
— of 18 ft., 136.
spikes, iron, 85.
spiral curvings, 163.
— design, 168; 185.
— motif, 166.
spire of temple, 189.
splashing waters, 78.
splendour of roof, 62.
spring below cliff, 192 n. 2.
springing-point of dome, 99; 103; 136; 154; 163; 168.
spring, natural, 205.
springs and watercourses, 1.
— now choked up, 160.
spur of plateau, 80.
square base, 132; 145; 191.
— chamber, 149.
— cistern, 169.
— panels, 150.
— plan, 148; 175; 207; 209.
— — of platform, 162.
— — of tomb, 138–40.
— platform, 199.

square rooms, 57; 61; 65; 77.
squinches, 45; 50; 55; 97; 117; 129; 135; 137; 140; 145; 148; 151; 161; 163; 165; 168; 184; 187; 191; 201; 209; 213.
stables, police, 104.
stages and steps, 85.
—, justification built in, 40.
—, upper and lower, 38.
staircase, 61; 76; 81; 160 n. 1.
— into well, 183.
— of 15 steps, 153.
—, rock-hewn, 40.
stalactites, 163.
stars, band of, 163.
star-shaped interiors, 50.
— octagon, 71.
— panels, 152.
— patterns, 160.
— plan, 25.
— squares, 96.
— temples, 21.
steel and iron weapons, 73 n. 1.
steps, 38 n. 2; 40.
—, flight of, 74; 103; 145.
— in passage, 41.
— inside walls, 143; 151.
— in thickness of wall, 134.
— of Samarra tower, 90 n. 2.
— up to passage, 84.
S-shaped court, 37.
stilt, 213.
— of arch, 79; 133.
— of dome, 150; 155; 163.
— showing Persian influences, 67–8.
— to apex, 138.
stone and mortar building, 28.
Stone, Henry, and Son, vii.
stone margins, 190.
— sarcophagi, 139–40; 151.
storage, 81; — of arms, 40.
store-rooms, 98; 173.
stores for goods, 105.
struts, 46; — of dome-wall, 55.
stucco decoration, 185.
— -work, 51; 57; 116; 130; 153; 188; 190.
subdued lighting, 97.
Subḥān Qulī, 128 n. 1.
subterranean canals of Naubād and Bidar, 205–6.
— channel, 97 n. 1.
— passage, 77–8.
Suburban Monuments, 176–213.
Ṣufic doctrine, 119; 127.
Ṣūfī terminology, 190.
Ṣūfiya School, Mosque Arch, 109 n. 2.
sugar cane, — — field, 204–5.
'sugar of gratitude', 123.
Śukla Tīrath, 1 n. 3.
sulphur springs, 210.
Sulṭān Fīroz Shāh, 148.
Sulṭān Maḥmūd Shāh, 144.
— Muḥammad Shāh, 144.
Sulṭāns of Delhi, 166; 209; 211.
sun and moon, 126.
svastika, 64.
Swāmīkannu Piḷḷai, 85–6 n. 2.
sweeper of the porch, 126.
swimming-bath, 72; 74–5.
swings, 211.
Syed Husain Bilgrami, 116 n. 1.
Sykes, P. M., '*A Fifth Journey*', 92 n. 3.
symbols on tombs, 201.
syncretism of Hindu & Muslim art, 27 *et passim*.
Syrinx in Hyrcania, 23 n. 1.

T

Ta'alluqdār, 19.
— of Bidar, 102 n. 1.
Ta'alluqdār's Court, 47; 58.
Ṭabaṭaba, Sayyid 'Alī, 5 n. 6; 66 & n. 1.
table-land, 41; 89.
table of succession, 115 n. 3; 119 n. 1.
'tablet' design, 151.
—, inscribed, 84 n. 2; 87 n. 1; 88 n. 1; 111 n. 2; 187; 210.
Tahdīd Khāna, 103.
Tahsīl Office, 59.
takhtī, 164; 200.
Takht-i-Fīroza, 10 n. 5; 64.
Takht-i-Kirmānī, 100–2 & 102 n. 1.
Takht Maḥall, vi; 6 n. 1; 28; 40; 42; 44; 65; 69; 91; 126; 153.
— —, site of, 28.
takīya, 190.
Talghāṭ Darwāza, 16; 83.
Talikota, battle at, 13–14.
ta'līm khānas, 103.
Ta'līm of Nūr Khān, 110.
— Pansāl, 104.
— Ṣiddīq Shāh, 105–6.
talisman texts, 127.
tamarind trees, 174; 189; 205.
tankah and *tumān* of Deccan, 66 n. 1.
tank at Kamthāna, 203; — at N.W. of fort, 80; — in old fort, 28.
tanks, 176; 203; 208.
tapering dome, 149.
— form, 94.
'Tārā Mīyān', 18.
Ta'rīkh-i-Fīroz Shāhī, 4 n. 1.
Tarkash Maḥall, 57–9; 60.
Tarn, W. W., 23 n. 1.
Tasker, Sir Theodore, vi; 66; 91.
Tasker's Walk, 44.
tawa, 181.
tawdry effect, 145.
Telingāna, 3; 5; 8; 10; 129; — country, 17.
temple, near bastion, 80.
—, on hill slope, 207 n. 2.
temples in Deccan, 21.
—, medieval, 59.
temporary tomb, 151.
terrace, 62; 81; 91.
terra-cotta jālīs, 65.
thickness of domes, 34.

thickness of masonry, 58.
thirty-six suites, 98.
thorns, iron, star-shaped, 73 n. 1.
Thousand Cells, 77–8.
three-apartment hall, 77.
three-compartmental building, 178.
three-grave tomb, 183.
three-storey building, 98.
— tower, 94.
threshold, 101 n. 2.
Throne Room, 69.
throne, royal, 67.
'throne verse' (*āyat-ul-kursī*), 36; 117; 128; 139.
thrust of dome, outwards, 55; 133.
Thulth script, 33; 95; 118; 127; 143; 158; 193; 206 n. 1; 210 n. 1.
tiger and rising sun, 70. *See* lion.
— effigies, 24; 101 & n. 3.
— in heraldry, 101 n. 3.
Tiger of God, 12 n. 3.
'tiger's gate', 12.
tile and stucco decoration, 161.
tiled panels, 24.
tile-work, 24; 172; 185; 200.
—, coloured, 45–7.
— in rampart rooms, 35 n. 1.
titles of 'Alā-ud-Dīn, 131 n. 1.
Todar Mal (Tondar Mal) Hazārī, 17.
toilet chamber, 45.
— requisites, 153.
Tomb and Mosque of Shāh 'Alī Qādirī, 202–3.
— at Naubād, 206.
Tombs:
'Abdullāh Maghribī, 167 & 168 n. 1.
Aḥmad Shāh al-Walī, 114–28.
— — al-Walī's son, 129–30.
'Alā-ud-Dīn, 105; 137.
— Shāh II, 130–2.
'Alī Barīd, 151–60.
Amīr Barīd, 150.
Badr-ud-Dīn Qādirī, 199–200.
Fakhr-ul-Mulk, 211.
Ghālib Khān, 191.
Ḥadrat Bībī Bandagī Ḥusainī, 169–70.
— Makhdūm Qādirī, 200.
— Multānī Pādshāh, 107–9.
— Niẓām-ud-Dīn, 172.
— Nūr Samnānī, 191–2.
— Sayyid Amīr Ḥamza Qādirī, 189.
— Sayyid-us-Sādāt, 208–11.
— Shāh Zain-ud-Dīn Kunj Nishīn, 174–5.
Ibrāhīm Barīd, 160–1.
Khān Jahān Barīd, 167–9.
Khāṣṣ Maḥall, 190–1.
Maḥmūd Gāwān, 192.
— Shāh Baihmanī, 136–7.
Malika-i-Jahān, 135–6.
Muḥammad Ḥusain Imām-ul-Mudarrisīn, 195.
Qāsim Barīd and that of his consort, 149 n. 2.
— — II, 162–5.
Shāh 'Alī, 197–9.
— Muḥibb-Ullāh, 212–13.
Shāh Rājū, 148.
— Rukh Khān, 139–40.
Shaikh Badr-ud-Dīn, 199–220.
Sulṭan Aḥmad Shāh's wife, 128–9.
— Humāyūn, 132–4.
— Kalīm-Ullāh, 138.
— Muḥammad Shāh II Lashkarī, 134–5.
— Niẓām Shāh, 134–5.
— Walī-Ullāh, 137.
'Tomb of the Barber', 166–7; 168 n. 1.
'Tomb of the Dog', 171–2.
Tomb of Walī-Ullāh, 110.
tombstones, 57 n. 2.
tombs under nīm tree, 146–8.
tonga, v.
top-heavy dome, 152; 158.
Top-i-be mithlī, 85–6.
Top-i-Ḥaidarī, 42.
Top-i-Ilāhī, 36 n. 1.
Top-i-Maḥmūd Shāhī, 82; 85–6 n. 1.
top in *Firishta*, 29.
torches held by pūjārīs, 179 n. 1.
tortuous passage, 85.
tower, royal, 44.
towers, 85; — slender, octagonal, 26.
town, enclosure, 90.
trabeate style, 70; 134.
tracery, 97; —, delicate, 100; — in niches, 132; — of windows, 55.
tracts on Ṣufī doctrine, 115.
Transactions VIIth All-India Oriental Confer., 12 n. 1.
transitoriness of this world (فاني), 156.
transport of stone, 31.
trap-dykes, 63 n. 1.
trapezoid form of well, 78.
trap masonry, 83; 154; 160; 182; 191.
trappean bed, 205.
trap slabs, 174.
— stone from Gulbarga district, 31.
'traverse line', 38–9.
treasures of divinity, 123.
trefoil arch-heads, 200–1.
— design or pattern, 59; 61; 110; 113; 141; 154; 193; 196 n. 1.
— parapet, 144; 163–4; 168; 170; 183; 199.
trellis-work, 34; 93–6; 117; 136; 171.
triangular corbels, 133.
triple channel of moat, 30.
triple moat, 23.
T-shaped gateway, 41.
Tudor arch, 67; 131.
— design, 59–60.
Tughluq architecture, 22.
— tombs, 166.
Tughra, 43; 118 & n. 2; 141.
—, device, 119.
— style, 101.
Tunis, 103.
tunnel, cut in rock, 37.
—, rain-water, 80.
Turkish architects, 29.

Turkish engineers, 23.
— ladies, 59.
— mercenaries build fortifications, 23.
— origin of Qāsim Barīd, 12.
Turks of Egypt & Arabia, 29 n. 5.
'turnip-shaped' domes, 25; 211.
turquoise, bluish-green, 158.
Turquoise Throne, 10 n. 5; 64; 144.
turrets, 105; 111; 174.
— at corners, 167; 191.
— with tile-work, 32.
twelve-sided figure, 191.
two-grave tomb, 164.
two mosques in grove of Zain-ud-Dīn, 175-6.
two-storied building, 145.

U

Udgīr, 205; 208.
—, fortress, 12; 13.
—, garden at, 16 n. 9.
— road, 162; 171.
Ulugh Beg's Madrasa, 92.
— Khān, 3; 28.
underground chambers, 81.
— room, plan of, 77.
uniform dimensions, 64; 77–8.
— plan, 97.
— plan of rooms, 77.
— surface monotony, 68.
Unity, Divine, 124.
— and Multiplicity, 122.
Unknown, part of, 126 n. 2.
unknown tomb with dome, 183.
'untouchables', 211.
upper apartments, 57 n. 2.
— floor, 191.
— storey, 62; 97; 153.
— — of Tarkash Maḥall, 60 n. 3.
'Ur, 164 n. 1.
urban populations, 20.
Urdū language, 60 n. 1.
'Urs, 116 & n. 2; 148; 184–5; 192.
Ustād Yār Muḥammad, 104.

V

vagaries, religious, 116.
Vakīl-us-Salṭanat, 8; 9 n. 3.
vandalism, 63; 173.
vantage-point, 71.
variety, love of, 67.
Vasco da Gama, 29 n. 5.
vase-motif design, 160; 170.
vault below floor, 183.
—, lantern-shaped, 48.
— of Divine Light, 157.
— of King's Room, 24.
'vault of nine apartments', 206 n. 1.
vaulted ceilings, 103–4; 107; 159; 162; 167; 169; 171; 173; 176; 178; 188; 191; 195; 197; 200–1; 209; 212.
— roof, 153.
— roof of gateway, 43.
vaulted rooms, 49; 51.
vaults, 33; 61.
vazīr, 84 n. 1.
vegetation, overgrown, 93.
veranda, 45; 51; 98.
verdure, luxurious, 177.
verge of plateau, 89.
vermilion and gold, 72, 117; 118.
vertical carvings, series of, 21.
vestibules, 72.
Vidarbha, 3.
view of city wall, 78.
views from walls, 192.
Vijayanagar, 6; 9; 13.
vine-creeper leaves, 64.
vines, canes, fruits, 2.
Vīragaṛh, 9 n. 4.
Vīrasanghayya, hero, 80.
Vīrasanghayya's temple, 28; 80–1.
Vishagaṛh, 9.
Vishṇu Narasiṁha, 101 n. 3.
vistas of lowlands, 71.
votaries, 103.
—, motley groups of, 177.
— of temple, 179.
voussoirs, 133.
vulnerability, 83.
vulnerable points. 85.

W

'walī', 115 & n. 2.
Walī-Ullāh Shāh, Baihmanī 12; 111; 137-8; 147 n. 2; 149–50; 169.
walk on walls, 143.
Walk, Tasker's, on glacis, vi & n. 1.
walls 11 ft. thick, 151.
waning of Bidar glory, 27.
Warangal, 3; 6; 21; 82 n. 3; 133 & n. 4; 203.
wardrobe (or toilet) chamber, 45.
washing clothes, 211.
Wāṣil Ganj, 17.
— Khān, Senr. and Junr., 17.
watchmen and drummers, 107.
water-channels, 50; 53; 56; 176; 187.
water cistern, 103.
water-flagons and jars, 73.
water from the rock, 176.
Water-miller's School, 104.
water of life, 122.
waterworks, 48.
weapons and armour, 73 n. 1.
weathering damage, 167.
weather-staining, 100.
well in forecourt, 97 n. 1.
— of mosque, 197.
wells, 105; 140; 160; 191.
—, deep, 77–8; 186.
—, old, 39; 53.
western arcades, 60.
Western Asiatic countries, 24.
— — mosques, 90.
western enclosure wall, 51.

western hall, 98 n. 1.
— side of court, 70.
white and gold letters, 118.
— ants (termites), 99.
Whitehead, *Cat. of Coins in Punjab Museum*, 15 n. 4.
white lettering, 158.
whitewash, 184–5.
wide span, 104.
wide-spanned arches, 153.
wife of Shāh Walī Ullāh, 171.
— of Sulṭān Humāyūn, 135.
wild beasts kept in moat, 61.
Wilmott, C., 116 n. 1.
windows of palace, 44.
— opening on moat, 93.
—, double, 95.
—, pierced in fort-walls, 33.
wing of hall, 65.
wings of building 84 n. 1; 93; 97.
wood-carving, 25; 44; 48.
wooden columns, 25; 196.
— doors, 47.
— —, iron-studded, 84.
— pillars, 63.
— shafts, 74.
women's graves, 199; 203.
wreaths and medallions, 159.

Y

Yadu'llāh, 39 n. 1.
Yādavas, 3.
Yād-Ullāh, 113 & n. 1.
Yāfiʻī, ʻAbd-Ullāh, 115 n. 5; 116.
Yakka Tāz Jang Bahādur, 19.
Yamīn-Ullāh, 186.
Yamīn-ur-Raḥmān, 186.
Yates, *Khurasan and Sistan*, 92 n. 3.
Yazdī, ʻAlī Shihāb-ud-Dīn, 12.
yellow, blue, and white tiles, 96; 130.
—, green, and blue tiles, 76; 187.
yellowish-white plaster, 194.
yogīs, 180.
yonī and linga, 80; 179; 207.
Yūsuf ʻAdil Khān, 11.

Z

Zachcha Bachcha, 56.
Ẓafarābād, 15 & n. 4; 177.
Ẓafar Khān, 4 & n. 5.
Ẓafar-ul-Mulk ʻAlawī, 182.
Ẓahīrābād, 1 n. 2.
Zain-ud-Dīn, 174.
Zain-ul-ʻĀbidīn Khān, 18 n. 3.
Zamān Khān, 113.
Zamorin, 29 n. 5.
Zanāna enclosure, 62.
— Maḥallāt, 51.
Zanānī Masjid, 54–6.
zeal of votaries, 80.
zenana, 110.
zig-zag passages, 37.
— plan, 87.
zilʻa-dārī system, 19.

THE FIRST GATEWAY OF THE FORT

II

THE TRIPLE MOAT

THE SHARZA DARWĀZA

THE SHARZA DARWĀZA AND PARAPET: VIEW FROM THE SOUTH-WEST

THE RAMPARTS OF THE FORT FACING THE SOUTH-EAST

V

VI

THE GUṂBAD DARWĀZA

VIEW OF THE INTERIOR OF THE FORT FROM THE GUṂBAD DARWĀZA

VIII

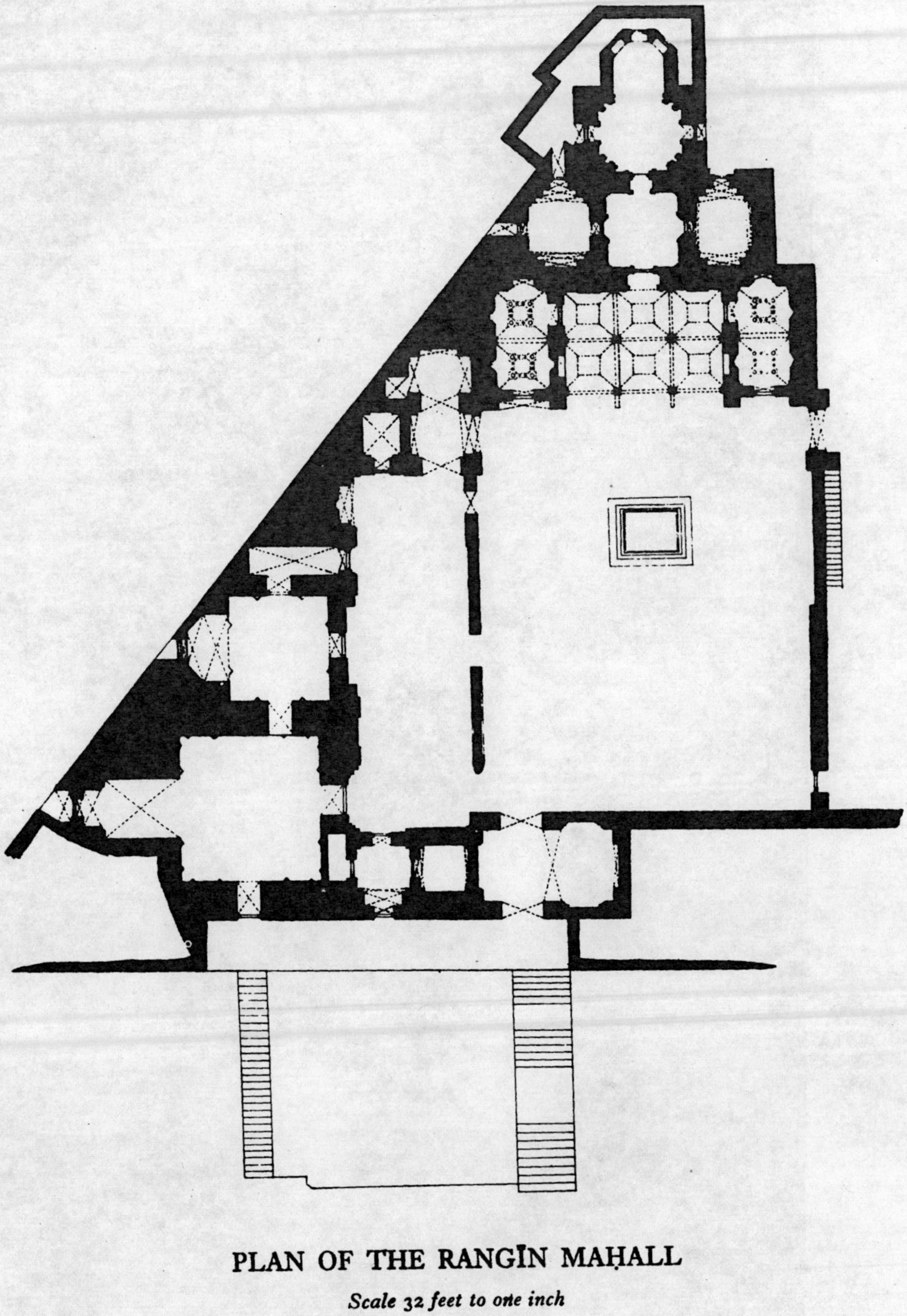

PLAN OF THE RANGĪN MAHALL

Scale 32 feet to one inch

TILE-WORK ON THE UPPER WALLS OF THE RANGĪN MAḤALL

COLUMNS OF WOOD: RANGĪN MAḤALL

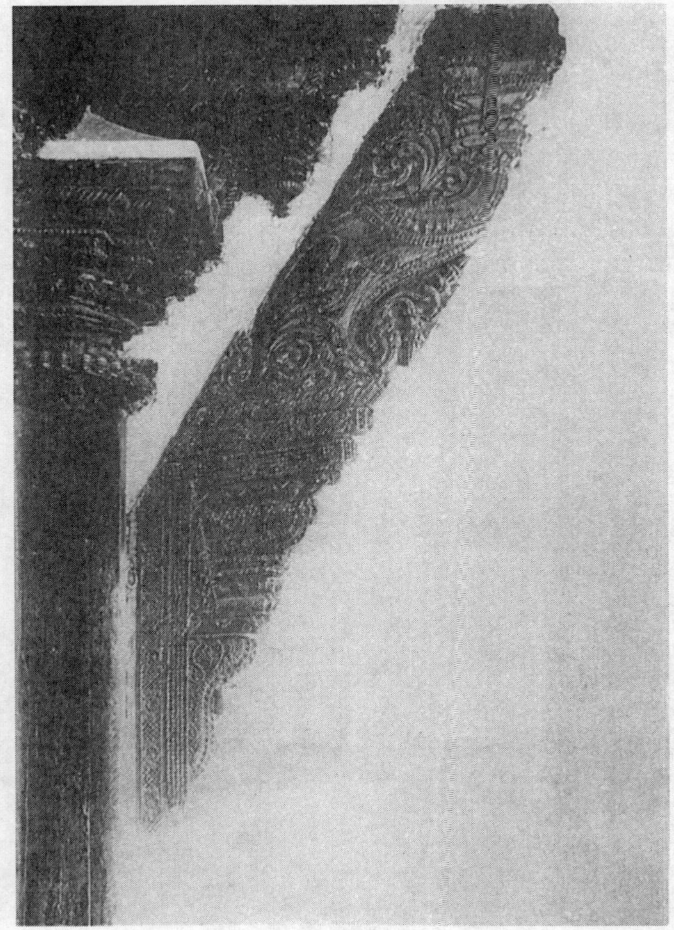

DESIGNS OF WOOD CARVING: RANGĪN MAHALL

(*a*) MUSLIM PATTERNS, (*b*) HINDU DEVICES

XII

TILE-WORK ON THE DOORWAY OF THE ROYAL PAVILION: RANGĪN MAḤALL

MOTHER-OF-PEARL WORK ON THE INNER DOORWAY OF THE ROYAL PAVILION: RANGĪN MAḤALL

XIV

TILE-WORK OF THE DADO: RANGĪN MAḤALL

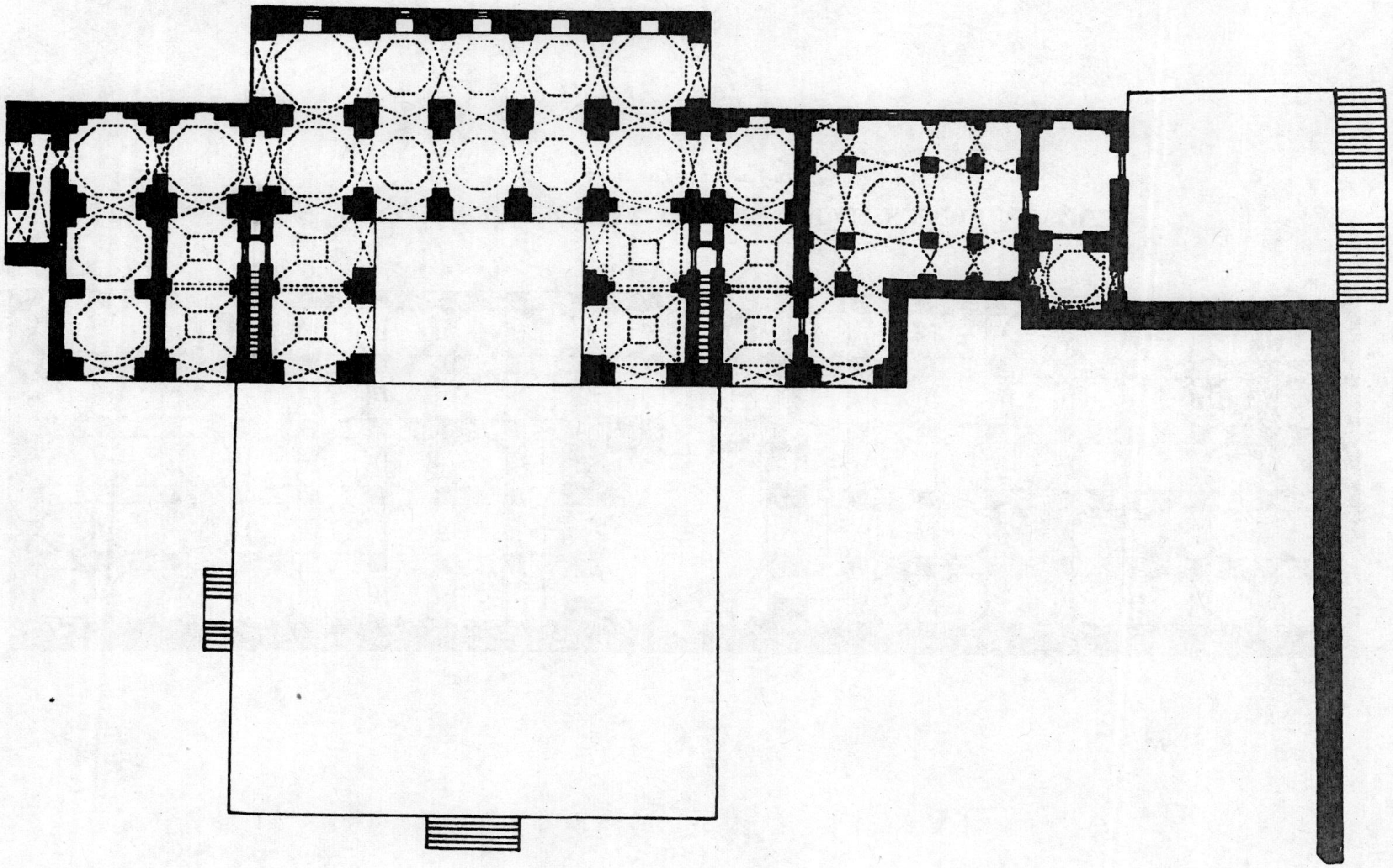

PLAN OF THE ROYAL BATH

Scale 24 feet to one inch

XVI

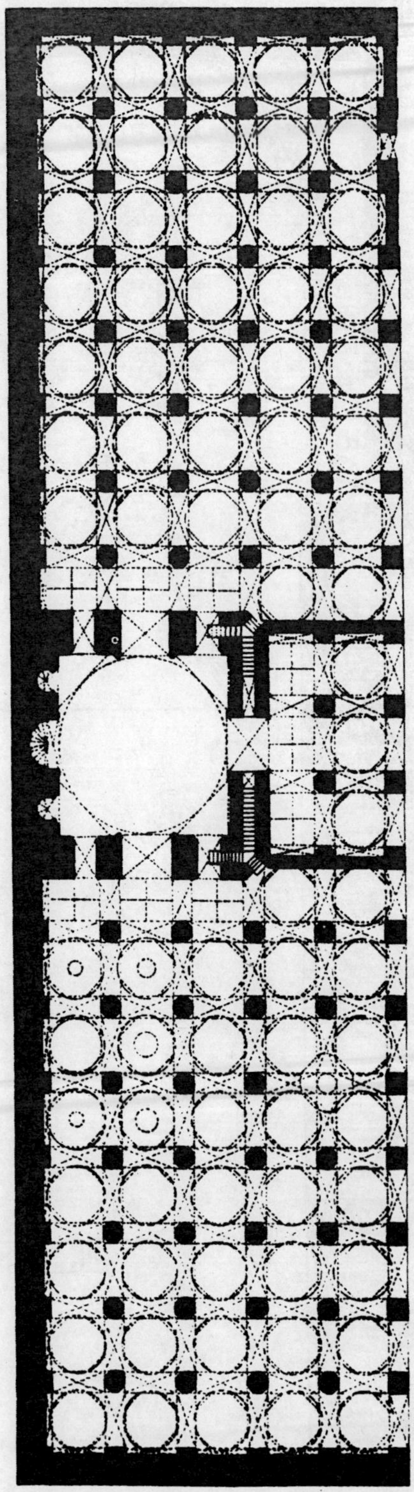

PLAN OF THE PRAYER-HALL OF THE SOLAH KHAMB MOSQUE

Scale 40 feet to one inch

XVII

THE SOLAH KHAMB MOSQUE: GENERAL VIEW

Before conservation

XVIII

THE SOLAH KHAMB MOSQUE: INTERIOR

THE TARKASH MAHALL (?): DECORATIVE FEATURES

PLASTER-WORK OF THE TARKA<u>SH</u> MAḤALL (?)

THE TARKASH MAHALL (?): SOUTHERN WING

XXII

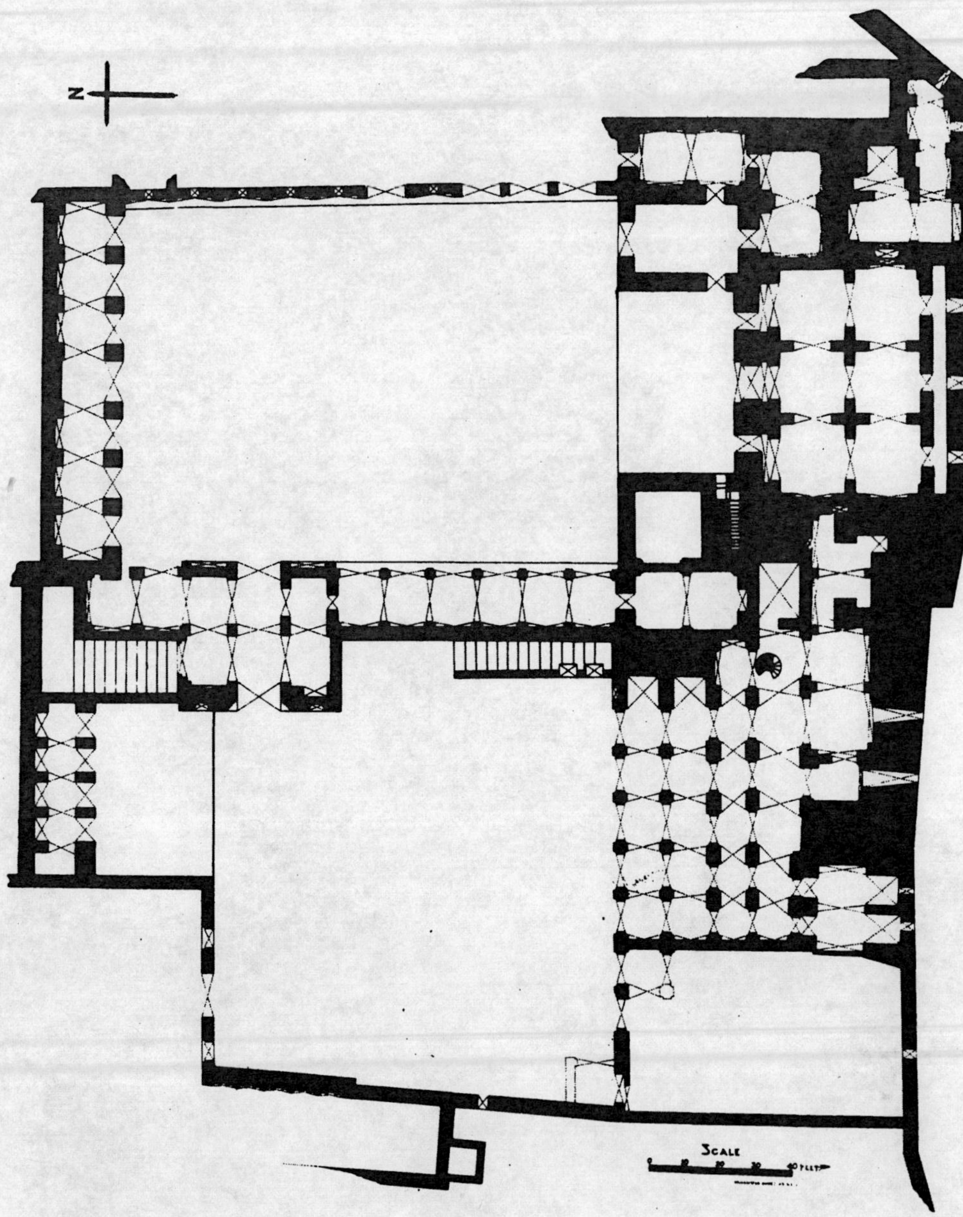

PLAN OF THE GAGAṆ MAḤALL

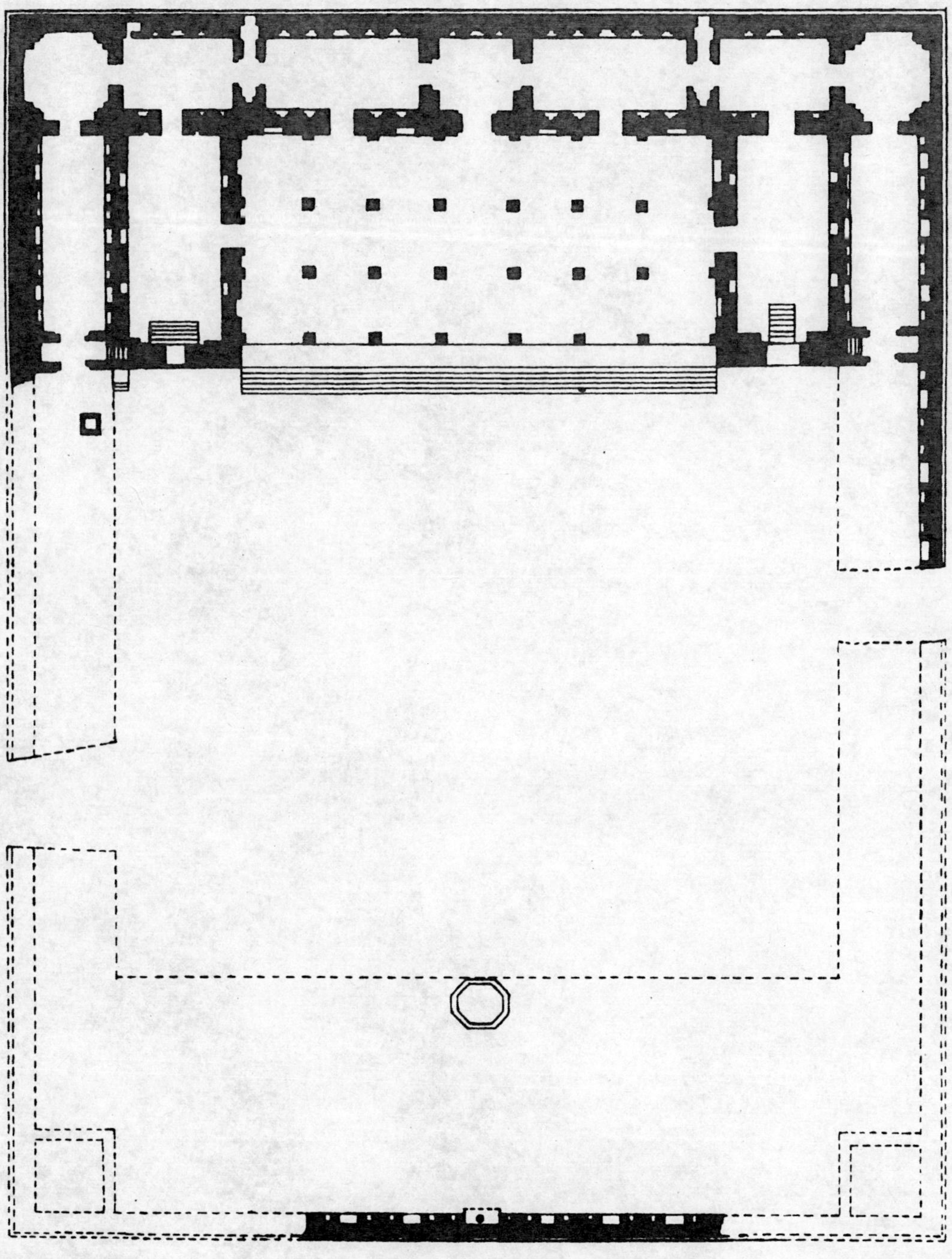

PLAN OF THE HALL OF AUDIENCE

Scale 40 feet to one inch

XXIV

THE HALL OF AUDIENCE: GENERAL VIEW

THE HALL OF AUDIENCE

XXVI

THE MINISTER'S ROOM

XXVII

DESIGNS OF THE TILE-WORK: AUDIENCE HALL

XXVIII

DESIGNS OF THE TILE-WORK: AUDIENCE HALL

DESIGNS OF THE TILE-WORK: AUDIENCE HALL

PAVEMENT OF THE ROYAL CHAMBER: AUDIENCE HALL

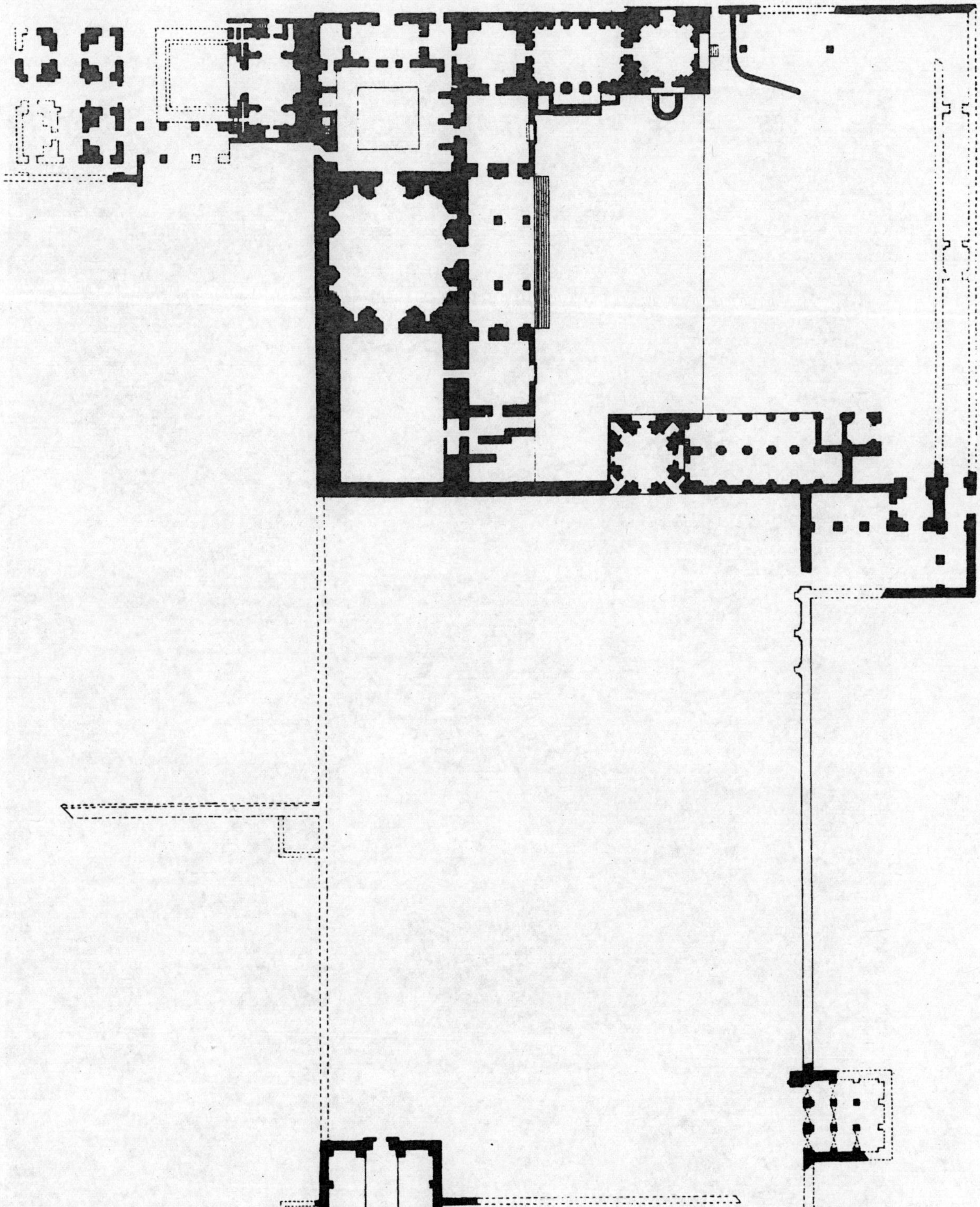

PLAN OF THE TAKHT MAHALL

Scale 75 feet to one inch

THE GATEWAY OF THE OUTER COURT OF THE TAKHT MAHALL

ROOMS IN THE OUTER COURT OF THE TAKHT MAHALL

Before conservation

GATEWAY OF THE INNER COURT OF THE TAKHT MAḤALL
Before conservation

THE TAKHT MAHALL: GENERAL VIEW DURING EXCAVATION

FACADE OF THE ROYAL CHAMBER: TAKHT MAḤALL

THE TIGER AND SUN EMBLEM ON THE FAÇADE OF THE ROYAL CHAMBER

ROOM ON THE LEFT SIDE OF THE ROYAL CHAMBER AFTER EXCAVATION

APARTMENTS OF THE TAKHT MAHALL TOWARDS THE SOUTH-WEST AFTER EXCAVATION

THE SOUTHERN WING OF THE TAKHT MAHALL AFTER EXCAVATION

PAVILION TO THE SOUTH-WEST OF THE TAKHT MAHALL AFTER EXCAVATION

GATEWAY TO THE NORTH OF THE TAKHT MAHALL: VIEW FROM THE WEST

GUARD-ROOMS: VIEW FROM THE EAST

XLIV

THE KALYĀNĪ BURJ

THE DOUBLE LINE OF FORTIFICATIONS

THE LONG GUN

THE LARGE GUN

THE MONKEYS ENJOYING THEIR NOON MEAL

THE GUN ON THE MUṆḌĀ BURJ

L

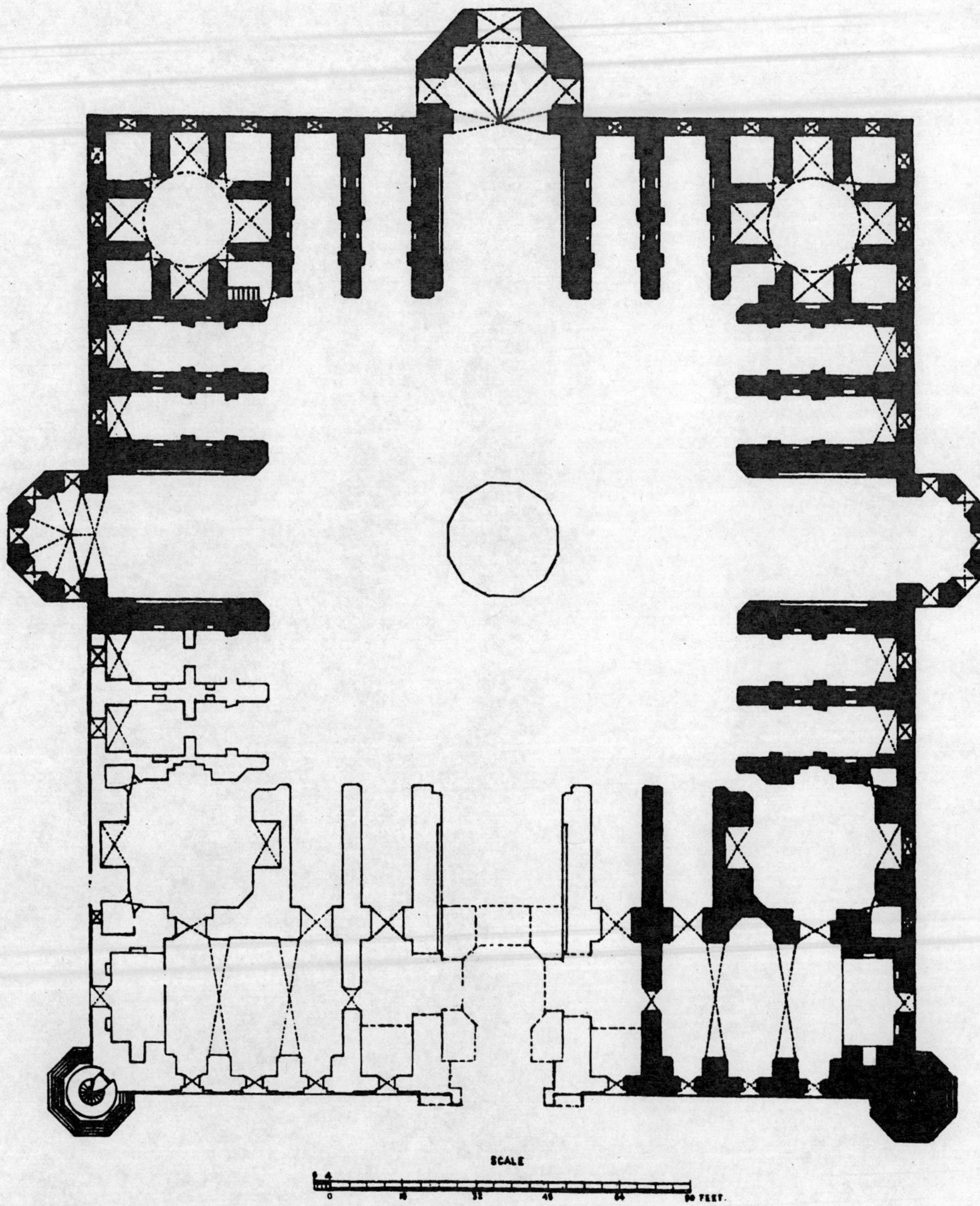

PLAN OF THE MADRASA OF MAḤMŪD GĀWĀN

FAÇADE OF THE MADRASA OF MAḤMŪD GĀWĀN

FAÇADE OF THE MADRASA OF MAḤMŪD GĀWĀN: DETAIL OF TILE-WORK

MADRASA OF MAHMŪD GĀWĀN: GENERAL VIEW

Before conservation

MADRASA OF MAḤMŪD GĀWĀN: VIEW FROM THE SOUTH-EAST

MADRASA OF MAḤMŪD GĀWĀN: INTERIOR: VIEW FROM THE EAST

MADRASA OF MAḤMŪD GĀWĀN: EXTERIOR: VIEW FROM THE NORTH-EAST

THE FATḤ DARWĀZA: BIDAR TOWN

LVIII

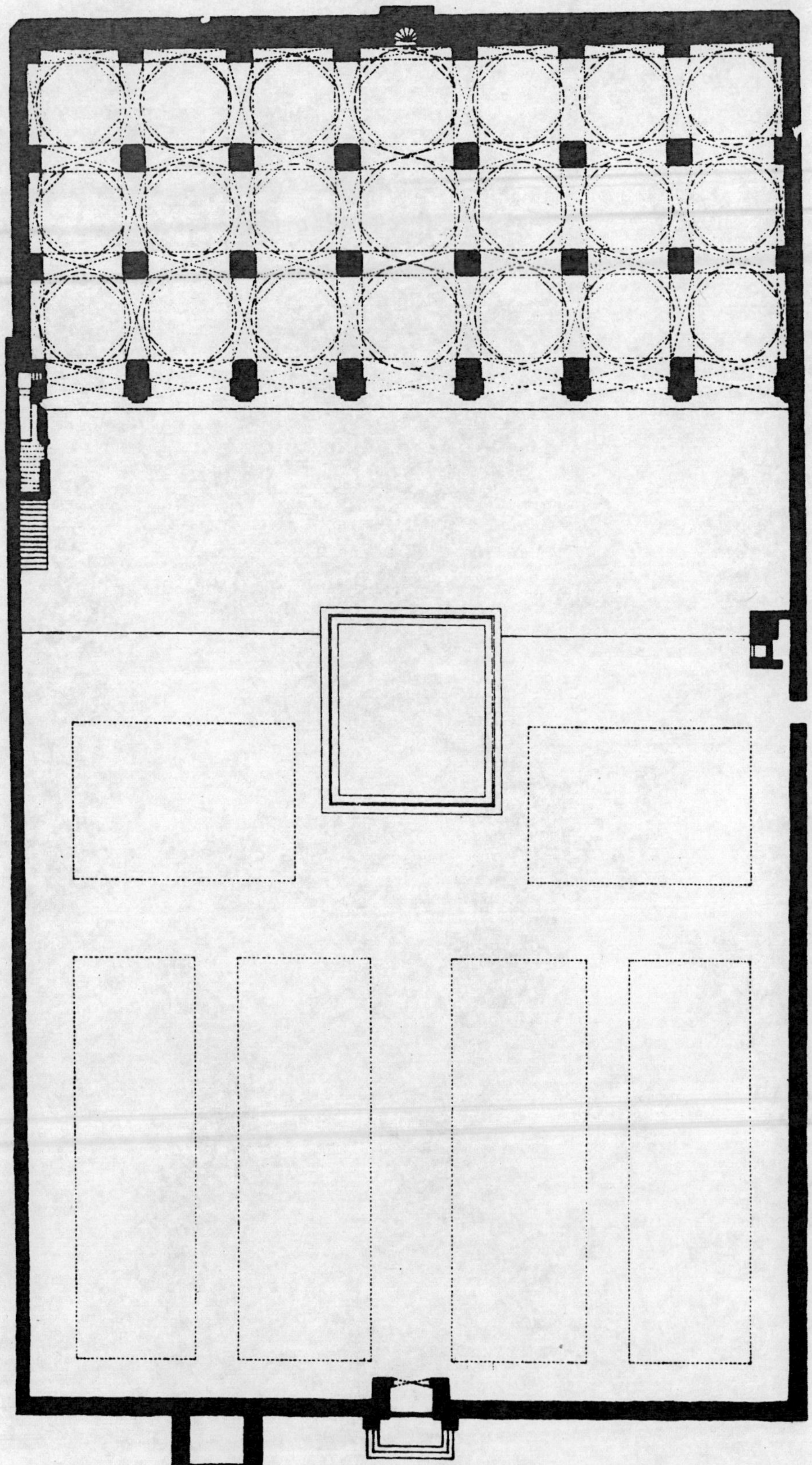

PLAN OF THE JĀMI' MASJID

Scale 32 feet to one inch

THE JĀMIʿ MASJID: GENERAL VIEW

LX

THE JĀMI' MASJID: INTERIOR

THE DULHAN DARWĀZA: VIEW FROM THE EAST

LXII

THE TALGHĀṬ DARWĀZA: VIEW FROM THE NORTH

THE PATH LEADING TO THE TALGHĀṬ DARWĀZA

THE C̲HAUBĀRA

THE TAKHT-I-KIRMĀNĪ

LXVI

A MOSQUE NEAR THE DULHAN DARWĀZA

THE BAIHMANĪ TOMBS: VIEW FROM THE SOUTH-EAST

PLAN OF THE TOMB OF SULṬĀN AḤMAD SHĀH WALĪ BAIHMANĪ

Scale 12 feet to one inch

THE TOMB OF SULṬĀN AḤMAD SHĀH WALĪ BAIHMANĪ : VIEW FROM THE NORTH

FLORAL AND CALLIGRAPHIC DESIGNS OVER THE SOUTHERN DOORWAY OF AḤMAD S̲H̲ĀH WALĪ'S TOMB

GEOMETRIC AND CALLIGRAPHIC DEVICES ON THE SOUTHERN WALL OF AḤMAD SHĀH WALĪ'S TOMB

CALLIGRAPHIC AND FLORAL PATTERNS ON THE EASTERN WALL OF AḤMAD SHĀH WALĪ'S TOMB

FLORAL DESIGNS ON THE EASTERN ARCH OF AḤMAD SHĀH WALĪ'S ṬOMB

LXXIV

THE CEILING OF AḤMAD SHĀH WALĪ BAIHMANĪ'S TOMB

THE *JANGAM* WITH HIS PARAPHERNALIA AT THE *'URS* OF AḤMAD S͟HĀH WALĪ BAIHMANĪ

LXXVI

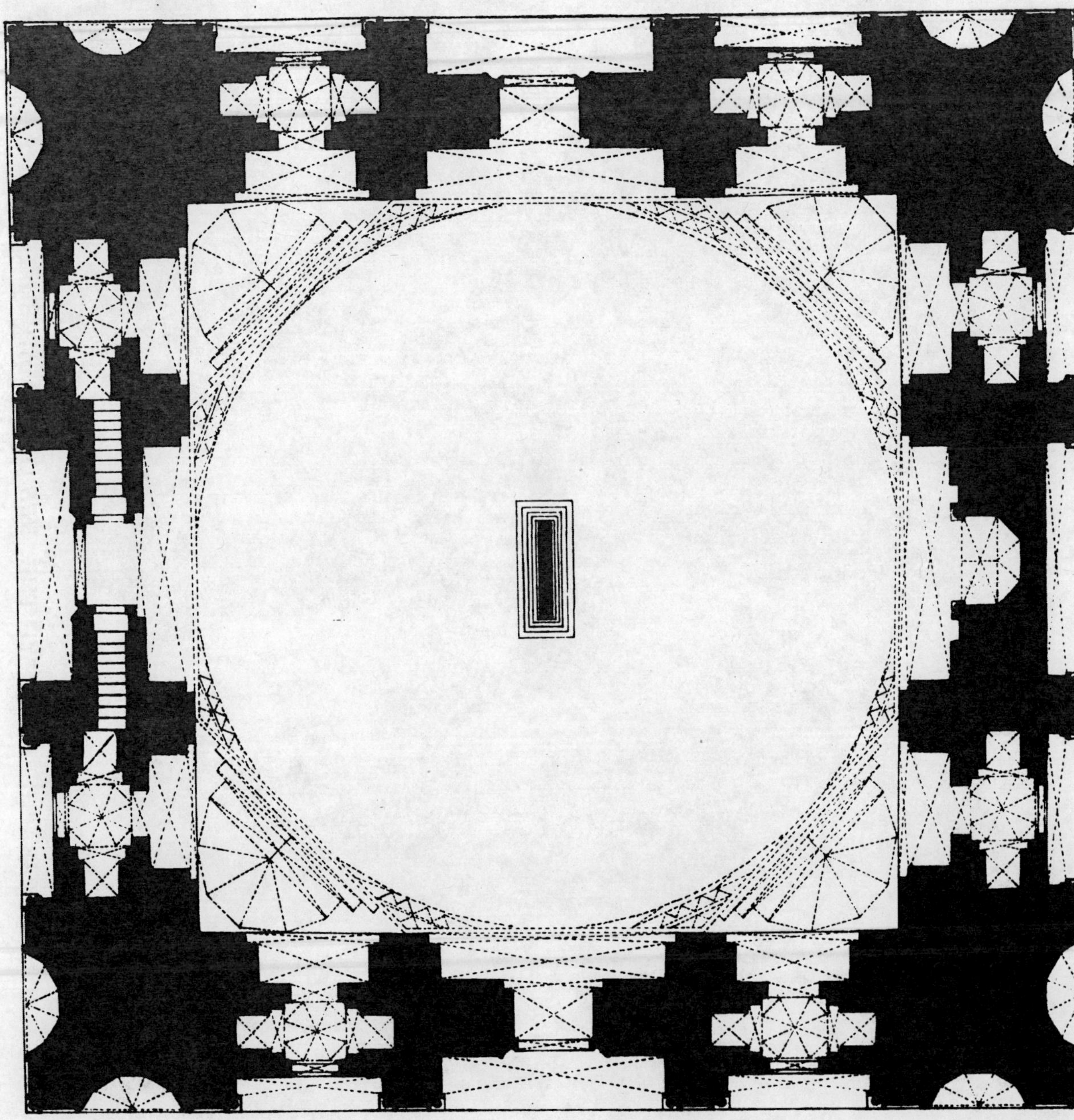

PLAN OF THE TOMB OF 'ALĀ-UD-DĪN BAIHMANĪ

Scale 12 feet to one inch

(*a*) THE TOMB OF 'ALĀ-UD-DĪN BAIHMANĪ: VIEW FROM THE NORTH

(*b*) THE SAME: DETAIL OF TILE-WORK: VIEW FROM THE SOUTH

THE TOMB OF SULṬĀN HUMĀYŪN

THE TOMB OF MAHMŪD SHĀH BAIHMANĪ: VIEW FROM THE SOUTH

LXXX

THE TOMB OF MAḤMŪD SHĀH BAIHMANĪ: VIEW FROM THE NORTH

THE TOMBS OF WALĪ-ULLĀH AND KALĪM-ULLĀH BAIHMANĪ

SECTION ON A B

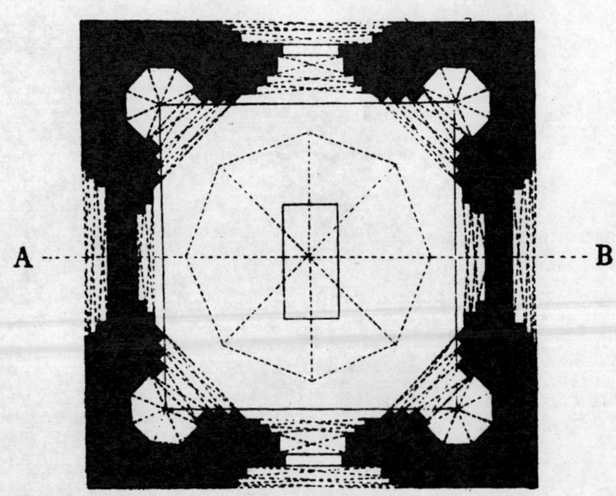

PLAN AND SECTION OF SULṬĀN KALĪM-ULLĀH'S TOMB

Scale 12 feet to one inch

PLAN OF THE *CHAUKHAṆḌĪ* OF ḤAḌRAT KHALĪL-ULLĀH

Scale 16 feet to one inch

THE *CHAUKHAṆḌĪ* OF ḤAḌRAT KHALĪL-ULLĀH: GENERAL VIEW

THE *CH̲AUKHAṆḌĪ* OF ḤAḌRAT K̲H̲ALĪL-ULLĀH: DETAIL OF CARVING

A TOMB TO THE EAST OF ḤAḌRAT KHALĪL-ULLĀH'S *CHAUKHANḌĪ*: VIEW FROM THE SOUTH

A TOMB TO THE EAST OF ḤAḌRAT KHALĪL-ULLĀH'S *CHAUKHAṆḌĪ*: INTERIOR: STUCCO DECORATION

A TOMB TO THE SOUTH-WEST OF ḤAḌRAT KHALĪL-ULLĀH'S *CHAUKHAṆḌĪ*:
INTERIOR: STUCCO DECORATION

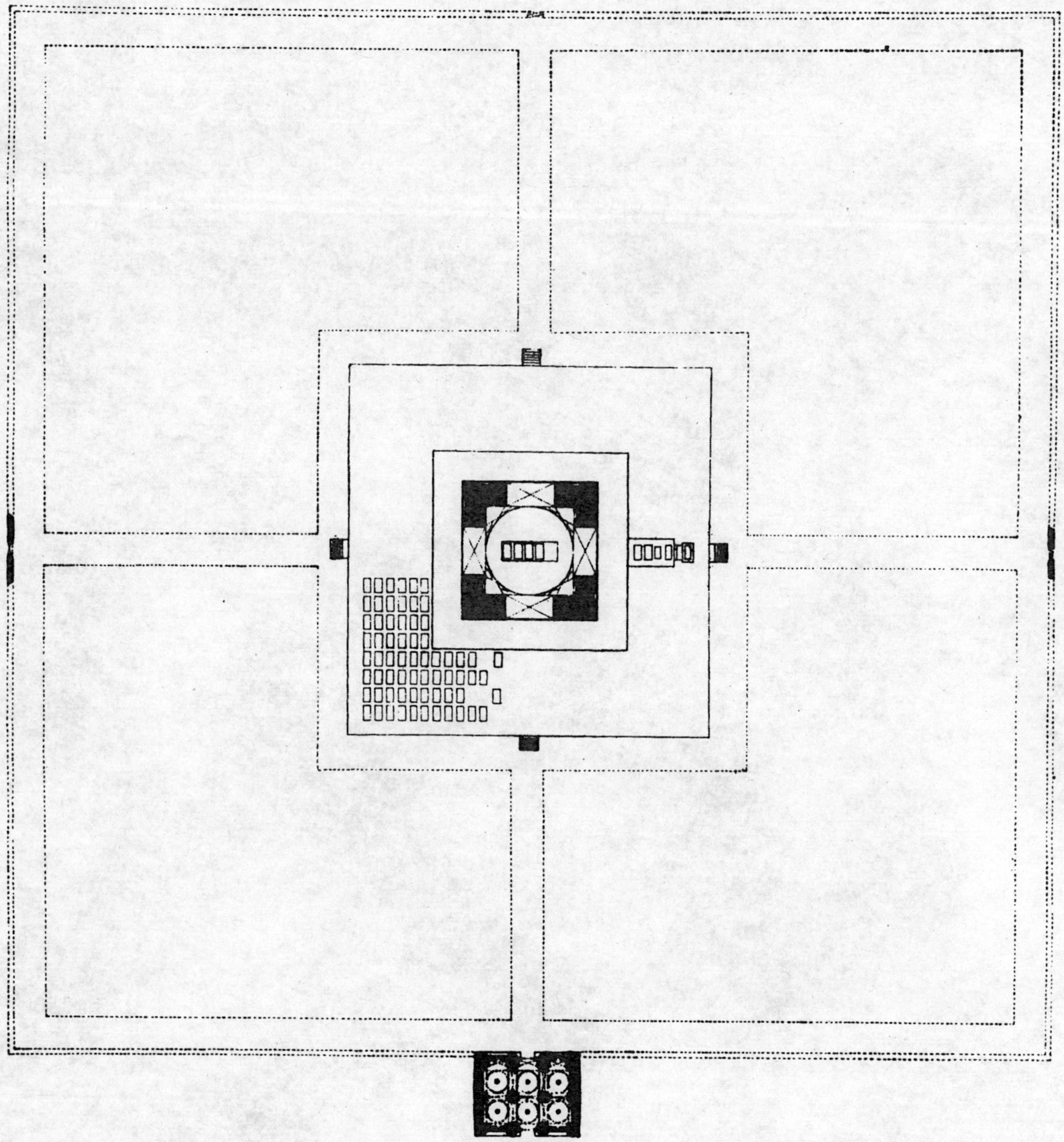

PLAN OF THE TOMB OF SULṬĀN 'ALĪ BARĪD

Scale 72 feet to one inch

THE SOUTHERN GATEWAY OF 'ALĪ BARĪD'S TOMB

THE HALL ON THE FIRST FLOOR OF THE SOUTHERN GATEWAY:
TOMB OF 'ALĪ BARĪD

THE TOMB OF SULṬĀN 'ALĪ BARĪD: VIEW FROM THE SOUTH-EAST

THE TOMB OF 'ALĪ BARĪD: VIEW FROM THE WEST

THE BLACK-STONE SARCOPHAGUS: TOMB OF 'ALĪ BARĪD

AN INSCRIPTION ON THE WESTERN WALL OF THE TOMB OF 'ALĪ BARĪD

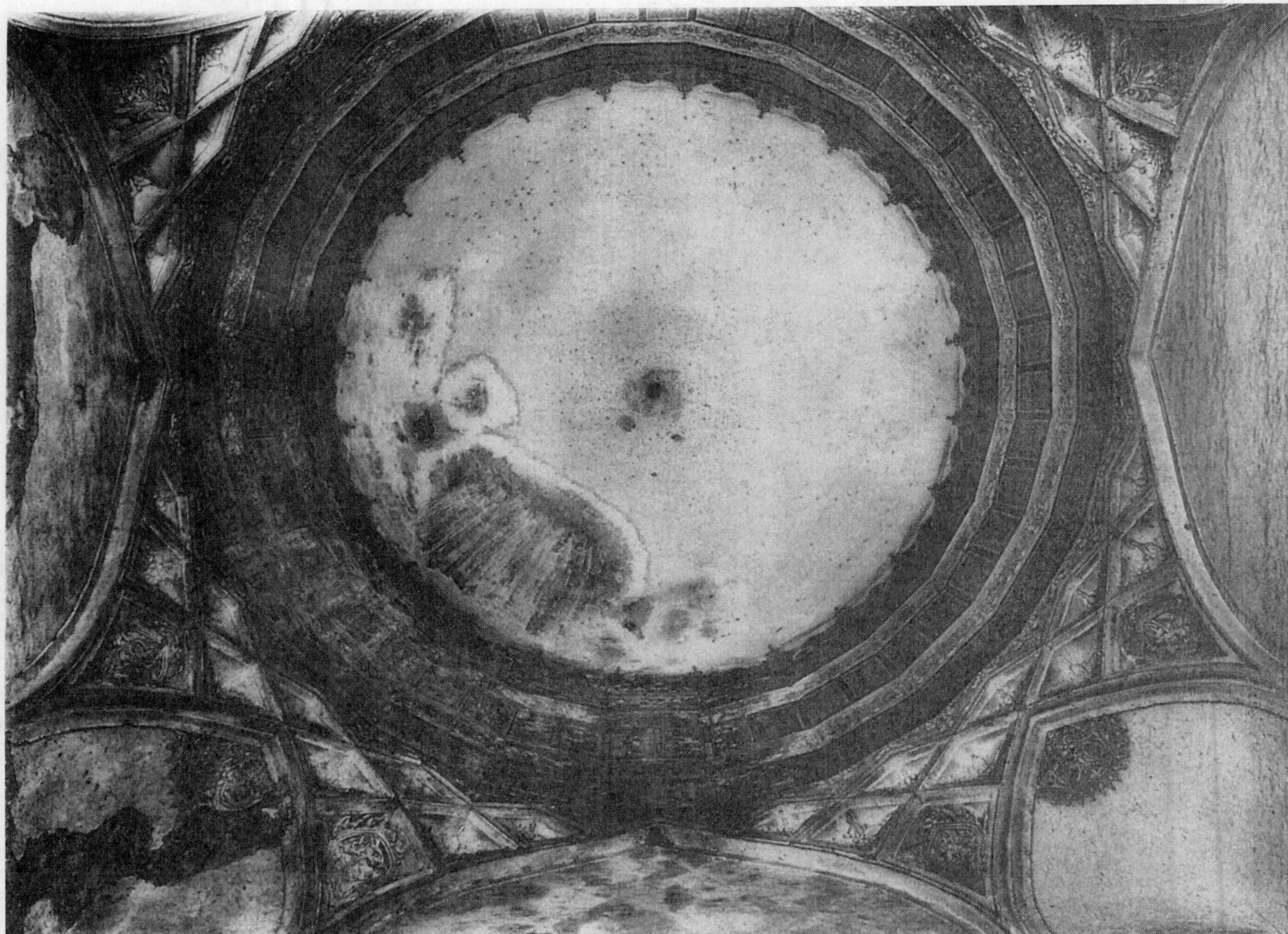

THE CEILING OF 'ALĪ BARĪD'S TOMB

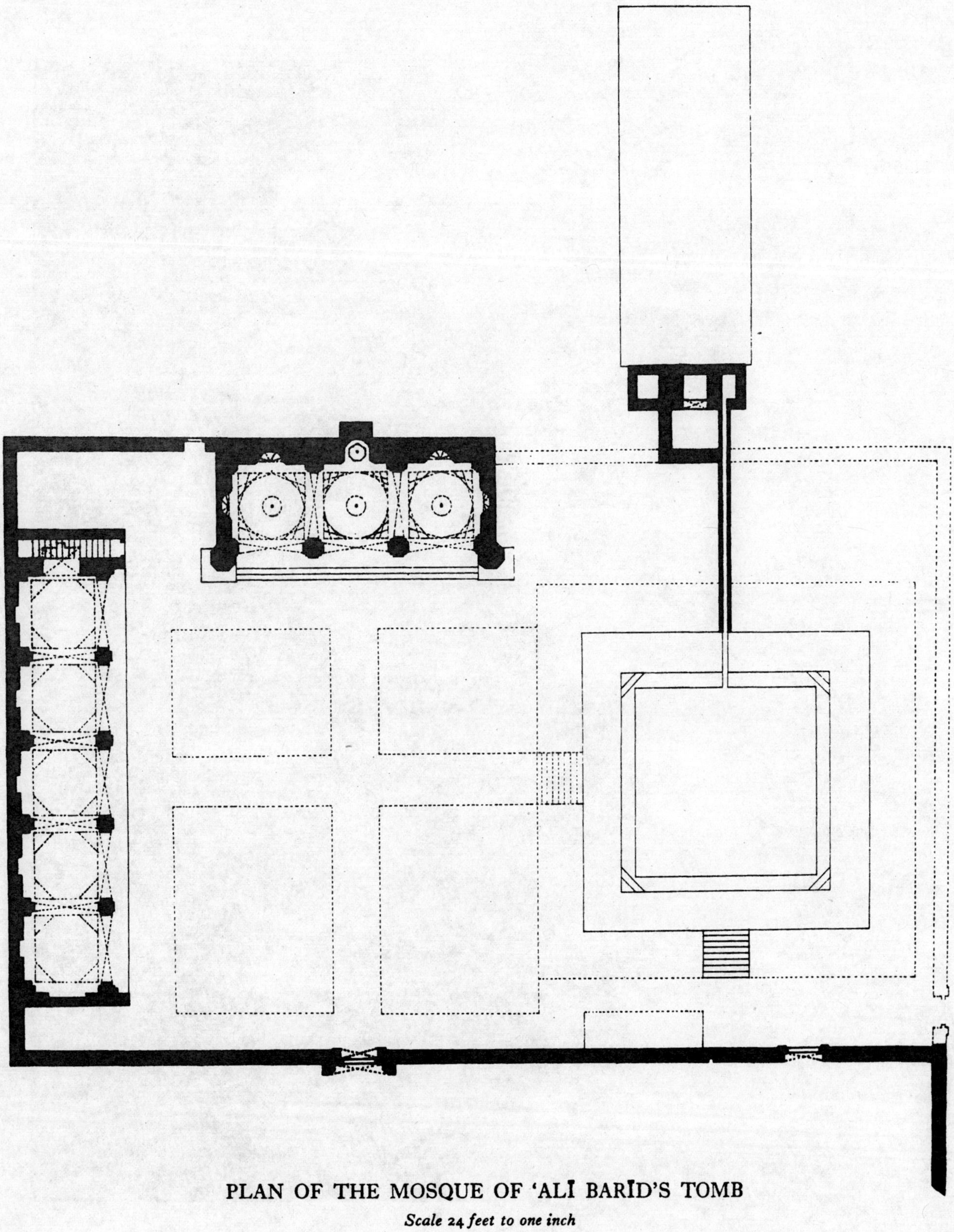

PLAN OF THE MOSQUE OF 'ALĪ BARĪD'S TOMB

Scale 24 feet to one inch

THE MOSQUE OF 'ALĪ BARĪD'S TOMB: FAÇADE

THE MOSQUE OF 'ALĪ BARĪD'S TOMB: INTERIOR

C

THE MOSQUE OF 'ALĪ BARĪD'S TOMB: VIEW FROM THE NORTH-WEST

THE TOMB OF IBRĀHĪM BARĪD

THE CEILING OF IBRĀHĪM BARĪD'S TOMB

A CARVED PILLAR: TOMB OF IBRĀHĪM BARĪD

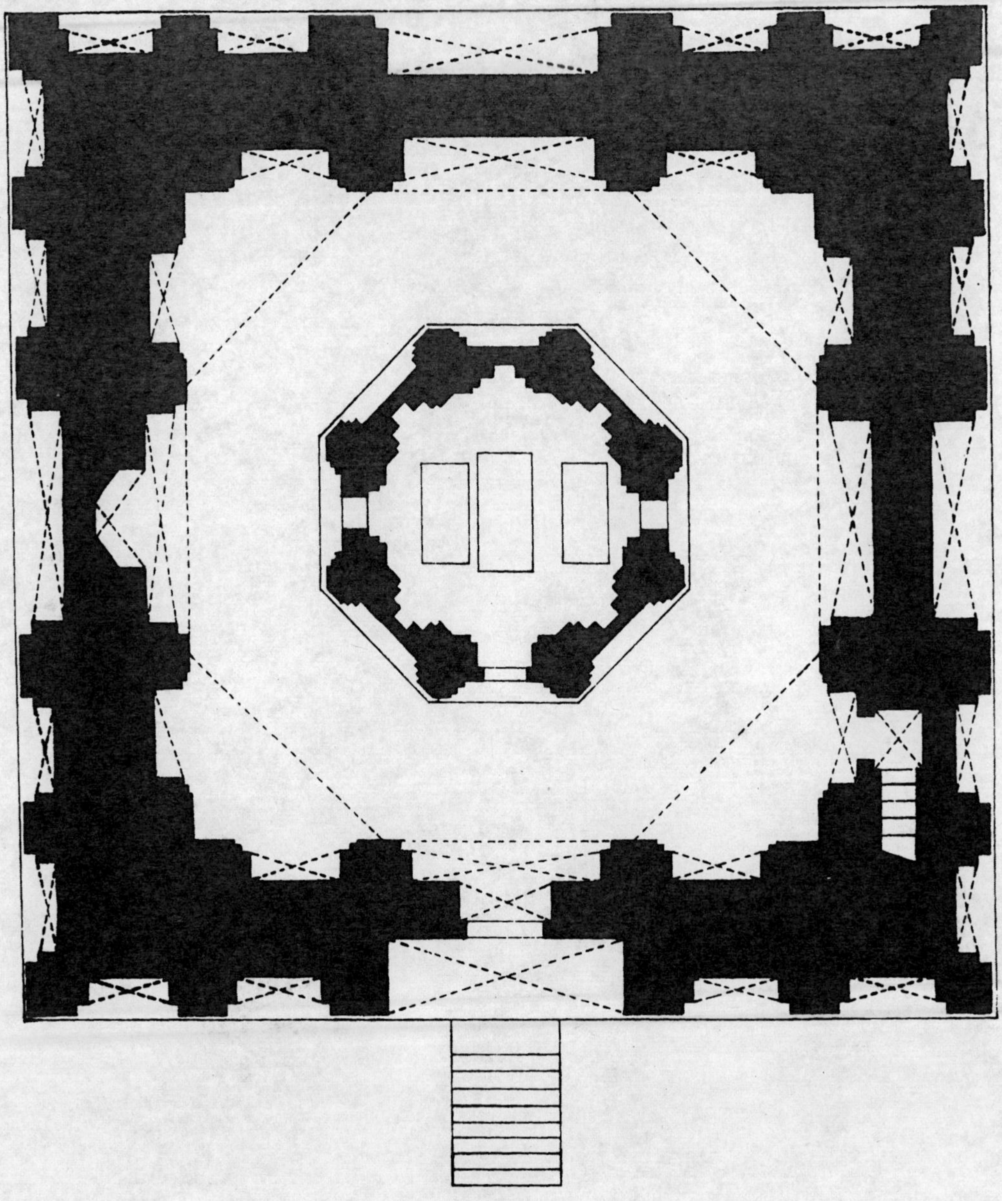

PLAN OF THE TOMB OF AMĪR BARĪD

Scale 12 feet to one inch

(*a*) THE TOMB OF AMĪR BARĪD: VIEW FROM THE SOUTH-WEST

(*b*) THE SAME: VIEW FROM THE SOUTH

Before conservation

CVI

AN ANONYMOUS TOMB: INTERIOR

THE *RAṆ KHAMB* OR POLO POSTS (?)

THE TOMB OF QĀSIM BARĪD II

AN ANONYMOUS TOMB

CX

THE TOMB OF A LADY (C̲H̲ĀND SULṬĀNA?)

THE SARCOPHAGUS OF A LADY'S TOMB

CXII

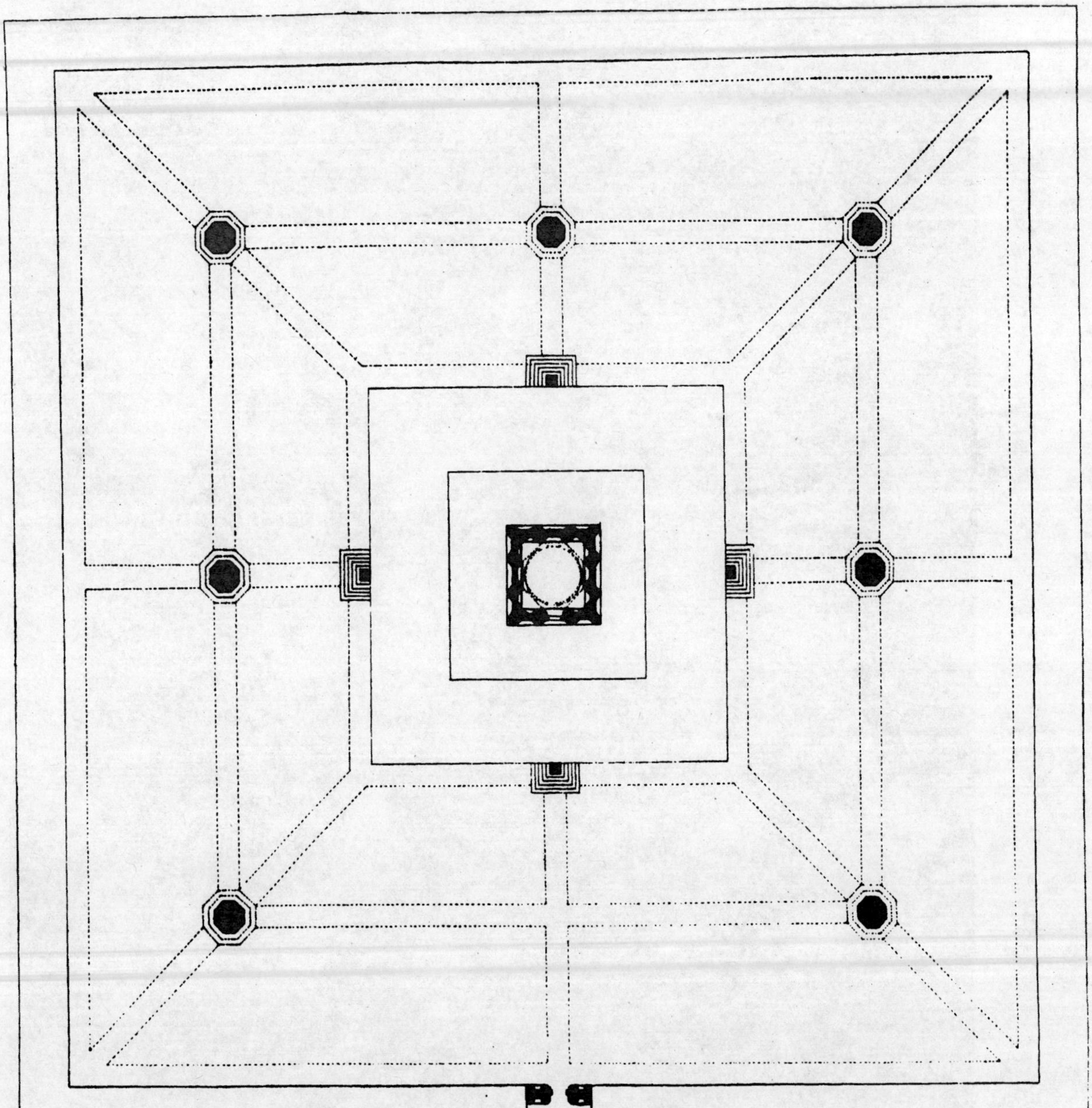

PLAN OF THE TOMB OF KHĀN JAHĀN BARĪD

Scale 48 feet to one inch

THE TOMB OF K͟HĀN JAHĀN BARĪD

THE TOMB OF KHĀN JAHĀN BARĪD: CUT-PLASTER DECORATION

THE BARBER'S TOMB AND MOSQUE
Before conservation

THE TOMB OF ḤAḌRAT ʿABDULLĀH MAGHRIBĪ

Before conservation

(*a*) THE DOG'S TOMB (?)
Before conservation

(*b*) AN ANONYMOUS TOMB
Before conservation

CXVIII

THE FARḤ BĀGH

THE ḤABSHĪ KOṬ: PRINCIPAL TOMB

CXX

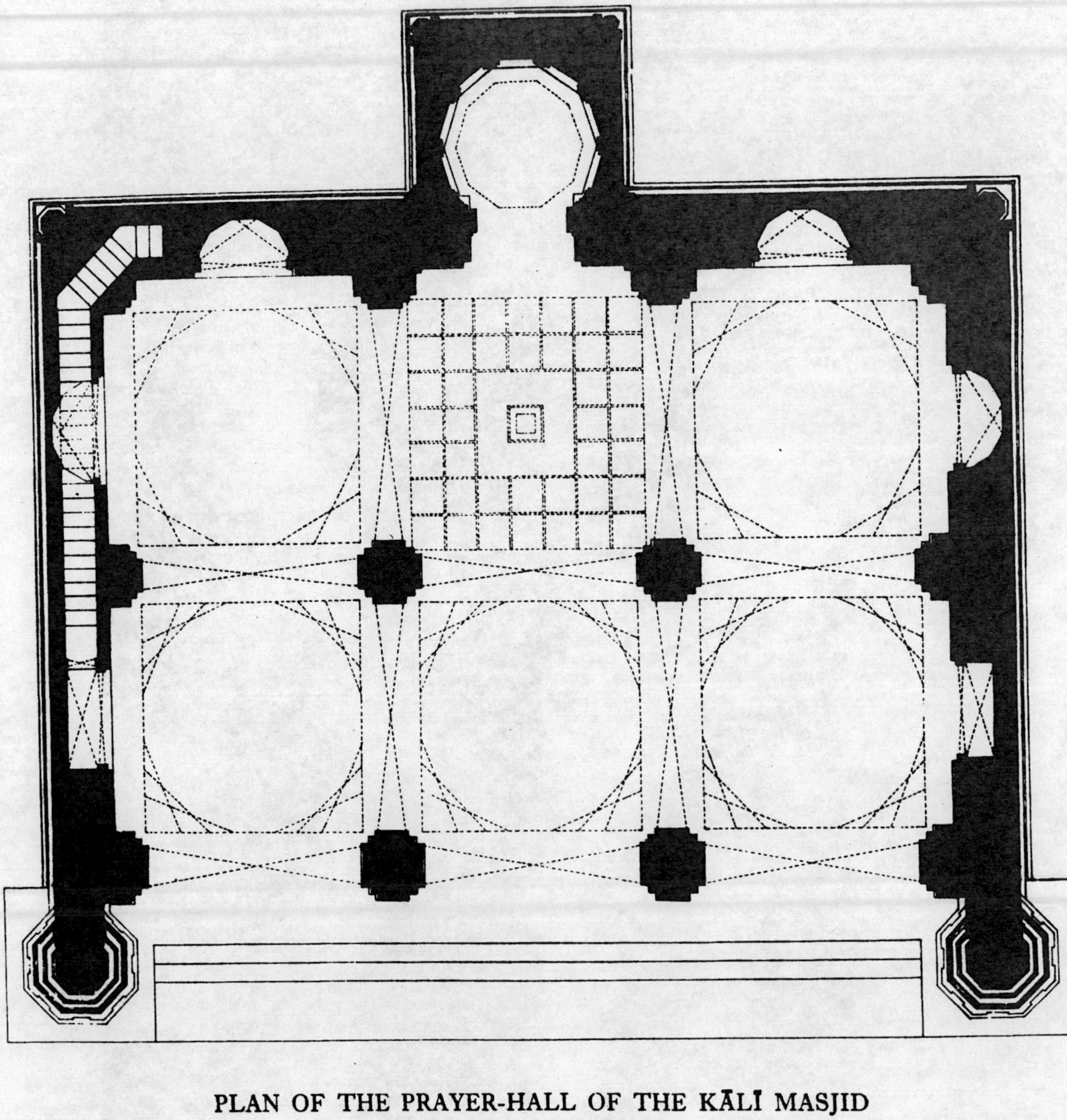

PLAN OF THE PRAYER-HALL OF THE KĀLĪ MASJID

Scale 9 feet to one inch

THE KĀLĪ MASJID: FAÇADE

THE KĀLĪ MASJID: VIEW FROM THE SOUTH-WEST

THE TOMB OF ḤAḌRAT SH̲ĀH ABŪ-'L-FAIḌ: GENERAL VIEW

THE TOMB OF ḤAḌRAT SHĀH ABŪ-'L-FAIḌ: DOORWAY

THE TOMB OF ḤAḌRAT MAKHDŪM QĀDIRĪ: VIEW FROM THE SOUTH-EAST

A MOSQUE NEAR THE TOMB OF ḤAḌRAT MAKHDŪM QĀDIRĪ

CXXVII

THE *PĀPNĀS* SPRING

CXXVIII

THE TOMB OF ḤAḌRAT SAYYID-US-SĀDĀT

PLAN OF THE TOMB AT FATHPŪR

Scale 32 feet to one inch

THE TOMB AT FATHPŪR